Regional Accountability and Executive Power in Europe

This book discusses the major issues currently affecting the accountability of executive power in Europe. The work is divided into three parts. The first examines the territorial dimension including unitary, regional and federal. It discusses how territorial actors participate in strengthening or weakening the implementation of accountability of executive power in modern democratic States. The second part explores the links between national traditions and European accountability of executive power to establish a common European culture. The third and final part focuses on how to build a truly multidisciplinary approach to accountability of executive power and draws on legal, historical and political approaches. The volume will be an invaluable resource for researchers, academics and policy-makers in constitutional law and politics, public law, comparative law, legal history and government.

Marcel Morabito is Professor Emeritus of Legal History at Sciences Po, Paris, and member of the Institut Louis Favoreu, Aix-Marseille University, France.

Guillaume Tusseau is Professor of Public Law at Sciences Po Law School, Paris, Fellow of the Institut Universitaire de France.

Routledge Research in Constitutional Law

This series features thought-provoking and original scholarship on constitutional law and theory. Books explore key topics, themes and questions in the field with a particular emphasis on comparative studies. Where relevant, titles will engage with political and social theory, philosophy and history in order to offer a rounded analysis of constitutions and constitutional law. Series Editor: David Marrani

Available titles in this series include:

Law and the Philosophy of Language
The Ordinariness of Law
Pascal Richard

Human Rights Defenders and the Law
A Constitutional and International Legal Approach
Núria Saura-Freixes

Law, Localism and the Constitution
A Comparative Perspective
John Stanton

Constitutional Reform and Brexit
Gary Wilson

Comparative Executive Power in Europe
Perspectives on Accountability from Law, History and Political Science
Edited by Marcel Morabito and Guillaume Tusseau

Regional Accountability and Executive Power in Europe
Edited by Marcel Morabito and Guillaume Tusseau

For more information about this series, please visit: www.routledge.com/Routledge-Research-in-Constitutional-Law/book-series/CONSTLAW

Regional Accountability and Executive Power in Europe

Edited by Marcel Morabito
and Guillaume Tusseau

Routledge
Taylor & Francis Group
LONDON AND NEW YORK

First published 2024
by Routledge
4 Park Square, Milton Park, Abingdon, Oxon OX14 4RN

and by Routledge
605 Third Avenue, New York, NY 10158

Routledge is an imprint of the Taylor & Francis Group, an informa business

British Library Cataloguing-in-Publication Data
A catalogue record for this book is available from the British Library

Library of Congress Cataloging-in-Publication Data
Names: Morabito, Marcel, editor. | Tusseau, Guillaume, editor.
Title: Regional accountability and executive power in Europe / edited by Marcel Morabito and Guillaume Tusseau.
Description: Abingdon, Oxon [UK] ; New York, NY : Routledge, 2024. | Series: Routledge research in constitutional law | Includes bibliographical references and index. | Summary: Provided by publisher.
Identifiers: LCCN 2023051220 (print) | LCCN 2023051221 (ebook) | ISBN 9781032251004 (hardback) | ISBN 9781032251011 (paperback) | ISBN 9781003281559 (ebook)
Subjects: LCSH: Executive power—European Union countries. | Federal government—European Union countries. | Constitutional law—European Union countries. | European Union countries—Politics and government.
Classification: LCC KJE5329 .R44 2024 (print) | LCC KJE5329 (ebook) | DDC 342.4/06—dc23/eng/20231108
LC record available at https://lccn.loc.gov/2023051220
LC ebook record available at https://lccn.loc.gov/2023051221

ISBN: 978-1-032-25100-4 (hbk)
ISBN: 978-1-032-25101-1 (pbk)
ISBN: 978-1-003-28155-9 (ebk)

DOI: 10.4324/9781003281559

Typeset in Galliard
by Apex CoVantage, LLC

Contents

Contributors

Juan F. López Aguilar is Professor of Constitutional Law at the University of Las Palmas de Gran Canaria, Spain, and Chair of the Committee of Liberties, Justice and Home Affairs of the European Parliament

Audrey Bachert-Peretti is Associate Professor of Public Law at Aix-Marseille University, France

Hafida Belrhali is Professor of Public Law at the University of Grenoble Alpes, France

Malik Bozzo-Rey is Research Professor in Ethics at the Catholic University of Lille, France

Mercedes Bresso is a member of the European Parliament. She is former President of the COR (Committee of the European Regions), President of the Piemonte Region and of the Province of Torino, in Italy. She was Professor of Economics, specialised in Environmental Economics, at the Politecnico of Torino and other Universities.

Laurent Carrié is Prefect for the Gers department, France

Claus Dieter Classen is Professor of Public, European and Public International Law at the University of Greifswald, Germany

Virginie Donier is Professor of Public Law at the University of Toulon, France

Jean-Baptiste Donnier is Professor of Private Law and Criminal Sciences at the Aix-Marseille University, France

Amaia Errecart is Senior Lecturer in Information and Communication Sciences at the University of Sorbonne Paris Nord, France

Aurore Gaillet is Professor of Public Law at the University of Toulouse Capitole, and a member of the Institut Universitaire de France

Cécile Guérin-Bargues is Professor of Constitutional Law at the University of Paris-Panthéon-Assas, France

Jean Paul Jacqué is Professor Emeritus of European Law at the University of Strasbourg, France, and Honorary Director General of the Council of the European Union

Luigi Lacchè is Professor of Legal History at the University of Macerata, Italy

Clémentine Legendre is Professor of Private Law and Criminal Sciences at the University of Lorraine, France

Xavier Magnon is Professor of Constitutional Law at Aix-Marseille University, and Head of the Louis Favoreu Institute, France

Marcel Morabito is Professor Emeritus of Legal History at Sciences Po, Paris, and member of the Institut Louis Favoreu, Aix-Marseille University, France

Stéphane Mouton is Professor of Public Law at the University of Toulouse Capitole, France

Julien Padovani is Associate Professor of Public Law at the University of Paris 1, Panthéon-Sorbonne, France

Fabienne Péraldi-Leneuf is Professor of European Law at the University of Paris 1, Panthéon-Sorbonne, France

Paolo Ponzano is Professor of European Governance at the European College of Parma, Italy, and a former Director of the European Commission

Hanan Qazbir is Associate Professor of Public Law at the University of Toulouse Capitole, France

François Quastana is Professor of Legal History at Aix-Marseille University, France

Emilien Quinart is Associate Professor of Public Law at the University of Paris 1, Panthéon-Sorbonne, France

Olivier Rozenberg is Associate Professor of Political Science at Sciences Po, Paris, France

Guillaume Tusseau is Professor of Public Law at Sciences Po Law School, Paris, and a member of the Institut Universitaire de France

Sophie in 't Veld is a member of the Committee of Liberties, Justice and Home Affairs of the European Parliament, Renew Europe Group, The Netherlands

Yoan Vilain is a researcher at Humboldt-Universität, Berlin, Germany.

André Viola is Senior Lecturer of Public Law at the University of Toulouse Capitole, France, and a Councillor of Aude Department

Jacques Ziller is Professor of Public Law and European Union Law, formerly at the University of Paris 1, Panthéon-Sorbonne, Paris, France, and at the University of Pavia, Italy

Introduction

Marcel Morabito

This book has been written within the framework of the REGALIEN Project (*Responsibility of Governments, Accountability and Legitimacy in European Nations*) led by Professor Guillaume Tusseau and myself from Sciences Po Paris. It follows a first volume which was published recently in the same collection under the title, *Comparative Executive Power in Europe: Perspectives on Accountability from Law, History and Political Science*. The first volume described the paths taken by constitutionalism on the topic of the political responsibility of the executive power, which is a major topic of our political life, in sixteen European states: Belgium, France, Germany, Greece, Hungary, Italy, the Netherlands, Scandinavia (Denmark, Norway, Sweden), Poland, Portugal, Romania, Spain, Switzerland and the United Kingdom. This second volume aims to extend those monographs by opening new perspectives, first by going beyond the framework of the academic approach to allow grassroots actors to speak, on the local scale as well as on the European one, and, second, by trying to enrich the academic approach by crossing disciplinary perspectives.

Regional Accountability and Executive Power in Europe, in line with the REGALIEN Project, is a collective work, which associates Sciences Po Law School (Paris), Institut Louis Favoreu (Aix-Marseille Université) and Institut Maurice Hauriou (Université Toulouse Capitole), a trio which has been reinforced by Institut de Recherche en Droit International et Européen de la Sorbonne (Université Paris 1 Panthéon-Sorbonne). That cooperation has led to three symposia, the results of which are gathered in this volume: 'The point of view of local authorities' (Toulouse, 21 January 2022), 'National traditions and European legal culture' (Paris, 20 May 2022) and 'Read-across perspectives' (Aix-en-Provence, 7 October 2022).

The first event on 'The point of view of local authorities', which was organised at Toulouse by Institut Maurice Hauriou, endeavoured to confront the academic reflections and the practice of different local actors. That local dimension seemed necessary since a political decision only makes sense when it has gone through a field test, which is the only thing that allows to measure its merits and to implement it efficiently. The expression 'local authorities' here is

DOI: 10.4324/9781003281559-1

obviously understood in a generic sense, and reality may differ widely depending on the modes of organisation of the State. The federal or regional form of the State thus favours the interactions between the central power and the local authorities. However, France's difficulties in completing real decentralisation show that this exercise may come up against some limits, since the dialogue between the local authorities and the central power often meets difficulties. However, the fundamental issue remains the same: how do local actors participate in holding the national executive power to account in the European States? Answering that question implies determining the very existence of that responsibility, highlighting its modes and measuring its impact.

The contributions to this symposium, now gathered in this volume, which deal with those different aspects, speak in favour of the existence of a responsibility of the national Executive towards the local authorities. Indeed, the field of responsibilities is not limited to the relations between the governments and the parliamentary assemblies. In other words, the manifestations of responsibility are not limited to parliamentary control. As the comparative approach clearly shows, democracy requires regular interactions between the decision-makers of different levels. This dialogue may undoubtedly vary depending on the complexity of the local authorities, their competences or even the democratic tools that are available to the people. There is no doubt either that the modes of holding the Executive to account may consequently vary. Still, the work of this first symposium helps us to better grasp the limits and the evolution of that responsibility. Parliamentary control is giving way to increasingly significant judicialisation. Responsibility-assessment firmly stands next to responsibility-sanction. Far from questioning the importance of responsibility, those renewed forms confirm that it is a crucial stake in a democracy. What happens at the European Union level?

That question was the focus of the second symposium, which was organised by Paris Sciences Po Law School and Institut de Recherche en Droit International et Européen de la Sorbonne, on the topic of 'National traditions and European legal culture'. The relation between Member States and the European Union is unquestionably, and in several respects, a crucial stake. First of all, is it possible to identify common national traditions as to the responsibility of the executive power? Though there are many works on fundamental rights and the essential role they have in the European constitutional legacy, the domain of the institutions, without being neglected, is less the focus of research studies. Yet, the legacy of history as to the organisation of power is far from being insignificant. Despite differences of context, the English and American experiments – and even more the dense and tumultuous laboratory that France used to be – have left indelible traces in our constitutional culture. What are their common elements, what have their vectors been? Studying that common foundation is an absolutely necessary stage to grasp the responsibility of the executive power at the level of the European Union.

Once that has been done, other questions immediately arise. To what extent have the traditions of the Member States had an impact of the European policy of responsibility? Is there a common European culture in that respect? The European academics and institutional actors confront their visions, give us their convictions. From those dialogues, what appears is how difficult it is to think about a real culture of the responsibility of the Executive in the European Union system. The first difficulty is due to an institutional blurring which results from both the difficulty of identifying an executive power and the functional split of the holders of the executive power in the Member States and their administrations, which act as bodies of both the States and the European Union. Second, the procedures do not always produce the expected effects. Technical rationality prevails over political orientations so that, although treaties are amended, practices do not change. Last, the topic of responsibility in the European Union system attracts less interest than in the case of the national parliamentary systems. The European model seems too far from the latter. One should note however that despite the complexity and originality of the European institutional system, both academics and actors underline how topical the issue is today and make suggestions of actions which will undoubtedly hold the readers' attention.

The symposium which was organised in Aix-en-Provence by Institut Louis Favoreu on 'Read-across perspectives on responsibility' was the third and last part of the triptych. Providing a more strictly academic perspective than the previous ones, it focused on deciphering how everyone, in their own field, tackles the issue of responsibility. Thus, analyses of specialists of constitutional, administrative, civil and sports law, history of law, philosophy, political science or even information and communication sciences were presented, dealing with issues such as how key notions – fault, risk, damage, harm, causality, sanction, reparation – are understood in each of those disciplines. Is there a consensus on their definition? Is it possible to take some distance from one's own speciality, go beyond disciplinary perspectives and claim a multidisciplinary approach of the concept of responsibility? While many such questions remain open, one thing is certain. In an environment in which the executive power has been significantly reinforced, the means of holding it to account are now more than ever at the core of the democratic stakes. May this book contribute even more to convincing those who, at different levels, participate in decision-making that this is indeed the case.

Part I

The responsibility of the national executive power from the point of view of local territories

Section 1

Theoretical reflections

1 A European perspective

Mercedes Bresso

Local actors in the EU

In Europe, there is a tendency towards an increase of the powers and responsibilities of local actors, especially of the regional governments (in many cases the names are different, they may for example be called 'provinces'). There are fundamentally two main types of regions: those which have a legislative power (Germany, Belgium, Austria, Italy, Spain) and those which only have administrative competences (France, Greece, Sweden, Finland, the Netherlands, Portugal, Croatia, Denmark). Normally, smaller countries manage funds on the basis of territorial subdivisions which are only statistic ones.

Several factors have led to the strong increase of the powers of regional governments over the years. These include the availability of funds, the direct relation with the Commission and the European institutions, as well as the participation in the Committee of the Regions, which has developed the principle of multilevel governance and which increasingly puts the emphasis on subsidiarity as a fundamental element of the European construction.

This trend is due, first, to the structure of regional policies (structural funds and cohesion fund), which aim at reducing socio-economic inequalities in the Union and compel Member States to manage funds on a regional basis and, if possible, to have them directly managed by their administrative regions. Some regions, like those in Belgium, are directly represented on the EU Councils in matters dealing with their competences. Others, like those in Italy, may participate in the Councils together with the ministers of their government, again on matters related to their competences. In other cases, as in Spain, the government informs the regions of the topics being discussed in the Council and shares the decision of the position of the country with them.

Moreover, through the Committee of the Regions (COR), the EU maintains close relations with the regional governments and the other levels of subnational powers – cities, provinces, districts, delegations – which are consulted on a regular basis and invited to partake in debates or concrete initiatives, as for example the 'Covenant of Mayors', which was set up by the Commission and the COR to directly involve cities in the policy against climate change.

DOI: 10.4324/9781003281559-4

These arrangements have resulted in a reinforcement of traditional organisations of the local powers (such as the Council of European Municipalities and Regions, CEMR) and the birth of new ones which represent big cities (EUROCITIES) or regions with a legislative power (Conference of European Regional Legislative Assemblies, CERLA) or all the regions (Assembly of European Regions, AER), and many other thematic organisations. All those organisations are periodically invited to participate in consultations on directives and regulations which concern them (which are very numerous) and the president of the Commission invites their presidents to a yearly meeting to confront all the European policies that concern them.

All that has obviously modified – sometimes deeply modified – the status and responsibilities of subnational powers at a national level, too.

The existence of a responsibility of the national executive power to the local actors

I will take the example of the Italian case which I have experienced directly as the President of the Province of Turin (an equivalent of a French *département*), from 1995 to 2004 as well as that of the Piedmont Region from 2005 to 2010.

In Italy, the Minister of the Interior is accountable for local authorities, while the Minister of Regional Affairs is accountable for regions. It is the latter who presides over the State-Regions Conference, which is composed of all the presidents of the regions or their delegates, and deputies for matters in question. Usually, it is the presidents who participate.

The Conference debates all the bills of the government about the regions, the ministers being present. It gives advice, which is sometimes mandatory, on those bills or on other issues, such as the negotiations on the EU structural funds, the distribution of funds for health (one of the fundamental competences of the regions), and, in general, the distribution of all the contributions of the State to the regional budgets, which have their own but insufficient taxes. In some cases, agreement is mandatory, in others, after a double vote of the Conference, the government may proceed without an agreement. It is a mandatory moment of consultation, provided for in the law, which represents the main forum of agreements (and disputes) between the government and the regions.

There was an attempt at creating a Senate of the Regions, like the German *Bundesrat*, which entailed a constitutional amendment that was approved by the Chambers but rejected by popular vote. This situation created a paradox, since a former constitutional reform – which had significantly increased the competences of the region – was de facto annulled by the national legislator, which should have adopted laws to transfer competences to the regions, but never did. In addition, the reform of the Senate, which would have created a necessary forum for discussion and, simultaneously, reduced the excess of competence attribution of the previous constitutional reform (which had been approved by popular vote), was eliminated by popular vote.

This occurred because public opinion, which was very much in favour of regions at the end of the last century, rapidly changed and has since adopted a negative attitude towards regional empowerment. This created a paradoxical situation from a legal point of view: a formal constitution that would have transferred almost everything to the regions was neutralised by a de facto constitution which opposed and prevented the transfer of competencies, even if the reductions of the regional powers had been rejected by referendum.

There is also a so-called Unified Conference, which gathers the representatives of municipalities, other local authorities and the presidents of the regions, and is presided over by the Minister of Regional Affairs. The Conference enables local authorities to give their opinions on all the issues that concern them, such as bills, funds and budgets.

The lesson that can be drawn from the attempts at 'federalising' in Italy is that because of a very complex transfer of legislative powers, it would have been simpler to transfer administrative and management powers, together with a decent tax reform to ensure necessary resources. A similar process of federalism happened in Spain and my impression is that there were similar problems, which were probably enhanced by the Catalan issue. One can also think of the difficult relations between the Belgian regions and central government. The situation in Germany, by contrast, is different due to the fact that it has been a federal state since its beginning.

More generally, I consider that while an appropriate regionalisation may be useful, a 'double legislative power' makes relations with the EU and the lives of citizens more complicated, as they are necessarily more confused by a triple level of legislation, if we take European law into consideration as well.

The modes of the Executive's responsibility: towards reciprocal responsibility?

There is no doubt that the existence of local actors with important powers for the life of local authorities entails responsibilities for the national Executive for several reasons. First and foremost of these is to ensure there are the necessary resources for the effective management of the attributed competences. Secondly, there is the need to coordinate planning actions and projects with both a national interest and an impact on territories, and, then finally to also ensure that the requirements of local actors are finally taken into consideration.

Consultation moments, on the model of the State-Regions Conference, may be useful to avoid forms of 'individual' consultations (national government-local authority on a project, for example) which may create situations of privilege or exclusion. However, this type of consultation is made increasingly difficult by the intervention of the media and opinion movements, which tend to oppose any large-scale project and force local actors to follow them on positions that are often populist and against the general interest. From that point of view, a senate which represents local actors is undoubtedly useful to guarantee that the State-local authority consultation is balanced when it is especially difficult to conciliate diverging interests (local/regional/national/European).

What are the effects of the responsibility of the executive power towards local actors?

The issue of the Executive taking the opinion of local actors into account is one of the most debated ones. It starts at the European level, where the Committee of the Regions complains that its opinions – which are mandatory – are not well taken into consideration by the Commission, nor by the Parliament nor even by the Council. In reality, the European decision-making process is very complex. Everybody participates and is heard, but in the end, when it is about an ordinary legislative procedure (co-decision), negotiation and the Parliament-Council agreement will prevail. Even the Commission, in the final phase, intervenes cautiously and the COR and the European Economic and Social Committee (EESC) are of course not consulted.

However, it is not true that the Commission does not take into account local interests and the interests of social partners when it presents a text, and Parliament always considers the role of local authorities and regions in decisions that concern them, such as those on the environment, the economy, the social issues, structural funds, etc. Furthermore, Member States, which are represented on the Council, are sometimes compelled to associate the regions and their laws in the European legislative process. They usually do this domestically, unless, as in the case of Belgium, their laws provide that they should be present on the EU Council. At the European level, it is mainly regions which are formally involved but the associations of local authorities remain very powerful and listened to.

On the national level there are significant differences between Member States. In countries such as the Netherlands or Finland, the mayor is a civil servant who is nominated by the central government in association with the majority of the Municipal Council. In other countries such as France and Italy, prefects, who represent the Executive for many issues related to security, organisation or intervention in times of crisis, still have an important role. In Italy, for example, it is the prefect who dissolves the Municipal Council in case of crisis and appoints an official. That situation sometimes creates the impression of a far away and hostile Executive. The relations between the State and the local authorities then are established via Members of Parliament or senators of the same political family.

Sanctions are essentially linked to the budget, since local authorities which are experiencing structural deficit or are too much in debt may be dissolved if the Executive does not intervene and provides aid. In Italy, in relation to the regions' competences, the non-application of a European directive may be sanctioned, and the concerned region will have to pay the fines decided by the EU.

In addition, the mayors and presidents of the regions are directly elected. This process tends to create very powerful and famous political protagonists, who often oppose the national power.

The president of a region considers themselves above a minister and almost on par with the Prime Minister who is not elected by the people as they are.

Such an institutional context does not facilitate relationships, and the mediation of political families tends to prevail.

The same tensions between the local, regional and national levels may be seen throughout Europe, but, in my view, they are stronger when local actors have more competences and when their elected members are more visible.

2 The responsibility of the national executive power in Germany from the point of view of local territories

Claus Dieter Classen, Aurore Gaillet and Yoan Vilain

When examining the organisation of the administration in Germany, it is important to keep in mind the determining impact of federalism, which leads to the distinction that must be made between the Federation (*Bund*) and the federated states (*Länder*). There is also a third level, which French people know less, but which is no less essential in the organisation of 'territories': at the lowest level, the 'municipality level' encompasses municipalities and counties (*Kreise*),[1] of which Article 28(2) of the Basic Law guarantees the autonomy. They have direct relations with the *Länder*, but not with the federal administration.

Such an organisation has several consequences in relation to our topic: in some areas, there is no national executive power; when there is, it only has relations with the *Länder*; the relations between the national executive power and the *Länder* – treated first – are quite different from those between the executive power of the *Länder* and the local level treated thereafter.

The federal and the *Länder*

The limits of the national executive power

In Germany, the national executive power only plays a limited role. This is due first to the fact that the Federation only has the legislative competences provided for in the domains enumerated in the Basic Law[2] (hereafter BL): in principle, if there is no legislative power, there is no administration either. That is one of the reasons why Germany is sometimes represented at the European Council by the minister of a *Land* (Article 16(2) TEU) – when, in the relevant domain, there is no ministry at the national level (see Article 23(6) BL, e.g., school education, culture or broadcasting).

1 See for example on that point: A. Gaillet, T. Hochmann, N. Marsch, Y. Vilain, and M. Wendel, *Droits constitutionnels français et allemand* (Paris: LGDJ, 2019), pp. 123 ff.; A. Jacquemet-Gauché, *Droit administratif allemand* (Paris: LGDJ, 2022).

2 A. Gaillet, et al., *Droits constitutionnels français et allemand*, pp. 202 ff.

DOI: 10.4324/9781003281559-5

Even more, the scope of the federal legislative power (which remains significant, as reforms of federalism are implemented) does not have any determining impact on the administrative organisation: pursuant to the aforementioned German 'executive federalism', the BL provides that, 'The Länder shall execute federal laws in their own right insofar as this Basic Law does not otherwise provide or permit' (Article 83 BL).[3] The Federation itself therefore rarely executes laws. One could quote the foreign service, the federal financial administration (Article 87(1) BL), transport infrastructures (federal roads and motorways, railways, waterways, air transport – Articles 90, 87(e), 89, and 87(d) BL), federal armed forces (Article 87(a) and (b) BL) and some security authorities (Article 87(1) BL). The same is true for social insurance institutions (Article 87(2) BL). Admittedly, the legislator may also create superior federal authorities (Article 87(3) BL), but here, that possibility has only been used in a limited way (e.g., for the environment and health).

One of the translations of that organisation is seen at the level of the distribution of civil servants: in 2019/2020, in France, out of 5.5 million people working in the civil service, 44 percent worked for the central government, 34.4 percent for local territories (and the rest for the hospital public service, which has disappeared in Germany since the 1970s); in Germany, out of 4.9 million *Beschäftigte im öffentlichen Dienst* (people working in the public administration/public sector), 10.41 percent worked for the Federal Government, 50.38 percent for *Länder*, 31.39 percent for local authorities (and 7.81 percent for social security services).

Federal administration(s)

When there is a federal level of administration, the main actors of the executive power are the ministries, which are all headed by a minister. In Germany, it is usual to divide the operating principles into the 'Chancellor's leading principle' (*Kanzlerprinzip*) (who 'shall determine and be responsible for the general guidelines of policy', Article 65(1) BL); the 'principle of the autonomy of ministerial departments' (*Ressortprinzip*), which supposes that, within the framework of their competences, the ministers take their decisions 'independently and on [their] own responsibility' (Article 65(2) BL); and the 'Cabinet principle' (*Kabinettsprinzip*), according to which the government is a collegial body – which also limits the powers of the Chancellor, because of the weight of the political parties on the practice of government coalitions.[4]

Beyond ministries, there are several administrative authorities. Most of them are subordinated to a federal ministry, which differentiates them from

3 All translations of BL from: www.gesetze-im-internet.de/englisch_gg/englisch_gg.html#p0452

4 N. Hubé, 'Le Gouvernement peut-il parler d'une seule voix? Institutionnalisation et délimitation du rôle du porte-parole du gouvernement fédéral allemand (1949–2015)', *Revue française d'administration publique* 171, no. 3 (2019): pp. 681–696.

the French independent administrative authorities. That specificity is due to a specific conception of the principle of democratic legitimacy,[5] according to which the legitimacy of the administration can only be guaranteed if there is parliamentary oversight, even if it is indirect. That is only possible through a minister, who is accountable to Parliament, which, in return, gives the latter scrutiny power over the administration.

Maintained role of the Federation

In the areas where the *Länder* execute the federal laws, the Federal Government keeps some normative power: 'The Federal Government, a Federal Minister . . . may be authorised by a law to issue statutory instruments' (Article 80(1) BL). Similarly, '[t]he Federal Government, with the consent of the Bundesrat, may issue general administrative provisions' (Article 84(2) BL). However, in both cases, the approval of the *Bundesrat*, the institution which represents the governments of the *Länder*, is necessary. Even though the Federal Government has the power to control that the *Länder* and their authorities 'execute federal laws in accordance with the law' (Article 84(3) BL), in practice, that power has only very limited importance. Lastly, if a dispute arises in that context, the Federation must call upon the *Bundesrat*, the decision of which may be challenged before the Federal Constitutional Court (Article 84(4) and (5) BL) – a proceeding that has never been triggered.

The relations between the federal executive power and the *Länder*

The importance of the Bundesrat

The *Länder* partake in the exercise of the federal power, mainly through the *Bundesrat*, which '[consists] of members of the Land governments' (Article 51 BL), and, through it, 'The *Länder* shall participate in the legislation and administration of the Federation and in matters concerning the European Union' (Article 50 BL). That second chamber is very different from the French Senate. First, it is composed not of elected members, not even indirectly, but of members of the governments of the *Länder*; second, the *Bundesrat* thus directly represents the *Länder*, unlike the French Senate, which may represent

5 C. D. Classen, 'La notion constitutionnelle de démocratie en Allemagne et en France', *Jus Politicum*, no. 18 (2017): p. 247. R. Wiedemann, 'Les autorités administratives indépendantes et la jurisprudence de la Cour constitutionnelle fédérale sur la légitimation démocratique', in *Le modèle des autorités de régulation en France et en Allemagne*, eds. G. Marcou and J. Masing (Paris: Société de législation comparée, 2011), pp. 53–62. For a historical perspective: A. Gaillet, *La Cour constitutionnelle fédérale allemande. Reconstruire une démocratie par le droit (1945–1961)* (Paris: La Mémoire du Droit, 2021), pp. 370 ff.

the local territories, but in a more indirect way.[6] Members of the *Bundesrat* must also vote as a unit (Article 51(3) BL) and are bound by an imperative mandate, which distinguishes them from the members of the *Bundestag*, who are independent when they vote.

The *Bundesrat* has some legislative powers. It also participates in the execution of laws through its right of approval of federal regulations and circulars (*supra*). In all those cases, its refusal will result in the failure of the measures. Even though, within German parliamentarianism, the Federal Government is only accountable to the *Bundestag* (which may overthrow it), the *Bundesrat* has some powers of control, for it may demand that members of the Federal Government attend, and ask them questions, and it must be 'kept informed by the Federal Government with regard to the conduct of its affairs' (Article 53 BL). In practice, however, those two provisions are not really determining, since the governments of the *Länder* have other information channels at their disposal, such as the direct links between the Federal Government and that of the *Länder*.

Other channels of influence of the Länder

It is a tradition that a deputy minister in charge of the coordination of the relations between the Federation and the *Länder* and a representative of the government for East Germany are nominated within the Federal Chancellery. In addition, the 'conferences' which gather either the ministers-presidents of the *Länder* (heads of the executive bodies) and the Head of the Federal Government (Chancellor), or ministers of the *Länder* and of the Federation of a given domain are important. The organisation of those conferences is somewhat similar to the organisation of the Council of Ministers of the European Union.

The management of the COVID-related crises has given many examples of that coordinated organisation: most of the main political decisions were taken within the framework of conferences of the Chancellor (Angela Merkel, until December 2021) and ministers-presidents of the *Länder*. It is all the more surprising that those conferences do not have any legal basis, which is criticised in Germany – and seems strange for a State which is often held as a model for its legal rigour.

The relations between the federal power and the local level

Considered only from the federal level's perspective, the local level of administration has no significant importance (except the three towns of Berlin, Hamburg and Bremen which are also organised as *Länder* – and subject to a few conclusion remarks *infra*): the *Länder* consider they are the main representatives of the interests of the local level at the national level. However, there are

6 A. Gaillet, et al., *Droits constitutionnels français et allemand*, pp. 355 ff.

associations which allow for a coordinated political representation at the federal level: the *Landkreistag* (for the districts), the *Städte-und Gemeindebund* (for towns and municipalities) and the *Deutscher Städtetag* (for cities). The *Bundestag* has even provided, in its standing orders, for the obligation for a committee debating a bill on the interests of the municipalities to hear those associations and report on it to the *Bundestag*.[7]

The *Länder* and the local level

As to the lower levels, at the federal level, the *Länder* should be distinguished from the local level, which encompasses municipalities and districts. The two levels are different especially because of the autonomous – and not derived – state power of the *Länder*. Each *Land* is free to organise its executive power and its administration as it wishes, which explains the diversity of organisation models in Germany. The municipalities and counties are made up by the *Länder* and are subordinate to the authority of the latter. Similarly, the *Länder* are responsible for the general conditions in which the municipalities and counties manage their finances.

In order to clarify responsibilities, the constitutional review of 2006 specified that 'Federal laws may not entrust municipalities and associations of municipalities with any tasks' (Article 84(1) BL): if the Federation cannot or does not want to carry out some tasks, it has to entrust them to the *Länder*. Then they have to decide, under their own responsibility, if they choose to involve the municipal level in the execution of the given task. In addition, almost all the constitutions of the *Länder* impose on the latter to grant adequate compensation for the additional costs they may incur when they give additional tasks to municipalities or counties.[8] That taking into consideration of the municipal level is echoed in constitutional case law, as the Federal Constitutional Court has granted municipalities and counties the right to be heard by the Parliament of the *Land* before a federated bill on their existence is put to the vote.[9]

To conclude that short overview, a few nuances may be brought, which will also qualify the three-way split of the responsibilities of the 'Executive' in Germany and the quasi-absence of direct responsibility between the municipal level and the Federation. From a political and media point of view, all the actors could claim some responsibility within the framework of their respective capacities. Moreover, the German political culture is characterised by

7 Rules of Procedure of the German Bundestag and Rules of Procedure of the Mediation Committee (2022), Rule 66(2), Rule 69(5), and Rule 70(4).

8 For the *Land* of Mecklenburg-Vorpommern, see the Basic Law for the Federal Republic of Germany, Article 72(3).

9 *BVerfG* [Federal Constitutional Court], Judgement of 12 May 1992 2 BvR 470, 650 707/90.

enhanced attention to compromise seeking – the coalition contracts being a perfect example of it. In addition, regional balances within parties are taken into account when the government is formed and play a moderating role in the taking into account of regional interests at the federal level. Last, the constitutional courts may be called upon to play a mediation role by deciding disputes between the Federation and the *Länder* (Federal Constitutional Court) and between municipalities and *Länder* (federated constitutional courts).[10]

10 A. Gaillet, et al., *Droits constitutionnels français et allemand*, p. 590; for the control of the obligation mentioned at note 7 see Constitutional Court of this Land, decisions of 17 June 2021 (9/19) and of 19 August 2021 (2 et 3/19 et 1/20).

3 Is calling upon the court a way to acknowledge the responsibility of the Executive?

Virginie Donier

On a formal level, an analysis of the rules of French domestic law shows that no provision allows for local authorities to make the Executive responsible. That is due to the French conception of the unitary State, according to which decentralisation is only a mode of organisation of the State. The principle of free administration is exercised in accordance with the conditions defined by the law. Case law shows that the pliability of the principle of free administration has little allowed the local authorities to defend their local autonomy against the central government, regardless of whether that autonomy was claimed against the law or against the national regulatory power.[1] The State-local authorities relation is therefore unequal, and that is consequently also true of that between the executive power and the local authorities.

However, that first observation must be qualified because of the movement of judicialisation which is increasingly characteristic of the relations between the State and the decentralised authorities, and therefore the relation with the Executive. Indeed, local authorities benefit from a right to collective redress as ruled by the *Conseil Constitutionnel* in its QPC Decision of 23 October 2013, *Commune de Pré-Saint-Gervais.*[2] It is also protected under Article 11 of the European Charter of Local Self-Government, which gives it a legal foundation, even though the direct effect of some provisions of that charter is not recognised. That does not mean that the right to collective redress allows the local authorities to have the court consecrate a demanding conception of free administration, for jurisprudence has regularly underlined the reserve of the *Conseil Constitutionnel* on that point.[3] In that respect, the introduction of the

1 J. H. Stahl, 'Le principe de libre administration a-t-il une portée normative?', *Nouveaux cahiers du Conseil constitutionnel*, no. 42 (January 2014): p. 31.

2 Conseil Constitutionnel (CC) [Constitutional Court], décision no. 2013-350 QPC, 25 October 2013, *Commune du Pré-Saint-Gervais.*

3 J. H. Stahl, 'Le principe de libre administration a-t-il une portée normative?'; H. Alcaraz, 'Le principe de libre administration des collectivités territoriales dans la jurisprudence constitutionnelle après la révision constitutionnelle du 28 mars 2003', *Revue française de droit administratif* (*RFDA*) (2009): p. 497.

DOI: 10.4324/9781003281559-6

priority preliminary ruling on constitutionality has not turned out as promising as expected.[4]

However, local authorities tend to increasingly ask the court, and first, the Administrative Court, to settle a dispute in which they rise up against the State, and the Executive in particular. Examples could be the decision of the *Conseil d'État* of 29 June 2005, *Commune de Puteaux*, on the right to the State's respect of the goods belonging to local authorities,[5] or the decision of the *Conseil d'État* of 26 July 2011, *Département de la Seine-Saint-Denis*, on the guarantee of sufficient resources deriving from the principle of financial autonomy.[6] In line with the latter decision, it must be underlined that the dispute case law relative to the principle of financial compensation is quite abundant.[7] Moreover, within the framework of the application of that principle, dispute case law is developing, when the State miscalculates the sums granted to the decentralised authorities.[8]

That tends to show that by calling upon the courts, local authorities do not hesitate to remind the Executive of its duties and commitments. The debate on the insufficient funding accompanying decentralisation, and more precisely, the transfer of competences, is an eminently political debate, but it tends to shift to the litigation arena. The court *de facto* becomes an arbitrator of the relations between the State and the local authorities, and more precisely between the executive power and the local authorities when the issue is about a regulatory decision. The judicialisation movement that local authorities have launched and developed is therefore a way of holding the Executive to account.

A recent dispute in the environment area, i.e., *Commune de Grande Synthe*, which needs to be detailed, provides a good example, for that case shows an evolution.[9] The municipality, represented by its mayor, and the mayor filing independently too, had challenged the implicit refusal of the President of the Republic, the Prime Minister and the Minister for the Ecological Transition

4 P. de Montalivet, 'QPC et droit des collectivités territoriales', *Actualité juridique Droit administratif* (*AJDA*) (2016): p. 586.

5 Decision No. 264714. It was a claim against a decree on the reclassification and transfer of property, to the benefit of the State, of public lands and buildings belonging to a local authority.

6 Decision No. 340041. The claim was against the Prime Minister's refusal to abrogate the decree on child welfare funding.

7 See for example, Conseil d'État (CE) [Highest Administrative Court: Sits in Sub-Section], 2 March 2010, région Rhône-Alpes, no. 322 781, on the creation of a new statutory allowance for civil servants including those working for local authorities.

8 X. Cabannes, 'Le contentieux des relations financières entre l'État et les CT', *AJDA*, no. 11 (2016): p. 598.

9 Conseil d'État (CE), 19 November 2020, commune de Grande Synthe et autres, *AJDA* (2021), p. 217, note H. Delzangles; see also, A. Van Lang, A. Perrin, and M. Deffairi, 'Le contentieux climatique devant le juge administratif', *RFDA*, no. 4 (July–August 2021): p. 747; see also, Conseil d'État (CE), 1 July 2021, commune de Grande Synthe, *RFDA* 2021, p. 777 with the conclusions by S. Hoynck.

and Solidarity, to grant their request that the State take all the measures necessary to reduce greenhouse gas emissions on the national territory, to make the climate priority an obligation and to implement immediate measures of adaptation to climate change. The analysis of the decision forcefully shows that the local authorities no longer hesitate to use the tools of administrative litigation to hold the Executive to account in the fight against climate change. Though decentralised authorities do not have all the levers for action in that area, they dare resort to administrative litigation to compel the State to act. More precisely, it is interesting to consider two aspects: the interest in bringing proceedings on the one hand, and the use of the injunction power on the other. The second point is especially important given the strategy of the claimants, as the objective of the claim is to get from the *Conseil d'État* an injunction forcing the government to take the requested measures within six months.

As to the interest in bringing proceedings, the decision grants such an interest to the municipality, but refuses it to the mayor claiming as such or as a private citizen. The fact that climate change affects the whole national territory does not bar the acknowledgement of the interest to act of the municipality of Grande Synthe, given the risks to which it is especially exposed by the year 2030 because it is located on the coastline. The *Conseil d'État* indicates that climate change will have a certain and indirect impact on the situation of the municipality and on the interests it defends. The conception of the interest in bringing proceedings sustained by the Administrative Court here gives legitimacy to the claim of the municipality, which tends to support the idea that litigation may be a way to remind the State of its responsibilities and commitments, which derive especially from international conventions, and specifically from the Paris Agreement of 12 December 2015.

The acknowledgement of the municipality's interest in bringing proceedings is the first stone that allows the authority's legitimacy to file in court to challenge the failure of the Executive to be recognised. Moreover, the claim of the claimant shows that local authorities have got hold of all the tools of administrative litigation to bring a conflict that is not devoid of political features to the litigation arena. Though the injunction first aims to guarantee the good execution of court decisions, in the present case, the municipality's request did not belong to that framework. The aim of the claim for an injunction was to compel the executive power to discharge a duty it had ignored until then. It was therefore by relying on the existence of a power of injunction independently of the execution of a court decision that the municipality tried to prevail.[10] The injunction aimed to point to the failures of the Executive and to force it to take more efficient measures. Behind that request therefore was hidden an issue inherent in the responsibility of the Executive.

However, the indirect holding of the responsibility of the Executive comes up against some limits, and especially the theory of government acts. The

10 A. Van Lang, et al., 'Le contentieux climatique devant le juge administratif'.

injunction can only go as far as asking the Executive to introduce a bill in Parliament to make climate priority mandatory. The judicialisation movement that is being described here is not limitless, some acts benefiting, pursuant to consistent case law, from jurisdictional immunity. It can be deduced that the government act allows for implicitly drawing the boundaries of the responsibility of the Executive.

However, as to the other requests, the decision rendered by the *Conseil d'État* on 1 July 2021 in the same case shows that they were founded. The Decision of 19 November 2020 is a preliminary judgement requiring further investigation. At the end of that additional investigation, the *Conseil d'État* eventually ordered the State to take all the necessary measures to meet its commitments related to the reduction of greenhouse gas emissions before 31 March 2022. The implicit refusal of the President of the Republic, of the Prime Ministers and of the Minister of the Ecological Transition and Solidarity was therefore annulled. This tends to show that the municipality managed, by using the different weapons of administrative litigation, to hold the State responsible in the especially sensitive area of climate change. If the reasoning of the court about the interest in bringing proceedings and that about the power of injunction are considered together, it seems that a municipality which is especially concerned by the consequences of climate change is entitled to remind the State, and more specifically the Executive, of its commitments and responsibility in that respect. Calling upon the court is a way to compensate for the failure of the Executive, which tends to demonstrate that there is indeed a possibility, for local authorities, to hold the Executive to account, even when it is not explicitly provided for in the law. That possibility is the result of a conquest of decentralised authorities which rely on access to court and to the jurisdictional arena to solve a dispute which is also political.

Beyond the first-rate lessons which derive from that case, it seems that some issues remain: in addition to the domain of the environment, what could be the field of application of that form of liability case? The challenge of the Executive through litigation is not limited to the environment, it also exists in relation to the application of the principle of financial compensation as has already been mentioned. However, those claims are only rarely successful given the Administrative Court's restrictive interpretation of that principle, in line with the *Conseil Constitutionnel* case law. The issue is therefore tricky, and one may wonder if the *Commune de Grande Synthe* case may be a starting point or an isolated case.

There nonetheless remains that such a challenge of the executive power through litigation reveals a new form of responsibility which is not only political in nature. According to Tocqueville, 'When judicial power raises its head that means that political power is caving in'. That sentence may be fully meaningful if it is admitted that calling upon courts is a way of making the relations between the State and local authorities less unequal.

Section 2

Regional realities

4 The point of view of a State representative

Laurent Carrié

The argument of the previous chapters, which I completely share, is that of an Executive which is looking for political legitimacy in the eyes of local actors. Is this a form of political responsibility which would offset the weakening of the political accountability of the Government to the Assemblies? I do not know. However, I can confirm that I have lived and observed that shift with the previous Prime Ministers I have worked for and especially Prime Minister Jean Castex. He accepted that political logic of looking for legitimacy in local territories and made it his own. It is also that of the President of the Republic in the Marseille en Grand Plan.

If I had to give a date for this search for political legitimacy with local authorities, I would choose the great national debate of the first semester of 2019. The President of the Republic, after the yellow vest crisis, started a whole series of trips outside Paris (the first being to Souillac on 19 January 2019) to meet mayors and find solutions to end the crisis with local actors, to make those solutions acceptable and make them legitimate in the eyes of the public opinion. That approach was strengthened and amplified by Jean Castex after he assumed his duties. He clearly told me, when I was his counsellor for local territories at Matignon, that he wanted to sign a maximum of agreements with the main associations of local elected representatives, main local authorities and main local executive bodies during his time as Prime Minister.

The agreements with the main associations of local elected representatives

That is why a political agreement with *Régions de France* was signed soon after he assumed his duties at the end of July 2020. It was the first deal that was obtained with a real negotiation with the President, Renaud Muselier. It led to a commitment of the Regions to support a certain number of dispositions that the Government intended to introduce into a certain number of texts, especially the 3Ds Bill, but also to sign revival agreements with the State in each region. It provided for counterparts, though. The State, for example, granted the Regions 600 million Euros in accordance with the revival plan, which was delegated to the Regions *préfets* to support the Regions' in-the-field

DOI: 10.4324/9781003281559-8

projects (mobility, heating rehabilitation of high schools, etc.). It was also given concrete expression with the *Assemblée des départements de France* in December 2020, with which the Prime Minister signed an agreement integrating a certain number of provisions which would be adopted in the different Draft Budget Bills and 3Ds Bill. The Head of Government thus entered into an agreement with *France Urbaine* in February 2021.

The Prime Minister then committed to supporting a certain number of provisions in accordance with the 3Ds Act in favour of metropolises, while paying contributions to the credit sums for the calls for projects supporting the mobility projects of urban local authorities (metropolises, urban communities and conurbations).

The revival and ecological transition contracts (RETC)

The national authorities' search for legitimacy and responsibility in the eyes of local ones can be seen in the revival and ecological transition contracts that the Prime Minister wanted to establish as soon as he assumed office. That contract is a single contract of the State with the local authorities which gathers all the projects within the competences of the State and local authorities on an intercommunal territory. It gives complete visibility to the actions of the State, to those of the local authority and to the funding dedicated to a territory. The starting idea is to have only one contract since there used to exist more than a dozen thematic contracts within the competence of different ministries. Indeed, before the RETC, the inter-ministerial contract policy with local authorities relied on multiple thematic contracts: conventions on inner city action, city contracts, conventions for industrial territories, contracts for the revival of inner cities, ecological transition contracts, contracts for the revival of defence sites, contracts for tourist resorts, etc.

That situation made the State's action for territories – the local representatives of which found it really difficult to give consistency to those systems – opaque. To respond to those difficulties, it was decided to reorganise all the contract policy of the State. The objective is now to have only one contract and the challenge has almost been met since the whole national territory is covered by the RETCs, even if in practice that simplification itself raises many issues.

Prime Minister Jean Castex signed contracts with the presidents of Toulouse, Nantes, Rennes, Nice and Toulon. The systematic objective of the national Executive was to sign agreements with the main local executives to anchor its action on the territory.

The Marseille en Grand Plan

During his trip to Marseille on 2 September 2021, the President of the Republic determined the axes of an action plan of more than 5 billion Euros for Marseille and its metropolis. 'Marseille en Grand' is thus articulated around seven ambitions: security, education, mobility, housing, employment, health and big projects.

If I had to characterise Marseille en Grand, I would say it is a political contract. Nothing was signed except protocols signed by the Prime Minister on specific topics (schools, mobility), but there was a foundational speech of the President, which was a political speech, which stated that the State put means on the table in exchange for returns. The President made a commitment and expected a return from the territory. Concretely speaking, in case of a disagreement, it is not a contract that is brought to the Administrative Court, but each party can at any time point to the inaction of the other, either politically or in the media.

That is why our aim is that the objectives of the President be realised rapidly. For example, about schools, funding corresponding to 254 million Euros was adopted in the first weeks of October in the Draft Budget Bill. It aimed to support the exceptional plan dedicated to schools in Marseille.

As to transportation and mobility, a billion Euro funding was adopted under the form of advances and subsidies to support the projects of Marseille and its metropolis.

For the ANRU (the national agency for the urban renewal) funds, the President of the Republic decided to double the sum from 300 to 600 million Euros. There again, funds were released very quickly.

In that plan, a certain number of returns are expected from the local authorities, especially the reform of the Aix-Marseille-Provence metropolis. It is a complex institution since it covers the whole *département*. The President therefore asked that the elected representatives and the Minister for the Cohesion of the Territories work to create a more agile and reformed structure. A discussion between the local actors and the minister on the elaboration of a bill was launched. The latter was examined in January 2022 at the National Assembly by the Joint Committee on the 3Ds Bill.

As to returns, the President and the Government also asked for a certain number of additional commitments to be made. On the implementation of low-emission zones, for example, the local authorities fulfilled their commitments. The Local Plan for Housing (LPH) was to be adopted at the end of 2022 by the metropolis. It was closely monitored by the *Préfecture*.

Towards a new type of political responsibility?

Is this the sign of a shift from a search for legitimacy to a new form of political responsibility? If that is the case, how is this new responsibility of national authorities working with the local actors?

It is undeniable that this is a political responsibility since, in the case of Marseille en Grand, the President himself committed himself to a certain number of decisions being taken quickly in order to improve the situation of Marseille. The President of the Republic has met his commitments, and if he had not done so, there would undoubtedly have been reactions of elected representatives and media on the topic. The reliability of the word of the President would have been weakened, and he would have been held responsible.

This is in a way a moral and political contract which relies on the fact that each party to it must meet its commitments. It is a new phenomenon which results in decisions made by the national Executive in close collaboration with the local executive bodies. The President of the Republic travelled to Marseille, just like the Prime Minister came to wrap up the last discussions with the mayor of Marseille, the president of the metropolis and the president of the Region.

As I said in the introduction, this new phenomenon dates back to the great national debate and the yellow vest crisis. It may be explained by the fact that the national authorities consider that the strongest legitimacy is that of the local authorities and try to strengthen theirs by reaching agreements with them. For me, that trend is related to the disconnection created by the end of the possibility to hold multiple offices, which put an end to the local and national legitimacy that Parliamentarians used to have concurrently.

5 The point of view of a local elected official

André Viola

I think it is the local actor and not the academic that has been invited, and I will naturally rely on my experience as a local representative for more than 25 years, so let me specify first from where I speak. I am a councillor of Bram (3,200 inhabitants). I have been a councillor since 1995 and was mayor from 2003 to 2011. I have been a councillor of the Aude *département* (of which I was president from 2011 to 2020) since 2001. I could have relied upon concrete examples of issues for which I had to directly negotiate with the Executive and give you my opinion, but I have preferred to refer to the experience I have had for a dozen years as a *département* councillor and a member of the governing bodies of the *Assemblée des Départements de France*, which led me to participate in many discussions and negotiations at the national level with the different successive governments. Last, of course, I have started from the list of questions raised by the organisers of that round table which I would sum up as follows: what are the modes of consultation and communication between the government and the local authorities? What means are available to the local authorities to exert pressure on the government? Can they rely on the Senate? How to improve the relations between the local authorities and the Executive?

First, asking how to improve the relations between the Executive and the local authorities implies that they are not good, or that there is some margin for improvement. . . . Well, I share this impression. Relations are not good. You could answer, is it not the politician who is answering, and who, not being very complacent with the current government, seizes the opportunity to have a dig at it? No, I am trying to be objective and honest. When I look at the past and the three presidential terms during which I have had the possibility to debate with the different governments, things are more complicated today and have been since Emmanuel Macron was elected. Beware, I am not speaking of the content of the policies. Each President of the Republic has faced strong oppositions, and blockades on the part of local authorities. Things have never been all rosy. Let us remember that Nicolas Sarkozy met the opposition of the local authorities on his project of local councillor and forced merger of intercommunalities, which, for the first time in the history of the Fifth Republic, led to the right's loss of the Senate; or that François Hollande is

DOI: 10.4324/9781003281559-9

still being reproached by many local councillors for the NOTRe Act, and, for what is specific to *départements*, the most advanced attempt, even though it failed, to cancel that level. Thus, the last two Presidents of the Republic have encountered huge difficulties with local authorities, as Emmanuel Macron has throughout this term. But I am here speaking of form. Local representatives, since the beginning of the term, have had the feeling that they are not heard, that they are not even listened to. All the governments have started discussions, negotiations with associations of local representatives, and even though those governments held strong positions, discussions and changes were possible. Since 2017, negotiations have looked more like the presentation of positions that may not be changed. . . .

We are about to celebrate the 40th anniversary of decentralisation and I have had the opportunity to say, in a contribution I was asked to make on that occasion, that local authorities were not the first concern of the current president, to say the least. I am not developing that point any further; people may answer that that is very subjective, but know that many local councillors think the same. They may also be in bad faith. . . . However, and in the defence of the current president, I think that there is a phenomenon, regardless of which president would have been elected after François Hollande, which has deeply modified the relations between the Executive and the local authorities. The induced effects of that phenomenon have not been thought through enough: I am talking of the end of the holding of multiple offices of parliamentarian and leader of the local executive since 2014, which was enforced during the legislative elections of 2017. Let me say that from the start, I was and still am in favour of that prohibition. However, it is evident that it resulted in separating parliamentarians from local affairs, especially with the wave of new MPs in 2017 who had no local experience. If I come back to very local issues, how many such issues were solved in the corridors of the National Assembly before 2017 thanks to a simple discussion between a minister and an MP-mayor? And if one looks at the larger picture, it was much simpler, before 2017, to tackle issues about local authorities at the National Assembly, because many parliamentarians had first-hand experience of the issue. However, does one need to have experience of an issue to legislate on it? Of course not. Thus, some suggest putting an end to the prohibition of holding multiple offices to find again that contact and improve the relations between the Executive and the local authorities and make them more fluid. I am not, again, in favour of it. That allows me to incidentally answer another question of the organisers of this symposium: yes, undeniably, the Senate has become a considerable support (the only one?) for local authorities for the past five years. It was recognised as the representative of local authorities in 2003, at the moment of the second cycle of decentralisation, and it has never represented them so well as during the past term. The discussions between the Executive and the assemblies of local authorities were so complex, and ineffective, that the debates in the Senate were the only ones, the only forum where the local authorities could have their claims heard. The debate on the bill on the differentiation, decentralisation and de-concentration and different measures of simplification of the local public action (known as the 3Ds Bill) is the best example of it.

Then, does the government consult the local authorities, do the latter have means of pressure, apart from the Senate, on the Executive? The local authorities are consulted, of course, and have been during this term, as in previous ones and I have had the opportunity of participating in debates, each time, almost, a bill impacted a competence of the local authorities – the association representing that level of local authorities being consulted beforehand. Over the last three terms, and as a member of the *Assemblée des Départements de France* (ADF), I even participated in long-term negotiations on an issue that has been a feature of the relations between the State and the *départements*, that is, the management of the *Revenu de Solidarité Active* (RSA, a form of French social welfare). Whereas some *départements*, managed by a left-wing Executive, wanted the State to manage the RSA, considering that that was part of the national solidarity, the great majority of *départements* wanted that the State at least better compensate the funding of the RSA, since the *Conseil Constitutionnel* had refused 'rolling compensation', which had created considerable frustration among the ADF. The debates never led to a consensus, the ADF often obtaining a simple rise of the compensation of the share of the State or an increase of means (e.g., the right to increase the transfer duty in 2013 under the Ayrault Government). Pursuant to the 3Ds Act, an experiment of recentralisation of the funding of the RSA will be implemented in some volunteer *départements*.

There are therefore many exchanges between the State and the local authorities, and when Edouard Philippe was prime minister, he tried to formalise a forum in which they could all exchange views: it was the *Conférence Nationale des Territoires* that Emmanuel Macron had promised during the presidential campaign. It was to be a twice-yearly meeting which aimed to 'get out of the often sterile, sometimes distrustful confrontation' between the State and the local authorities, according to what he said. Unfortunately, that Conference never reached its objective. The format was not the right one: there was very little time for debates (three hours every six months), the agenda was completely decided by the Executive, so that the Conference simply became a platform for the two sides, with a succession of little-constructive monologues. Local authorities reproach the Executive with taking unilateral decisions, without even mentioning them at the Conference. It was during one of those conferences, which was held at Cahors, that the famous 'Pact of Cahors', a system that imposed on the biggest local authorities to limit the increase of their operating expenditures – the increase could not exceed 1.2 percent on average (downward and upward adjustments depending on the authorities were provided for in the law which formalised that system) – subject to 'financial sanctions', was presented. The system did not please, to say the least, many local authorities, which refused to sign the 'pact' (and risked heavier financial penalties if they did not respect the supervision rate), arguing that this was a serious violation of the free administration of local authorities (an argument that was not upheld by the *Conseil Constitutionnel* which had to decide the case).

There was a strong tension between the State and the local authorities, and the feeling of distrust grew over time. That distrust even led some associations of local councillors, which was thought to be impossible, to gather in '*Territoires Unis*' in September 2018. The objective of that association was to oppose the government, since the local authorities did not want the Executive to try to divide them by playing a level of local authorities against another. The creation of that association was a turning point in the term, the local authorities then having, at least in the media, a more important means of pressure, and even though the government has never invited that association as such to negotiate, the local authorities have constantly relied on '*Territoires Unis*' to act.

To conclude, I will come back to the last question I had to address: how to improve the relations between the Executive and the local authorities? Should one leave it there, saying that the Senate is where everything should be done, but then, for me, the Senate should be made a real forum for debates between the local authorities and the government, it should be much more focused on those topics than today, and maybe there should be a reform of its organisation, of its role? Should a new space of consultation be created? But then it should not be a gadget and must be made official in the law to become credible. In the end, for me, things cannot stay as they are. I am convinced that the impact of the end of the holding of multiple offices for parliamentarians at the level of relations between the Executive and the local authorities has not been thought through. Should we step back? I would not wish it. We should invent a system to solve that difficulty, for it is one. Today, in many areas where the State wants to act, the local authorities now have jurisdiction. It is necessary, and even crucial, for the State and the local authorities to debate and negotiate, that is, work together. It is necessary to set up a new organisation and I hope this symposium will open up avenues on that topic.

Conclusion

How do local actors participate in the strengthening or in the weakening of the holding to account of the Executive within modern democratic States?

Stéphane Mouton

How do local actors participate in the strengthening or the weakening of the holding to account of the Executive within modern democratic States? Answering that question was not an easy task, for two reasons:

The first reason: in light of its evolutions, political responsibility remains a principle that is difficult to define and to legally determine, for academics as well as for local actors, as Marc Péré underlinedduring the debates.

First, the notion of responsibility is an evolving notion, with a changing nature: from penal, individual and punitive, it became political, collective and afflictive following the evolutions of the parliamentary regime. Second, that political responsibility itself expanded out of the strict considerations of holding the higher bodies of the State to account, to the point that its political and penal dimensions tend to reconnect in modern political regimes. That is what is shown in the virtuous evolution of the criminal liability of the members of the government – even though its legal modelling in its current form causes serious debates and even disputes[1] (*Cour de Justice de la République*) – and the putting into perspective of the executive power in the administrative area. There is an emerging domain, that of a possible responsibility that is 'administrative' in nature, which is apparently appearing under the increasing influence of the action of some actors legally linked to the Executive (inner circle . . .). It is a complex phenomenon which exists in several constitutional systems, like that of Switzerland, for example, but also of France now. Responsibility is therefore multifarious depending on the States' organisation and their concerns.

The second reason: it is hard to define, and it remains a mechanism that is difficult to limit in the law of the Constitution.

First, it is true that, being considered as the heart of the constitutional engineering of modern political regimes, political responsibility has been subjected to the increasing control of constitutional law, to the point that

1 An example would be the unsatisfactory organisation of the criminal liability of the members of the Government before the French *Cour de Justice de la République* created in 1993.

DOI: 10.4324/9781003281559-10

the mechanisms related to the political organisation of the government have become a matrix for the assertion of modern constitutional law in democratic States. Despite that legal hold, however, the principle of the political responsibility of the Executive has always resisted the logics imposed by constitutional dictates. It remains a principle the motives of which are conditioned by the institutional balance of powers which escapes them.

Second, in addition to that difficult legal determination, its implementation in the institutions has always been subjected to the tribulations of a constitutional system which, since the 1789 Revolution, and beyond the different regimes, has never managed to conjugate the principles of balance and trust that are so important for it to be well implemented in a modern parliamentary regime. The efforts to make parliamentarianism rational, which have never compensated the tempestuous habits of a constitutional history, which did not find at once the principles that would be useful to its modern development, with the wisdom of the law. Yes, as comparative law shows, it is difficult to build a 'concordance' democracy,[2] as Thierry Tanquerel called it, in France as in other constitutional regimes.

Despite those difficulties, the issue of the political responsibility of the national government cannot be left aside, for it remains at the heart of the democratic organisation of the power of the State. Based on a double logic of checks and balances the aim of which is that 'power stops power', the issue of the political responsibility of the government is one of the main benefits of the modern forms of political constitutionalism and of the modes of implementation of the separation of powers.

Though Montesquieu's theorem has never ceased to inspire the different modes of the implementation of the 'horizontal' separation of powers among the constitutional bodies entrusted with exercising the sovereign power of the State since 1791, it has never been conceived as a principle that may develop a requirement of responsibility on the part of local authorities.

However, in itself, that idea does not seem incongruous. Couldn't one imagine the development of such a responsibility of the national constitutional bodies and of the executive power for example towards the 'intermediary bodies' in order to answer to that second separation of powers, which this time is 'vertical', and which is necessary to the good organisation of the political go-betweens through which the 'sovereign power of the State flows' towards local authorities? Wasn't it possible to imagine, following a principle of reciprocity in return for the exercise of sovereignty, the principle of a political responsibility of the national constitutional bodies towards those 'social forces', as Montesquieu underlined, which determine the dynamics of the organisation of the sovereign power within them?

2 See also Thierry Tanquerel's study on the responsibility of the national executive power in Switzerland', in *Comparative Executive Power in Europe: Perspectives on Accountability from Law, History and Political Science*, eds. M. Morabito and G. Tusseau (Oxfordshire: Routledge, 2023), pp. 213–231.

It was due to the French political and constitutional culture, which is built upon an excessive exhalation of the principle of sovereignty of the State institution within the nation that that second separation of powers was overshadowed. It therefore stifled any will to develop an organisation of power that would have made local authorities real political partners in decision-making and/or a counterpower with power of control. In France, as Virginie Donier remarks, 'The relation between the State and the local actors has always been unequal'.

Here is the starting point. Imagining a principle of the national executive power's political responsibility to local authorities relies on a constitutional void. Is this observation critical? Does it make it impossible to think about the national executive power's responsibility towards local authorities in France? No, and for two reasons.

The first one is that such absence is the result of a truncated conception of the exercise of power in a democracy. Foreign examples show it. In Germany, for example, as in other European democracies, the network of political decision-making is based on a multiplicity of national and local actors and their increasing interaction in the management of political affairs, which in itself generates a principle of responsibility of those actors among themselves.

The second one is that the development of public policies, which are increasingly complex and diverse to implement, can no longer be reduced to a conceptualisation and implementation following a top-to-bottom impulse, from the national executive bodies to local authorities. Such an evolution strengthens the obligation for the national executive power to 'give accounts' to its local partners.

Such was the aim of that symposium: what was at stake was the highlighting of the political relation between local authorities[3] and national ones – which is realised through a game of political influence, assessment or even control – and bringing to light a dimension that remains in the shadow of the constitutional law of political responsibility but is nonetheless an essential living dimension of the democratic life of modern nations.

In order to meet that stake, three questions deserved to be raised and debated by contributors: Why is there a responsibility of the national Executives to local authorities? How does that responsibility of the national Executive to local authorities manifest itself? What are the effects of the responsibility of the national Executive towards local authorities?

Why is there a responsibility of the national Executives to local authorities?

The first interesting conclusion of that symposium is that there is indeed a political responsibility of the national Executive to local authorities. It does not derive from the constitutional texts, but from the necessary consequences

3 As Serge Regourd noted, from a legal point of view, local actors should be understood to be 'local Executives'.

of an institutional system the building and operation of which in France show signs of weakness. Indeed, that political responsibility compensates for two strong failures of the political system under the Fifth Republic.

Compensating the failures of the institutional system

The establishment of a link between the national Executive in France and the local authorities first aims to by-pass the pitfalls of the French presidential system. Concretely speaking, as Chloë Geynet-Dussauze underlined,[4] it is a political phenomenon which aims to fight against power 'capture' by the Executive, the consequence of which is to undermine the principle of accountability to Parliament. For Mathieu Carpentier, that 'de facto responsibility', which is not to be found in constitutional law, may therefore be imagined as a political mechanism trying to compensate for the pitfalls of a rationalised parliamentarianism which neutralises any implementation of the principle of the political responsibility of the government.[5]

That is exactly what Senator Philippe Bonnecarrère said too. For him, the weakening of the principle of classic political responsibility results in generating 'a phenomenon of multiplication and plurality of responsibilities'. The increasingly obvious 'dysfunctioning' of the political accountability of the government to the Parliament results in the emergence and assertion of government responsibility to other authorities and powers, among which local ones are the first. Quite simply, and like a virtuous democratic political-constitutional phenomenon, 'the weaker the Government's political responsibility to the Parliament is, the stronger it becomes to local authorities'.

That is a new manifestation of the will to regenerate, from bottom, a principle of trust in the political authority which comes from the top, to quote an expression from Sieyès. That is the reason why new actors appear and multiply in the political arena. Several of our contributors have underlined a phenomenon which, from that point of view, is developing both at a national and a European level.

Thus, at the local level, the *Association des Maires de France*, which is a classic representative of political territories, to which are added new institutional actors, the *maisons des régions*, the *maisons de départements* in main cities, *intercommunalités*, the *France Urbaine* association, as underlined by Laurent

4 See also C. Geynet-Dussauze and P. Jensel-Monge, 'France', in *Comparative Executive Power in Europe: Perspectives on Accountability from Law, History and Political Science*, eds. M. Morabito and G. Tusseau (Oxfordshire: Routledge, 2023), pp. 23–40.

5 See also M. Carpentier, 'Quelques points aveugles de l'irresponsabilité du président de la République', *Les Cahiers Portalis* 9, (2022): pp. 111–125.

Carrié,[6] André Viola[7] and Marc Péré, turn up as new political actors emerging opposite the State. They establish themselves as representatives and spokespersons of expectations of local authorities in front of the public policies which are coordinated by State administrations. What is important to highlight here is that such an assertion is not limited to a technical dimension with a purely administrative implementation, but that it results in a decision-making alternative within a logic of consultation and partnership. It is a dynamic that has been taken into account quite well by the European institutions. In that sense, Fabienne Péraldi-Leneuf noted that the Committee of the Regions, an intermediary between the EU and local authorities, has taken into consideration that new culture of local actors opposite the State and its administrations in the determination and conduct of public policies at the European, nation and local levels.

In front of the too classic phenomenon of avoidance of the local representation by the national Executive, several local intermediaries are built which compel the State to take into account those forms of expression. For the State, there is a reality that looks like a political obligation to respond to the requirement that the local authorities accept its decisions and policies.

Answering the demands as to the democratic legitimisation of power

As Laurent Carrié has shown in his chapter and his report mentioned earlier, the State itself is asking for that relation with local actors 'in order to assert its legitimacy on the territory'. That new relation answers the concern, which is clearly displayed by the State, of reinforcing the acceptance of its action by different players, from the regional to the local levels.

This new political stake naturally engenders a new channel of responsibility which is not limited to an institutional stake between national bodies. It expands into a relation between the national constitutional bodies and the local authorities. As highlighted by Philippe Bonnecarrère, the issue of responsibility remains a central one in democratic life: 'without it, there is no democracy'.

The ramping up of local actors forces the State to change cultures. It encourages the implementation of a dynamic of coordination of decisions and of cooperation of public policies compelling the national executive power to develop mechanisms of consultation and dialogue with local actors which assert themselves as political interlocutors to which it is accountable. Undoubtedly,

6 L. Carrié's report ('The Point of View of a State Representative, Chapter 4'), in this volume, *Regional Accountability and Executive Power in Europe*, eds. M. Morabito and G. Tusseau (Oxfordshire: Routledge, 2023).

7 A. Viola, 'The Point of View of a Local Elected Official' (Chapter 5), in this volume, *Regional Accountability and Executive Power in Europe*, eds. M. Morabito and G. Tusseau (Oxfordshire: Routledge, 2023).

such an evolution consecrates 'a new generation of political contracts'[8] (we will come back to that), between the national Executive and the local actors which naturally relies on the birth of 'a new form of political responsibility'.[9] It has been very clearly expressed for a few years and especially in the organisation of the great national debate organised by Emmanuel Macron, and the revival and ecological transition contracts (*contrats de relance et de relance écologique*, CRTE).[10]

In light of this change of cultures, this symposium has highlighted the shift of the responsibility issue, from an institutional interaction among national bodies towards a new form of political vertical reciprocity between national and local bodies. It is an evolution which therefore requires that the local territories, which are the actors of the development of that new responsibility, be considered anew.

Comparative law shows that the good organisation of democracy implies interaction among actors. New forms of political control are developing within different States of the European Union. They are new forms of oversight which are not necessarily analysed in terms of classic constitutional counter powers. They assert themselves rather in terms of collaboration, co-legislation, which the law increasingly takes into account. The Conference of Ministers-Presidents, the coalition contracts in Belgium, as exposed by Marc Verdussen,[11] and even the assertion of an administrative type of federalism as suggested by Jacques Ziller,[12] show those new forms of political interaction between the national bodies and the local actors.

How does that responsibility of the national Executive to local authorities manifest itself?

Far from being old-fashioned or hackneyed, the issue of the responsibility of national Executives remains highly topical. Though it is a classic one, given the evolutions shown earlier, it is undergoing deep evolutions in all the European States. To quote Marc Verdussen on that point, in that area today, 'lines are shifting'.

What does it mean?

It means that, concretely, the forms of expression of that responsibility are changing, or rather are transforming in order to take on a new institutional,

8 See L. Carrié, 'The Point of View of a State Representative (Chapter 4)'.

9 L. Carrié, 'The Point of View of a State Representative (Chapter 4)'.

10 L. Carrié, 'The Point of View of a State Representative (Chapter 4)'.

11 See also M. Verdussen, 'Belgium', in *Comparative Executive Power in Europe: Perspectives on Accountability from Law, History and Political Science*, eds. M. Morabito and G. Tusseau (Oxfordshire: Routledge, 2023), pp. 6–22.

12 See also J. Ziller, 'Functional Duplication and Political Accountability of the Executive in the EU Member States' (Chapter 8), in this volume, *Regional Accountability and Executive Power in Europe*, eds. M. Morabito and G. Tusseau (Oxfordshire: Routledge, 2023).

political and legal appearance. In the light of the evolutions of modern parliamentary regimes and of the acceptance of the political domination of the government power in Parliament, especially in the operation of the institutions, the principle of the political responsibility of the government has already failed: responsibility-assessment tends to assert itself next to responsibility-sanction. Though this evolution today is characteristic of how relations between the Executive and Parliament work in the implementation of the 'horizontal' separation of powers, it is now expanding in the field of the new political relations between local actors and the Executive and its administrations. Now, a new political responsibility is developing inside the institutional folds of those new relations that the national Executive has with local actors.

That symposium has clearly shown a specific phenomenon, that of the judicialisation of the political responsibility of national Executives (A). It is a phenomenon which opens a modern democratic process of transformation, of unheard-of 'politicisation' of the very classic administrative responsibility (B).

The judicialisation of the local authorities holding national Executives accountable

It is a meeting point of the reflections and discussions of that day. The responsibility of the national Executives is being judicialised. Philippe Bonnecarrère underlines that the judicialisation of French life is a reality that modifies the responsibility of the State to local authorities. This phenomenon is thought to have become quite strong with judicial review, which has become a means for local authorities to act against the law. The new mechanism of review opened by Article 61–1 C. 58 clearly participates in that judicialisation. It follows a groundswell – that of the assertion of the court in all the European systems. That is shown by the activism of the Portuguese Constitutional Court which, based on Article 223 of the Constitution, participates in the judicialisation of the link between national and local actors, within the framework of the referendum technique at the local level, which transmits a political tradition which is strongly anchored in some European countries like Switzerland.

Admittedly, that judicialisation also strengthens classic constitutional mechanisms of holding to account members of the national Executives, following special procedures like the one which is provided for by the *Cour de Justice de la République* in France. That movement participates in the revaluing of *criminal liability*, as Chloë Geynet-Dussauze underlined.[13]

It is also above all expressed through new institutional channels. 'The Executive's responsibility does not disappear, it is transformed!' It is exported into new fields and uses new actors. That is where one of the most interesting

13 See C. Geynet-Dussauze and P. Jensel-Monge, 'France', in *Comparative Executive Power in Europe: Perspectives on Accountability from Law, History and Political Science*, eds. M. Morabito and G. Tusseau (Oxfordshire: Routledge, 2023), pp. 23–40.

elements of the symposium lies. As underlined by several local actors who have participated in this symposium, Marc Péré and André Viola for example, local authorities use jurisdictional means to hold national rulers to account. That observation by political actors has been supported by the very interesting doctrinal analysis of Virginie Donier. She has demonstrated that local authorities use classic litigation paths to carry a new form of political responsibility. Local authorities, through their executive powers, now ask the court to observe, based on legal grounds, the national actors' failures, political abstentions and refusal to act.

She has also highlighted the double legal mechanism on which that judicialisation is founded. As to its legal foundation, it relies on the acknowledgement of the local authorities' right to file in court, based on Article 6 ECHR, of course, but also on the full acknowledgement of the *Conseil Constitutionnel* since its QPC decision of 25 October 2013. Courts acknowledge the local authorities' interest to act against the State. The efficiency of that judicialisation depends upon the implementation of the power of injunction. Thus, that evolution

> tends to show that by calling upon the courts, local authorities do not hesitate to remind the Executive of its duties and commitments. . . . The court de facto becomes an arbitrator of the relations between the State and the local authorities, and more precisely between the executive power and the local authorities when the issue is about a regulatory decision. The judicialisation movement that local authorities have launched and developed is therefore a way of holding the Executive to account.[14]

In that sense new litigations demonstrate it. The *Commune de Grande-Synthe* case of 19 November 2020 is its clearest expression today. By challenging the implicit refusal of the State to reduce its greenhouse gas emissions, the Grande-Synthe municipality uses a litigation instrument to support debates which are undeniably political in nature. Now, the interest to act is a legal lever which allows to hold the State accountable to local authorities and to point to the failures of the national Executive as to its international obligations, especially in terms of climate change.

Admittedly, the political dimension of administrative litigation has always existed. The administrative procedure has always been and remains the legal envelope of a claim or a challenge which can be analysed in political terms. But that political motivation used to remain within a litigation procedure which in a way reduced the political claim to a legal motive. The law rationalised the political in a classic function dedicated to administrative courts, within

14 See V. Donier, 'Is Calling upon the Courts a Way to Acknowledge the Responsibility of the Executive? (Chapter 3)', in this volume, *Regional Accountability and Executive Power in Europe*.

the framework of their function of institutionalisation of the State power and under the high authority of the *Conseil d'État*.

What is appearing now is the valuation of the political dimension of administrative litigation because that procedural channel compensates for the failures of the mechanisms of the political responsibility of the Executive. Not playing through the classic institutional channels of political representation through mechanisms of imposition of the administrative responsibility, the responsibility of the executive power shifts to administrative litigation.

The 'politicisation' of administrative responsibility

In support of that very relevant analysis, one thing must be added. It is a mechanism that is in the end a consistent one, from both a political and legal point of view. Indeed, that political reflex in litigation is logical in a State where the administration has always been considered as the institutional channel of diffusion of power. But it also results in generating an increase in the administrative responsibility of the State because of the failures of the national Executive to local authorities.

That is the most obvious consequence of judicialisation – the ramping-up of administrative responsibility. That is what Philippe Bonnecarrère underlines in his analyses, following a phenomenon of 'trivialisation of administrative control of all the acts', from urban planning of municipalities, for example, on the basis of an extensive conception of the legality check in relation to the letter of Article 72 C. 58. Later, resorting to '*référé-liberté*', which aims to protect individual liberties, tends to evolve into a power of injunction against the State for it to turn *droits-créances* into reality.

That phenomenon is taking on considerable significance in France. For us, it demonstrates the institutionalisation of a new form of responsibility of the national Executive to local authorities which accompanies the development of new forms of political responsibility, founded on the assessment rather than the sanction of the national executive power before the bodies which represent local territories.

As a consequence of the government's loss in political efficiency in front of the National Assembly through mechanisms defined in Articles 49 and 50 of the Constitution, the Senate is reasserting its supervisory function, through the legal levers that the Constitution grants it. From that point of view, the valuation of that new political role is already visible in Article 49(4) C. 59 which grants the government the possibility to ask the Senate for its approval of a policy address.

Above all, though, it is the development of the action of committees, the strengthening of the information and assessment means since the major constitutional reform of 2008, which has participated in the assertion of a real political activism of the Senate which indirectly shows a new channel of political responsibility between the national executive power and a parliamentary assembly linked to local territories and its actors. Thus, that new form of responsibility, which relies on a control-assessment function rather than a control-sanction one, participates in the assertion of a responsibility of the national executive power to local territories which revives a culture of counter powers that had become particularly blunted in the operation of the Fifth Republic.

That movement thus leads to a new reflection on the second parliamentary chamber, the role of which may, depending on the democracies, confirm that revaluation. Though it seems real in some parliamentary democracies, in Germany for example, it remains controversial and is even clearly challenged, as in Belgium, where a harmful atmosphere, and even the announced death of the second chamber, is alluded to.[15]

What are the effects of the responsibility of the national Executive towards local authorities?

There is no doubt that the development of a political responsibility of the national executive power by local actors is a new expression of the relations between the different local and national levels.

What is the real scope of such an evolution? Should it be considered as a real and deep evolution of political behaviours, or as an artificial phenomenon that is over-interpreted by a doctrine and actors who are tired or worried of seeing government action prosper outside any influence and political control?

There is, as all the contributors have shown, real resistance to that phenomenon. Even more, if that phenomenon existed indeed, would there not be an instrumentation of its scope by the executive power itself? Those are the two questions which have been suggested, or even raised by contributors.

Resistances

There is political resistance to the development of that responsibility in the first place. It is based on classic constitutional principles. As Marc Péré has emphasised, that new type of responsibility goes against the unity and indivisibility of the Republic, the logic of which is naturally averse to any construction of the political responsibility of the rulers by local territories.

Such data, which are so deeply rooted in the development of a democracy relying on the sovereign power of the State, have always resulted in the development of a logic of decentralisation, or even hyper-centralisation of the power by national representatives. 'I do not believe in the Girondin tale!' Serge Regourd told us. Moreover, how to support the development of a form of responsibility of the national executive power which would be founded on a relation of trust between national and local actors? To do so, relations must be based on trust here. However, as André Viola underlines, 'the relations between the State and the local territories are not good!' The

15 M. Verdussen, 'Belgium'.

increasing tensions under Nicolas Sarkozy's, François Hollande's and today Emmanuel Macron's terms of office between the national Executive and the local authorities because 'local representatives are not listened to' testify to it.[16]

It is true that the local authorities are completely absent of the building and organisation logic of the State power and are never included in the modes of exercise of the sovereign power of the State. Separated from the executive and judicial powers, they only very indirectly intervene in the 'forestalling functions' exercised by the Senate against the national executive power in the horizontal modes of responsibility between those two seats of national powers. From that point of view, the situation is singularly different from what exists in other States. In Germany, for example, Aurore Gaillet, Dieter Classen and Yoan Vilain have highlighted all the importance of the German *Bundesrat* in the implementation of the relations between the federal and *Länder* executives in a federal construction which is not composed of two but three levels – federal, federated and municipal – pursuant to Article 28(2) of the 1949 Basic Law.[17]

In France, the political-administrative reality tends to unavoidably push local actors into a field of action with a purely administrative scope. That is the consequence of a model of decentralisation which 'is not always authentic' by nature,[18] and quite 'imperfect' in a model where 'the State in theory [always] wants to build the game from afar but in reality always remains present'. Such is the logic that has repeatedly been implemented in France since the beginning of the 1980s despite a discourse that is increasingly favourable to a decentralised Republic, which has been recognised in the Constitution since 2003. There results from it a contradictory evolution. In a sense, it is true that the State 'is trying to reinforce the decentralisation process by developing a more sustained delegation of competences to local authorities', as Jean-Michel Lattes has underlined. It is the internal logic that has been asserted in so-called decentralisation laws since the LOTI Act of 1982 and in more recent Acts, such as the MAPTAM Act, the NOTRe Act, the LOM Act, or, even more recently, the *Resilience and Climate* Act. However, despite that declared will, in fact, the culture of the subordination of local authorities resists, in spite of a discourse that revalues their political role. Concretely speaking, those evolutions do not translate into what Chloë Geynet-Dussauze presented as 'a withdrawal of the State from the local political game'.[19]

And if one adds the observation of a 'timorous' court, as Virginie Donier calls it in her reflections, or 'unadventurous' by culture as Mathieu Carpentier notes when it is asked to defend local authorities against the State, the new

16 A. Viola, 'The Point of View of a Local Elected Official' (Chapter 5).

17 A. Gaillet, D. Classen, Y. Vilain, "The Responsibility of the National Executive Power in Germany from the Point of View of Local Territories' (Chapter 2), in this volume, *Regional Accountability and Executive Power in Europe*.

18 A. Viola, 'The Point of View of a Local Elected Official' (Chapter 5).

19 See also C. Geynet-Dussauze and P. Jensel-Monge, 'France'.

forms of responsibility of the executive power to the territories eventually seem to support more an implicit logic of a new reinforcement of the power of the national Executive which is subject to a political logic of 'presidentialisation' of the regime encouraging the increasingly absolute centralisation of power.

Admittedly, such a dynamic is supported by the inner logic of the institutions of the Fifth Republic, but it is also corroborated by the institutional logic of the European Union. By developing a politics relying on treaties among States, the Union increasingly generates centralisation in fact, despite laws that are supposed to be more 'decentralising' in theory.[20]

Renew democracy?

That could be the direction. Today, there is a real dynamic of renewal of the links between the political levels and the mechanisms of political responsibility that link them together. It relies here on the deep development of a contractual culture which has progressively been institutionalised, especially since 1982. It was then institutionalised and has been valued in the processes of delegation of competences that the State has realised in favour of the local authorities in the different legislative texts over the past 15 years.

Those links are developed in the planning contracts between the Regions and the State. They are also visible through the development of a policy of agreements between the State and the main local authorities as shown in the agreements between the State and the Regions, *départements* and main conurbations.[21]

In short, there is a contractual impulse which, according to Laurent Carrié, 'gives birth to a new generation of contracts which renews the rights and obligation of the parties'.[22] The reason for that is to be found in the fact that those new contracts are free from a technical and administrative dimension, from the strict execution of decisions made by the State, and are now asserted in a more political dimension which is based on a requirement of cooperation in decision-making and execution. The *Marseille en Grand* Plan is the clearest expression of that change as the legal uncertainties that surround it show. As was noted in the preceding contributions and discussions, *Marseille en Grand* belongs to a new genre of political contract. It is not an administrative contract. Admittedly, the State-Regions planning contracts have always been considered as administrative ones, the provisions of which do not entail real legal dictates. Unlike the latter, the *Marseille en Grand* Plan is a convention which develops a political relation in which everyone can 'point to the inaction of the other' in the execution of their commitments (Laurent Carrié). It is therefore

20 J. Ziller, 'Functional Duplication and Political Accountability of the Executive in the EU Member States' (Chapter 8).

21 In that sense, see the *3DS* Act.

22 L. Carrié, 'The Point of View of a State Representative' (Chapter 4).

a new form of political responsibility based on the principles of incentives, consultation and dialogue, and built on the will to revalue the representation of local territories.

Here again, the example of several European States may open some perspectives. In Belgium, for example, a country that is marked by the federation culture, which is intertwined with that of the confederation, the local authorities are not subordinate. They are entities which are in a situation of 'equipollence' with the federal level which therefore contains very different, multiple and fragmented political responsibilities because the attribution of responsibilities relies on several federated and federal actors.[23] The Consultative Committee is a sui generis body which ensures the relation and organisation of relations among the federated, federal and European levels, following a logic of consultation.

In Germany too, the political dialogue is free from the classic relation between Federation and *Länder* to include that third category of actors, the municipalities and local administrations in a logic of the development of 'administrative federalism' where the *Länder* are the link, or the screen between the Federation and the local level.[24]

That political dynamic reveals the importance of the parliamentary chamber. In different ways, as the Swiss example shows, the Senate is the most efficient link to pass on the issue of responsibility.

Indeed, and that will be the last point of this report, that general reflection on the responsibility of the national Executive towards the local authorities implies a certain valorisation of the second parliamentary chamber at the national level since, first, it is a representative of the local authorities and, second, it has a function of political control of the executive power. As there is no possibility in France to politically overthrow the government, it is nonetheless a very efficient chamber of assessment and control.

Then, a last main political and constitutional issue has been raised here. On the level of the necessary representation of the second chamber, it is the issue of the holding of multiple offices which is quite acute in France. It is a sensitive subject, an 'elephant in the room' as Jacques Ziller said, and despite all the controversies it is the subject of, the issue of the holding of multiple offices remains unthought of by constitutional law, even though it conveys very strong political questions, linked to a sensitive concrete political reality.

As shown by the divergent assessments made on this issue, it is necessary to look anew at the holding of multiple, national and local offices. There were those 'for it' like Serge Regourd, those who were 'undecided', like Senator Philippe Bonnecarère who noted that the 'ultra-fast' reform of the holding of multiple offices has hidden a human and political reality, or, like André Viola,

23 M. Verdussen, 'Belgium'.

24 A. Gaillet, D. Classen, Y. Vilain, "The Responsibility of the National Executive Power in Germany from the Point of View of Local Territories' (Chapter 2).

who remarked that the 2014 reform on that issue which came into force in 2017, which was virtuous in itself from a democratic point of view, has not solved the shortcoming of reinforcing the political distance between the national representatives and the local territories. Ineluctably, it encourages a loss of practice, of continuous information of parliamentarians and ministers, a remoteness of local information circuits, which is in practice compensated for by the new contractual logic which tries to avoid the pitfalls of that downward slide.

The conclusion of that symposium is therefore self-evident. Yes, there is a responsibility of the national Executive to the local territories. Though it remains implicit in its statement, heterogeneous in its implementation and uncertain in its consequences, it nonetheless shows the will and even the necessity to rethink the different levels of the building and organisation of a national power the legitimacy and efficiency of which must rely on the trust and support of all the actors that are useful for its implementation.

Part II

National traditions and European culture

Section 3

What impact do the traditions of the Member States have on the European practice of responsibility?

6 Are there common national traditions regarding the responsibility of the executive power?

Luigi Lacchè

Introductory remarks

Answering the question (reflected in the title) posed by the organisers of this conference[1] is very difficult, if not impossible. So, I take this request first and foremost as a provocative incitement to reflect. Certainly, the *REGALIEN Project*, broadly comparative and interdisciplinary as it is, offers a wide 'data set' useful to the comparative constitutional history approach that I am trying to follow and develop.[2]

Today – from a global perspective – comparative constitutional history can help us to better understand, among other things, the unity/diversity dialectic that is at the heart of the arduous European integration processes. Between the nineteenth and the twentieth centuries historical comparison was one of the ways to (think to) strengthen or 'invent' national identities. Today it seems to us more appropriate and useful to 'deconstruct' these histories, going beyond boundaries,[3] de-nationalising them. This point of view helps us to demystify the excessively simplified use of 'general' typologies, models and clichés. We need to transcend the disciplinary divide between comparative constitutional history and other disciplines in the social sciences that study the same set of phenomena.[4] This vision may prove to be helpful also in dealing with the notions of 'constitutional heritage' and 'common constitutional traditions'. In

1 'La responsabilité du pouvoir exécutif: Traditions nationales et culture juridique européenne' [National traditions and European legal culture], Conference of the 'Projet REGALIEN (Responsibility of Governments, Accountability and Legitimacy)', Paris, 20 May 2022.

2 L. Lacchè, 'Crossing Boundaries. Comparative Constitutional History as a Space of Communication', *Glossae European Journal of Legal History*, no. 15 (2018): pp. 126–139.

3 About several kinds of boundaries – subject-matter, disciplinary and geographical – in current comparative law, see M. Tushnet, 'The Boundaries of Comparative Law', *European Constitutional Law Review* 13, no. 1 (2017): pp. 13–22.

4 See A. von Bogdandy, 'National Legal Scholarship in the European Legal Area: A Manifesto', *International Journal of Constitutional Law* 10, no. 3 (2012): p. 624; R. Hirschl, *Comparative Matters. The Renaissance of Comparative Constitutional Law* (Oxford: Oxford University Press, 2014), pp. 191–192.

DOI: 10.4324/9781003281559-13

fact, comparative constitutional history[5] can perhaps provide an opportunity to better decipher two very important issues of our own times: first of all, assessing the identity and the constitutional substance of a European living common core of constitutional traditions; second, considering constitutional history as a useful tool to address different levels of global constitutionalism and new trends of governance.

Constitutional history, considered as a 'particular' space of communication, can help us to reflect on developments within a European legal culture of constitutionalism. The demystifying and critique of the excessive and ahistorical use of 'constitutional' models are important elements in the fashioning of a renewed history. In this way constitutional history can enhance other research outlooks, for example comparative constitutional law and political science. One of the issues addressed by constitutional history concerns the 'making' of constitutional texts. This history has often been reduced simply to a sort of history of genealogies. The use of 'models'[6] as prescriptive frameworks suggests that there are 'original' and 'derivative' constitutions. I for my part believe that constitutional phenomena always deal with *place-specific experiences.* Sometimes we happen to read that in a constitution a significant proportion of its articles are copied from texts or principles deriving from other nations. But what does it mean to transpose or copy certain articles? It is evident that to copy really means to invent or to reinvent. Texts move, they are compared and also 'copied', and yet every text becomes specific and 'original' once again, because, on each occasion, contexts, circumstances, times, places, authors and factors change. A constitution is at the same time a factor of sharing and of separation, of identity and of difference. A constitution is always a *patchwork* composed of different elements. For this reason, it would seem better to embrace a dynamic and interactive concept of constitutional change through texts, social contexts, political practices, constitutional interpretation and communication.

In this chapter I will try to deal with the theme of the responsibility[7] of the Executive from this methodological perspective, using the comparative historical approach. This can only be a first attempt given the evident complexity of the topic.

5 See L. Lacchè, *History & Constitution. Developments in European Constitutionalism: The Comparative Experience of Italy, France, Switzerland and Belgium, 19th–20th Centuries* (Frankfurt-on-Main: V. Klostermann, 2016).

6 Some reflections in A. G. Manca, 'Introduzione', in *L'istituzione parlamentare nel XIX secolo: Una prospettiva comparata/Die parlamentarische Institution im 19. Jahrhundert: Eine Perspektive im Vergleich*, eds. A. G. Manca and W. Brauneder (Bologna: il Mulino/Berlin: Duncker & Humblot, 2000), pp. 12 ff.

7 I will use, first of all, the word responsibility as it best represents the historical-constitutional conceptualisation of our topic.

The founding experiences

The responsibility of the executive power is, as is well known, a key element enabling us to determine the nature of a political-constitutional regime. Thus, the history of this highly important 'machinery' is relevant to the reframing of contemporary issues in terms of principles and general frameworks. It can be useful to grasp the *longue durée* and structural elements and logics of the responsibility of the Executive. Our aim is simply to highlight certain aspects that emerged in the course of the nineteenth century. Yet it was of course the 'Atlantic triangle' involving Great Britain, the United States of America and France in the course of the eighteenth century that determined the basic contours of the concept, developing three different constitutional experiences. You could say that the basic grammar was formed then and in these contexts.

The gradual sedimentation of the principle that, 'The king can do no wrong' throughout the historical development of English legal thought offers an opportunity to understand the constitution from a historical perspective.[8] 'The king can do no wrong' can therefore serve as a heuristic tool allowing us to apprehend the various dimensions and institutions of the constitution in the light of historical development.[9] British history shows how long and complex the path from the fourteenth to the eighteenth century was as it became possible to distinguish between 'criminal' impeachment and political responsibility as a factor of *civilisation* concerning conflict in the 'parliamentarisation' process of the constitutional regime.

The American experience[10] of impeachment, with its originality and highly specific genetically republican and presidential features, draws on the

8 On this perspective see J. W. F. Allison, *The English Historical Constitution: Continuity, Change and European Effects* (Cambridge: Cambridge University Press, 2007); J. W. F. Allison, 'The Spirits of the Constitution', in *Accountability in the Contemporary Constitution*, eds. N. Bamford and P. Leyland (Oxford: Oxford University Press, 2014), pp. 27–56.

9 C. Roberts, *The Growth of Responsible Government in Stuart England* (Cambridge: Cambridge University Press, 1966); J. Greenberg, 'Our Grand Maxim of State: "The King Can Do No Wrong"', *History of Political Thought* 12, no. 2 (1991): pp. 209–228; J. L. Malcolm, 'Doing No Wrong: Law, Liberty, and the Constraint of Kings', *Journal of British Studies* 38, no. 2 (1999): pp. 161–186; D. Baranger, *Parlementarisme des origines: essai sur les conditions de formation d'un exécutif responsable en Angleterre (des années 1740 au début de l'âge victorien)* (Paris: PUF, 1999); and now, above all, M.-F. Fortin, 'A Historical Constitutional Approach to The King Can Do No Wrong: Revisiting Crown Liability' (PhD diss., University of Cambridge, 2019); M.-F. Fortin, 'Rule of Law, Parliamentary Sovereignty and Executive Accountability in English Legal Thinking: The Recent Revival of The King Can Do No Wrong', *Journal of Constitutional History/Giornale di storia costituzionale* 2, no. 44 (2022); P. Daly, 'The United Kingdom', in *Comparative Executive Power Accountability in Europe: Perspectives from Law, History and Political Science*, eds. M. Morabito and G. Tusseau (Oxfordshire: Routledge, 2023).

10 In the context of a vast literature see among the most recent contributions, W. H. Rehnquist, *Grand Inquests. The Historic Impeachments of Justice Samuel Chase and President Andrew Johnson* (New York: Morrow, 1992); M. J. Gerhardt, 'The Lessons of Impeachment History', *The George Washington Law Review* 67, no. 3 (1999): pp. 603–625; R. Berger, *Impeachment:*

'monarchical-parliamentary' legacy of the former motherland, tracing however a new pattern of accountability. The French debate after the Revolution of 1789, for its part, opened up a new and important laboratory,[11] destined to foster reflection on the original imprinting (the fight against ministerial despotism and the subordination of the executive to the legislative power) – revolutionary thought impregnated with the penal dimension of ministerial responsibility.[12]

These three founding experiences reveal very important differences reflected in various historical episodes and institutional choices. But a question arises spontaneously: are there in any case common elements between these three constitutional cultures regarding the accountability of the executive power? From this perspective we could say that these three contexts have in common the reference to two great 'machines of modernity'. The first is the impossibility or perhaps the difficulty of maintaining and managing a space of compatibility between the ancient culture of immunity and privilege (*Immunitas id est privilegium*) and the assertion of the principle of the equal submission of one and all to the law. At the beginning is the idea that modern peoples consider the constitution to be based on mistrust. If representative government requests that power be temporarily entrusted to representatives, one of the corollaries is that they must be constantly monitored to avoid abuses and crimes against the State, nation or people. So the privilege of immunity is no longer fully compatible with the 'government of the moderns'. But finding a balance between the two needs (the full exercise of power and the control of rulers) would prove extremely difficult. Jacques Necker understood this issue

The Constitutional Problems (Cambridge: Harvard University Press, 1999); M. Oliviero, *L'impeachment: Dalle origini inglesi all'esperienza degli Stati Uniti d'America* (Turin: Giappichelli, 2001); J. A. Engel, P. Baker, T. Naftali, and J. Meacham, *Impeachment: An American History* (New York: Modern Library, 2018); L. H. Tribe and J. Matz, *To End a Presidency: The Power of Impeachment* (New York: Basic Books, 2018); A. Hirsch, *Impeaching the President: Past, Present, and Future* (San Francisco: City Lights Books, 2019).

11 On the concepts of executive power and government in France see in the *Journal of Constitutional History/Giornale di storia costituzionale* 2, no. 28 (special issue) (2014) the following: E. Marguin-Hamon, 'Le pouvoir exécutif en France (Révolution/Vème République). Une révolution achevée?'/'The Executive Power in France (Revolution/Fifth Republic). An accomplished revolution?', pp. 5–10; M. Troper, 'Le pouvoir exécutif en France (Révolution/Vème République). Introduction', pp. 11–15 and 'Démocratie et Pouvoir exécutif dans les constitutions révolutionnaires. Du pouvoir exécutif au gouvernement', pp. 127–134; as well as A. Le Pillouër, 'Le dualisme de l'Exécutif sous la Révolution française', pp. 19–32; M. Morabito, 'La responsabilité du chef de l'État', pp. 43–49.

12 See V. Azimi, 'Aux origines de la responsabilité ministérielle', in *1791. La première constitution française*, eds. J. Bart and F. Naudin-Patriat (Paris: Economica, 1993), pp. 216–269; D. Amson, 'La responsabilité politique et pénale des ministres de 1789 à 1958', *Pouvoirs*, no. 92 (January 2000): pp. 31–60; M. Morabito, *Histoire constitutionnelle de la France de 1789 à nos jours* (Paris: LGDJ, 2020), pp. 77 ff.; C. Geynet-Dussauze and P. Jensel-Monge, 'France', in *Comparative Executive Power Accountability in Europe: Perspectives from Law, History and Political Science*, eds. M. Morabito and G. Tusseau (Oxfordshire: Routledge, 2023).

very well: 'Being accountable for the executive power without altering the dignity of the Government, and executing that responsibility without causing trouble in the State – here may lie the greatest political difficulty'.[13] It is not by chance that Necker is evoked here. Two authors in particular, both thinkers and politicians, and on either side of the Atlantic, contributed a great deal to defining the original problem of responsibility.[14] The time was that of the '80s of the eighteenth century. The *Dictionnaire critique de la langue française* of Abbot Jean-François Féraud[15] attributed to Jacques Necker, the finance minister of Louis XVI, the introduction, into the political-institutional lexicon, of the word *responsabilité* ('Responsabilité est un mot de M. Necker'). *The Oxford English Dictionary* assigns the authorship of the word 'responsibility' to Alexander Hamilton in *The Federalist*.[16]

These two references are important. Necker reflects on the formation of a public space of responsibility. The basic notion is that the government (and even the monarch) must be accountable to the *tribunal de l'opinion publique*. *The Federalist* contains the most extraordinary reflection on the different aspects of responsibility emerging from the American Constitution but always in comparison with the British experience.

What 'common' starting point?

If we refer – as it is this that specifically concerns us – to the nineteenth-century European continental history of executive power accountability, we must ask ourselves a first question: what does it mean to speak of common national traditions? Most assuredly, we are faced with a highly varied and complex panorama.[17] The dynamics of responsibility shift depending on times

13 J. Necker, 'Dernières vues de politique et de finance', in *Oeuvres complètes*, vol. 11 (Paris: Treuttel et Würtz, 1820–1821), p. 155.

14 L. Lacchè, 'Responsabilità ministeriale', in *History & Constitution* (Frankfurt-on-Main: V. Klostermann, 2016), p. 381.

15 A. J. F. Féraud, *Dictionnaire critique de la langue française*, vol. 3 (Marseille: Chez Jean Mossy Père et Fils, 1788), p. 456. Cf. F. Brunot, 'Responsabilité', in *A Grammatical Miscellany Offered to Otto Jespersen on His Seventieth Birthday*, eds. N. Bøgholm, A. Brusendorff, and C. A. Bodelsen (Copenhagen: Levin & Munksgaard/London: Allen & Unwin, 1930), pp. 401–404; G. Proschwitz, 'Responsabilité: l'idée et le mot dans le débat politique du XVIIIe siècle', in *Actes du Xe Congrès de linguistique et philologie romanes* (Paris: Klincksieck, 1965), pp. 385–397; J. Henriot, 'Note sur la date et le sens de l'apparition du mot 'responsabilité', *Archives de philosophie du droit* 22 (1977): pp. 59–62.

16 *The Oxford English Dictionary*, 2nd ed., vol. 8 (Oxford: Oxford University Press, 1989), p. 542. The reference is to *Federalist* #63.

17 For a wide overview, cf. P. Brandt, M. Kirsch, and A. Schlegelmilch, eds., *Handbuch der europäischen Verfassungsgeschichte im 19. Jahrhundert. Institutionen und Rechtspraxis im gesellschaftlichen Wandel: Um 1800*, vol. 1 (Bonn: Dietz, 2006); W. Daum, ed., with the collaboration of P. Brandt, M. Kirsch, and A. Schlegelmilch, *Handbuch der europäischen Verfassungsgeschichte im 19. Jahrhundert. Institutionen und Rechtspraxis im gesellschaftlichen Wandel, 1815–1847*, vol. 2 (Bonn: Dietz, 2012); P. Brandt, M. Kirsch, and A. Schlegelmilch,

and contexts. Constitutionalism granted by monarchies (e.g., the French Constitutional Charter of 1814, the Bavarian *Verfassungsurkunde* of 1818, the Brazilian/Portuguese Charters of 1824 and 1826, the Italian '*Statuti*' and especially the '*Statuto*' granted in March 1848 by the King of Sardinia) opened one path; 'constituent' constitutionalism (e.g., Portugal 1822, French *Charte* of 1830 with its ambiguity on legitimation and sovereignty issues, the Belgian liberal-democratic Constitution of 1831. . .) traced another; polymorphic constitutionalism characterised by the alternation of monarchical and republican regimes (France, Spain, etc.) brought yet other elements to take into consideration, namely, a republican constitutionalism linked to various mechanisms developed within the constitutional monarchy framework.[18] On the other hand, the weight of written constitutions should not be overestimated, taking into account as we should the constitutional 'anthropology' of European liberals: for them written texts are only a part of the 'whole constitution'. Practices, customs, conventions and behaviours are also very important.

Being mindful of these general premises, I believe that the best starting point for understanding the historical design at issue is represented by Article 13 of the French *Charte Constitutionnelle* of 1814 whose text reads as follows: 'The person of the king is inviolable and sacred. His ministers are responsible. To the king alone belongs the executive power'.[19] This text represents an attempt to fix the historical British practice but with a great and fundamental difference: in England the principle is the point of arrival of a long history, whereas in France and on the European Continent this evasive formula became all at once – without it being informed by any real experience – a constitutional rule which was meant to take root in political customs. Article 13 contains three principles: 'The king can do no wrong', the *monarchisches Prinzip* 'à

eds., *Handbuch der europäischen Verfassungsgeschichte im 19. Jahrhundert. Institutionen und Rechtspraxis im gesellschaftlichen Wandel, 1848–1870*, vol. 3 (Bonn: Dietz, 2019). See also M. Kirsch and P. Schiera, eds., *Denken und Umsetzung des Konstitutionalismus in Deutschland und anderen europäischen Ländern in der ersten Hälfte des 19. Jahrhunderts* (Berlin: Duncker & Humblot, 1999); H. Dippel, ed., *Executive and Legislative Powers in the Constitutions of 1848–49* (Berlin: Duncker & Humblot, 1999); M. Kirsch and P. Schiera, eds., *Verfassungswandel um 1848 im europäischen Vergleich* (Berlin: Duncker & Humblot, 2001); **A. G. Manca and W. Brauneder, eds., L'istituzione parlamentare nel XIX secolo. Una prospettiva comparata**; A. G. Manca and L. Lacchè, eds., *Parlamento e Costituzione nei sistemi costituzionali europei ottocenteschi/Parlament und Verfassung in den konstitutionellen Verfassungssystemen Europas* (Bologna; il Mulino/Berlin: Duncker & Humblot, 2003); L. Lacchè, *History & Constitution* (Frankfurt-on-Main: V. Klostermann, 2016); U. Müßig, ed., *Reconsidering Constitutional Formation I National Sovereignty: A Comparative Analysis of the Juridification by Constitution* (New York: Springer, 2016); U. Müßig, ed., *Reconsidering Constitutional Formation II Decisive Constitutional Normativity: From Old Liberties to New Precedence* (New York: Springer, 2018).

18 Just recall the example of the French Republic after the constitutional laws of 1875 and the connection with the doctrines of Orleanism: M. Morabito, *Histoire constitutionnelle de la France*, pp. 318 ff.

19 The exact same formula was repeated in Article12 of the 1830 Charter.

la française' and ministerial responsibility. This article defines the external boundaries of the responsibility in question, but it leaves to institutional practice the task of problem solving with regard to the constitutional regime. The article establishes the pillars of representative monarchical government, but it does not necessarily prevent an evolution towards a parliamentary one.

Beyond the cliché of the 'natural' assertion of parliamentary systems, the ambivalence, flexibility and laconic nature of the formula made it the most important *constitutional programme* in nineteenth-century Europe,[20] a programme to be interpreted and filled out with whatever content might be deemed appropriate. A number of similar written provisions (e.g., Sweden 1809; Spain 1812; France 1814; Norway 1814; Netherlands 1815; Bavaria 1818; France 1830; Belgium 1831; Sardinia 1848; Prussia 1851; Spain 1876, etc.) served to justify a wide range of constitutional monarchies and contrast politico-constitutional regimes of executive power responsibility. The nineteenth century was the century of monarchy, so much so that even the handful of republican experiments had a monarchical Head of State as point of reference and term of comparison.[21]

The theory of ministerial responsibility – the great Italian jurist Vittorio Emanuele Orlando noted in 1909 –

> encompasses in itself and summarizes all modern constitutional law. In fact, each of the institutions of parliamentary government coordinates with this theory, goes back to it or necessarily descends from it. Without it, neither can the right of control of Parliament be conceived, nor could the prerogative of the Head of State be exercised: this combination, which constitutes the essential character of parliamentary forms, is integrated into the Responsibility of Ministers.[22]

Circulation of constitutional doctrines, a key author: Benjamin Constant

An important aspect of the European debate concerns the elaboration of a broad *corpus* of doctrinal works dedicated to the principle of ministerial responsibility. A number of prominent authors published, at different moments,

20 On these aspects A. G. Manca and L. Lacchè, ed., *Parlamento e Costituzione nei sistemi costituzionali europei ottocenteschi.*

21 Cf. M. Kirsch, *Monarch und Parlament im 19. Jahrhundert. Der Monarchische Konstitutionalismus als europäischer Verfassungstyp: Frankreich im Vergleich* (Göttingen: Vandenhoeck & Ruprecht, 1999). Cf. A. G. Manca, 'La monarchia costituzionale nell'Europa del lungo Ottocento: da forma a strumento di governo', in *Dottrine e istituzioni in Occidente*, ed. L. Blanco (Bologna: il Mulino, 2011), pp. 151–184.

22 V. E. Orlando, 'Prefazione' to V. Teixeira De Mattos, *Accusa parlamentare e Responsabilità Ministeriale* (Milan: Vallardi, 1909), p. IX.

authoritative monographs. I could quote, for example, Robert Mohl[23] in the German context, Oswald de Kerchove[24] in Belgium or Camillo Montalcini[25] in Italy. These and many other scholars helped circulate national cases comparing them and elaborating common ideas and categories. But no writer has had such a founding role in Europe as Benjamin Constant. His pamphlet *De la responsabilité des ministres*[26] was very popular indeed, and most scholars took it as their starting point.

There are at least two reasons for the great influence exerted by Constant's pamphlet. First of all, his intellectual links with Madame de Staël and Jacques Necker, and more broadly with the so-called Coppet Group, should be borne in mind. They were familiar with British constitutional history, starting from 1714 and the advent of the Hanoverian dynasty.[27] An adequate knowledge of the British experience enabled this circle to grasp three major dynamics: the development of the principle of the monarch's inviolability and the emergence of a Cabinet headed by a Prime Minister; the progressive weakening of criminal impeachment in favour of the autonomy of political responsibility; and the growing weight of public opinion in orienting governmental choices.[28]

These authors reflected in depth on the crucial problem of the executive power and the role of the Head of State.[29] They did so in both monarchical and republican contexts. The British splitting of the executive power between monarchical ownership (*puissance*) and ministerial exercise (*responsabilité*) appeared as a favourable condition for establishing a balance between stability and change. As we have seen, Necker was perfectly aware of this. It was no coincidence that he was a banker and finance minister, in a country, France, which was crushed under a huge public debt. He used the vocabulary

23 R. von Mohl, *Die Verantnortlickeit der Minister in Einherrschaften mit Volksvertretung, rechtlich, politisch und geschichtlich entwickelt* (Tübingen: Lauppschen Buchhandlung, 1837).

24 O. K. de Denterghem, *De la responsabilité des ministres dans le droit public belge* (Paris: Auguste Durand, 1867).

25 C. Montalcini, *L'istituzione regia e la responsabilità ministeriale* (Turin: UTE, 1887).

26 B. Constant, *De la responsabilité des ministres* (Paris: H. Nicolle, 1815).

27 D. Baranger, *Parlementarisme des origines.*

28 See A. Laquièze, 'Le modèle anglais et la responsabilité ministérielle selon le groupe de Coppet', in *Coppet, creuset de l'esprit libéral. Les idées politiques et constitutionnelles du groupe de Madame de Staël*, ed. L. Jaume (Paris: Economica, 2000), pp. 157–176.

29 M. Morabito, 'Necker et la question du 'chef de l'État', in *Coppet, creuset de l'esprit libéral. Les idées politiques et constitutionnelles du groupe de Madame de Staël*, ed. L. Jaume (Paris: Economica, 2000), pp. 41–54; M. Morabito, *Le chef d'État en France* (Paris: Montchrestien, 1996); M. Morabito, *Il comando negato. Rivoluzione Francese e potere esecutivo* (Manduria, Bari, Rome: Piero Lacaita Editore, 1997). Cf. also H. Grange, *Les idées de Necker* (Paris: Klincksieck, 1974), pp. 307–349; L. Jaume, 'L'esprit de Coppet et l'organisation du pouvoir exécutif', in *La Constitution de l'an III ou l'ordre républicain*, eds. J. Bart, J.-J. Clere, C. Courvoisier, and M. Verpeaux (Dijon: Éditions Universitaires de Dijon, 1998); L. Lacchè, 'Coppet et la percée de l'État libéral constitutionnel', in *Coppet, creuset de l'esprit libéral. Les idées politiques et constitutionnelles du groupe de Madame de Staël*, ed. L. Jaume (Paris: Economica, 2000), pp. 147–149.

of *Commercial Society*: the minister, a public official, governing in the name of the King, must have credit if he is to gain the trust of public opinion.[30]

Therefore, we can say that between the end of the eighteenth and the beginning of the nineteenth century no other group pondered the problem of the responsibility of the executive power as deeply as the Coppet circle did. It is important also to follow the genealogy of Benjamin Constant's ideas, from his unpublished *Fragments*[31] to the *Réflexions sur les constitutions*[32] and *De la responsabilité des ministres*, embracing also a number of changes made to his *Cours de politique constitutionnelle*.[33]

The incipit of *De la responsabilité* is very famous, and there Constant explains his theory of neutral power:

> The responsibility of ministers is the necessary condition of any constitutional monarchy. It is that responsibility which places the King in a separate sphere, above all the agitations of the Government proper. By distinguishing between the royal power and the executive or ministerial power, it makes of the former a neutral and preserving authority, which decides between the active powers when they disagree and which, remaining calm in any circumstances because it is never compromised, restores peace by putting an end to conflicts, and action by removing obstacles.[34]

This initial statement should immediately warn the reader against interpreting Constant's work through the contemporary, 'rationalised' category of the political responsibility of ministers. Only by adopting a specific viewpoint can we hope to understand Constant's theory, as well as that of most scholars

30 J.-D. Bredin, 'Necker et l'opinion publique', in *Coppet, creuset de l'esprit libéral. Les idées politiques et constitutionnelles du groupe de Madame de Staël*, ed. L. Jaume (Paris: Economica, 2000), pp. 25–40; L. Jaume, 'Tra concetto e idea-forza: l'opinione pubblica secondo Necker', *Giornale di storia costituzionale* 6 (2003): pp. 129–144.

31 B. Constant, *Fragments d'un ouvrage abandonné sur la possibilité d'une constitution républicaine dans un grand pays*, ed. H. Grange (Paris: Aubier, 1991).

32 B. Constant, *Réflexions sur les constitutions, la distribution des pouvoirs, et les garanties dans une monarchie constitutionnelle* (Paris: H. Nicolle, Gide fils, 1814).

33 B. Constant, *Collection complète des ouvrages publiés sur le Gouvernement représentatif et la Constitution actuelle de la France, formant une espèce de Cours de politique constitutionnelle*, vol. 2 (Paris: Chez P. Plancher, 1818). On the evolution of Constant's thought about this topic from the beginning, see L. Jaume, 'Le concept de "responsabilité des ministres" chez Benjamin Constant', *Revue française de Droit constitutionnel*, no. 42 (2000): pp. 227–243; L. Jaume, 'Introduction', in *De la responsabilité des ministres*, *Œuvres complètes de Benjamin Constant*, vol. IX, eds. O. Devaux and K. Kloocke (Tübingen: Max Niemeyer Verlag, 2001); B. Constant, *Principes de politique et autres écrits (juin 1814-juillet 1815)*, *Œuvres complètes*, vol. XI, eds. O. Devaux and K. Kloocke (Tübingen: Max Niemeyer Verlag, 2001), pp. 415–438.

34 The critical edition of *De la responsabilité des ministres*, with the text edited by K. Kloocke and the 'Introduction' and notes by L. Jaume, is now very useful, p. 441.

during the nineteenth century. After the Restoration, (constitutional) monarchy – according to the English vulgate – seemed to be the natural institution for affirming the 'government of the moderns' based on the inviolability of the Head of State and ministerial responsibility. Necker had already focused on the specificity of the monarchical condition.[35] Its features (prestige, inheritance, stability. . .) allowed for the responsibility of the Executive (a pillar of free government) without destroying the power of the State. The *fil rouge* connecting Constant's remarks from the republican to the monarchical context is given by the notion of *neutral power* and its capacity to preserve an effectual balance of powers. Its jurisdictional dimension is evident: the monarch, who is in so many respects that neutral power, is, when there is a conflict between public opinion and the government, a sort of 'judicial power' of the other powers.[36]

The constitutional architecture at the basis of Constant's discourse deals with the reality of the French order at the beginning of the Restoration period. The Lausanne thinker was familiar with the British political context and the growing distinction between criminal/legal and political responsibility. But France is not Great Britain. It is necessary to bear in mind the basic difference between the British experience and the European continental situation at the beginning of the nineteenth century. In England the construction of the executive power and ministerial responsibility was the outcome of a centuries-old history, historical events and specific circumstances. In France, as well as in Europe, the starting point was a written text intended to establish a new political-constitutional system. Article 13 of the French Constitutional Charter is paradigmatic. It looks, first of all, at *impeachment*, but its ambiguity, flexibility and its laconic phrasing allow for further solutions. 'The person of the king is inviolable and sacred. His ministers are responsible. To the king alone

35 J. Necker, 'Dernières vues de politique et de finance', p. 71.

36 'In a representative monarchy, the essence of Royalty is the independence of the nominations it is granted. The King never acts in his own name. Being at the apex of all the powers, he creates some of them, moderates the others and leads political action, tempering it without participating in it. That is where his inviolability comes from. This prerogative should therefore be left untouched and respected. His right to choose should never be contested. Assemblies should not arrogate the right to exclude – a right which, when it is exercised persistently, finally implies that of nominating. I will not be accused, I think, of being too favourable to absolute authority, but I want Royalty to be invested with all the strength and surrounded by all the reverence which are necessary to it for the salvation of the people and the dignity of the throne. Deliberations of the assemblies should be perfectly free; support from the press, freed from any constraint, should encourage and enlighten them; the Opposition should enjoy all the privileges of the most daring debate – do not deny it any constitutional means to deprive the ministry of its majority. But do not open a path for it towards which, once it will have been opened, it will constantly rush. The declaration that is proposed will in turns become a formula of no consequence and a weapon in the hands of factions'. (B. Constant, 'De la déclaration que les Ministres sont indignes de la confiance publique (Chapter 7)', in *De la responsabilité des ministres*, in *Principes de politique et autres écrits (juin 1814-juillet 1815)*, *Œuvres complètes*, vol. XI, eds. O. Devaux and K. Kloocke (Tübingen: Max Niemeyer Verlag, 2001), p. 464).

belongs the executive power' contains three principles that are theoretically 'compatible' with different constitutional regimes, covering a wide spectrum, from the *Monarchisches Prinzip* to the parliamentary system.

Benjamin Constant, as well as other publicists, was aware of these conditions. He distinguished between the legal use of power and an illegal one, when ministers do not behave as officers authorised by the law but as private individuals who violate the law.[37] This distinction shows how different the point of view is. On the other hand, it is quite evident how familiar these authors were with the institutional features of political responsibility. Ministers lose public trust when they lose the majority in the assemblies.

> *When we have what we do not yet have*, but which is an absolute necessity in any constitutional monarchy, I mean, a ministry that acts in concert, a stable majority and an Opposition well separated from that majority, no ministry will be able to remain in power if it is not supported by the greatest number of votes, unless it calls upon the people in new elections. Then, those new elections will be the touchstone of the trust granted to that minister.[38]

The distinction between legal and political responsibility is in theory clear enough but Article 13 of the *Charte* simply inaugurated the long nineteenth century. So, we could say that political responsibility can be seen as the 'battlefield' of the representative regimes: 'parliamentarisation' is a momentous historical process, a complex and mutable one according to national contexts, especially given *place-specific* conditions, to quote Constant's formula. Continental constitutional regimes started to experiment, and to experience ministerial responsibility, the pillar of the new political systems after the Restoration.[39] This was a process driving several forces: public opinion, political groups, prerogatives and the great resources at the disposal of monarchs who

37 Lucien Jaume connects this position also to Constant's determination to overcome Article 75 of the Constitution of the year VIII ('Introduction' to *De la responsabilité des ministres*, pp. 420–421).

38 B. Constant, 'De la déclaration que les Ministres sont indignes de la confiance publique (Chapter 7)', in *De la responsabilité des ministres*, in *Principes de politique et autres écrits (juin 1814-juillet 1815)*, *Œuvres complètes*, vol. XI, eds. O. Devaux and K. Kloocke (Tübingen: Max Niemeyer Verlag, 2001), p. 463 (italicisation not original).

39 On the attempt to create a fully rounded parliamentary regime in France (1814–1848) see especially M. Morabito, *Histoire constitutionnelle de la France*, pp. 197–227; P. Rosanvallon, *La monarchie impossible. Les Chartes de 1814 et de 1830* (Paris: Fayard, 1994); A. Laquièze, *Les origines du régime parlementaires en France (1814–1848)* (Paris: PUF, 2002); L. Lacchè, 'Constitución, Monarquía, Parlamento: Francia y Bélgica ante los problemas y "modelos" del constitucionalismo europeo (1814–1848)', in *History & Constitution* (Frankfurt-on-Main: V. Klostermann, 2016), pp. 167–180; L. Lacchè, 'Governo rappresentativo e principio parlamentare: le *Chartes* francesi del 1814 e 1830', in *History & Constitution* (Frankfurt-on-Main: V. Klostermann, 2016), pp. 303–327; L. Lacchè, 'La razionalizzazione ottocentesca: il

reign but also *influence* the scene. Most of the institutional techniques had been established but it was by no means easy to find a lasting and effective balance.[40] The conflict between representative government and parliamentary principles, between *régner* and *gouverner*,[41] was not the solution but the main problem of the nineteenth century. Executive power responsibility was at the heart of this 'fight' and of a vast network of doctrinal contributions and controversies. For these same reasons it was not simple to 'separate' practically political accountability from *impeachment*, with the threat sometimes being made that a minister or a government would be forced to resign.[42]

Once again it is useful to read Constant on the true purposes of accountability:

> Responsibility seems to me to have to achieve two objectives – that of depriving guilty ministers of power and that of maintaining, in the Nation, through the vigilance of its Representatives, the publicizing of their debates, and the freedom of the press applied to the analysis of all the ministerial acts, a spirit of analysis, a common interest in the maintaining of the State Constitution, a constant participation in government matters, in short, an animated feeling of political life.[43]

The line between guilt and innocence is blurred in political matters. The important thing is to take power away from the minister and to strengthen the vigilance of the representatives of the nation and the public spirit. The corollary is well known:

> From all the previous provisions there results that ministers will often be denounced, sometimes accused, seldom condemned and almost never punished.[44]

---

problema dell'affermazione del modello parlamentare nell'età delle Chartes', in *La Costituzione francese/La Constitution français* (Turin: Giappichelli, 2009), pp. 329–354.

40 See A. Laquièze, *Les origines du régime parlementaires en France (1814–1848)*, pp. 151 ff.

41 On this distinction see L. Lacchè, 'Gouverner n'est point administrer. Régner est encore autre chose que gouverner. Le retour d'un vieillard: P. L. Roederer et le problème du "gouvernement" pendant la Monarchie de Juillet (1835)', in *History & Constitution* (Frankfurt-on-Main: V. Klostermann, 2016), pp. 355–377.

42 P. Desmottes, *De la responsabilité pénale des ministres en régime parlementaire français* (Paris: LGDJ, 1968); J.-J. Clère, 'La mise en œuvre de la responsabilité pénale des ministres sous la monarchie de juillet: théories et réalités', in *Les ministres devant la justice*, ed. Association française pour l'histoire de la justice (Arles: Actes Sud, 1997), pp. 79–115; N. Havas, 'De la manière de penser la responsabilité des ministres sous la Restauration', *Jus Politicum*, no. 1 (2008).

43 B. Constant, 'Résultat des Dispositions précédentes, relativement aux effets de la Responsabilité (Chapter XIII)', in *De la responsabilité des ministres*, in *Principes de politique et autres écrits (juin 1814-juillet 1815)*, *Œuvres complètes*, vol. XI, eds. O. Devaux and K. Kloocke (Tübingen: Max Niemeyer Verlag, 2001), p. 481.

44 B. Constant, 'Résultat des Dispositions précédentes, relativement aux effets de la Responsabilité (Chapter XIII)', p. 481.

Some aspects of ministerial responsibility in Europe during the nineteenth century

Constant's thought was immediately debated in France[45] and some critical remarks contributed also to change some of his views, but it was in Europe that the great publicist became the most widely cited 'authority' in the course of the nineteenth century. All this shows us not what we think we should find in that debate according to our viewpoints but what was relevant at the time according to the then current concepts and concerns. What for us sounds like ambiguity if not confusion is precisely the specificity of the nineteenth-century discourse on the responsibility of the executive power. This methodological vision should guide us in our analysis of the main aspects of our topic. Here I can only point out some of the aspects that had a more general impact.

A history of executive accountability in Europe should combine two dimensions: on the one hand trying to bring out the common elements, on the other pointing out the elements of specificity. It is taken for granted that national experiences are characterized by their own special features. So, just by way of example, French constitutional history offers an extraordinary, tumultuous and very rich 'inventory' of all the forms and practices of responsibility. The most important theme probably concerns the difficulty involved in 'transferring' the mechanisms developed in the context of the 'monarchical condition' to republican and presidential regimes. A linear history is therefore impossible, and the 'politicisation' of responsibility continued to be a problem until the Fifth Republic.

If instead we turn our gaze to the German lands the *leitmotif* could be another category, that of the guaranteeing of the Constitution[46] and the construction of the *Rechtsstaat*. For the jurists and politicians who were faithful to the *Monarchisches Prinzip* – starting with Friedrich Julius von Stahl[47] – ministerial responsibility can exist only for the purposes of constitutionality and not, as in England, at the behest of the parliamentary government. Legal responsibility guarantees that any government action conforms to the Constitution and not to the will of the representative assemblies. In reality, conservative exponents, Stahl among them, tried to weaken the principle of responsibility, as in the Prussian case.[48] On the other hand, most German liberals did not

45 L. Jaume, 'Introduction' to *De la responsabilité des ministres*, pp. 431–434.

46 On this category see A. G. Manca, L. Lacchè, eds., *Parlamento e Costituzione nei sistemi costituzionali europei ottocenteschi*.

47 F. J. Stahl, *Die Philosophie des Rechts. II. Rechts-und Staatslehre auf der Grundlage christlicher Weltanschauung*, 2nd ed. (Tübingen: Mohr, 1846).

48 F. Hartung, 'Verantwortliche Regierung, Kabinette und Nebenregierungen im konstitutionellen Preussen, 1848–1918', *Forschungen zur Brandenburgischen und PreuBischen Geschichte*, no. 44 (1932): pp. 1–45; E. Hahn, 'Ministerial Responsibility and Impeachment in Prussia 1848–63', *Central European History* 10, no. 1 (1977): pp. 3–27.

think they would be able to establish a regime predicated upon the political or parliamentary responsibility of ministers on the British model.[49]

As Robert Mohl stated in 1837, a law on ministerial responsibility appeared to be a capstone of the *Rechtsstaat*:[50] the chamber's right to impeach ministers would have been the appropriate way to guarantee the constitutional regime and to strengthen the principle of the irresponsibility of the sovereign. For Mohl, political and legal elements interpenetrate in ministerial responsibility. The purpose is political, but the means is legal. So only ministerial crimes that violate the Constitution and individual rights must be prosecuted. In 1833 Mohl defended the Minister of the Interior, Hassenpflug, in the Hessian electoral assembly (*Kurhessen*). He was accused by the lower chamber of dissolving the Assembly and violating its privilege to check elections.[51] This was the only case of impeachment in Germany before 1848 and the minister was acquitted.

Despite the differences existing among continental political-constitutional systems, for a conspicuous part of the doctrine there is a common need in the constitutional monarchical regimes for the ministers to have a special responsibility, which completes and integrates the principle of irresponsibility of the sovereign. What may appear to be a conceptual difficulty in separating or confusing impeachment and political accountability is in reality another characteristic of the nineteenth century. For a long time, the idea persisted – in contrast to what Constant thought – that political responsibility was not enough because the minister, accused or, on very rare occasions, actually condemned, could always return to power. Responsibility serves, first of all, to defend and guarantee the Constitution and then eventually to lay the blame on the minister. In addition, for many liberals the complete and strong assertion of political responsibility would strengthen beyond measure the elected assemblies and political majorities, by the same token weakening the constitutional monarchy and the need for balance between *power* and *accountability*.

This aspect however gives rise to a further question. Can the responsibility of the executive power really be regulated? For in the case of political responsibility, it depends on a complex mosaic of 'techniques' and dynamics. You can perhaps say that its history coincides with the history of parliamentarianism and modern constitutionalism, hence it is based above all on practices,

49 O. Pflanze, 'Juridical and Political Responsibility in Nineteenth Century Germany', in *The Responsibility of Power: Historical Essays in Honor of Hajo Holborn*, ed. L. Krieger and F. Stern (New York: Doubleday, 1967), pp. 162–182. On Ludwig von Rönne's theory regarding ministerial responsibility see A. G. Manca, *La sfida delle riforme. Costituzione e politica nel liberalismo prussiano, 1850–1866* (Bologna: il Mulino, 1995), pp. 156 ff.

50 R. Mohl, *Die Verantnortlickeit der Minister in Einherrschaften mit Volksvertretung*, p. 1.

51 E. R. Huber, *Deutsche Verfassungsgeschichte seit 1789*, vol. 2 (Stuttgart: Kohlhammer Verlag, 1960), pp. 70–73; P. Popp, *Ministerverantwortlichkeit und Ministeranklage im Spannungsfeld zwischen Verfassungsgebung und Verfassungswirklichkeit. Ein Beitrag zur Verfassungsgeschichte des Kurfürstentums Hessen* (Münster: Lit, 1996).

customs and conventions. When all is said and done it was only in the second half of the nineteenth century that political responsibility was explicitly stated in a European constitutional text.[52] In reality, it was legal responsibility that gave rise to most questions. First of all, there was a huge debate on the nature and boundaries of ministerial offences. And even before that, legislators and scholars had wondered if it was either possible or useful to draw up a law regarding responsibility. From the beginning, Constant grasped the essential nature of the problem, reckoning that in this regard any attempt to draft a precise and detailed law, as criminal laws should properly be, would be illusory. He was sceptical:

> If each of those manners of harming the State had to be mentioned and specified in a law, the Code of Responsibility would become a treatise on history and politics and its provision would only be about the past. Ministers would easily find other means of avoiding them in the future.[53]

Constant's doubts were widely shared. In many cases the constitutional promise to draft a law on legal responsibility was never kept. This was the fate of nations like Great Britain, France, Belgium, Italy, Prussia or Spain.[54] There were in some national experiences many attempts to discipline legal responsibility, but they remained no more than projects. The arguments referred to in order not to regulate legal responsibility were linked both to the constitutional ideology of the liberals in favour of the fluidity and elasticity of representative government and the belief – just read Benjamin Constant or Pellegrino Rossi – that politics, being protean, cannot be legally 'regulated'.

Conversely, Sweden (1810), Württemberg (1819), the Grand Duchy of Baden (1820), Portugal (1826), Norway (1828), Saxony (1838), Hungary

52 'The ministers are jointly responsible to the Chambers for the general policy of the Government and individually for their personal acts' (Article 6 of the French constitutional law, 25 February 1875). Cf. M. Morabito, *Histoire constitutionnelle de la France*, pp. 323–324.

53 B. Constant, 'De la Responsabilité proprement dite (Chapter VI)', in *De la responsabilité des ministres*, in *Principes de politique et autres écrits (juin 1814-juillet 1815)*, *Œuvres complètes*, vol. XI, eds. O. Devaux and K. Kloocke (Tübingen: Max Niemeyer Verlag, 2001), p. 460.

54 For example, Article 56 of the French *Charte* of 1814: 'Special laws will specify this kind of crimes, and will determine its indictment'; Article 69 French *Charte* of 1830: 'There will be provided successively by separate laws, and that with the shortest possible delay, for the following subjects: . . . 2. The responsibility of ministers and the secondary agents of government'; Article 134 of Belgian Constitution of 1831: 'Until provision is made with a law, the House of Representatives will have a discretionary power to accuse a minister, and the Court of Cassation to judge him, characterizing the crime and determining the penalty. However, the penalty cannot exceed imprisonment, without prejudice to the cases expressly provided for by the criminal laws'; Article 61 of the Prussian Constitution of 1850: 'The rules concerning the cases of ministerial responsibility, the prosecution in this regard and the penalties to be applied will form the subject of a particular law'. On Spain see the 'Prologue' by J. Varela Suanzes in *Poder y libertad: los origines de la responsabilidad del Ejecutivo en España (1808–1823)*, ed. I. Fernandez Sarasola (Madrid: Centro de Estudios Politicos y Constitucionales, 2001).

(1848), Bavaria (1848–1850), Switzerland (1850), Denmark (1852), the Netherlands (1855), the Austrian Empire (1867), Greece (1876–77), Bulgaria (1879), Romania (1879), Serbia (1891) etc. approved laws on ministerial crimes and related legal procedures. These laws were heterogeneous, and in some cases, they sought to implement a constitutional promise. But this fact certainly did not ensure the effectiveness of the approved provisions. There were very few cases of the actual application of the impeachment of ministers.

Another European common principle – in the wake of the English experience and regardless of constitutions and laws – concerns who is to judge ministers. The gold standard is that the Chamber elected by the people impeaches and the second Chamber, appointed by the sovereign or with other characteristics, has to judge the ministers.[55] For the indictment there are several possibilities: the formation of ad hoc Commissions, when necessary, or of a permanent Council composed at the beginning of each term (e.g., Sweden, Portugal). As for the judgment, history shows that a number of other solutions, in certain circumstances, were also adopted: the *Cour de Cassation* in Belgium; the *Haute Cour de Justice* in France (France, 1791 and 1848); a State court *(Staatsgerichtshof)* in Bavaria (1850) or Austria, composed of 24 citizens elected by the two Chambers.

The lack of a specific discipline or of a real effectiveness turned out to be the defining feature of the accountability of the executive power in Europe during the nineteenth century. Uncertainties and contradictions were part and parcel of the difficult implementation of the *konstitutionelle Verfassungen*. The nineteenth century was largely the century of monarchical imprinting and not of parliamentary regimes. It must not be forgotten that the executive power originally belongs to the Head of State, and this has crucial consequences for the concrete working of responsibility. The distinction between political and legal responsibility is 'clear' in theory but, in reality, these two faces have to be seen together, intertwined with each other. The basic idea for liberals is that the Constitution is threatened, first of all, by those who exercise the executive power whereas impeachment, in still uncertain constitutional systems, remains a 'communicative' resource serving to reassure public opinion.

Conclusion

Another aspect that must be emphasised is that the nature and limits of the executive power radically changed at the beginning of the twentieth century. The 'long' nineteenth century ended with the outbreak of the First World War. The REGALIEN Project arises from the observation of the current generalised

55 Once again, the French *Charte constitutionnelle* of 1814 is the European text which best 'translates' the English experience: 'The Chamber of Deputies has the right to accuse the ministers, and to bring them before the Chamber of Peers, which alone has the right to judge them' (Article 55).

strengthening of the executive power in Europe. This trend has to be seen within a longer historical process initiated a century ago. The First World War represented the turning point of the process of strengthening the executive marked by deep remodelling of the intervention of the State in all the sectors of social life. In the transformation of public law, before and after the Great War, the normative power of the government (regulations, decrees, provisions . . .) was not episodic or arbitrary, but a symptom of a specific historical phenomenon, of a constitutional transformation.[56] In France – the nation that had developed ***parlementarisme absolu*** during the Third Republic[57] – the controversial formula *Gouvernement législateur*,[58] discussed first only in the opening two decades of the twentieth century, anyway opened the new phase.[59]

56 This aspect was especially thorough in France: the public law debate is very well presented by M.-J. Redor, *De l'État légal à l'État de droit. L'évolution des conceptions de la doctrine publiciste française, 1879–1914* (Paris: Economica, 1992), pp. 137 ff. Cf. also G. Sacriste, *La République des constitutionnalistes: professeurs de droit et légitimation de l'Etat en France, 1870–1914* (Paris: Presses de Sciences Po, 2011). For a comparison see H. S. Jones, *The French State in Question. Public Law and Political Argument in the Third Republic* (Cambridge: Cambridge University Press, 1993); C. Laborde, *Pluralist Thought and the State in Britain and France, 1900–1925* (London: Palgrave Macmillan, 2000); M. Stolleis, *Origins of the German Welfare State Social Policy in Germany to 1945* (New York: Springer, 2013); M. Fioravanti, *La costituzione democratica. Modelli e itinerari del diritto pubblico del ventesimo secolo* (Milan: Giuffrè, 2018); L. Lacchè, *La Costituzione nel Novecento. Percorsi e vicissitudini dello Stato di diritto* (Turin: Giappichelli, 2023).

57 J.-P. Machelon, *La République contre les libertés? Les restrictions aux libertés publiques de 1879 à 1914* (Paris: FNSP, 1976); J.-P. Machelon, 'Parlementarisme absolu, État de droit relatif: à propos du contrôle de la constitutionnalité des lois en France sous la Troisième République (Positions et controverses)', *La Revue administrative* 48, no. 288 (November–December 1995): pp. 628–634; O. Rudelle, 'La République absolue. Aux origines de l'instabilité constitutionnelle de la France Républicaine, 1859–1875', *Revue française de science politique* 33, no. 3 (1983); E. Maulin, *La théorie de l'État de Carré de Malberg* (Paris: PUF, 2003); M. Morabito, *Histoire constitutionnelle de la France*, pp. 349 ff.

58 G. Cahen, *Le gouvernement législateur. La loi et le règlement* (Paris: Rousseau, 1903); J. Barthélemy, 'Le gouvernement législateur. Le projet de délégation du pouvoir exécutif', *Revue politique et parlementaire* (April 1917): pp. 5–20. Cf. F. Bock, *Un parlementarisme de guerre, 1914–1919* (Paris: Belin, 2002); E. Lemaire, 'Le désaccord du parlement et du gouvernement sur la "Constitution du pouvoir politique en temps de guerre": l'échec du projet Briand sur les décrets-lois (déc. 1916–jan. 1917)', *Jus Politicum*, no. 15, https://juspoliticum.com/article/Le-desaccord-du-parlement-et-du-gouvernement-sur-la-Constitution-du-pouvoir-politique-en-temps-de-guerre-l-echec-du-projet-Briand-sur-les-decrets-lois-dec-1916-jan-1917-1065.html; E. Quinart, 'L'émancipation du pouvoir réglementaire (1914–1958)' (PhD diss., Université de Lille, 2019), pp. 44 ff., 99 ff.

59 J. Barthélemy, *Le rôle du pouvoir exécutif dans les républiques modernes* (Paris: Giard et Brière, 1906), p. 9: 'The theoretician naturally tends to given the most important role to the legislative function, because, together with the judicial function, it is the most characteristic feature of the specific activity of the State, which is to establish the law and guarantee it. However, the legislative and judicial functions are only the abstract life of the State; its concrete life is the management of public affairs, it is the administration, in a very broad sense, but that administration is the natural attribute of the Executive'. Cf. F. Saulnier, *Joseph-Barthélemy 1874–1945. La crise du constitutionnalisme libéral sous la IIIe République* (Paris: LGDJ, 2004), pp. 393 ff.

The rationalisation of parliamentary systems in the course of the twentieth century strengthened the status of the executive power vis-à-vis parliaments and broadened their scope.

A first attempt to sketch a comparative constitutional history of executive power responsibility may serve to bring out some common features and to answer affirmatively, albeit in general, the question contained in the title of this chapter. At the same time, it shows us the multiplicity and variety of experiences and tools, highlighting several turning points, phases, contexts and different modes of legitimation. The fact that we use the same words (executive power, government, responsibility, impeachment, etc.) does not mean that nothing has changed. The greater part of the concepts and issues regarding Europe today are linked to a long historical legacy rich in deviations, changes and intertwinings. A glance at the historical dimension can be useful first of all for realising that Europe has been involved for several decades now with certain 'new' phenomena: the growth of competing forms of responsibility serving to compensate for some defects linked to 'pure' political responsibility;[60] new kinds of connection between political and legal responsibility, especially through parliamentary oversight;[61] the re-emergence of legal responsibility and its growing 'politicisation'; the expansion of the concept of responsibility towards social media and civil society; the 'corporatisation' of political cultures and systems focusing on the concepts of accountability[62] and compliance (responsibility of governance). Once again, history is *magistra vitae* but within a multidisciplinary approach.

60 O. Beaud, 'La responsabilité politique face à d'autres formes de responsabilité des gouvernants', *Pouvoirs*, no. 92 (2000): pp. 17–30.

61 E. Giglio, *Parliamentary Oversight of the Executives. Tools and Procedures in Europe* (Oxford: Hart Publishing, 2020).

62 P. Avril, 'Responsabilité et accountability', in *La responsabilité des gouvernants*, eds. O. Beaud and J. M. Blanquer (Paris: Descartes et compagnie, 1999), pp. 85–93.

7 The accountability of the EU Commission, as the EU's Executive

Paolo Ponzano

Tasks of the EU Commission

The (executive or non-executive) tasks of the EU Commission are the following:

- Carrying out political tasks that are comparable to those of a national government, such as introducing bills, executing the budget and representing the EU abroad;
- Operating as a central administrative body in the domain of economic regulation, including competition, while performing administrative tasks in different areas, alone or in cooperation with Member States and the Union agencies – from applying the legal norms decided by the European legislator to controlling Member State application of those norms. Those tasks – which give the Commission a wide margin of discretionary appreciation – are not normally fulfilled by national governments but rather by executive agencies, which may be monitored by the government;
- Being the guarantor of the Treaty, which implies that when it brings actions before the European Court of Justice for violation of a Union law, it has a role similar to that of a general prosecutor, thus exercising a quasi-judicial function; to which was added more recently the role of guaranteeing the values of the Union, such as the rule of law, as provided for in Article 7 of the Lisbon Treaty;
- Carrying out tasks involving significant political discretion within an institutional framework aiming to ensure budget discipline, coordination of national economic policies, and financial aid to Member States against banking and sovereign debt crises in the Euro Zone and more recently against the pandemics;
- In 2020, the Commission was charged with buying vaccines and distributing them to Member States and, in a more innovating way, getting the resources necessary to the financing of NextGenerationEU (a common debt of about 750 billion Euros) on the capital market. Moreover, the Commission is tasked with monitoring the content of national recovery

DOI: 10.4324/9781003281559-14

and resilience plans and grants Member States the financial aid provided for in Article 122 TFEU;

- Now, the Commission receives real 'mandates' from the European Council asking it to submit proposals in several domains, including in matters that are outside the competences of the Union, such as sanction against third-party countries or measures of energy policy.

Statistical data about the executive tasks of the European Commission

- Since the mid-1960s, the Commission has adopted about 120,000 executive acts under its own responsibility – but with the help of about 260 committees composed of representatives of Member States – to implement the decisions of the European Legislator and apply the about 15,000 European laws that are currently in force (regulations or directives). There were 4,094 such executive acts (or ministerial orders in national law) in 2020 and 4,017 in 2021 (data from the services of the European Union). Those data do not include the delegated acts (or orders in French law) that the Commission has been deciding since the Lisbon Treaty under the supervision of the European Legislator (European Council and Parliament). There were 135 delegated acts in 2020 and 230 in 2021.
- To my knowledge, there has been no case of revocation, by the Council or by the EU Parliament, of the delegation granted to the Commission to decide a delegated act. However, there were a dozen cases in which the Council or the EU Parliament raised objections to the exercise of the competence delegated to the Commission in a specific case (which compelled the Commission to amend the content of its delegated act).
- Before the Lisbon Treaty came into force, no distinction was made between the executive and delegated acts, so that the European Commission, following the so-called Comitology procedure, adopted implementation measures of European laws as well as measures aiming to amend or complement existing European Laws (directives related to food products, positive or negative lists of authorised or forbidden goods or services, measures about financial services, etc.). The 2002–2003 work of the European Convention put an end to that broad interpretation of executive acts and gave birth to the delegated acts procedure (i.e., 'orders'), which was included in the Lisbon Treaty.

The European Parliament has always challenged the so-called Comitology procedure which allowed the Commission to amend the content of a European law without the approval of the European Legislator. The coming into force of the Lisbon Treaty which subjected the enactment of a delegated act (i.e., order) to the tacit or explicit approval of the legislator concretely put an end to the dispute with the EU Parliament on the so-called Comitology procedure.

Changes in the role of the Commission

Initially, under the Treaty of Rome, the Commission was granted tasks that were essentially of an executive nature and was only given little room to take political decisions. Despite that, the Treaty of Rome already provided for some political accountability of the Commission to the EU Parliament since it granted the (not-yet-elected) Parliament the possibility to vote by a two-thirds majority on a motion of censure against the Commission which would have forced the latter to resign. That procedure was difficult to implement since the EU Parliament, until the Maastricht Treaty, did not have the right to approve the appointment of a new Commission. Consequently, if a motion of censure had been passed, the EU Parliament would not have been able to oppose the Member States' choice of a new Commission that would have been even less inclined to follow the positions of the EU Parliament. That explains why the EU Parliament never passed a motion of censure against the Commission.

The case of the Santer Commission was a particular one in that respect, for the EU Parliament did not directly pass a motion of censure but asked an independent expert committee to write a report on the dysfunction cases imputed to the Commission in the financial management of some executive measures. Since the report of the expert committee was critical of the behaviour of the Commission and its final conclusion indicated that the committee had found no civil servant of the Commission acknowledging any accountability in the decisions that had been taken, the College of Commissioners preferred to collectively resign before the Parliament voted on a motion of censure which was likely to get the necessary majority. Within the Commission and sometimes outside of it, that event was presented as the confirmation of a change in the role of the Commission towards the status of a 'government', since, at a national level, governments have to resign when they have lost the political confidence of their parliamentary majority. The collective resignation of the Santer Commission resulted in an important administrative reform of the Commission (the Prodi-Kinnock Reform) which included a regular rotation of the Directors-General and Heads of Units as well as a significant reinforcement of the financial supervision applicable to its executive measures. Independently of the change in the status of the Commission following the resignation of the Santer-presided College, there remains that the Commission underwent an increasing 'politicisation'. Indeed, under the Treaty, the European Parliament acquired the right to vote upon the nomination of the Commission and to approve the choice of the President of the Commission made by the European Council (which led in 2014 to the '*Spitzenkandidat*' procedure). What may have contributed to the reinforcement of the legitimacy of the Commission and its political role is the procedure of the hearings of Commissioners established by the European Parliament in 1994 for the Santer Commission. While a debate within the College during the last months of the Delors Commission had decided that the procedure of the hearings was inapplicable (not being provided for in the Treaty), the candidate Commissioners of the Santer

Commission all attended the hearings summoned by the European Parliament for they would have reinforced their political legitimacy and facilitated the appointment vote of the College.

A reinforcement of the increasing 'politicisation' of the Commission and its relation of political trust with the European Parliament may have been the fruit of the bilateral agreements concluded between the Commission and the European Parliament after the choice of the President of the Commission and the vote of approval of the new College (see the Codes of Conduct agreed to in 1990 by the Delors Commission and in 1995 by the Santer Commission and the Framework Agreements concluded by the successive following Commissions: in 2000 by the Prodi Commission, in 2005 and 2010 by the Barroso Commissions and in 2016 by the Juncker Commission, see the *Appendix* at the end of this chapter). The practice of political orientations given by the President of the Commission to each of the Commissioners individually has taken the form of 'engagement letters' under Article 17(6) of the Lisbon Treaty. That practice was amended at Point 2 of the Framework Agreement between the Barroso Commission and the European Parliament in 2010 as the precondition to the agreement of the European Parliament to the election of the President of the Commission.

The theory of the functional split and the Commission

According to the theory of the functional split applied by some academics to national governments, the latter's representatives have a double role: they represent the national interests when they act within the State legal order but represent the interest of the International Organisation when they act within the international legal system. That theory applies easily to the double role of the national Executives when their representatives act within the community decision-making process. For example, the members of the COREPER obviously defend national interests when they decide on a proposal of the Commission, but they do not neglect the European Union's interest in taking a decision which will further the integration process. Several examples of the concrete application of that theory within the Council of the European Union could be given (see for example the unanimous agreement (with two abstentions) on the 'Bolkestein' directive which was at the centre of controversies during the referendum debate in France).

That theory obviously does not apply to the European Commission. This derives not only from the obligation of independence mentioned in Article 17(3) of the Treaty and from the oath sworn by the commissioners before the Court of Justice but also from the three existing safeguards that concretely ensure that such obligation is respected: (1) the fact that the Commission is composed of a multinational administration which could hardly promote purely national interests in the elaboration of bills or executive decision proposals; (2) the fact that the commissioners are supposed to favour the interests of their portfolio rather than the interests of their countries of origin (see the example of Pascal Lamy who voted in favour of the agriculture policy that was challenged in France for it was in line with his portfolio of commercial policy; see also the case of Martin Bangenmann who asked for a longer transitory period for the introduction of catalysts although the German industry could have adapted earlier and that of Carlo Ripa di Meana who on the contrary asked for tighter environment norms although the Italian industry could not have applied them, etc.); and (3) the fact that the decisions of the Commission are made by a simple majority (even if it prefers consensus and rarely resorts to voting). If a commissioner suddenly wanted to refer a proposal in line with the interests of his country of origin to the decision of the Commission, they could easily be outvoted. A Hungarian commissioner could not have opposed a proposal for an embargo on petroleum whereas Hungary could veto it in the Council.

That the independence of the Commission is respected is confirmed by practice. I could count on the fingers of one hand the number of cases when a Commissioner made the Commission adopt a proposal that conformed to the interests of his country of origin (for example proposals respectively from Commissioners Loyola de Palacio and Neil Kinnock about the legal status of Gibraltar's airport vis-à-vis Union law because of a dispute between the United Kingdom and Spain; proposal of Leon Brittan on the creation of a free-exchange Zone between Europe and the United States). A particular case was that of a proposal of an executive measure by the Commission on the prohibition of the use of some genetically modified products. Given that the Member States serving on the Committees which had to decide on the Commission's proposed measures systematically voted for or against a proposed measure for ideological reasons (in general one half for and the other against), President Barroso decided that the Commission would decide by consensus and orally to avoid commissioners voting for or against the proposal in writing depending on the ideological stance of their country of origin. A more national behaviour sometimes showed at the level of the Heads of Cabinet of the Commissioners (who swear no oath to the Court of Justice), half of whom being national civil servants and half Union civil servants.

The double legitimacy of the Commission derived from European citizens (via the European Parliament) and Member States (via the European Council and the Council)

We have already seen that the changes resulting from the Treaties (Maastricht, Amsterdam and Lisbon) have substantially established the appointment of the Commission by the European Parliament and, therefore, its political legitimacy (see earlier). The President of the Commission and their colleagues are aware of their political accountability to the European Parliament because the latter has different means to hold them accountable in the implementation of the political orientations on the basis of which the President of the Commission has been elected and has obtained the vote of confidence by the whole

College. The '*Spitzenkandidat*' procedure has reinforced that trend and has made the election of the President of the Commission more transparent and legitimate (even though the election of Ursula Von der Leyen in 2019 did not confirm that procedure). In practice, this means that the support of a coalition of political groups in the European Parliament is necessary to guarantee the College of Commissioners will exercise its political action and that the Commission has therefore become an eminently political institution, legitimised by the European Parliament (even though, unlike what prevails in national parliaments, it is not always easy to clearly distinguish a political majority from a political minority within the European Parliament, which gives the Commission more freedom to act).

Since the European Union is not a State, and therefore the Commission is not the government of a parliamentary State, there follows that the Commission is more an institution – endowed with above all executive competences – of a Union of citizens and States which draws its legitimacy from the European Parliament and the States which proceed to its nomination after the European Parliament's approval. That second source of legitimacy has modified that which used to prevail since the Lisbon Treaty (Article 17(7)) provides that its appointment is made by the Council as an institution of the Union by a qualified majority and not by the Member States anymore. Although since the Treaty of Rome the Commission has been conceived and remains an institution independent from the States, its double legitimacy allows it to optimally ensure the general interest of the Union it is supposed to promote.

The accountability of the Commission via a series of checks and balances

Political accountability

That accountability is to the European Parliament via the passing of a motion of censure (Articles 17(8) TEU and 234 TFEU). Admittedly, the European Parliament has never adopted one of the eight motions of censure presented against the Commission (mainly because of the very high threshold of the required two-thirds majority). In the case of the Santer Commission, the European Parliament refused to give the Commission the discharge of the budget but did not vote on the motion of censure because the Commission collectively resigned after the report by the committee of independent experts (see earlier).

The Treaties did not provide for the individual accountability of the Commissioners but considered the Commission as a collegial body accountable to the European Parliament. However, pursuant to the 2010 Framework Agreement between the Commission and the European Parliament, the latter may ask the President of the Commission to withdraw their confidence in an individual Commissioner or to change their portfolio. To date, that disposition has never been applied.

Pursuant to Article 226 TFEU, the European Parliament may establish a temporary committee of inquiry tasked with examining the cases of violation of or maladministration in the application of European law. Since 2009, the European Parliament has set up two committees of inquiry, one on the measures of emission monitoring in the automotive industry ('Dieselgate') and the other on tax evasion after the publication of the 'Panama Papers'.

The European Parliament, like the Council, has the right to withdraw the delegation of power granted to the Commission for the adoption of a delegated act, but it has not used that right yet. It cannot do the same for the adoption of an executive act, but it could check that the Commission has not acted *ultra vires* (15 October 2014 Decision of the Court of Justice).

Article 230(2) TFEU allows the European Parliament to ask the Commission oral and written questions (about 45,000 since the beginning) and it may organise question-time sessions. Moreover, the Commission is obliged to present its action programme, make report and provide the European Parliament with information under the Framework Agreements concluded between the two institutions (see earlier).

Article 225 TFEU allows the European Parliament to ask the Commission to present a proposal as to the application of the Treaties within three months. The current Commission has politically committed to deliberate at its own level (oral procedure within the College) all the resolutions voted on by the European Parliament and based on Article 225 TFEU. The Vice-President in charge of interinstitutional issues (currently Mr. Sefcovic) will then inform the European Parliament of the Commission's answer.

The political accountability of the Commission is only to the European Parliament and not to the Council or the European Council. The dispositions which allow the Council to ask the Commission to present a proposal (Article 241 TFEU) or to start a dialogue on its work programme (IIA of 13 April 2016) or to ask the Court that a commissioner resign or be deprived of their rights (Articles 245 and 247 TFEU) are commitments of the Commission but do not entail political accountability on its part.

Legal accountability

The Treaty grants the Court of Justice the role of judge or referee of the disputes that may arise between the Union institutions about the legal acts that the Union has adopted. Consequently, the Court of Justice has to decide on actions brought to annul acts of the Commission, for damages, and to issue preliminary decisions on the validity of an act of the Commission referred to it by a national court (including for the violation of a fundamental right). Whether the application of competition law (when the Commission acts at the same time as investigator, prosecutor and judge) is compatible with the principle of the right to an impartial judge provided for in Article 47 of the Charter of Fundamental Rights has been raised. The decisions of the Court of Justice and the Court of Human Rights have confirmed that compatibility since the decisions of the Commission may still be reviewed by the European Court of Justice.

Some academics or theoreticians of European integration have suggested that the powers of the Commission that are more technical, especially those about the application of European law, be entrusted to the agencies (executive agencies as opposed to regulatory agencies). However, that proposal disregards the fact that the most important powers have been granted to the Commission by the Treaty itself (in the domains of competition, anti-dumping measures and the Stability and Growth Pact) and that the Treaty would therefore have to be amended. Moreover, one may wonder whether those agencies (there are 35 of them today) may be able to fulfil those tasks in a more objective way, given that the governance of most of the agencies entrusts decisive powers to the representatives of the Member States, and the most recent ones even provide for majority votes (European Banking Authority, European Securities and Markets Authority, etc.). One should consider that in the application of European law it is necessary to assess and take into account different public interests and to ensure the different policies of the Union are consistent – a role that the Commission, supported by a unique administration having appropriate expertise, is better placed to play. In addition, the Court of Justice case law (*Meroni* decision 1958, confirmed in 2014 by the C-270/12 decision, *UK v Commission*) forbids the institutions of the Union to delegate to the agencies the powers that require the exercise of a discretionary political power. Moreover, delegating executive powers to the agencies would imply a subsequent dispersion of the executive power within the European Union, thus creating additional problems of legitimacy and accountability.

Bad administration

The European Commission is accountable for bad administration in its activities to the European Ombudsman, who is designated by the European Parliament, which has the power to conduct investigations on its own or based on claims which lead to a report to the European Parliament (Article 228(1) TFEU). Over the 2017/2018 period, the Ombudsman opened 445 inquiries, some of which were examined by the Budget Control Committee of the European Parliament, which is the driving force behind the discharge procedure, the refusal of which led to the resignation of the Santer Commission.

Financial management

As to financial management, the Commission is not accountable only to the European Parliament for the discharge procedure, but also to the European Court of Auditors (CoA), which has important powers to fulfil the mission of the Treaty to review the legitimacy and legality of all the revenue and expenditure of the Union (Article 287 TFEU). Pursuant to that article, the Court of Auditors provides the European Parliament and the Council with a statement of insurance about the reliability of the accounts and the legality and regularity of the conducted operations. The CoA examines whether the financial management of the Commission was correct and also assesses in its special reports whether the objectives of the policies and programmes of the Union have been reached and results obtained efficiently. One must note, among others, the especially critical reports of the Court of Auditors on the financial management of the Common Agricultural Policy and the migrant crisis. The Commission has often been reluctant to follow the recommendations of the Court of Auditors to improve the budget management of common policies as that could have put Member States in a difficult position since they share accountability for financial management.

The discharge procedure, in Article 319 TFEU, allows the European Parliament upon the recommendation of the Council to exonerate the Commission of any accountability in the execution of the budget. Until now, there have been only two cases in which the European Parliament has refused the discharge to the Commission (in 1984 and 1998). The latter case led, among others, to the resignation of the Santer Commission (after the report by the Committee of Wise Men) and to the creation of the European Anti-Fraud Office (OLAF). Structurally speaking, OLAF is a service of the Commission, but it has very broad independence since its Director-General cannot receive instructions from any Member State or the Commission or other institutions of the Union. OLAF may conduct independent inquiries within the institutions and may bring a claim before the European Court against the Commission were its independence challenged. In November 2017, within the framework of reinforced cooperation, the Council established the Office of the European Public Prosecutor, who is responsible for investigating and sanctioning some crimes which affect the financial interests of the EU, which complements OLAF's inquiries.

Transparency and accountability to citizens

Pursuant to Article 15 of the Lisbon Treaty, in order to promote good governance and ensure that civil society participates, the institutions and other bodies of the Union are supposed to work with utmost respect of the principle of openness. The public's access to the documents of the institutions of the Union (Commission, Council and EP) is regulated by Regulation (EC) No 1049/2001. Checking the effective use of those rules over a given year has shown that in 2017 there were 6,255 requests for access to the documents of the Commission, of which 3,200 were completely accepted, 1,043 were partially accepted and 930 were refused (the others did not meet the criteria or the document did not exist). Pleas were entered against the refusal of the Commission to the Court of Justice, which tends to restrictively interpret the exceptions to the rule of access contained in the regulation. In a significant decision of the Court of Justice *Turco v Commission* (2008), it was specified that the public's access to the documents of the institutions 'enables citizens to participate more closely in the decision-making process and guarantees that the administration enjoys greater legitimacy and is more effective and more accountable to the citizen in a democratic system'.

The Commission took a series of measures to ensure that its action was transparent through decisions about the contacts of its Commissioners and General Directors with Associations and their collaborators, rules of transparency to be respected when it has an external expert evaluation of Committees and lobbies carried out and the proposal of a mandatory register that must be agreed upon by institutions (not adopted by the Council and European Parliament yet).

Relations with national parliaments and advisory boards

The Lisbon Treaty added yet another control procedure by allowing each national parliament to challenge any (legislative) act which would violate the principles of subsidiarity and proportionality. In particular, when at least one third of national parliaments (at the level of the bicameral chamber) question a European bill, the latter must be examined by the Commission (the 'yellow card' procedure). If that threshold reaches at least a simple majority of the national parliaments (i.e., 27 chambers out of 54), then the Council and the EP must give their view on whether the bill is compatible with the subsidiarity principle ('orange card' procedure). Finally, if there is a 55 percent majority of the members of the Council or a simple majority in the EP who say that the bill is not compatible with the subsidiarity principle, it will not be adopted ('red card'). The thresholds provided for in the Lisbon Treaty are obviously very high, so that only the 'yellow card' procedure has been applied two or three times against the Commission. The latter re-examined its proposals but only in one case (the Monti II Bill on the regulation of posted workers) did it withdraw its proposal (about which some academics concluded that it had made no fault). In another case (that of the proposal as to the creation of the European Public Prosecutor's Office, aimed at by the Treaty itself), the Commission kept its proposal which was then adopted by the Council within the framework of reinforced cooperation.

In order to compensate for the circumstance according to which a more or less important number of national parliaments raised objections against the proposal of the Commission (most of the time based on the content of the proposal and not on subsidiarity), the Commission pledged itself to directly answer the opinions of the national parliaments regardless of the threshold (Barroso procedure after the name of the President of the Commission who made that commitment). That procedure of political dialogue between the Commission and the national parliaments has led to hundreds or even thousands of opinions of the Commission which have allowed to clarify the real content of its proposals without blocking or slowing down the decision-making process. Moreover, the Committee of the Regions, which would have a right to file ex-post to the Court of Justice if the subsidiarity principle were violated, has never used it so far.

The advisory bodies of the Union (Committee of the Regions, and European Economic and Social Committee) are supposed to give their opinion on the proposals of the Commission which are about their own prerogatives or areas of expertise under the Treaty. However, since 1993, the Council's practice and the ordinary legislative procedure between the Council and the European Parliament have shown that the opinions of the advisory bodies are rarely taken into consideration in the Community decision-making process. In order to compensate for that issue, the Commission has promised those bodies it will consult them before it makes any legislative proposal on the basis of communications, green or white papers or other consultation documents, in order to use their suggestions or opinions before it officially issues its proposals.

Conclusions

Following Max Weber's theory, a political regime or institution which exercises some authority is legitimated insofar as the recipients of its action have a certain level of trust in it. The European Commission has – or has been supported by – a system of checks and balances which should ensure such trust. Of course, that does not prevent measures from being taken later to guarantee that trust. One should not forget however that the role of the Commission has evolved over time, from an independent institution charged with elaborating and defending the general interest of the Union (as defined by Jean Monnet) to an institution that is politically accountable, mainly to the European Parliament (see the bilateral agreements which multiply the commitments of the Commission), but which at the same time must take into consideration the balance to ensure among an increasing number of (big and small) Member States. Moreover, the fact that the Commission entered into many bilateral agreements with the European Parliament (see the following *Appendix*) and that it considers that it is bound by the conclusions of the European Council on which its President sits, makes one conclude that its responsibilities and powers in the Treaties are not autonomously exercised, but rather as a joint responsibility with the European Parliament and the European Council. That blurring of responsibilities among institutions makes it more difficult to identify the institution which is responsible (and therefore accountable) for a legal act of the Union. The revision of the Lisbon Treaty, the procedure of which the European Parliament aims to activate under Article 48 TEU, should be the occasion of clarifying the respective roles of the different Union institutions and give back its real meaning to Max Weber's theory.

Appendix

The interinstitutional agreements concluded between the European Commission and the other institutions, among which the European Parliament

1. The European Commission has concluded a series of tripartite agreements on financial prospects with the European Council and Parliament which frame the exercise of its budget powers. Those agreements range from the Common Statement of 30 June 1982 which contains a list of so-called compulsory expenditures and non-compulsory expenditures (OJ C 194 of 28.07.1982) to the last Interinstitutional Agreement of 2020 which sets the multi-year financial prospects for the 2021–2027 period (OJ 433/2020);
2. The Commission has concluded agreements with the other institutions on the practical application of the so-called Comitology process (Plumb-Delors exchange of letters in 1988, Modus vivendi between the three institutions in 1994, 1996 Samland-Williamson agreement, commitment of the Prodi Commission on the application of the Lamfalussy process on the financial services in 2001) which aimed to give the European Parliament better control over the application of the executive measures of the Commission. Those agreements are now outdated by the new dispositions of the Lisbon Treaty about the executive and delegated acts;
3. The Commission has concluded agreements with the other institutions (European Council and Parliament) on the best way to legislate at the European level ('Better Regulation'). Those agreements aim to frame the Commission's exercise of its right to initiate bills and imply other institutions in the legislative agenda of the Commission (examination of the yearly political strategy, of the working programmes of the Commission, withdrawal of proposition process, etc.);
4. The Commission has concluded bilateral agreements with the European Parliament to reinforce its political accountability and legitimacy through additional commitments to the EP about the exercise of its institutional prerogatives. Those Agreements range from the Delors Commission Code of Conduct concluded in 1990 and 1995, to the Framework Agreements concluded by all the following Commissions before or after their vote of approval (2000, 2005, 2010 and 2016). In those agreements, the Commission pledged itself, among other things, to put the EP at the same level as the Council when giving information about its activities and sending

its documents and to take utmost consideration of the EP in relation to the presentation of new proposals, their legal basis, the withdrawal of its proposals etc. Moreover, the President of the Commission has promised to take into account the EP's requests about the resignation, replacement or change of portfolio of a commissioner.

8 Functional duplication and political accountability of the Executive in the EU Member States

Jacques Ziller

Introduction

The development of European integration since the establishment of the European Coal and Steel Community (ECSC) by the Treaty of Paris of 21 April 1951 – which entered into force on 23 July 1952 – has had a growing impact not only on public opinion, but also on many political actors as well as on public law and political science scholarship. In order to understand why and how European integration has significantly changed the issue of democratic accountability of the Executives of Member States since the early 1950s, we have to understand the institutional organisation of the EU and the dynamics that it generates.

It is essential to consider that the EU is not a federal State, neither in the sense of law nor in the sense of political science.

In international law, as well as in constitutional law, for there to be a State there must be a territory, a population and a sovereign government. The EU does not have a territory of its own: the rules set up by the EU apply to the territories of its Member States only insofar as they have agreed to such application.[1] The EU does not have a population of its own: it is the Member States, and they alone, who determine the criteria for acquiring European citizenship – and, if necessary, for losing it – because EU citizenship is the direct consequence of a Member State's citizenship;[2] moreover, it is the States that have the power to welcome, or not, third-country nationals on their territory. A sovereign government means institutions with the power of final decision on the rules that apply to the territory and its population, and which have effective enforcement powers over that territory: the latter is not true for the EU, which depends on the authorities of its Member States for enforcement.

From a formal point of view, the EU is a form of confederation, i.e., a group of sovereign States bound by an international agreement which creates

1 See Articles 55 TEU and 355 TFEU.

2 Article 9 TEU: 'Every national of a Member State shall be a citizen of the Union. Citizenship of the Union shall be additional to and not replace national citizenship'.

DOI: 10.4324/9781003281559-15

common institutions for the exercise of powers which the States party to that treaty consider necessary to exercise jointly. This is reflected, inter alia, in the procedure for amending treaties (Article 48 TEU). The Articles of Confederation and Perpetual Union of 1777 were likewise an international treaty between the 13 American colonies that had declared their independence from the English Crown. Confederations, like international governmental organisations and the European Union, can only exercise the powers delegated to them by their Member States: this is the principle of attribution (Article 5(2). TEU 2). Conversely, in the case of federal States, the distribution of powers between the centre (the Federation) and the members (the States) is determined in the federal constitution, which generally specifies the level to which powers not mentioned in the constitution belong.

From the point of view of political science there exists no commonly accepted definition of a federation though the concept of federal State is being studied essentially as opposed to that of unitary State. An important point is that it is generally accepted that federal States have particular powers in the fields of defence and international relations and have their own budget and taxes. On the contrary, the EU's competences[3] in the field of defence and international relations are particularly weak and the Union does not levy its own taxes yet.

This being said, it has to be stressed that from the beginning in the 1950s the European Communities were conceived from a political point of view as a federation in the making, which might have become the United States of Europe. This was explicit in the Schuman Declaration of 9 May 1950:

> By pooling basic production and by instituting a new High Authority, whose decisions will bind France, Germany and other member countries, this proposal will lead to the realization of the first concrete foundation of a European federation indispensable to the preservation of peace.[4]

Although we cannot speak of a European federal State in 2022, it is undeniable that federalism as a political concept remains present in debates on the EU.

In order to understand how the institutions and their decision-making procedures set up for European integration since the 1950s have impacted the accountability of Member State Executives, the analysis of role splitting (*dédoublement fonctionnel*), a concept developed by Georges Scelle in the 1930s, is particularly useful (Section I). Furthermore, a comparison between EU and German federalism is essential and benefits from the concept of joint-decision trap (*Politikverflechtungsfalle*) developed by Fritz W. Scharpf in the

3 The word for the concept of powers is 'competence' (not competency) in EU law, a word which has been taken from Latin and corresponds to the German *Zuständigkeit*.

4 Official translation from the French available at: https://europa.eu/european-union/about-eu/symbols/europe-day/schuman-declaration_en

1980s. We will explain these two theories by examining how the institutional modalities of European federalism have undoubtedly led to a strengthening of the role of the Executive, which contributes to put it at the centre of political action (Section 2), without solving the problem of its accountability in this area because of the decrease in legibility of political action, the joint-decision trap and the sectorisation of the Executives (Section 3).

Role splitting and European federalism

It must be emphasised that the forms of federalism that are characteristic of the EU's institution as well as of its decision-making and enforcement system are in no way similar to those of the United States of America or of Switzerland; nor, for that matter, to those of Belgium or Austria or Spain. EU federalism strongly resembles German federalism.[5] This resemblance appears most clearly when comparing the Council of the EU on the one hand and the *Bundesrat* on the other. In the United States of America, senators are elected – by state congresses until 1913, directly by citizens in the states since then – and they hold the sole office of senator. On the contrary, the *Bundesrat* – a word which, by the way, precisely means Federal Council – is composed of serving members of the *Länder*'s Executives: very often the Head of Government (*Ministerpräsident*), the Minister of Finance, the Minister of Justice, etc., who may be supplemented by a higher civil servant of their ministerial department. Moreover, and again unlike the US Senate, the members of the *Bundesrat* do not vote in a personal capacity but as a group (three for smaller *Länder*, five for bigger ones), in accordance with the position defined by their government; in the same way, the members of the EU Council do not vote in a personal capacity, but as State representatives.

When preparing the Schuman Declaration in 1950, Jean Monnet and his collaborators Paul Reuter and Pierre Uri chose on purpose to set up a Special Council of Ministers composed of members of the Member States' central governments alongside the High Authority – the predecessor of the Commission, and like the latter completely independent. It was indeed obvious that neither the French nor the German Government – and those of the other future Member States, i.e., Belgium, Italy, Luxembourg, the Netherlands and possibly the United Kingdom[6] – and their parliaments even less, could accept the establishment of a supranational authority with binding powers if the latter's decisions were not subject to some form of approval by the governments themselves. Monnet's revolutionary idea was that this would not necessarily be

5 For more details see, J. Ziller, 'Multilevel Governance and Executive Federalism: Comparing Germany and the European Union', in *The European Union Legal Order after Lisbon*, eds. P. Birkinshaw and M. Varney (The Hague: Kluwer Law International, 2010), pp. 257–275.

6 At the beginning of June 1950, the UK government was invited to take part in the preparation of the future ECSC Treaty, but it renounced participating when it became clear that the independent High Authority would be established without a full veto right for the Member States.

unanimous approval. In his memoirs, Monnet refers to the speech of Konrad Adenauer, who chaired the first meeting of the Special Council of Ministers on 8 September 1952, with the words: 'Adenauer explained how he saw the role of the Council: it has never been better explained, indeed, than at that first meeting'.[7]

Indeed, this speech is worth quoting, especially since Adenauer, while sitting as German Foreign Minister – a portfolio he himself held at the time –, was clearly speaking as a Federal Chancellor. This situation was foreshadowing the contemporary European Council.

> [The Council] is the federal institution of the Community. As such, it has a double mission according to the Treaty. On the one hand, it will act as an institution of the Community i.e., an institution of the supranational formation, with its own sovereign rights and independent of the states. As an institution of the Community, the Council participates in the settlement and management of sovereign rights which the Member States have excluded from their sphere of action and have ceded to the Community. In this capacity, it is called upon by the Treaty to participate actively in the creation of regulations by the Community. It will be heard on all important measures of the High Authority. Its approval or decision is required in important cases. Its unanimous agreement is required for matters of major importance. On the other hand, the Council of Ministers has a second mission. It does not only defend the interests of the Community in the field of the sovereign rights that have been transferred to them, but also the interests of the Member States in the field of the sovereign rights that they retain. . . . The Council of Ministers thus has a linking and mediating role. It is at the intersection of two sovereignties, one supranational and one national. It must serve the interests of the Community in the same way as those of the states and strike a balance that gives them what belongs to them respectively. As the Treaty stipulates, it must harmonise mutual interests. As an institution, it is thus given a priority task which concerns all those who are working towards the unification of Europe.[8]

This speech deserves to be read in the light of sociological objectivism and above all of the theory of 'role splitting' (*dédoublement fonctionnel*) of the

7 J. Monnet, *Mémoires* (Paris: Fayard, 1976), p. 564. For the English version, see, *Memoirs, Introduction by George W. Ball, Translated from the French by Richard Mayne* (Garden City, NY: Doubleday & Company, 1978), p. 380, https://archive.org/stream/MonnetJeanMemoirs/Monnet%2C%20Jean%20-%20Memoirs_djvu.txt.

8 Translation by this author from the text available in French at: www.cvce.eu/obj/discours_de_konrad_adenauer_8_septembre_1952-fr-61b9e46a-be38-4742-9bc1-103732a82aaa.html. NB: The Chancellor was speaking in German and the term 'organ' has to be translated as 'institution' and not 'organ', as done in the French text.

French international lawyer Georges Scelle (1978–1961).[9] The Council of the Union, and perhaps even more so the European Council, are a striking illustration of role splitting, with all its advantages but also all its shortcomings. Let us by the way recall that Jean Monnet himself was one of the most ardent promoters of Meetings of the Heads of State or Government that became the European Council with the Action Committee for the United States of Europe[10] which he set up, because he was convinced that it was essential for them to consider themselves accountable for the progress of European integration.

Scelle's doctrine of 'role splitting' has been particularly well explained in English by Antonio Cassese, himself one of the best contemporary Italian international lawyers:[11]

> The great jurist observes at the outset that the 'original and persistent flaw of the international legal order' is the lack of legislative, judicial and enforcement organs acting on behalf of the whole community. This being so, and in view of the necessity for any legal order to rest on the three aforementioned functions, the inescapable consequence for Scelle is that the three social functions do exist in the world community but are organized in a quite unique fashion. As there are no 'specifically international rulers and agents' (*gouvernants et agents spécifiquement Internationaux*), national members of the executive as well as state officials fulfil a 'dual' role: they act as state organs whenever they operate within the national legal system; they act qua international agents when they operate within the international legal system. Thus, when the head of state or the state legislature take part in the formation of a law-making treaty, they act as international law-making bodies . . . similarly, any time one or more state officials undertake an enforcement action (resort to force short of war, reprisals, armed intervention, war proper) they act as international enforcement agencies (*agents exécutifs internationaux*). To avoid possible misunderstandings, it should be emphasized that for Scelle national officials do not have double roles which are fulfilled simultaneously, but a dual role in the sense that they operate in a Dr. Jakyll [sic] and Mr. Hyde manner, exhibiting a split personality. In other words, although from the point of view of their legal status they

9 G. Scelle, *Précis de droit des gens – Principes et systématique* (Paris: Sirey, 1932); G. Scelle, 'Règles générales du droit de la paix', in *Collected Courses of the Hague Academy of International Law*, vol. 46 (The Hague: RCADI, 1933), pp. 358–359.

10 See, among others, M.-T. Bitsch, 'Jean Monnet et la création du Conseil européen', in *Jean Monnet L'Europe et les chemins de la paix*, eds. G. Boussuat and A. Wilkens (Paris: Editions de la Sorbonne, 2020), pp. 399–410, https://books.openedition.org/psorbonne/47378?lang=fr

11 A. Cassese, 'Remarks on Scelle's Theory of "Role Splitting" in International Law', *European Journal of International Law* 1, no. 1 (1990): pp. 210 ff.

> are and remain national organs, they can function either as national or as international agents.

It is clear that the ECSC High Authority was a fundamental step in the direction indicated by Scelle of 'superstate authorities [that] would become emanations of [a global community] and no longer representatives of each of the components'.[12] However, both the practice of the ECSC and the Treaties of Rome have given the Council a more important role than Monnet and his team had foreseen. Doctrine generally analyses the roles of the different institutions according to the supranational vs. intergovernmental key; it seems to us that Scelle's categories are more refined, in particular thanks to their sociological theory dimension.

Role splitting putting the Executives at the centre of political action

As a result of role splitting, the position of Member States' central Executives has been strengthened both at the expense of central parliaments as in relation to local and regional authorities.

Strengthening the position of the Executive at the expense of the Parliament

To understand role splitting in EU affairs it is not sufficient to look at the European Council where Heads of State or Government meet. It is indispensable to also have a closer look at the Council (of the EU) and its preparatory bodies.

Role splitting: the Council of the European Union and its preparatory bodies

The Council of the EU (not to be confused with the European Council) has decision-making power in the legislative function of the EU in all fields, in most cases as co-legislator with the European Parliament, while the latter has no decision-making power in some specific fields where special legislative procedures apply. Until the Maastricht Treaty, which came into force on 1 October 1993, the Council was even the only institution exercising legislative power. In theory the Council was also holder of regulatory power, which it could delegate to the Commission if it so wished for the implementation of the acts it had adopted, as it did increasingly from the 1980s. When delegating the power to adopt acts of general and individual scope for implementation, the Council usually established control mechanisms in the form of committees of Member State representatives, a phenomenon known as 'comitology'. With the Lisbon Treaty, this mechanism was formalised with

12 G. Scelle, '*Règles générales*', pp. 429–430.

the provisions on delegated and implementing acts in Articles 290 and 291 TFEU. Through comitology, the governments of the Member States participate in the executive function of the Council, just as they participate in its legislative function, since the Council is always a legislator.

The Council is composed of members of the central governments of the Member States – or, where appropriate, a member of a regional government duly authorised to represent the Member State in the Council. This is a point worth emphasising, and it distinguishes the Council both from the usual bodies of international organisations, where States are in practice represented by their ambassadors or permanent representatives, and from the German *Bundesrat*, whose members are very often replaced by their deputies who are senior officials, not politicians. In the case of international organisations, diplomats are of course instructed by their ministers and are only accountable to them. In Germany, it is the *Land* government that gives voting instructions to its representatives, but they have a single vote for the *Land*.

The Member States of the Union all have a Permanent Representation (embassy) to the institutions of the Union seated in Brussels, but the Permanent Representatives never sit in a Council meeting. However, it should be noted that these meetings are prepared by the Committee of Permanent Representatives (COREPER), as recalled by Article 16(7) TEU. The Permanent Representatives and their deputies meet once a week to check their countries' positions and prepare compromises; they do not, of course, vote, but they indicate, if necessary, what their government's representative would do in case of a vote.

At Council meetings the agenda is divided into 'A items', to be approved without debate following an agreement within COREPER, and 'B items', which require a debate. B items are very few in number, so it can be said that it is in practice the Permanent Representatives who express the position of their Member States. In most cases, the compromise established in COREPER is the result of prior negotiation in a Council preparatory body (most of them called working parties) where governments are represented by officials from the administrations concerned or by officials based in the Permanent Representation. There are hundreds of such preparatory bodies, who meet from about two to ten times a year. This way of proceeding applies whatever the function exercised by the Council, including and primarily the legislative function. This way of functioning leads to the depoliticisation of the exercise of the Council's functions, with strong repercussions on the political accountability of the Executive, as we shall see in the second section.

One issue that is central to the question of accountability and that has been dealt with frequently in legal and political literature is that of the public nature of Council debates. Gradually, first with the Treaty of Amsterdam (1997) and then with the Treaty of Lisbon (2007), it was established in the treaties that the Council's meetings in which it acts as a legislator must be public. The idea is that legislative activities have to be public as they are in national parliaments, whereas cabinet meetings usually are not public and hence the Council does not need to hold public meetings when it does not act as a legislator. The

Council's legislative meetings can be followed in streaming mode in real time and the recordings remain accessible. This however can hardly be an effective accountability mechanism because of the extremely small number of B items on the agenda of the meetings. Furthermore, it is well known that one of the perverse effects of publicising debates is that in some cases the representative of a Member State ostensibly votes against a proposal when in fact the government agrees with the compromise reached in COREPER; the purpose is simply to be able to tell the public opinion or parliament that the country's interests were defended to the end. There has never been to our knowledge any suggestion of making COREPER meetings public. If those meetings were public, the problem of transparency would shift to working groups. In reality, the best way for a State to defend its interests is to participate as actively as possible at all levels in the negotiations leading to a compromise position of the Council. This is a strategy in which the British in particular were masters before the UK left the EU.

Another issue that has been discussed at length by scholarship and in politics is the question of how the Council votes: unanimity or qualified majority. In cases which are reduced in quantity but important in quality, as for example in the case of tax harmonisation, the Council votes by unanimity. In most cases however, the Council is supposed to vote by qualified majority, representing 55 percent of the Member States and 65 percent of their population. With unanimity, accountability may seem simpler to ensure: the position of a government in Council is known and its consequence is particularly visible if it has prevented the adoption of a decision. This being said, the possibility for a Member State to use its veto right is limited from a political point of view, as shown by the studies on the use of the Luxembourg compromise[13] that was the result of the 'empty chair crisis' provoked by General de Gaulle in July 1965.[14] It should be recalled that from 1967 to 1985 the Council refrained from voting by qualified majority when the treaty provided for it, and this had the effect of considerably slowing down the decision-making process; it only voted twice in such cases before the entry into force of the Single European Act (SEA), to the ire of Margaret Thatcher whose government was defeated on one issue of agricultural policy and on the opening of the intergovernmental conference which prepared the SEA.

As a matter of fact, there is always a complex negotiation upstream of the Council's decisions, whatever the voting method. There is negotiation between Member States, but also negotiation between them and the Commission, which has a monopoly on legislative initiative, and negotiation with Parliament in all the cases where Parliament acts as co-legislator.

13 H. Wallace, P. Winand, and J.-M. Palayret, *Visions, Votes, and Vetoes: The Empty Chair Crisis and the Luxembourg Compromise Forty Years On* (Brussels: Peter Lang, 2006).

14 J. Ziller, 'Defiance for European Influence – The Empty Chair and France', in *The Enforcement of EU Law and Values – Ensuring Member State's Compliance*, eds. A. Jakab and D. Kochenov (Oxford: OUP, 2017), pp. 422–435.

In many Member States, most notably in Denmark since the 1980s, the parliaments have put in place mechanisms to hold their government to account for the progress of negotiations for a Council decision. In our view, there is no indisputable evidence that this has significantly increased the political accountability of the Executive; it is well known in practice that overly precise directives from parliament deprive the government of room for manoeuvre, with the risk that it cannot participate effectively in the adoption of a compromise. It is also well known that many governments do not hesitate to use the weapon of a 'parliamentary reserve', according to which they have to report to parliament before making their final position known. However, this type of blackmailing can backfire on the government exercising it, as can the threat of a veto in cases where unanimity is required for a Council decision.

Role splitting in the European Council

The Treaty of Lisbon formally established the status of the European Council as an institution of the Union with Article 15 TEU, which contains a series of details on its functions, organisation and operation. The wording of these provisions is a clear expression of the role splitting of the political Heads of the Member States' Executives, in application of Article 10(2)(2) TEU: 'Member States are represented in the European Council by their Heads of State or Government and in the Council by their governments, themselves democratically accountable either to their national parliaments, or to their citizens'. It should be stressed that although the European Council has had a permanent president since the Treaty of Lisbon – appointed by its members for two and a half years and renewable only once – this president does not have the right to vote, which belongs solely to the heads of the Member States' Executives – another clear sign of role splitting of Member States' Executives. The President of the European Council can at most exercise moral suasion because s/he chairs the meetings and therefore chooses when to propose the formulation of a consensus or to vote.

In practice, the European Council has existed since the Paris summit of 10–11 February 1961, held at the invitation of French President De Gaulle, who wished to advance his project for European political cooperation, the 'Fouchet Plan'. This summit was followed eight years later by a summit in The Hague at the invitation of the Dutch Government on 1–2 December 1969. The agenda and composition were in fact dictated by Georges Pompidou. Pompidou had been elected President of the French Republic on 15 June. This summit, attended by the Head of State of France and the Heads of Government of the other five Member States, as well as by the President of the Commission, was particularly important for the relaunching of European integration, with three important decisions for the future.

Further summit meetings took place from then on. The Paris Summit of 19–21 October 1972 was organised by Pompidou at the request of the

European Parliament, which was not yet elected by direct universal suffrage. The Copenhagen Summit of 13–14 December 1973 was organised by the Danish Government following a letter from Pompidou, who felt that world problems should be discussed together before the possible visit of US President Richard Nixon to Europe in early 1974. The only decision at this summit was that the Heads of State and Government should meet more often.

The creation of the European Council was proclaimed at the Paris Summit of 9 and 10 December 1974 on the initiative of the new French President Valéry Giscard d'Estaing, who endorsed Monnet's proposal to create a European authority composed of Heads of State and Government. Giscard d'Estaing pointed out that between 1969 and 1974, the leaders of the Communities had met only three times, while they had met many more times with the Presidents of the United States and the Soviet Union. He said it was 'an anomaly for Europe'.[15] However, it was not until the Dublin Summit of 10–11 March 1975 that the European Council started meeting regularly, usually three times a year, under the chairmanship of the Head of the Executive of the State holding the six-monthly Council presidency.

The President of the European Commission, Belgian Jean Rey, had played a significant role at the Paris Summit in December 1969, but his successors, Dutch Sicco Mansholt and French François-Xavier Ortoli, had been marginalised. It was only Roy Jenkins – British President of the Commission from January 1977 to January 1981 – who succeeded in imposing his presence at European Council meetings, including during the discussions on foreign policy which were not the Commission's responsibility. In our opinion, the sidelining of the Commission until 1977 is a typical consequence of role splitting: Valéry Giscard d'Estaing in particular was convinced that it was the Heads of the Executive who had the legitimacy to give impetus to the Communities, not the Head of the Commission.

It should also be noted that while the President of the Commission has since then participated in all the European Council meetings, he or she does not have the right to vote and cannot prevent consensus building without the support of at least one Member State. It should further be noted that the democratisation of the European Parliament by direct universal suffrage election in 1979 has not led to the regular participation of its President in the European Council, although he or she is sometimes invited. Unlike the President of the Commission, the President of the Parliament is not a member of the European Council.

It is also worth pointing out that the media and the political world often confuse the Council Presidency with the Presidency of the European Council, especially when it is a powerful Member State that holds the rotating

15 Statement by Valéry Giscard D'Estaing after the Paris Summit (10 December 1974). See at: www.cvce.eu/obj/fr-6d60fe44-595d-481a-9e83-1ed2a5d9d790.

presidency.[16] It is a constant temptation for Heads of Government to present themselves to their potential electorate as the 'President of Europe', even if only for six months. While the Head of the Executive of the country holding the presidency usually tries to take credit for decisions that are supposedly well received by public opinion, he or she is usually careful not to underline the role of the presidency in decisions that are perceived as negative by public opinion.

For the members of both the Council and the European Council, role splitting contributes to strengthening the national Executive in relation to the Parliament. The European Parliament's control over the Council is certainly exercised through its function as co-legislator, but it has no sanction of its own. The Parliament's control over the European Council is limited to the hearing of the Head of State or Government of the State holding the six-monthly presidency. As for the national parliament, its control is necessarily limited by the collective nature of the decisions of the Council or the European Council.

The strengthening of the Executive at the expense of Parliament which is due to the role splitting of Heads of State and Government reinforces a phenomenon that can be observed in most pluralist democracies independently from the participation or not in European integration. It is not the only element of change in the Member States that is undeniably due to the institutional framework of European integration. On the contrary, the strengthening of the central government in relation to local and regional authorities, also due to European integration, is only sometimes concomitant with a strengthening of the central government for other reasons; on the contrary it is often concomitant with decentralisation.

Strengthening of central Executives in relation to local and regional authorities

The 1970s and 1980s were a period of significant decentralisation in several EU countries. In Italy the Constitution of 1947 provided for the establishment of regions, but it was not until the law of 16 May 1970 and the implementing decree of 15 January 1972 that the regions were established as territorial authorities throughout the whole peninsula. The movement of decentralisation continued in particular during the 1990s, not only towards the regions, but also towards local authorities (*comuni*). The case of Spain is even more significant: the 1978 Constitution provided for the establishment of Autonomous Communities, which were set up during the 1980s. The case of France is also important, with a number of decentralising reforms in the 1960s and

16 Article 16(9) TEU: 'The Presidency of Council configurations, other than that of Foreign Affairs, shall be held by Member State representatives in the Council on the basis of equal rotation, in accordance with the conditions established in accordance with Article 236 of the Treaty on the Functioning of the European Union'.

1970s and above all the major decentralisation laws of the early 1980s. Finally, Greece can be mentioned, where after a period of adopting regionalisation laws that never came into force, regions were finally established at the end of the 1980s. In all those countries there was some chronological correlation with deepening of European integration.

In the United Kingdom, decentralisation started a few years after accession to the European Communities, with the beginning of gradual devolution to Scotland, Wales and Northern Ireland in 1979. Devolution was mainly due to James Callaghan's government seeking parliamentary support. The government of Margaret Thatcher did not reverse devolution, but it enacted a strong centralisation at the expense of local authorities by taking over or controlling more strictly functions traditionally carried out at the local level, and by reducing the levels of local authorities.

There is some political science literature, and also legal literature, which attributes the creation of regions to European integration, making a confusion between chronological correlation and causality. The scholarship in question wrongly deduces an influence of the EU on the creation of political regions as a result of the establishment of 'NUTS-2 regions' for the implementation of regional policy in the 1970s and 1980s. This type of argument is based on a misinterpretation of the creation of the Unified Nomenclature of Statistical Territories (NUTS), an accounting operation for the establishment of subnational statistics relating to the development of GDP and unemployment. Such a nomenclature was necessary for the application of Article 107(3)(a) TFEU – already present in the Treaty of Rome – according to which, in derogation from the prohibition of State aid which may distort competition, the Commission could authorise 'aid to promote the economic development of areas where the standard of living is abnormally low or where there is serious underemployment'. Evidence of the wrongness of such an interpretation is provided by countries as different as Ireland, Portugal, the Netherlands and the Nordic countries, where NUTS 2 regions do not correspond to institutionalised regions.

An analysis of the impact of European integration on the powers of the German *Länder* shows to what extent the institutional development of the Union has led, on the contrary, to a centralisation in favour of the federal government. Let us remember that the *Länder* are much older than European integration. They are the product of federalism by aggregation, which first took place in a short-lived manner with the Frankfurt Constitution of 1848, then with the creation of the German Empire by the Constitution of 16 April 1871, continued by the Weimar Constitution of 11 August 1919, and again by the Basic Law of 1949. The annihilation of the *Länder* as well as of communal autonomy by the National Socialist regime between 1933 and 1945 should not hide the ancient nature of German federalism.

One must also take into account the particular nature of German federalism, which is above all a form of executive federalism. The existence of quantitatively and qualitatively important federal legislation has traditionally been compensated for by the fact that the implementation of these laws is carried out by the *Länder* administration. In contrast, the legislative powers of the *Länder* have always been reduced in economic and social matters, because of the wording of the Basic Law and the social homogeneity of Western Germany. Important competences have been transferred in those fields to the EU by the Rome Treaty of 1957 and the Single European Act of 1986 for the establishment and consolidation of the internal market.

In the areas where the *Länder* have legislative competences, and especially in the areas where they are implementing federal legislation, it is nonetheless the federal government that is represented in the Council, in COREPER and in its working groups. The *Länder* obtained therefore the presence of an 'Observer' (*Länder Beobachter*) within the Permanent Representation of their country to the European Communities as early as 1957. This Observer was responsible for transmitting directly to the *Länder* governments the proposals drawn up by the Commission that, according to him, were likely to have an impact on the exercise of their administrative and legislative functions.

With the Single European Act of 1986 there was an acceleration of the European decision-making process planned for the completion of the internal market by 31 December 1992. It was therefore foreseeable that the traditional mechanisms of consultation with the *Länder* and, above all, their participation in the federal legislative procedure through the *Bundesrat* would become less and less effective. This is why when Jacques Delors visited several *Länder* during the preparation of the acts for the completion of the internal market, several political leaders explained the principle of subsidiarity to him: Delors therefore asked that it be included as a fundamental principle of the Union in what was to become the Maastricht Treaty. It is worth noting that following earlier reports prepared at the request of the European Council on integration developments, such as the Tindemans Project 1975, the draft Treaty establishing the European Union adopted by the European Parliament on 14 February 1984, known as the Spinelli Project,[17] stated in its preamble: 'Intending to entrust common institutions, in accordance with the principle of subsidiarity, only with those powers required to complete successfully the tasks they may carry out more satisfactorily than the States acting independently'. Furthermore, the wording of the provision on the composition of the Council was modified in order to allow for a member of a subnational government to sit in its meetings. This occurs for Belgium and Germany in fields like Education, but the relevant politician is representing the Member State and expresses a position which is the result of coordination of both the relevant subcentral and central governments. Role splitting is thus further extended but remains fundamental.

17 Available at: www.cvce.eu/obj/draft_treaty_establishing_the_european_union_14_february_1984-en-0c1f92e8-db44-4408-b569-c464cc1e73c9.html

The centralising impact of European integration was even more visible in Spain. After the period of establishment of the Autonomous Communities between 1979 and 1983, the negotiations for the accession of Spain and Portugal to the European Communities, which had begun during this period, culminated in the Accession Treaty of 1985 that entered into force on 1 January 1986. For some years, the governments of the Communities, especially those of Catalonia and the Basque Country, were under the illusion that accession would enable them to negotiate directly with the Commission to obtain more powers, but they were disappointed to find that it was the central government alone that benefited from the role splitting resulting from its participation in the Council.

This being said, it must be taken into account that the centralising impact of European integration is felt very differently from one Member State to another, as the forms of decentralisation are extremely heterogeneous. In some Member States, in particular the Nordic countries, as well as Belgium and the Netherlands, but also Portugal, it is above all the municipal level which is the locus of a decentralisation that already existed for a century or more – even if this is partly masked by Belgium's federal development in the 1980s. The municipal level has also gained in competences in countries like Italy. France remains the exception, with its large number of communes – nearly 35,000 – compared with about 8,000 for countries of comparable size such as Germany, Spain and Italy, and with de facto heterogeneity in the exercise of communal competences in France although they are in principle the same for all.

The centralisation due to participation in the Council is also very noticeable and known to local political actors in countries where decentralisation mainly concerns the communal level, such as Denmark or the Netherlands. It has to be added that Member States are liable for their failure to comply with the obligations of the treaties and secondary legislation. They may therefore be subject to an infringement procedure triggered by the Commission – or another Member State – which may lead to a judicial procedure before the Court of Justice. Infringement procedures – and the exchange of information that may eventually lead to such a procedure – are formally involving only the central government and the Commission, although the Member State is liable for action or abstention of all authorities, be they located at a central, regional or local level. Even though a certain number of Member States have developed institutional mechanisms to involve regional and local authorities in the establishment of the State's position to be conveyed to the Commission, at the end of the day, and especially in case of emergency, it is the central Executive that decides.

The dual phenomenon of strengthening the Executive through European integration at the expense of the parliament and at the expense of local and regional authorities is not accompanied by appropriate accountability mechanisms. Apart from strictly endogenous causes which impede a good functioning of accountability mechanisms, this is partly due to the institutional system of the Union and its functioning; it is also due to the functioning of EU federalism.

The reduced legibility of political action of Member States' Executives

The institutional setting and procedures of the EU which have created a joint-decision trap comparable to that of Germany and the sectorisation of decision-making which is linked to the competences that have been gradually transferred to the EU have a strong impact on the autonomy of Member States' institutions, which contributes to blurring accountability lines.

Role splitting and joint-decision trap

The consequences of role splitting in the EU institutions were analysed in 1988 by German Political Scientist Fritz W. Scharpf as a 'joint-decision trap' (*Politikverflechtungsfalle*),[18] which results from the particular kind of political intertwining (*Politikverflechtung*) of the German federal system as well as of that of the European Union.

In Scharpf's own words:[19]

> In Germany as in the European Community/Union, important policy choices at the centre, and also all institutional changes, depend on the support of constituent governments (of the Länder or Member States) either by unanimous agreement or by qualified majority votes. In contrast to the ideological or class-based factions of national parliaments, the Bundesrat and the Council of Ministers are supposed to represent territorially-based interests. But unlike the US Senate and the second chambers of all other parliamentary federal states, their members will not only represent the interests of citizens and firms in their respective territories but are also able to defend directly the institutional self-interests of their governments.
>
> . . . as in Germany, EU governments have generally been searching for consensus and avoiding decisions that would violate the vital interests of a Member State . . . I used the metaphor of the 'joint-decision trap' to summarize the arguments explaining these practices. They start from the fact that, on issues of institutional reform, member governments represent not only the interests of their constituents but also their own institutional self-interest which, in the present context, can be interpreted as a concern for autonomy and influence. If problems within their territories can no longer be resolved through autonomous policy choices, these governments may reluctantly delegate competencies [sic] to higher-level institutions. But they will nevertheless try to maintain as much influence

18 F. W. Scharpf, 'The Joint-Decision Trap. Lessons From German Federalism and European Integration', *Public Administration* 66, no. 2 (1988): pp. 239–278.

19 F. W. Scharpf, 'The Joint-Decision Trap Revisited', *Journal of Common Market Studies* 44, no. 4 (2006): pp. 845–864.

> as possible over the exercise of these competencies. In order to prevent decisions violating their own preferences, they will insist on unanimity or qualified majority voting even though the outcomes are likely to be inefficient from a problem-solving perspective.

Scharpf's analysis thus acknowledges role splitting and adds an explanation of the reasons why actors when exercising their EU role do not base their positions on the optimisation of their national interests. In order to fully understand the nature of the EU joint-decision trap and its consequences, a supplementary element needs to be added, which complements Scharpf's analysis, i.e., the growth of sectorisation of policies. This sectorisation in turn reduces the legibility of political action and makes democratic accountability more difficult.

Sectorisation of policy making

As we have seen, in the Schuman Declaration of 9 May 1950, which announced the future Paris Treaty of 1951, the ECSC was conceived with an institutional apparatus particularly well suited to its objectives. In the short term, the aim was to bring Germany back into the fold of Western Europe and to organise the coal and steel industries – which were essential from the point of view of State sovereignty – according to the principles of an open economy that would prevent the return of the vertical and horizontal concentrations that had contributed to the outbreak of the two world wars. In the medium term, the aim was to lay the foundations for a future federal Europe, whose competences would gradually include defence and other important policy areas.

The failure of France to ratify the European Defence Community Treaty in 1954 led to a reorientation of the short- and medium-term objectives and from an institutional point of view to a strengthening of the Council in relation to the Commission/High Authority. The Treaties of Rome of 1957 added to the coal and steel sector not only the nascent atomic energy sector and thus the development of civil nuclear power, but also the establishment of a common market for all products (goods and services) and factors of production (labour and capital), as well as an initial series of accompanying policies: agriculture, transport, commerce (trade agreements with third countries), social policy and a system of association of the overseas countries and territories of Belgium, France, Italy and the Netherlands. These policies did not have at the time specific common institutional elements, with very few exceptions. The development of the policies embedded in the Rome treaties has strongly increased the sectorisation of Member States' central Executives. It was thus necessary to set up coordination structures, which do not always function well. Moreover, the development of new policies means that few sectors escape the phenomenon of Europeanisation, which increasingly reduces the margins of autonomy of the Member States' Executives.

Sectorisation as a consequence of the transfer of competences

In the Treaties of Rome – which are still in force as TFEU and Euratom Treaty – there are rarely specific institutional settings for single common policies, with a few exceptions.

First, the Euratom Treaty provides for the possibility of establishing joint undertakings, particularly in the field of procurement and research, without specifying the institutional content of their status. This allows, where appropriate, to set up structures that do not depend on the Member States but only on the Commission, such as the Euratom Supply Agency the ITER Common enterprise.

Second, the EEC Treaty of 1957 established the European Investment Bank (EIB), with an institutional system based on role splitting. The Protocol on the EIB stipulates that the main institution, the Board of Governors, 'shall consist of the ministers designated by the Member States' (Article 7(1)). The Treaty also expressly mentioned committees appointed by the Council. An Advisory Committee on Transport was provided for in Article 83 (now Article 99 TFEU).[20] Article 105 provided for the establishment of a Monetary Committee of an advisory nature, responsible for promoting cooperation between Member States' policies on monetary matters, for the composition of which each Member State and the Commission appointed two members (Article 105). A special committee responsible for monitoring the Commission's negotiation of trade agreements with third countries was established in Article 113 (now Article 207 TFEU).[21] Article 124 of the Treaty (now Article 163 TFEU) provided for the setting up of a committee to assist the Commission in managing the European Social Fund, chaired by a Member of the Commission, and composed of representatives of governments and of workers' and employers' organisations, on the model of the International Labour Organisation. It may be useful to clarify that EU 'Funds' – e.g., Social Fund (ESF), Agricultural Guidance and Guarantee Fund (EAGGF) – are merely budget lines and not institutional structures. Apart from the Social Fund, the EEC Treaty itself did not provide for their management to be dependent on a committee representing the Member States.

Since the 1970s there has been a gradual extension of common policy sectors, which was formalised in the treaties starting with the Single European Act which came into force on 1 July 1987. Some of those policies had already been developed in practice before, such as environmental policy and regional policy, which were set up after the first enlargement in 1973.

20 'An Advisory Committee consisting of experts designated by the governments of Member States shall be attached to the Commission. The Commission, whenever it considers it desirable, shall consult the Committee on transport matters'.

21 Article 105(2)(3) EEC: 'the Commission shall conduct these negotiations in consultation with a special committee appointed by the Council to assist it in this task and within the framework of such directives as the Council may issue to it'.

With the increase of sectorial policies at EU level, the various departments of Member States' Executives – and even the members of government – have become increasingly placed in a matrix system of relationships. On the one hand, the internal relations of the Executive – between members of government and between central administrative services – have grown in complexity. On the other hand, external relations of central government ministers and services with their counterparts in other Member States and the Commission have been added to internal relations. These external relations, which are not any longer a monopoly of the Ministry of Foreign Affairs, have created epistemic communities of Member State specialists in their policy fields – agriculture, transport, etc. – which do not easily fit in the Member State system of accountability. There is a well-known tendency of experts to feel more linked to their counterparts in other Member States than to politicians and experts of other policy fields in their own Member State.[22]

Variety of policy coordination systems across the EU Member States

The progressive Europeanisation of public policies has generated an increasing need for coordination within the Executive. The responses to that are very different from one Member State to another, with different consequences on the accountability channels of the Executive.

Two Member States have early on set up sophisticated and effective coordination systems. In France, the government soon started relying on a specific structure, the General Secretariat of the Interministerial Committee for European Economic Cooperation (SGCI), which had as a matter of fact been set up in 1947 by Robert Schuman, then Prime Minister, for the management of the Marshall Plan funds. The SGCI became the General Secretariat for European Affairs (SGAE) in 2005. The SGCI/SGAE structure is particularly well adapted to the organisation of the French Executive, especially when its Secretary-General is also a member of the Cabinet of the President of the Republic, as has been most often the case since the election of François Mitterrand in 1981, or a member of the Cabinet of the Prime Minister.

In the United Kingdom, a European Secretariat was set up within the Cabinet Office as early as for the negotiations leading up to the United Kingdom's accession to the Communities on 1 January 1973; it became the European and Global Issues Secretariat in 2007. For a long time, the UK system was also a particularly well-adapted and efficient coordination system, until it collapsed after the referendum of 23 June 2016 on *Brexit*, due to the internal division

22 See, amongst others, H. Siedentopf and J. Ziller, eds., *Making European Policies Work – The Implementation of Community Legislation in the Member States* (London: Sage, 1988). Also published in French under the title, *L'Europe des administrations? – La mise en œuvre de la législation communautaire dans les États membres* (Brussels: Bruylant – Institut Européen d'Administration Publique, 1988).

in Teresa May's Government and later to how Boris Johnson chose to conduct his country's relations with the EU.[23]

A number of other Member States have tried to emulate the coordination systems of France and the UK, with varying results, as is the case in Spain and Italy. In both countries, the requirements of government coalitions and the complexities of regionalism (especially in Spain) prevent the structures responsible for coordination from operating with the efficiency and effectiveness necessary for a strong influence on European decision-making procedures.

Strong coordination systems may facilitate the Executive's accountability to parliament if the political level so chooses or if parliament is strong enough. But there is too often a temptation for politicians to blame 'Brussels' rather than to take responsibility for the choices they have made under the constraints of the joint-decision trap.

In contrast, Germany has always had a relatively weak system of coordination, due to two central elements of its constitution. First, executive federalism implies that coordination of executive functions is most often done horizontally between the *Länder*, without the federal government usually having the means to impose its views. This phenomenon is increased by the difference in majority coalitions between the federal parliament (*Bundestag*) and the parliaments of the *Länder*. The same party can be part of the majority coalition in the federal parliament and of a government coalition at *Land* level that includes parties which are in opposition in the *Bundestag*. In such a case the representatives of the *Land* in the *Bundesrat* may well vote against the federal government's proposals. Second, the federal chancellor has only limited power over federal ministers, the *Richtlinienkompetenz* (competence in the form of directives), which does not allow her/him to interfere with the autonomy of ministerial departments. These patterns of the typically German joint-decision trap render the accountability of the Executive even more complicated than in other Member States.

An anecdotal case illustrates the difficulties of coordination in Germany's federal government particularly well, i.e., the issue of glyphosate in November 2017. The Commission had proposed an extension of the moratorium on the possible ban of Monsanto's herbicide, which is under suspicion of causing considerable damage to health and the environment, on the European market. The Commission, according to EU rules on implementing acts, submitted this proposal to the competent committee. France, Italy and many other Member States were opposed to the moratorium and in the summer, the German government indicated that it would abstain. Nevertheless, during the vote in the Committee, the German representative voted in favour of the proposed moratorium instead of abstaining, thus permitting the extension of the moratorium. This triggered the ire of Chancellor Merkel who could however do nothing else than declare that the vote did not correspond to the position of

23 See M. Barnier, *La grande illusion, Journal secret du Brexit (2016–2020)* (Paris: Gallimard, 2021).

the German government; it was too late to change the Committee's statement of position and the subsequent Commission decision. As a matter of fact, the German representative was a civil servant of the Federal Ministry of Agriculture; he had simply followed the directives of his minister, who wanted to keep the favour of many farmers who used this herbicide. At the time, negotiations were underway to establish a new government coalition after the September elections, and the federal government was therefore in principle only dealing with current affairs. For those who know how the German coordination system works, the fact that the civil servant simply followed his minister's directive rather than alert his colleagues in the Chancellor's Office was not surprising: the exceptional nature of the affair was only due to the fact that the change in the German position embarrassed the Chancellor vis-à-vis her colleagues in the European Council.

With comitology committees, there is thus an increase in sectorisation due to the role splitting of executive power holders and civil servants from different ministerial departments who are part of European epistemic communities as well as their own national administration. This phenomenon also appears in most of the European agencies that have been set up since the end of the 1990s, as they very often have an organisational structure that reproduces the Union system, with representatives of the Commission and representatives of the Executives of the Member States in their decision-making organs.

The strongest reaction to the difficulty of establishing clear lines of accountability has come for several decades from Germany, as mentioned in the previous section. As soon as the Single European Act was implemented, the *Länder* governments began to call for the establishment in the European treaties of a 'catalogue of competences', which they claimed was intended to prevent the 'creeping increase' of competences of the Union to the detriment of the institutions of the Member States. In Germany, a number of politicians and public law professors, as well as judges of the Federal Constitutional Court very often blame the Commission and the Court of Justice of the EU for the growth of EU action, and they simply ignore the fact that the Council is the main EU legislator, and that Germany usually has the means to counter a decision that would go against its most important interests even if it does not act, due to the joint-decision trap.

The interlocking of EU institutions and Member States' central Executives not only leads to an increasing sectorisation of the latter, but it also results in a reduction of their policy autonomy as explained with the concept of joint-decision trap. Both phenomena are blurring the lines of accountability in Member States.

The reduced autonomy of the Executive

While the institutional set-up and decision-making processes of the EU strengthen the Executive at the expense of parliaments, this strengthening is accompanied by a reduction in the decision-making autonomy of the Executive in all common policy areas. This is true of most policy sectors, and it is reinforced by the voting system applicable to the Council and the European Council.

In the sectors where the treaties provide for unanimous decision-making, the Executive maintains its autonomy at least in theory. These are important sectors, but basically few in number. For the Council, unanimity is necessary in cases such as harmonisation of taxation, free movement of persons and workers' rights and interests, as well as for the common foreign and security policy and a number of provisions relating to the area of security, freedom and justice. As the votes in Council on legislative proposals are known because of the transparency of the Council's work, it is easy to know whether a government representative has impeded the adoption of a decision, a directive or a regulation deemed contrary to national interests, or whether s/he has allowed for its adoption by a positive vote. However, in many cases it is better for the government to participate in the compromise on a text that will be eventually adopted than to remain isolated and out of the game.

In areas where the Council decides by qualified majority, which is the case for most policy areas, the Executive does not have the theoretical weapon of a veto to guarantee its autonomy. If a government wishes to have a Commission proposal modified, it is forced to make alliances with other governments and it also needs to take into account the position of the European Parliament.

As already mentioned, in most cases the Council does not vote, because a compromise has been reached beforehand in COREPER, whose work is not subject to the principle of transparency. Hence the legibility of the Executives' political action is blurred due to the fact that EU decisions depend on negotiations between Member States, which are mainly conducted at expert level.

Indeed, justifying a compromise position is more complex and requires far more explanations than explaining a blunt veto. Typically, the UK government has for years participated in the negotiations leading to directives or regulations in the field of immigration as well as police and criminal justice, and only decided to opt-out at the last moment, as was possible due to the special protocol on the UK. It was then often too late for the other Member States to resume negotiations between them, and the UK thus influenced the content of EU acts that were not applicable to its territory. Instead of explaining this phenomenon to the British electorate, many members of government preferred the blame game of attributing to the EU rules what they were in fact supporting.

As far as the European Council is concerned, the decision-making rule is usually consensus, which differs from unanimity in that no vote is taken; however, it is sufficient for one Head of State or Government to oppose in order to impede consensus. This being said, opposing a common position in the European Council can be very costly in terms of relations with other Member States. This was illustrated by the participation of the Italian Prime Minister Giuseppe Conte in the first European Council after he was appointed in June 2018: after each item of the agenda had been discussed he thought it useful to express an objection, until French President Macron openly told him during the meeting that this was not a way to behave in a European summit where consensus is being sought.

European Council meetings are prepared in COREPER, and by ministers of European affairs meeting in the General Affairs Council. There are usually prior negotiations between sherpas of the Heads of State or Government, all of which are not subject to transparency. The obvious result is that accountability of the Heads of State or Government of Member States for the positions of the European Council both to parliaments and to voters is quite difficult to establish.

The loss of autonomy described here is to a deal variable according to the political and economic weight of a Member State. In the case of small Member States the loss of autonomy is certainly more important and more constant than in large ones; that is why the governments of smaller Member States tend to rely all the more on the Commission, which must defend the general interest of the Union as already understood by Monnet and his team when preparing the ECSC Treaty. This being said, even in the case of the larger Member States such as France, Germany, Italy and the UK before Brexit, the autonomy of the Executives is reduced, because consensus between Member States should always be sought as far as possible, or at least coalitions established.

The glyphosate case, already mentioned, also illustrates the loss of autonomy of the Executive in France. President Emmanuel Macron had announced after the comitology decision in autumn 2017 that the use of glyphosate would anyway be banned in France; eventually, he had to face up to the fact that if France did not want to incur an infringement procedure, he had to support a compromise and postpone the ban until later.

The reduction in autonomy of the Executives leads to the depoliticisation of the European level consensus, for reasons explained by Scharpf with the concept of joint-decision trap. Such a depoliticisation explains also to a great extent the perception of the Union as a bureaucratic system; however, it is not the bureaucracy of the Commission that is at fault, or at least not primarily.

The loss of autonomy leads many among the Member States' Executives to blame 'Brussels' rather than to explain the reasons for European consensus and its ultimate benefits for each country, above and beyond the concessions that needed to be made. It is quite common for a Head of Government or a minister to say that a measure must be adopted 'because Europe asks us to do so', while they avoid specifying their role in the decisions taken by the European institutions.

On the other hand, it is quite common for members of the Executive to take credit for policies that are well received by the electorate, even when they are merely the implementation of European decisions, notably the transposition of directives.

The blurring of accountability lines is certainly heightened by the importance of cross-financing for the implementation of EU policies. With cross financing each level can take credit for successful interventions, or on the contrary complain about the lack of investment by the other level. This is a phenomenon that is also well known within the Member States, where it leads to low involvement of the electorate in local or regional elections in cases where there is no strong identification of the inhabitants with their territory.

Conclusion

The executive federalism based on role splitting that characterises the EU institutions and decision-making procedures and the resulting joint-decision trap mechanism have a twofold impact: the institutions of the Union, especially the Commission, are perceived by citizens as a cumbersome machine that is remote from their concerns; the institutions of the Member States, in particular the parliaments, but also the Executives, are perceived as being weak in protecting citizens, and also far removed from their concerns. This is a phenomenon that needs to be understood and its reasons explained. Furthermore, the ultimate benefits of common decision-making at European level need to be explained clearly and as simply as possible.

Whether the system can be reformed to make the lines of responsibility and accountability clearer is another matter, and one that is also well known in federal, regional, or decentralised States. A 'layer cake' system where each level is solely responsible for policy choices would certainly be more in line with effective democratic participation and control, but the increasing complexity of public policies is better served by a 'marble cake' system which is also well known in the USA's dual federalism although there is no joint-decision trap in that system.

The purpose of this chapter is not to make recommendations for reform, but only to better understand the problem of executive accountability in the EU as it has been constructed since the ECSC Treaty. At any rate, reforming the EU institutions depends on a consensus that has not always been present among the governments of the Member States. The complexity of the system induces scepticism in growing parts of the electorate of many Member States and this in turn impedes the adoption of radical institutional reforms. In the absence of visible economic advantages for most of the population of Member States – as was the case in the 'post-war boom' – the narrow path is that of explaining, explaining and explaining again.

9 Political accountability within the European system

Fabienne Péraldi-Leneuf

Quite surprisingly, the issue of political accountability in relation to the European Union system is little studied by French and foreign constitutionalists and the Europeanist doctrine, although it fascinates the observers of democracy in domestic parliamentary systems. This is probably due to the originality and complexity of the European institutional system, or even to the lasting impression that the European model is too different from those of national parliamentarianism. That issue is nonetheless just as topical as ever. Indeed, the European system is completely different from 'Communities' of old. Though the distinction between powers was blurred for a long time, and there was some 'appearance of diffused and permanent negotiation between scattered and ill-identified interests'[1] which went against the representative principle, time has passed. Democracy has spread, powers and interests are better identified, if only because, since the Lisbon Treaty,[2] the composition of the official Executive (the European Commission) has been linked to the results of the European legislative elections.

Based on the analysis grid as defined in the REGALIEN Project, the reflection on accountability in the Union system will include the same questions as those that are raised as to the accountability of the Member States of the EU: identification of the executive power, identification of who is holding to accounts, identification of the acts for which the Executive must account and identification of the consequences of accountability.

Starting from the initial treaties, the chapter will mention the appearance of the principle of political accountability in the ECSC Treaty through the sole tool of the motion of censure. It will be observed that the concept then went through an evolution that was inherent in the evolution of the Union's political system. The first part will study the transformations of that accountability. Beyond censorship, which never officially led to the overthrow of the

1 O. Costa and P. Magnette, 'Les transformations de la responsabilité politique dans l'union européenne', *Politiques et Management Public* 19, no. 1 (2001): pp. 103–120.

2 J. Ziller, *Les nouveaux traités européens: Lisbonne et après* (Paris: LGDJ-Clefs, 2008).

DOI: 10.4324/9781003281559-16

Commission, other mechanisms appeared, which were inspired from the constitutional traditions of the Member States, with and between the institutions, which revealed cultural and institutional discrepancies. Those mechanisms, which are consecrated in the texts (designation, nomination, censorship, parliamentary committees, oral written questions, budget discharge) allow today to assert that the system is parliamentary, even though they only reflect a minimal shared culture of accountability at the European scale ('Looking for European parliamentarianism').

In the second part, the chapter will focus on the failures/shortfalls of political accountability of the EU. Indeed, since the beginning, it has only targeted the Commission and its relations with the European Parliament. No tool involves the Council of the European Union, the second component of the European legislative power, nor even when it exceptionally plays an executive role. The same is true of the European Council, which is composed of the national heads of the executive branches.[3] Those two councils nonetheless represent the States and their governments which are 'democratically accountable, either to their national parliaments or their citizens' (Article 10 TEU). Their role should undoubtedly be seriously reconsidered from the angle of accountability. The Conference on the Future of Europe launched by the institutions with a view to an impending reform of the treaties gives the opportunity to think about it and for citizens to express their wishes from a democratic point of view. This chapter will try to mention the current lines of thinking ('The limits of European political accountability').

A third part will tackle accountability from a particular angle – that of European good governance. The classic mechanisms of political accountability being maybe incomplete and probably ill-adapted to guarantee efficient counter-powers, the Union has developed new forms of broader, societal, inclusive forms of accountability, starting from its 2001 white paper on European governance. The consequence is the orientation of the European policies towards a culture of systematic assessment, undoubtedly for purposes of decision-making power legitimisation. The sophistication of those mechanisms results in the apprehension of accountability in a pluralistic and original way which goes beyond Enlightenment parliamentarianism and will probably also spread, if it has not already done so, at the national level ('The other side of accountability in the European Union').

3 See J. Ziller, 'Functional duplication and political accountability of the Executive in the EU Member States', in *Regional Accountability and Executive Power in Europe*, eds. M. Morabito and G. Tusseau (London: Routledge, 2023).

Looking for European parliamentarianism

From the appearance of the accountability principle . . .

The inclusion of the motion of censure, a traditional element of political accountability,[4] in community treaties dates back to the drafting of the ECSC Treaty (Article 24). That it did not raise any debate at the time[5] is probably due to the relatively simple organisation of the institutional system. It was indeed articulated around the sole cooperation between two institutions, the High Authority, which became the European Commission in the 1957 EEC and EAEC Treaties, and the Council of Ministers, which shared decision-making and executive powers.

The parliamentary assembly had no legislative or budget role, only that supervision power. Moreover, the motion of censure was organised 'in a theoretically restrictive way',[6] i.e., in favour of the European Commission. To be adopted by the Members of the Assembly, it must meet two requirements: a two-thirds majority of votes cast and the majority of the Assembly Members.[7] The founding fathers, maybe hardened by the pitfalls of the French Fourth Republic parliamentarianism, had thus carefully framed that beginning of European accountability, and had in addition reserved it to the sole yearly discussion of the general report that the ECSC High Authority had to present to the parliamentary assembly.

One should also remember that the ECSC Treaty was signed only one year after the creation of the Council of Europe among six States which were also members of that organisation. That historical concomitance generated

4 C. Geynet-Dussauze and P. Jensel-Monge, 'France', in *Comparative Executive Power in Europe: Perspectives on Accountability from Law, History and Political Science*, eds. M. Morabito and G. Tusseau (London: Routledge, 2023).

5 The first works date back from the 1980s. See M. Chauchat, *Le contrôle politique du Parlement européen sur les exécutifs communautaires* (Paris: LGDJ, 1989); C. Hiscock-Lageot, 'Le traité établissant une Constitution pour l'Europe: une occasion manquée d'instaurer un régime parlementaire', *Revue française de droit constitutionnel (RFDC)* 2, no. 66 *(2006): pp. 303–320; A. Vauchez, Démocratiser l'Europe* (Paris: Seuil, 2014); H. Oberdorf, 'Vers une démocratie trans-parlementaire européenne?', in *La responsabilité politique des exécutifs des États membres de l'Union du fait de leur action européenne*, eds. C. Geslot, P.-Y. Monjal, and J. Rossetto (Brussels: Bruylant, 2016), pp. 241–256; L. Guilloud-Colliat, 'Contours et détours du contrôle du Parlement européen sur le Conseil européen et le Conseil', in *La responsabilité politique des exécutifs des États membres de l'Union du fait de leur action européenne* (Brussels: Bruylant, 2016), p. 257.

6 Report of the French Senate: M. Haenel, R. Badinter, P. Fauchon, L. Lanier, A. de Montesquiou, and X. de Villepin, 'La réforme des institutions de l'Union européenne dans la perspective de la Conférence intergouvernementale de l'an 2000', no. 148, Session ordinaire 1999–2000, https://www.senat.fr/rap/r99-148/r99-148.html.

7 Those voting conditions are still in force today. See Article 234 TFEU.

strong inspirations at the institutional level.[8] The EAEC Assembly was like the reproduction of the Advisory Assembly of the Council of Europe. A protocol appended to the ECSC Treaty on the 'Relations with the Council of Europe' even recommended that members of the Assembly 'should preferably be chosen from among the representatives in the Consultative Assembly of the Council of Europe' (Article 1). It was also provided that the ECSC Assembly '[would] forward annually to the Consultative Assembly of the Council of Europe a report on its activity'. The High Authority had to send the same general report as that provided in Article 17 of the Treaty on which a motion of censure would be voted to the Ministers' Committee and to the Consultative Committee of the Council of Europe.

The non-separation of powers, added to the absence of political consistency of the Assembly, which for a long time fuelled critical discourses on the 'democratic deficit'[9] of the Communities did not allow to reason analogically with the models of national parliamentarianism. As time passed, with institutional organisations, the interdependency link with the Council of Europe came undone[10] and the relations between the European Commission and the European Parliament changed. That process followed three main stages. The first and most fundamental one was of course the direct universal suffrage election of the European Parliament. European representatives are no longer 'delegates' nominated by the States, but rather elected by the peoples and they form a cross-sectional representation. The second stage was the parallel and unavoidable increase of the decision-making powers of the Parliament thanks to the progressive development of new procedures: cooperation, assent, co-decision, and, since the Lisbon Treaty, the ordinary and special legislative procedures. The third step was undoubtedly the 1986 decision *Les Verts v European Parliament*.[11] In line with its case law which consecrated fundamental rights in the Community legal order,[12] the Court of Justice, pushed by the German Constitutional Court, considered that the treaties were the 'Basic Constitutional Charter of the Communities' and that the latter were a 'Community of law'. The European Parliament had complete, both passive and active, legitimacy[13] capable of supporting its democratic expansion.

8 J. P. Jacqué, *Droit institutionnel de l'Union européenne* (Paris: Dalloz, 2018).

9 A. Moravcsik, 'Le mythe du déficit démocratique européen', *Raisons Politiques* 2, no. 10 (2003): pp. 87–105.

10 There is no reference to the Council of Europe in the EEC Treaty.

11 CJEU, Case 294/83, *Parti écologiste 'Les Verts' v Parlement européen*, 23 April 1986, ECR 1986-01339.

12 For the first see: CJEU, Case 29-69, *Erich Stauder v City of Ulm – Sozialamt*, 12 November 1969; CJEU, Case 11-70, *Internationale Handelsgesellschaft mbH v Einfuhr- und Vorratsstelle für Getreide und Futtermittel*, 17 December 1970; CJEU, Case 36-75, *Roland Rutili v Ministre de l'intérieur*, 28 October 1975, ECR 1975-01219.

13 Many other decisions or opinions reinforced that case law. See, for example, CJEU, 3 September 2008, *Kadi et Al Barakaat, aff. jtes* C-402/05 P et C-415/05 P, ECLI:EU:C:2008:461; CJEU, 18 December 2014, *Avis* 2/13, EC.LI:EU:C:2014:2454.

Research in the reports and archive documents shows that the topic of accountability started to fuel political debate in 1999.[14] The balance of powers being re-balanced, the European representatives at last took hold of their prerogative of political control. From 1997, because of different malfunctions and affairs within the Commission related to its bad management and misappropriations, they tried to table several motions of censure against it, but without success.[15] Eventually, on 15 March 1999, faced with the real threat of a motion of censure,[16] the Commission chaired by Jacques Santer decided to resign quite dramatically before the vote in Parliament. That exceptional political crisis opened a new era in accountability. Today, even though no motion of censure has ever effectively succeeded, it has become a weapon of deterrence.[17] It has above all contributed to a transformation of accountability.

. . . to the transformations of accountability

That was why in 1999 a Senate report explicitly raised the issue of 'Parliament's oversight in the Union'[18] and suggested 'redefining the conditions of accountability of the Commission to the European Parliament'. It considered two possible evolutions, by analogy with what exists at national level: either introducing some accountability of the Commission to the Council or modifying the voting rules while reinforcing the collegiality of the accountability of the Commission. The first idea was due to the observation that in constitutional law, the Executive can only be accountable to the institution which has established it, and the second that one should avoid the custom of too tight a dependence of the Commission on the European Parliament which could force it to resign with a simple threat. The report strangely supported the weakening of parliamentary oversight since at that time the composition

14 See the website: www.cvce.eu/recherche. The CVCE.eu research infrastructure of University of Luxembourg gives access to thousands of documents and publications on the process of the European construction.

15 See D. Georgakakis, 'La démission de la Commission européenne: scandale et tournant institutionnel (octobre 1998–mars 1999)', *Cultures et conflits*, no. 38–39 (2001): pp. 39–71.

16 The Commission resigned for the first time following several affairs involving commissioners, but that act was not quite the first of its kind. On 17 December 1998, the European Parliament did not grant the Commission budget discharge for the execution of the general budget of the European Communities for the financial year 1996. After that vote, Mrs Pauline Green, the Leader of the Socialist group, tabled a motion of censure co-signed by 70 other members of the group. Those members thought that the vote on the discharge 'meant that the Commission was not certain it had the confidence of this assembly'.

17 Fifteen motions were tabled, but only five were voted upon: On 10 September 1992 against the role of the Commission of agriculture in the GATT negotiations; in February 1997 to condemn the bad management of the mad cow crisis; on 10 January 1999 on the bad financial management of the Commission; on 4 March 2005 on the Eurostar manager; and on 18 November 2014 against Jean-Claude Juncker, who was accused of tax evasion.

18 Report on the 'Reform of the European Union institutions in view of the intergovernmental Conference of 2000'.

of the Commission was determined by the governments of the Member States which nominated it together, even though the European Parliament had to approve it beforehand.

Those proposals did not succeed. Later revisions of the treaties did not alter the meaning of the texts.[19] Adopting a motion of censure today complies with the same rules as initially, with the nuance that the resignation of the Commission as a body now includes that of its Vice-President, who is also the High Representative of the Union for Foreign Affairs and Security Policy and a member of the European Council. That broadening of the College undoubtedly influences how the motion, which remains a weapon of deterrence but is under-used, is practised.

On the contrary, 'accountability' was included in the treaties. Today, in addition to Article 10 TFEU which states, 'The functioning of the Union shall be founded on representative democracy' Article 17 TEU provides, 'The Commission, as a body, shall be responsible to the European parliament'.[20] It is clearly identified as the executive and governmental organ of the EU. As the first, it exercises the functions of coordination, execution[21] and management. It is the institution which 'shall promote the general interest', 'take appropriate initiatives to that end', 'ensure the application of the Treaties', 'oversee the application of Union law under the control of the Court of Justice of the European Union' and 'execute the budget and manage programmes'. As the second, it is now a political organ. Its president is *elected* only by the European Parliament by a majority of the members, upon the proposal of the European Council, but the latter must '[take] into account the elections to the European Parliament' (Article 17(7) TEU). That provision at last gives European parliamentarianism what it had been lacking since the beginning: the politicisation of the administrative supranational body.[22] The legislative function is unambiguously granted to the European Parliament and to the Council of Europe, which are co-legislators. The role of the latter is above all a legislative one, if one disregards the executive function it has in foreign policy and security (Articles 24 and 26 TEU). That 'reclassification' as a legislative chamber is the result of the Convention on the Future of Europe of 2002–2004, which aimed to simplify the institutional diagram by mimicking

19 Entrusting the Council with the political supervision of the Commission raises difficulties due to its 'functional doubling up', for its members are from national governments and have been democratically selected, and to the fact that it is still the holder of the executive power together with the Commission, in addition to its decision-making functions.

20 Article 17(8) TEU provides: 'The Commission, as a body, shall be responsible to the European Parliament'.

21 Article 291 TFEU states, 'Where uniform conditions for implementing legally binding Union acts are needed, those acts shall confer implementing powers on the Commission'.

22 See Decision of the European Parliament of 7 February 2018 on the Review of the Framework Agreement on relations between the European Parliament and the European Commission (2017/2233(ACI)).

the 'European' model of separation of powers. One should specify though that, because of the influence during rotating presidency, the Council has a determining role in the definition of priorities and the coordination of policies in close cooperation with the European Council,[23] as well as in domains that are not submitted to community procedures.

Other mechanisms than 'sanction' have therefore appeared, following the evolution of functions, which correspond to the logic of the parliamentary regime. The trials and errors of national regimes over centuries have served the history of accountability. The European Parliament is still the only institution which exercises functions of political control (Article 14 TEU).[24] That is visible in the conditions for the designation and swearing in of the Commission (Articles 17(7) and 17(8) TEU), in the organisation of parliamentary debates (written and oral questions Article 230 TFEU), in the establishment of permanent and temporary parliamentary committees (Article 226 TFEU), in the discussion of the annual report of the Commission (Article 233 TFEU) and in the budget discharge procedure (Article 319 TFEU). One may consider that this is the reproduction of national constitutional elements, but the implementation of those measures is singular in that it relies on a framework agreement creating a 'special partnership' between the European Parliament and the European Commission,[25] which was signed to facilitate and organise their cooperation and the modes of their collaboration. The part entitled 'political responsibility' develops the strong link that exists between the two institutions. The agreement for example provides in addition that a State of the Union Address by the President of the European Commission[26] take stock every year of the current situation in the European Union and define future working priorities. It launches the interinstitutional process that leads to the new working programme of the Commission for the following year. The agreement innovates by providing for a form of indirect individual accountability of commissioners. The Parliament can ask the President of the Commission to withdraw their confidence in a member of the latter. In that case, the President 'will seriously consider whether to request that Member to resign, in accordance with Article 17(6) TEU. The President shall either require the resignation of that Member or explain his/her refusal to do so before Parliament in

23 Article 15 TEU.

24 Article 14 TEU: 'It shall exercise functions of political control and consultation'.

25 Review of the Framework Agreement on relations between the European Parliament and the European Commission, JO L 304 of 20 November 2010, pp. 47–62.

26 The agreement provides that 'Each year in the first part-session of September, a State of the Union debate will be held in which the President of the Commission shall deliver an address, taking stock of the current year and looking ahead to priorities for the following years. To that end, the President of the Commission will in parallel set out in writing to Parliament the main elements guiding the preparation of the Commission Work Programme for the following year'.

the following part-session'.[27] Other provisions involve the Parliament at all the stages of the life of the Commission within the framework of a 'constructive dialogue' or the participation of the Commission to the parliamentary work (plenary sessions and any organ of the Parliament), including if the President considers redistributing responsibilities among the members of the Commission during his term.

The multiplication of the control processes unquestionably reinforces the 'informative' weight of Parliament which tries to exercise an increasingly strong pressure on the Commission in domains where it can intervene, as it has done recently about the violations of the rule of law in Poland and in Hungary.[28] However, those actions remain founded on sophisticated modalities of counterpower which disturb the models of parliamentarianism. Limiting one's reflection by analogy to the national constitutional systems, one can note that there still exist insufficiencies in European political accountability. Must one necessarily reflect that way? The Union system cannot completely align on the 'majority rule', or at least on the parliament-government *continuum*.

The limits of European political accountability

In the past, the loopholes in European political accountability were due to both the confusion of powers and the lack of political link between the administrative and decision-making functions, as we have seen. Today, the situation is not the same anymore, but there still remain breaches: the insufficient identification of institutions which are subject to political supervision, the absence of accountability in 'non-community' domains, the absence of dissolution process, and the variability and complexity of the political game.

The insufficient identification of institutions subject to political supervision

Though powers are better identified, the question is however that of the scope of political control, not only in relation to the Commission, which has always been its target, but also in relation to other entities and institutions which do not, properly speaking, have an executory role but still have an essential role in

27 Framework Agreement on relations between the European Parliament and the European Commission, Official Journal of the European Union, 20 November 2010, L 304/47, access at: https://eur-lex.europa.eu/LexUriServ/LexUriServ.do?uri=OJ:L:2010:304:0047:0062:EN:PDF

28 Parliament was very active on the issue of the respect of fundamental rights in Hungary, since it adopted no fewer than seven resolutions on the situation in the country before launching the procedure provided for in Article 7 TEU against it. Hungary appealed to the CJEU against the launching of the procedure which was rejected. See CJEU, Case C-650/18, *Hungary v European Parliament*, 3 June 2021. See also its recent position on the recovery plan: www.europarl.europa.eu/news/fr/press-room/20211001IPR14015/hongrie-pologne-approbation-des-plans-de-relance-une-fois-les-craintes-levees

the definition and implementation of the Union's policies. One can think first of the accountability of the agencies and bodies which orbit the Commission's administrative cosmos. There are already *ex ante* modes of control by Parliament of their mission and the agencies which participate in the execution are implied, with the Commission, in the *ex-post* supervision, but their multiplication, especially in domains which are out of Parliament's control admittedly raises a far from trivial issue at the level of the democratic operation. One can think next of course of the Council of Europe and Council of the European Union which each represent the States in the institutional system. With the Lisbon Treaty, which reasserted their weight, the 'intergovernmental' contribution to the building of Europe has remained significant. Even if those institutions are composed of Executives that are democratically accountable to their parliamentary assemblies or citizens, that legitimacy is not enough for the good of European parliamentarianism or even more simply the democratic functioning of the Union. Obviously, what is important is whether it is not only opportune but also possible to set up mechanisms of political control over them.

That issue, in relation to the Council, could have been initially relevant, for it was, in the texts, the holder of the executory power which it delegated to the Commission (Article 222 TEC). That delegation was concretely realised in the creation of committees (comitology) composed of representatives of Member States, who were entrusted with accompanying the institution in the adoption of execution norms. Understandably, it was not easy to conceive that it could be the object of the motion of censure together with the Commission, given its composition and the interests it represents. Above all, the Council was also the only decision-making body.

The issue is raised anew today, but differently due to the evolution of its functions. There is no doubt that introducing political supervision would be inconsistent and counter-productive in the context of its quality as co-legislator. Moreover, Parliament is not without means against it, for several provisions of treaties provide that the Council should be accountable to it, by informing it of its programmes and actions.[29] On the contrary, the Council has determining influence on the coordination of policies, on the occasion of its rotating presidency, in cooperation with the Council of Europe. It also has prerogatives which are outside the decision-making process within the CFSP, in the field of the EMU, or under Article 7.[30] Limiting political supervision to the Commission only belonged to the process of functional integration and

29 Members of the European Parliament may ask oral or written questions to the Council to ask for new measures and under Article 15(6) TEU the Council of the EU presents a report to the EP after each meeting of the European Council.

30 See L. Guilloud-Colliat, 'Contours et détours du contrôle du Parlement européen sur le Conseil européen et le Conseil'. See also C. Hiscock-Lageot, 'Le traité établissant une Constitution pour l'Europe: une occasion manquée d'instaurer un régime parlementaire', pp. 303–320.

community method. Broadening the responsibility of the Council for some of those activities would give new and citizen legitimacy to the interventions of governments, which would also be another form of integration.

Those questions are *a fortiori* transposable for the Council of Europe. Debates about its quality are livelier, though. Some observers think that it should be considered as an Executive, that it is a 'political engine', in the domain of both 'internal policies' and 'external policies', including in the domain of security and defence. It has moreover been institutionally reinforced since 2009, since it can adopt normative acts in limited cases.[31] Those who support that idea also support a theory of integration founded on intergovernmentalism, which highlights that, in reality, the EU is governed by States more than by a supranational legal system.[32] It is true that recent economic, health and budget crises seem to support that point of view. For others, on the contrary,[33] even though the Council of Europe has indeed a function of representation and of leader of the policies of the Union, it never intervenes in their adoption or implementation. The principle of the separation of functions (or powers) does not concern it, therefore, so it cannot be considered as an executive, if it cannot be held accountable for its acts.

What consequences could then be formulated as to political accountability? The Council of Europe's role of impulse-giving and national legitimacy makes that institution a very special body. One could consider, as for the Council, specific mechanisms of accountability implying the European Parliament, even though there is no link with the European majority, especially in the domains that are outside the common law of the Union. One could also, if it is to become an Executive, look for a specific legitimacy that would correspond to its mission. That position would make it necessary to revise the treaties, for example, by proposing that the President of the Council of Europe be elected by universal suffrage, or that their function be fused with that of the President of the European Commission. Those ideas have been on the table for a long time. The consequences for the system would be far-reaching. . . . The results on the Conference on the Future of the Union will undoubtedly be decisive, provided citizens seize upon that issue which is eminently technical and political.[34]

31 Article 15 TEU.

32 See S. Fabbrini, 'Executive Power and Political Accountability: Assessing the European Union's Experience', *EU3D Research Papers*, no. 7 (June 2021), https://www.eu3d.uio.no/publications/eu3d-research-papers/2021/research-paper-07-fabbrini.html. Admittedly, the recent crisis period significantly enhanced the European Council's role of initiative and setting of the legislative agenda, as well as in the crisis recovery through the establishment of a recovery plan.

33 S. Fabbrini, 'Executive Power and Political Accountability'.

34 M. Herbillon and V. Gomez-Bassac, *Rapport d'information déposé par la Commission des Affaires Européennes sur les conventions démocratiques de refondation de l'Europe*, no. 482 (Assemblée Nationale, 7 December 2017), https://www.assemblee-nationale.fr/dyn/15/rapports/due/l15b0482_rapport-information; T. Chopin, 'Europe: répondre au double déficit exécutif et démocratique', *Fondation Robert Schuman, Question d'Europe*,

The absence of political supervision in strategic policies

The drawbacks of aforementioned accountability more generally speaking belong to strategic domains where the Union is subject to specific rules and procedures, i.e., to inter-governmental domains like the CFSP/ESDP,[35] or crisis-management mechanisms like the European Stability Mechanism (ESM)[36] from the Treaty on Stability, Coordination and Governance (TSCG), or the post-Covid recovery plan (NextGenerationEU) adopted on 20 July 2020. Currently, there is indeed no parliamentary political control of those policies. In the CFSP/ESDP, the Council of Europe and the Council are the only institutions competent to adopt those decisions, apart from the Commission, the Parliament and the Court of Justice for the review of the acts. The Council is not quite the same institution as in the pillar of integration. It is at the same time the only one to take decisions and the only holder of a mission of implementation[37] together with the High Representative of the Union for Foreign Affairs and Security Policy, who 'executes' the policy. Apart from the few provisions which allow Parliament to be informed,[38] there is indeed a 'blind spot'[39] of accountability. The mechanisms and other plans conceived under the form of treaties signed among States (members of the Euro-zone for the first two) belong to the same political void. In the ESM, the European Parliament does not have any power of control whereas national parliaments can give their opinion. As to NextGenerationEU, though it was approved by the European Parliament, in compliance with the treaties for that type of 27-member agreement, it has no relevance as to the control of its implementation by the European Commission. It is however involved in the adoption of the legislative regulation relative to the conditioning of the granting of funds to the respect of the rule of law,[40] but with the rather restrictive role of being informed, producing a report or asking for a 'structured' dialogue.

---

no. 444 (25 September 2017), https://www.robert-schuman.eu/questions-d-europe/0444-zone-euro-repondre-au-double-deficit-executif-et-democratique.

35 Adoption of legislative acts is excluded in the title of the TEU (Article 24 TEU).

36 Though the EP may invite the Commission, the President of the Council, the President of the European Council and/or the President of Eurogroup to debate or to present their activities during the European semester, (Article 121(5) TFEU), it does not have a real power of oversight, either over the ECB or within the framework of the EMU's policies.

37 Under Article 26 TEU, 'The Council shall frame the common foreign and security policy and take the decisions necessary for defining and implementing it on the basis of the general guidelines and strategic lines defined by the European Council'.

38 Articles 17(4) and 18(4) TEU: The High Representative, who is also the Vice-President of the European Commission, shall present a report to the EP twice a year as he chairs the Foreign Affairs Council (Articles 18(3) and 27(1) TEU).

39 See S. Soyeon, 'La coopération interparlementaire' (PhD diss., L'Université de Lille, September 2020).

40 Regulation of the European Parliament and of the Council of 16 December 2020 on a general regime of conditionality for the protection of the Union budget, 2020/2092, JOUEL 433I, 22 December 2020.

The situation could be solved by a revision of the texts allowing the Parliament to enter these fields and/or consecrating their 'communitisation'. Another solution which is supported by some people would be to reinforce the participation of national parliaments in the Union by allowing them to take part in the control of the acts of the Council and the High Representative[41] or intergovernmental bodies in the other cases. For many years indeed, there has been an intensive cooperation among them which led in 2009 to the consecration of their specific and new role in the control of the subsidiarity principle.[42] That cooperation, which is both horizontal and vertical, is being institutionalised today to the point that they claim they contribute to the democratic legitimacy of the EU. It is not certain that that solution is the best for the European Union's destiny and democracy.

The absence of dissolution

A third loophole could result from the fact that the European Executive does not have the possibility of dissolve the European Parliament. That weapon, which is characteristic of parliamentarian regimes, is conceived as favouring a balance of powers. Most of the Executives in Europe have it and it is one of the powers of the President of the French Republic.[43] In that sense would that lack of dissolution be a sign that the European democracy is incomplete?

The answer is rather negative. The European model of responsibility is founded, as has been mentioned, on power relations which are not similar to those which exist in national parliamentary systems. Dissolution is not in itself an instrument which may be available identically or which could be grafted onto all the systems. It is part of the history of the political regime or not. It is therefore difficult to apply it in favour of the Commission or even the Council of Europe. The level of the Commission is not relevant if dissolution is conceived as a referee power, or aims to resolve crises, or even to respond to a motion of censure. As to the Council of Europe, for us, it does not have the legitimacy that would allow it to dissolve the Parliament, with which it does not govern.

Those observations could eventually lead to consider that the EU parliamentary system is not that imperfect, except maybe as to the political game.

41 See S. Soyeon, 'La coopération interparlementaire'. The author asserts that there is a reinforcement of the supervision of the head of the EU institutions through the interparliamentary bodies which shows that the intra-parliamentary cooperation within the EU institutions is becoming a supervisory body.

42 That role is the subject of two protocols annexed to the Lisbon Treaty: Protocol No. 1 on 'The role of national parliaments in the European Union', and Protocol No. 2 on 'The application of the principles of subsidiarity and proportionality'.

43 Article 12 of the Constitution. There were five dissolutions under the French Fifth Republic: in 1962, in 1968, in 1981, in 1988 and in 1997. The last one resulted in cohabitation. In other countries, like the United Kingdom, it is decided by the Prime Minister.

The inconstancy and complexity of the political game

Undoubtedly, despite the election by direct suffrage, the absence of a uniform electoral procedure in Europe, of a political role of the European parties and of a European political campaign[44] have significantly limited the European Parliament in its political relations. Indeed, two main majority groups have agreed for decades to govern based on an agreement aiming to distribute the presidency of the Parliament and those of Parliamentary committees. At that time the notion of 'political commission' of course did not exist.

It was only the Lisbon Treaty in 2009, which, by establishing the principle of the election of the President of the Commission by Parliament, contributed to bring about a major change. For the first election under that regime, in 2014, the principle was accompanied with the process of *Spitzenkandidaten*, which allowed Jean-Claude Juncker, the new President of the Commission, to get unquestionable legitimacy, because it resulted from a vote. He therefore could rely for five years upon a centre-left and centre-right coalition to support his policy. It is often mentioned that that period indisputably marked the return of the 'political' against the technocrats, especially in relation to the Greek file, which allowed to save Greece from an exit from the Union.[45]

Maybe it was for that reason that the following election in 2019, and for the first time in a long time, showed some interest from citizens. However, despite that new stronger political dimension, the link between the Commission and the Parliament does not reflect a coordination based on a common political agenda. On the one hand, the Commission naturally looks for allies among governments as much as, and even more than, among citizens. It should be noted that Ursula von der Leyen was not elected according to the process of *Spitzenkandidaten*, but thanks to a difficult compromise between the Council of Europe and Parliament. She therefore does not have a clear majority. On the other hand, the election this time resulted in more diverse political positions and a more complex distribution of political groups in Parliament.[46] If one adds the fact that political groups are composed of members of different nationalities and from very diverse parties, trying to get a majority results in a constant quest for alliances or coalitions which makes it difficult to get both the support of the Commission and firm and consistent opposition against it.

How to make debates more political then? According to Martin Selmayr, the politicisation of the Commission is not due to a policy of the parties but

44 The principle of transnational lists was not adopted for the European elections of 2019 and citizens cannot directly vote for European political parties.

45 M. Selmeyr, 'La Commission européenne: moteur politique de l'intégration européenne, une conversation avec Martin Selmayr', interview by F. Mérand, *Revue Le Grand Continent*, 27 April 2021, https://legrandcontinent.eu/fr/2021/04/27/la-commission-europeenne-moteur-politique-de-lintegration-europeenne-une-conversation-avec-martin-selmayr-et-frederic-merand/

46 There are seven political groups within the European Parliament.

to group work which 'goes beyond the frontiers of nationalities and political allegiances'.[47] There lies the specificity of the European system: the European stakes are not only dependent on partisan logic. The political game does exist, but it is more complex since the Commission is not the interlocutor of only the European Parliament, and not the only one of Parliament. It also needs to be trusted by the 27 Member States to have legitimacy, as the negotiations on Brexit have shown.

That may be why another side of political accountability has developed with the principles of European 'governance' starting from 2001. Accountability must be considered differently, at the risk of modifying for the Union the perception that one could have of parliamentarianism.

The other side of accountability in the European Union: towards post-parliamentarianism?

The congenital loopholes of political accountability are undoubtedly at the origin of the 2001 white paper of the European Commission on European governance.[48] Indeed, that document follows the trajectory of the evolution of the Union and must be related to the effort to reinforce democracy. The white paper proposes 'opening up the policy-making process'. It 'promotes greater openness, accountability and responsibility'.[49] It is therefore about how the Union uses the powers it has been entrusted with and suggests solutions to make them more effective. Governance relies on five principles: '*Openness, participation, accountability, effectiveness and coherence*'. They are all tightly linked in order to 'connect the EU more closely to its citizens', enhance local powers, strengthen the citizens' trust in public decision-makers, clearly identify objectives and above all allow citizens to require that the institutions account for their decisions.

As to *accountability*, the white paper insists on the fact that each institution must explain its action and take responsibility for it, but Member States are even more targeted as well as and all those who participate in the elaboration and the implementation of the policies, whatever the level they work at. There is not accountability but multiple accountabilities. The institutions are the first

47 'That process must be organised, from communication to political decision, including the good functioning of the daily operations of the commissioners' college, which can thus operate like a government. If they want to succeed over the long term, the President of the Commission must be the captain of that team'.

48 Le livre blanc sur la gouvernance européenne: COM/2001/0428 final [European governance – A white paper COM/2001/0428 final]. In that text, the concept of 'governance' means 'rules, processes and behaviour that affect the way in which powers are exercised at European level, particularly as regards openness, participation, accountability, effectiveness and coherence'.

49 See, https://eur-lex.europa.eu/LexUriServ/LexUriServ.do?uri=COM:2001:0428:FIN:EN:PDF

concerned and must have a more consistent functioning and global action. First, the Commission must refocus on its executive mission, that is, tasks of policy initiation, execution, supervision and international representation. That refocus has several aspects: identification of key moments which punctuate the annual and five-year political life (Annual Political Strategy, State of the Union Address, annual report on subsidiarity and proportionality), the strengthening of the partnership with the European Council, and the execution of policies and legislation. The 'refocusing' of the other institutions (Parliament and Council) should allow to elaborate a more targeted, essential, accessible and clearer legislation. Thus, from now on, the commitment of institutional actors in the decision-making process will not only be redefined, but also assessed and potentially sanctioned. The justification for this is that 'the advent of a European political conscience reinforces the need for accountability in the exercise of powers'. The consequence is the orientation of European policies towards a culture of systematic assessment.[50]

The white paper resulted in the launching of the vast action, 'Better lawmaking' in 2003, which led to several interinstitutional agreements, many communications on 'smart regulation', 'regulatory fitness', 'better regulation', the establishment of 'toolboxes' to ensure its quality, the creation of the 'REFIT' platform to assess the policies and texts based on quality audit, the recent establishment of another platform composed of experts to collect data on the possibilities of a simplification, reduction of the burden and modernisation of the existing legislation of the EU to enlighten the Commission.[51]

Many works have followed that large-scale evolution of European governance of the EU,[52] which has also been marked by the different political objectives of the different Presidents of the Commission. There results from those 20 years a remarkable renewal of the decision-making process which today implies many actors, from the initial conception of the policies to their implementation in the Member States and at a local level. That very strong inclusivity of the interested parties contributes to the moving away, in the Union, from a vertical top-down or bottom-up vision of power to horizontal implication of all the networks. It is obvious that the tools and procedures

50 See F. Péraldi-Leneuf, 'L'évaluation législative dans le système de l'Union européenne', in *La qualité de la loi-Expériences française et européenne*, ed. P. Albertini (Paris: Mare & Martin, 2016).

51 All those documents are accessible on the dedicated website: https://ec.europa.eu/info/law/law-making-process/planning-and-proposing-law/better-regulation-why-and-how_fr#donnez-votre-avis-partagez-votre-point-de-vue-et-vos-idées

52 See F. Péraldi-Leneuf, 'L'élaboration du droit de l'Union européenne au regard des exigences de légistique – Simplification, sophistication et légitimation', *Revue de l'Union européenne* (2018), pp. 34–42; F. Péraldi-Leneuf, 'La simplification du droit dans l'UE: le programme pour une réglementation affûtée et performante (REFIT)', *Revue LeGeS*, no. 2 (2017), pp. 255–263; F. Péraldi-Leneuf and S. de La Rosa, eds., *L'Union européenne et l'idéal de la meilleure législation* (Paris: Éditions Pedone, 2023); F. Péraldi-Leneuf, ed., *La légistique dans le système de l'Union européenne* (Brussels: Bruylant, 2012).

that have thus been created (consultations, expert assessments, impact assessments, application of the subsidiarity and proportionality principles, *ex ante* assessment as to fundamental rights, etc.) have contributed to a strengthening of the Commission thanks to a better legitimacy of its action in the eyes of the civil society and citizens. Participation and dialogue are part not only of the Treaty (Article 11 TEU), but practically speaking of the relations with all the institutions, even if there remains some way to go to perfect that sketch of participatory democracy.[53]

The sophistication of the mechanisms thus leads one to understand accountability in the EU system in a plural and original way, which goes beyond Enlightenment parliamentarianism and will probably also instil the national orders, if it is not already the case. Even though an evolution of the forms of accountability towards the criminal can be seen at the national level, at the level of the European Union, it rather corresponds to a shift towards *a priori* legitimisation of the action of the Executive, that is, before the voting of the texts. That is why the Commission is always looking for a double legitimacy: not only that of citizens and society, but also of the Member States. Is the Executive trying to by-pass the political power? Representative democracy? Parliamentarianism? Or is it really simply a spontaneous *mise en abime* of accountability, the limits of which are not yet clearly defined?

53 F. Péraldi-Leneuf, 'La démocratie participative européenne, cet obscur objet du désir', in *Annuaire du droit de l'Union européenne (2018)*, eds. C. Blumann and F. Picod (Paris: LGDJ, 2020).

Section 4

A common culture? National traditions, European challenges

Questionnaire for discussion

Julien Padovani and Emilien Quinart

1. Is there a general feeling of political responsibility in the operation of the European Union?
   - Do you have the impression that there is a European parliamentarianism?
   - What is the nature of that responsibility: is it legal, democratic, political, technical, personal?
   - Who are the actors of that responsibility? On whose behalf and to whom is it exercised? Is it citizens, the Parliament, the Council of Ministers, the European Council, the national Executives, the national Parliaments, the Court, the political parties or the European or national political groups?
   - What are the concrete consequences of that responsibility? Does it modify the decision-making process? Does it reinforce its transparency?
2. What are the current forms of political responsibility in the operation of the European Union?
   - At what moment is the responsibility of the Commission the most intensely and efficiently exercised (depending on points of view)? Is it at the stage of the swearing into office? At the time motions of censure are tabled? At the moment of the informative control? When the budget is discharged?
   - Has the reinforcement of the legislative powers of the Parliament entailed by the Lisbon Treaty contributed to revaluing its powers of control?
   - How is democratic responsibility concretely exercised within the framework of intergovernmental decision-making procedures (CFSP, foreign affairs, justice and internal affairs, management of the financial crisis, etc.)? Are there formal mechanisms or informal attempts of control, by the European Parliament, of the Council of Ministers of the EU or of the European Council in those domains?
   - What is the role of national parliaments and of COSAC in the supervision of European decision-making processes? Is it effective? Does it entail original forms of responsibility?

DOI: 10.4324/9781003281559-18

3. What is the future of democratic responsibility in the operation of the European Union?

    - What are the shortcomings of the current system?
    - What do you think of the citizens' proposals of the Conference on the Future of Europe concerning the attribution of political decisions and responsibility?

        - Increased federalisation – election of the President of the European Council, the European Commission or a European Constituent Assembly by direct universal suffrage?
        - Creation of transnational electoral lists for the election of the Parliament?
        - Reinforcement of the citizens' participation and direct democracy (decisional or revocation referenda)?
        - Improvement of representativeness in the European Parliament, or creation of a chamber of the civil society?

10 Parliamentarianism and accountability of the executive power on a European scale

The experience of the European Parliament

Juan F. López Aguilar

Parliamentarianism: democracy and accountability

Parliamentary government is a variation of representative democracy, based on the institutional relationship of trust between the parliament and the cabinet (government, Council of Ministers). This means that, in a parliamentary democracy, the government is only possible through the *confidence* and political support of the parliament.

In other words, 'parliament' does not only mean an *elected assembly.* It also means that, wherever there is a parliament worthy of its name, the 'government' (the executive branch) is not directly put to a popular vote: indeed, it is the parliament that is put to a vote, i.e., it is the directly elected body. It is therefore the parliament's composition, seat by seat, which is periodically (every four or five years, depending on the specific, relevant constitutional dispensation of each parliamentary democracy) subject to citizen's universal suffrage. Now, once – and only once – the parliament has been properly constituted, it is the majority within it which is the actual decisive body empowered to invest the cabinet with parliamentary confidence. And this majority within parliament is to perform this function by establishing a so-called trust bond or trust relationship (*relación de confianza, treue, confiance, fiducia/ rapporto fiduciario*) with the parliamentary government (cabinet, in comparative standards).

The link between this 'trust bond' and the majority in parliament crucially lies in the adoption of the so-called vote of investiture (*investiture, investiture, investidura*) of the individual person/leading figure who is to head all governmental action and its administration, beginning with the very appointment of the members of the Council of Ministers along with the allocation of individual portfolios (*ministries, departments, dicasteri*): that person is the 'premier' or 'prime minister' (*presidente del consejo, presidente del gobierno*). He or she impersonates the leader of the cabinet's composition, political guidance and action. He or she is accountable for its delivery, and politically responsible for the whole executive branch.

DOI: 10.4324/9781003281559-19

Insofar as the 'trust bond' lives on, the government stays in office, fully fledged to lead and act, take legislative initiative and stand before parliament's scrutiny and control. As soon as the 'trust' fails or breaks, the whole cabinet falls, and the government is dismissed. The process of 'confidence building' through a whole new 'investiture vote' has to start again from scratch: the process of formation of the government starts all over again, depending on the applicable conventions, parliamentary rules or constitutional provisions in every particular case of parliamentary practice. On the grounds of *confidence*, i.e., trust bond, the cabinet is entitled to lead the executive branch and the administration. As long as confidence/trust remains, the cabinet carries out its constitutional powers and competences. As soon as this trust bond is broken, i.e., parliamentary confidence fails to sustain the government, the cabinet falls, so an overall new process of trust building is to be set in motion for a new cabinet to be put in place, via a renewed vote of confidence or via a new investiture vote.

A particular and most significant form of parliamentary democracy (PD) is the so-called prime minister (PM) parliamentary democracy (*kanzlerprinzip, parlamentarismo di primo ministro, parlamentarismo presidencialista*). Constitutional theory has built this category on the primacy of the Premier (PM) leadership both in the setting up of the confidence relationship (*relación fiduciaria*) and its dissolution, as well as in the whole process of forming and reshuffling the cabinet, all along the governmental action and its relevant decision-making. That is why constitutional and political theory have developed the so-called presidential type or presidential parliamentarianism doctrine. It means, in practice, that confidence is vested in the candidate to leadership of government action, namely the would-be prime minister. Once invested with the leading role as Head of Government, the PM impersonates the institutional link known as confidence and political trust.

Political accountability and political responsibility are hence component elements of PD. By 'political accountability' we are to understand the Executive's obligation to face account for its administration and management of public affairs and budgetary expenses and allowances. It comprises a correlated duty to provide parliament and MPs with all explanations and information about its governmental action and delivery which are deemed to be necessary or adequate to substantiate the continuity of the confidence/trust link between the elected representatives and members of the cabinet, including the PM.

By 'political responsibility' we are to understand the determinant nature of the confidence link between the parliament and cabinet, meaning in practise that the government ceases to fulfil its duties as soon as trust is called off or ceases to exist, be it through clear signals that the link has been cut, or through the activation of any of the institutional tools set forth by constitutional law and parliamentary rules (an explicit 'vote of no confidence' or 'censorship', *misstrauensvotum, mozione di sfiducia, moción de censura*).

In order to fill the range of 'political accountability' and 'political responsibility', constitutional law and parliamentary rules provide a variety of tools to verify the regular exercise of the cabinet's competences and relevant accomplishment of its public agenda. It is widely known as 'parliamentary control' and scrutiny of the cabinet. Its bottom-line is not only to overview the concrete results and achievements of government action, but also to check its quality in terms of efficiency, accuracy and political opportunity (its degree of correspondence to public opinion indicators of appropriateness depending on its set of priorities).

'Parliamentary control' encompasses, therefore, a wide set of instruments meant to open up access to transparent, regular and thorough information as to individual actions of the government and administration. It also comprehends a toolbox to inspect, overview and require political responsibility from the cabinet and the prime minister.

Insofar as the parliament is an elected assembly, representing (that is what *representation* is all about) a pluralistic social and political body, it is to be understood that the building up of the confidence and trust link is not supposed to be based on the whole of the chamber, but on its internal segment which enjoys an actual capacity to support the process of forming a government and governmental action, i.e., the majority within it. By the same token, it is to be understood that accountability and responsibility are to be regularly, as well as mainly, exercised from those Members of Parliament (MPs, parliamentary seats) who have not endorsed the motion of that confidence link, i.e., the minority/ies which lie(s) in the democratic function and role of the 'parliamentary opposition'.

That is why a parliamentary government is so narrowly linked with the constitutional and parliamentary protection of 'the opposition' (loyal opposition, HM's opposition, *leal oposición, opposizione parlamentare*, shadow cabinet). The wide array of institutional tools meant to protect the function of opposition (which belongs to the minorities opposing the government's policies and leading figures, at times under the shape of a so-called shadow cabinet, with its own shadow PM and shadow ministers responding to every governmental move with an opposite alternative) constitute altogether an expression of the maturity of a parliamentary government.

But, beyond that, it may be also a parameter of recognition and validity of its democratic credentials. In comparative politics, they include oversight powers (*poteri d'ispezione*, powers of scrutiny, *pouvoir d'enquête*), scrutiny and control, questions and interpellations (both written and oral), major political debates ('State of the Nation' kind), major parliamentary debates with a certain degree of protocol to the so-called Leader of the Opposition (the leading character of the largest minority in the House), and, as the case may be, access to judicial remedies (standing for constitutional review of legislative acts) along with various techniques with a sophisticated level of reassurance and political leverage.

The viability and feasibility of the political alternative (namely, the feasibility of legal pathways to accede to government, from the minority of today to the majority of tomorrow) thus emerges as a factor of *political legitimacy*:

recognition of 'the other' (and his or her right to an alternative) is the true validating motto of parliamentary government and democracy itself.

This principle implies that democracy is not, as is often said, 'the rule of the majority' (nor the 'rule by majority'): it is rather to be understood as the

> protection of minorities and the individual, inalienable fundamental liberties underlying every right to dissent, oppose and face majorities and majority-based decisions, as well as majority-based governments, coming up with an alternative which is meant to become the Government by, eventually, winning electoral support from a new social and political majority.

In other words, democracy does not mean *only* (neither consists only of) 'rule with support of majorities'. Democracy requires the majority rule, certainly: but the majority rule is not sufficient. Democracy requires much more beyond that: democracy requires constitutional rule of law (representative democracy based on free and fair elections), separation of powers, fundamental rights and liberties protected by an independent judiciary, equality before the law, no discrimination (no matter its grounds), political pluralism, protection of minorities and protection of the function of dissent and political opposition.

In practice, it actually means that parliamentary democracy is a specific form of representative democracy in which the political process is started in the electoral momentum, but once the representative assembly has been actually elected on the grounds of social, ideological and political pluralism, that pluralism lives on within the elective chamber. And it is precisely within the chamber where the first political alignment takes place, be it along majority or minority lines: voters have given their seats to those members (MPs) who are ready to align or coalesce into a majority willing to support the formation of the cabinet (single-party based, multiparty-coalition based, minority-government-based, etc.), as they have also placed in theirs a number of MPs who will not only be part of that majority but will oppose it thereafter, by taking the parliamentary opposition role.

Now, by the same token, the need to secure some level of legal protection of the basic right of every individual MP to freely express his/her views, opinions, votes, and to freely dissent and oppose the government's acts or policies of whatever kind without being charged, prosecuted or punished for it, has gradually evolved, over time, into the doctrine and institutionalisation of 'parliamentary prerogatives and immunities'. All parliamentary democracies provide for the MPs' 'inviolability' (prohibition of prosecution for opinions or speeches made while carrying out his/her representative duties), as well as the MPs' 'immunity' (forbidding any arrest, detention, criminal prosecution or charges brought against the parliamentarian or representative as long as he or she holds office, with the only exception of *ex flagrante delicto*) and the MPs' 'indemnity' (the right to perceive a salary or economic compensation for the expenses of election to parliamentary office).

Parliamentary government: factors, pillars, institutions

Electoral systems play a significant role in explaining the actual shape and functioning of every specific parliament. Accordingly, on the one hand, majority electoral systems often result in single-party majority governments and a clear-cut, well-defined main opposition party. The usual consequence of this major constitutional and parliamentary choice is a strong PM leadership on the majority side, answered by a well-defined opposition leadership role. Its correlation is a majority government facing a minority opposition with clear and express aspiration to become the majority and thus the new government in the next upcoming elections (it follows without saying that its 'opposition leader' makes a pledge to lead their party to electoral victory and hence become the next PM).

Plurality electoral systems, and especially proportional electoral systems, are, on the contrary, much more likely to produce a variety of multiparty parliaments and, hence, multiparty governments. As a consequence, multiparty majorities or coalition majorities will often support the process of forming a government through the so-called vote of confidence or investiture by working on a common, shared platform or (kind of) legislature contract. The way to formalise that political agreement results in a common vote upon the shoulders (and the program and/or manifesto) of the would-be prime minister *(presidente del consejo, primo ministro, kanzler)*. In such a scenario, on the other side of the spectrum, several parliamentary minorities will run against the government's action by facing it and standing up for their opposition role. At times, they might also compete among themselves for the opposition leadership (and its potential transformation into a future PM role), both in terms of gaining support in public opinion polls, and winning, in due time and process, the next electoral competition (hence, becoming the new majority to sustain a new government).

Once the elections have been completed, and a newly elected parliament is already in place, a very defining principle must be understood: just as a confidence or investiture vote is the very initial 'start-up moment' of cabinet formation and government action in a parliamentary government, the dissolution of the trust bond and/or the vote of no confidence becomes the crucial moment for that cabinet to step down (by loss of confidence or resignation): thus, after the loss of confidence, the government's action is to cease and come to a halt.

In the comparative pattern of the so-called rationalised parliamentarianism, all instruments which are meant to define the setting up of the confidence link, the sustainability of the trust relationship and, as the case may be, its breakup, are expressly institutionalised and dealt with by constitutional law and parliamentary rules. That is the way the dissolution of the confidence link is carried out by a specific modality of vote, known as 'motion of no confidence' or 'censure' (*sfiducia, misstrauensvotum, moción de censura*). In addition to this institutionalisation of the censure vote, there is also the possibility of refusing to grant the cabinet (i.e., the PM) a renewal of the confidence on specific votes which are singled out as deemed of particular importance: in those specific cases, should parliament deny or refuse to endorse the agenda, the reshuffling or the shifting of the political direction proposed, suggested or advanced by the PM in the convening of such 'confidence vote', the result would be tantamount to a censorship vote, namely the resignation of the cabinet and the fall of the current government, giving rise to a new process to form a new government with an equally renewed leadership or direction. It is also to be noted that, under a comparative law approach, a censure vote is regularly more demanding – both in procedure and substance – than a confidence vote, especially when it comes to the formalities, requirements, thresholds to meet for the right to activate the motion or implications thereafter. In practice, censure usually requires an absolute or qualified majority of the total amount of seats within parliament, whereas a confidence vote usually requires just a simple majority to sustain the continuation of the cabinet or, in case of failure to secure that simple majority, its compulsory resignation. Depending on the specific modality of the so-called constructive censure vote (*konstruktivemisstrauensvotum, mozione di censura costruttiva, moción de censura constructiva*), the adoption of the censure vote produces two simultaneous results: on the one hand, it equates both the compulsory dismissal of the incumbent PM and cabinet (resignation of the whole government) and simultaneous investiture ('constitutional nomination') of the so-called alternative PM, whose mandate to lead the cabinet is intertwined with the parliamentary removal of the outgoing PM. On the other hand, it merges the censure and dismissal of the outgoing prime minister with the affirmative support for the alternative PM, for the sake of the 'stability' of the legislature and mandate, thus allowing for the institutional shift of the leading character (and his or her supporting majority) without needing to resort to the call of a (snap) new election.

A most particular expression of this highly developed level of institutionalisation of PD is the discretionary power vested in the prime minister to 'dissolve' the parliament (parliament dissolution, *disolución parlamentaria, dissoluzione del parlamento, parlementsauflössung*), thereby calling for new elections for the citizens to decide as to the immediate future of the political process in an open competition for their electoral support.

So far, we have already summarised the main features and the itinerary of parliamentary government within the frame and experience of constitutionalism. Now it is time to link this historical process with the gradual emergence of a European type or pattern of parliamentarianism, embodied in the unique nature of the European Parliament, within the likewise unique nature of *European contemporary constitutionalism* and its own (supranational, democratic) decision-making process.

The European Parliament experience: political accountability in European constitutionalism

The European Parliament (EP) may be described as a unique institution. To begin with, it is the only democratically elected institution in the overall EU architecture. The only one in the European polity – 'European Government', a work in progress – to be directly legitimised by the universal suffrage of the European citizens. After *Brexit*, it currently consists of 705 elected members (MEPs), aligned in *political groups* (minimum of 25 MEPs, elected in at least seven Member States, MS), and a bench of non-attached, in accordance with their respective, distinctive political and ideological grounds.

The EP happens to be unique also in its nature and its representation. It is the only directly and democratically elected body of supranational scale in the world (450 million European citizens after Brexit), multilingual (24 official languages provided in translation and interpretation, even after Brexit) and multinational in its composition (after *Brexit*, 27 Member States' citizenships are represented), politically pluralistic in its internal structure (seven political groups, expressing both ideological and political cleavages across European lines, and a large number of non-attached MEPs), as well as a factory of supranational integration of diversity in its performance. Needless to remind: 'united in diversity' is the EU motto.

Although, historically speaking, that was not always the case, ever since the EC adopted its decision to give way to a democratically elected parliament (Council decision adopted in 1976, first implementation by means of a direct vote in the European elections of 1979), the once deliberative second-degree representative assembly was replaced by a truly elected parliament, which is meant to grow and act as a true parliament in every possible way.

The EP is now a *parliament* vested with legislative powers and budgetary authority in the EU decision-making process. Once free, fair and periodic elections take place (legislatures and terms of five years), the electoral result (the composition of parliament) determines the *rapport de forces* (i.e., the deciding majority facing opposing minorities) that will eventually support the investiture vote of the candidate to the office of President of the EU Commission and the overall College of Commissioners. By the same token, the EP also holds the power of censorship vote on the College of Commissioners, which, in case it is adopted, leads to the resignation of the College of Commissioners. The EP also exercises its parliamentary control upon the Commission's administration and its ongoing delivery, by means of a wide range of tools and competences, be it plenary or in the relevant committees of which the House consists (structured dialogues, hearings, oral questions in plenary and written questions).

Over the years, through a series of mandates in a row, the EP has institutionalised both its internal structure and its organisation, so it is governed, just like any other parliament, by its Presidency of the EP (elected every half term, for a two-and-a-half year term) and its Bureau (14 EP vice-presidencies), along with the deciding role of the Conference of Presidents of the political groups as a ruling body on the order of the day, in accordance with a comprehensive set of written rules of procedure.

The same principle applies as to the institutionalisation of its decision-making procedures (budgetary, legislative, nominations and appointments), notably on law-making files. Accordingly, it has increasingly weighted its control practises and parliamentary uses, especially as to the format of its political debates (i.e., the annual Convention on the State of the Union Debate, and the regular exchange of views held in plenary sessions with Heads of State or Government of the EU Member States). All these component elements are by now well established in the *interna corporis* according to EP rules of procedure ('standing rules', *regolamenti parlamentari, parliamentary statute, règlement parlementaire, reglamentos parlamentarios*).

As the current Treaty of Lisbon entered into force along with the Charter of Fundamental Rights of the European Citizens (1 December 2009), most parliamentary features of the unique EU constitutional structure have been subject to a process of institutionalisation and formalisation, the actual result of which allows a comparative analysis of the EP with the national parliaments of the varied Member States and the parliamentary *ideal type* itself.

And yet, there are many other additional features which may distinguish the EP as a unique form of parliament. Among them, the flexibility and openness of its internal procedures (less structured than national parliaments), the enhanced capacities of individual MPs (speaking times, individual voting lines, dissent within political groups, cross-interrogation techniques as the so-called blue cards for short lively cross debates among MPs).

Besides, the EP is particularly transparent through access to documents (Articles 40 and 41 of the Charter) and web streaming in all formats of its internal work and sessions. But there is a communication challenge that must be highlighted: how to reach to the European public, how to regularly communicate the work and delivery of any given mandate of the EP? The communication issue is a major challenge, not related to technologies (media box, access of media and journalists are largely provided) but to the insufficient level of conformation of a European public sphere, meaning 'European public space' consisting of European political cleavages expressed through European political parties competing for the vote of the European citizens on the arena of a European public opinion and European public debate truly worth its name.

However, the major challenge facing the EP, in its path to mature as a fully fledged example of parliamentary politics, is likely to be related to the insufficient density of what might be called the 'European demos'. A sense of *European belonging* is yet to be rooted and developed insofar as the potential of parliamentary politics is concerned. Certainly, a net of European media nurturing European-wide cleavages, in terms of public attitudes eventually to be converted into electoral behaviour, on a significant number of issues, would do a part of the trick.

Much has also been argued about the need to strengthen the European political arena with true European parties and their European foundations. The latest developments in this field have seen the initiative to launch European parties running for the office of the Presidency of the European Commission, under the format of a so-called *spitzenkandidat* (i.e., an individual character entrusted with a leading role in each particular European party campaign to win the European elections every five years).

The *spitzenkandidat* principle is meant to stimulate both the 'politicisation' of the electoral campaign for the EP (including massive rallies, media interviews, electoral debates on cross-party topics) and to impersonate the electoral manifesto behind his or her platform.

This principle is also meant to stir political participation and electoral turnout across the EU Member States, by means of making it visible that there is, first, ground for political confrontation and hence true competition, as well as a substantial say for the voters (all of the European citizens in all of the Member States) to decide. That say may have an impact on the Commission leadership, and thus on its whole agenda, its Commission working programme, its priorities, its discourse and narrative (leaning on conservative, progressive, liberal, or green values or whatever shades there might be in the political spectrum).

More to it: that 'politicisation' should also lead to the 'parliamentarisation' of European politics in all. Insofar as the *spitzenkandidat* principle is the basic ground on which the European Council is to assess the 'outcome of the European election for the European Parliament' (Article 17 TEU), the leadership of the Commission would be built on the assumption that the person embodies the likely confidence of the EP majority better than anyone else.

By producing this effect, the principle of political trust would entail a reinforcement of the political *legitimacy* of the College of Commissioners and its commitment to delivery over the five-year term. As a result, political accountability and political responsibility would also be improved, promoting a continued link between the initial stage of the Commission (the investiture vote with the confidence of the majority of the EP) and the continuous exercise of the powers to scrutinise and control the conduct of public policies, current affairs and EU administration by the Commission in office.

The intended political cycle of 'parliamentarisation' of the European politics could be further promoted by equating the term of office of incumbent EP and EU Commission with the scope of the so-called Multiannual Financial Framework (MFF), overcoming the current state of affairs, in which the negotiation of a seven-year term MFF inevitably overlaps with two different and successive terms of both the EP and EU Commission.

By bringing about that institutional change, European citizens would be given an additional reason to believe that in every EP election they actually do have a choice to make a decisive difference as to the budgetary magnitudes (the length and extent of resources to be mobilised in that five-year term) as well as to the budget priorities (which policies are to come first, which are the ones to be secured). And that is certainly a debate worth having, given its political nature and its ideological background. The underlying assumption is that an MFF with a certain orientation and degree of commitment to certain specific values and priorities is a choice of *political* nature that can and must be decided in a ballot, by universal suffrage of the European citizens in all the Member States.

As to its internal structure, the EP is organised according to the comparative standards of parliamentarianism. Its internal procedures, though, show some peculiarities which are suitable to the unique nature of the European integration process and experience. Its decision-making process is usually put into a comparative perspective under the federal pattern: in that regard, the EP would fit the role of a lower house (citizen's representation, accounting for the political pluralism across the European social fabric, consisting of the sum of its Member States), whereas the Council (meeting of members of national governments, one per Member State) would fit the role of an upper house (States representation). The European Council could be tantamount to a collegial Head of State (political leadership, guidance and impulse); the European Court of Justice (ECJ) would be a supreme court (mixture of constitutional and cassation competences corresponding to the various genetic prints of the European judicial architecture), in charge of the judicial guarantee of 'respect for the law' by establishing its binding interpretation. The European Commission (consisting of 27 members, one per Member State) would serve as a kind of permanent executive and administrative branch, working in a sort of dialogue with the European Council (meeting of Heads of State and Heads of Government), which is the leading institution to conduct the political process.

Under this comparative approach, all EP powers may be comprehended by usual *parliamentary* standards: legislative procedures, budgetary role, powers of appointment and dismissal of relevant public officials, and, most importantly, the power of scrutiny and control of the European institution in which the executive and administration powers are vested: the European Commission.

The institutional frame in which parliamentary scrutiny and control of the Commission takes place stems from the Treaty of Lisbon (TEU, TFEU, along with the EU Charter of Fundamental Rights, all of them in force since December 2009) and is based on the so-called Interinstitutional Agreement. The starting point for its dynamics is the regular election of the EP – every five years – and the subsequent constitution of the newly elected Parliament followed by the inauguration of the mandate and legislature (Article 217 TFEU).

The 'vote of investiture' of the nominee for the Presidency of the Commission is the initiating link of the chain of the political process (according to the principle of 'loyal cooperation' between EU institutions, Article 4 TEU). The confidence vested in the President-elect of the European Commission launches the consultations with the Member State national governments to supply the relevant candidates which are to be trusted with individual portfolios in the formation of the College. That process has to meet the requirements set forth by the president-elect in his or her investiture speech and debate before the EP: qualifications, ethical standards, gender balance, etc.

Once the College has been shaped, each and every one of the candidates for portfolios as commissioner nominees will have to pass an individual, thorough examination by the relevant EP committees before which they shall be accountable depending on their competences. That examination – first parliamentary hearing – will be based on two main axes: capacity and personal record and personal ability to fulfil the particular duties related to his or her portfolio. This particular procedure is far from irrelevant or protocolary: throughout the last series of processes of the formation of a new Commission, episodes of disapproval of certain candidates by the examining committees have proved to be decisive: a negative outcome of the committee vote after the hearing means the candidate – i.e., commissioner-nominee – has been rejected as considered unfit to fulfil his or her job. It means, in practise, that the national government of the particular Member State that originally made the choice shall be, much to its dismay, compelled to come up with a new proposal, a new candidate as commissioner-nominee, who will have to live through the whole examining procedure all the way again, from the outset to a potential final positive outcome (approval by the Committee).

It is only when the procedure of investiture of the whole College – i.e., commissioner-nominee after commissioner-nominee – has been successfully completed that the Commission is entitled to come before the plenary of the EP (Strasbourg session) to confirm the confidence vote by the majority of the House.

Parliamentary scrutiny takes place thereafter onwards, through the variety of tools which are widely known by parliamentary practices. Debates on Commission statements – including the regular annual 'Debate on the State of the Union', first plenary meeting in September after the summer break of August –, parliamentary questions (questions with oral answers, followed by a debate, round of speaking times and orators), debates on reports of a specific political nature or content (INI report on institutional matters), exchange of points of view with the Commission on the ground of policy matters (policy papers, agencies' annual reports on matters of parliamentary concern as it is the case of FRA, Europol, Eurojust or Frontex), or debates following the presentation on a specific subject by a European authority (the President of the ECB) or European official ('European Ombudsman') widen the scope of EP activities under the umbrella of scrutiny powers.

A very specific tool for the EP to play its role as an institution empowered to exert scrutiny and control over the EU Commission and EU administration is the inquiry committees (*unterschuchungsausschuss, commissione d'inchiesta, commission d'enquête, comisión de investigación*). It refers to a very special kind of single-issue committees which are meant to study, analyse or inspect a certain problem and to eventually produce a document of conclusions which will pave the way to improve the quality and efficiency of the European law. As to specialised procedures, it is worth mentioning that the budgetary procedure is rich in specific features. And yet, its first picture is to be completed with those procedures which are meant to deal with control of expenditure by the EU Commission, administration, agencies, as well as those which regulate the so-called discharge procedures and their subsequent votes by the EP plenary. In addition, the EP has developed a very unique range of techniques to exert some degree of scrutiny on implementing acts (Article 291 TFEU) adopted by the Commission according to mandates and standards that have been set in a specific piece of European legislation (i.e., legislative acts), as well as, to a lesser extent, implementing decisions (Article 292 TFEU) which, on the contrary, lack normative character. This whole field of activity has given rise to the so-called comitology, meaning the set of legal rules and practices which deal with specialized committees or administrative bodies through which the European Commission and the Member State administrations relate to complete the work of the European legislation.

European parliamentarianism from a constitutional perspective

One of the most relevant dimensions of the EP is related to the involvement of that institution in the overall operation of paving the way to constitutional debates ('interinstitutional conferences') on a European scale, and eventually to produce constitutional changes (Article 48 TEU).

The political dimension and constitutional scope of the EP – and the whole of the EU – is well expressed in the 'area of liberties, justice and security' established in Title V of the TFEU (Articles 67 to 89). The EP – especially its LIBE Committee – carries out a significant role as true law-making body in areas that used to belong to the exclusive domain of the sovereignty of MS, such as fundamental rights (GDPR, transparency), criminal law (terrorism, human trafficking, drugs, money laundering, corruption, misappropriation, fraud), procedural guarantees and legal aid and assistance (procedural rights package), judicial cooperation in criminal matters (European arrest warrant, European evidence warrant, e-evidence, etc.), as well as border management (Schengen package), migration (migration package), asylum management (asylum package) and security-related files (terrorist content online, interoperability package).

The same constitutional approach applies to the values and principles enshrined in Article 2 TEU (once called 'Copenhagen criteria': rule of law, representative democracy, fundamental rights, equality under the law, separation of powers, independence of the judiciary, pluralism, protection of minorities). Every case of 'serious risk' of 'breach' may expose any given Member State to the so-called Article 7 TEU procedure, which may lead to heavy sanctions and suspension of its voting rights in the Council. The cumbersome procedure has led the EP to adopt an 'EU Rule of Law, Fundamental Rights and Democracy Framework', on objective, regular and thorough examination upon all the Member States (upon the sample of EU justice scoreboard), as well as to a proposal to link access to EU budget and funds to full compliance with the rule of law standards.

This wide range of constitutional issues has been regularly dealt with by the EP through the most recent mandates, once the LT and the *Charter* eventually came into force (1 December 2009). Admittedly, for the past ten years the EP has seen its powers widened to an extent that was hardly foreseen at the outset of the integration process. In fact, it was the EP (during its 2009/2014 term) which was the first EU institution to take the initiative and the lead to launch the so-called Article 7 TEU procedure, upon the specific concerns raised by the 'illiberal democracies' (notably, Hungary and Poland under conservative governments) on matters of *rule of law, democracy and fundamental rights.* The abrupt sequency of constitutional and legislative measures imposed by the ruling majorities over a short period of time (in the course of a tight lapse, major impact was caused) gave rise to a series of EP plenary resolutions leading to the activation of the procedure established in Article 7 TEU to ascertain a 'clear risk' (by a two-thirds majority in the EP) of a systemic 'serious breach' of those principles enshrined in Article 2 TEU.

Though cumbersome in its internal structure and set of procedural requirements, the aforementioned procedure was actually triggered. Initiated under the EP impulse and support, the consequent range of infringement procedures launched by the Commission has been accompanied by actions brought to the ECJ, followed by relevant rulings, the compliance with which by the concerned Member State government is regrettably still pending on a number of issues.

Taking note of the background to these legitimate concerns, the EP has adopted two important measures to follow up: on the one hand, it has requested the EU Commission to come forward with a comprehensive 'EU Rule of Law, Fundamental Rights and Democracy Framework', meant to give account of the state of the implementation of those values and principles in all the Member States via a regular, periodic, objective and fact-based examination: this methodology builds on the precedent of the 'EU justice score board', which provides a thorough examination of the independence, efficiency and guarantees of all the judicial systems of all the EU Member States on a regular basis. On the other hand, the EP has endorsed the principle of linking access to EU budgeting and EU funds with compliance with the EU rule of law, democracy and fundamental rights standards enshrined in Article 2 TEU.

The essential assumption here is to overcome the challenge of the 'Copenhagen dilemma': the expression describes the puzzle posed by the fact that candidates for membership have to fulfil a whole path of constitutional and institutional reforms to qualify for those standards (through a lengthy process which includes up to 36 protocols of accession that have to be positively and unanimously assessed by the EU Member States), whereas, contradictory as it may seem, there is a lack of efficient tools to check the willingness to comply with those same standards once the candidate to accession has made its way into the club. That is precisely the point addressed in both the Hungarian and Polish backsliding into authoritarian types of regressive nationalism (increasingly Europhobic, both in record and behaviour), setting forth the conditions for a whole doctrine of 'constitutional breakdown'. . . within and from within the EU.

The dynamics of the EP have also endured, proving its resilience, the major political impact of the simultaneous entry into force of both the LT and the *Charter* and the outbreak of a series of episodes of crisis that started with the Great Recession (2009–2016), the 'refugee crisis', the eruption of populist forces leaning on Europhobic trends, the rise of so-called illiberal democracies among the Member State governments (notably Hungary's and Poland's),

Brexit (first time ever that a long experienced MS chose to depart from the EU, leaving the European process) . . . and, last but not least, the challenging Covid-19 pandemic and the EU deep crisis, thereafter, causing a major distress both to the European integration and to individual Member States.

All of these unprecedented situations have put the EP to a new stress test; more than that, it has put the whole of the EU to an existential test. But, yet, it has not stopped the EP in its persevering pathway to consolidate parliamentary behavioural patterns and standardised rules.

At the outset of the 7th EP, the president-elect of the European Commission, Ursula von der Leyen, expressed the VDL Commission's commitment to launch a comprehensive 'Conference on the Future of Europe'. As a call for the participation of European civil society, NGOs, academia, scholars, professions, entrepreneurs and the business sector, in order to have them all involved in an ambitious endeavour to rethink the EU architecture and its position in globalisation, it goes without saying that its outcome should pave the way for institutional reforms, that is to say, the reshaping of the European Parliament, by means of incorporating all of those aforementioned items (i.e., *Spitzenkandidat*, question time, fully fledged parliamentary legislative initiative, EP term matching with the MFF time frame, etc.) that could make it a more perfect European parliamentary experience encompassed within the frame of a 'more perfect EU'.

Concluding remark on the responsibility of the Executive on a European scale: national traditions and European legal culture of rule of law

Conventional wisdom suggests that social peace is only achieved if, at the same time as citizens are deprived of the possibility of using violence to defend their rights and interests, they are guaranteed effective protection through an independent and impartial judiciary. It is not surprising, therefore, that in a constitutional democracy – among the objectives of which is the achievement of this social peace – it is essential to shape public authorities so that they fit for this jurisdictional function. The right to access to justice and to an effective judicial protection hence plays a central role in the overall European fundamental rights system, as it is decisive for the configuration of the European rule of law. The very design of fundamental rights presupposes the existence of independent and impartial judges and courts that provide for the public service of justice. The quality of the rule of law and democracy itself depends, to a large extent, on how well or poorly it actually operates.

That is why a final remark comes along. When it comes to the debate on the 'decline (or backsliding) of rights and democracy in the EU', the EP – both in plenary and in committees, in particular in the EP committee responsible for freedoms, justice and home affairs (LIBE), which I am honoured to chair – has extensively addressed the challenge posed by the alarming signs of deterioration and regression of democracy and judicial independence in the EU during the 2009–2014 and 2014–2019 EP legislatures. This coincided with the EU's immersion in its worst crisis ever, the one that began in 2008, which we have come to call the Great Recession of the EU. It is true that this *backsliding* has been noticed not only in Hungary (under the Fydesz Government), and more recently in Poland (under the Pis Government), but in other latitudes and longitudes of Europe. But while it can be said that the setbacks in the EU have for some time now been particularly severe in what some commentators – I, among others – have graphically called the '*Putinisation*' of Hungary, it can also be said that, since the 'chronification' of the European crisis, over the course of a relatively short period of time, there has been a rapid and intense transition to what might well be called the '*Orbanisation*' of Poland (after the name of Viktor Orbán, the prime minister of Hungary since 2010 with an overwhelming two-thirds majority in the Hungarian Parliament). And from there to the 'Hungarianisation' of the political dynamics of some other Member States affected, in one way or the other, by a tendency to curtail information and media pluralism and public freedoms. It is, therefore, a more extensive and very worrying syndrome that, to a greater or lesser extent, is showing itself in a growing number of EU Member States, and not only – I repeat – in the last Member States to have joined us ('Great Enlargement' of 2004, with ten countries on board; 2007, Romania and Bulgaria; 2013, Croatia).

11 The scent of wild animals

Sophie in 't Veld

Introduction

In the Summer of 2021, I wrote a book called *The Scent of Wild Animals*, several months before the second Russian invasion of Ukraine began, and therefore, also several months before the EU put (more) sanctions on Russia, facilitated arms shipments to Ukraine, faced down an energy crisis and accelerated on its path to a European Energy Union. These steps constitute major strides in European integration, after equally big strides had been made during the pandemic.

There is a tendency to take the number of European competencies as an indication of the EU's health. I too believe that more EU competencies in a number of areas are welcome, long overdue even. At the same time, I believe that more competencies require a stronger European democracy. In other words, more European power should mean more accountability. Democratic accountability, that is. I believe that democratic accountability at the EU level has been too weak to begin with. Furthermore, I believe it is backsliding. When European powers increase, while democratic oversight weakens, then that is an altogether more disturbing bill of health for the EU. As you may realise by now, I am rather gloomy about the state of the EU. Fear not, there are also plenty recommendations in my book that will take Europe on a more democratic path.

This introduction is followed by a quartet of chapters from the book that I think have some resonance with recent events. To begin with, the worrying assaults on democracy in the United States and Brazil. Authoritarian former leaders instigated assaults on democratic institutions in these two very large, democratic states. In the US, the Congress was stormed, and in Brazil, all three federal branches of government were invaded. In Europe, we did not see this kind of open violence against our European democratic institutions. Nonetheless, I believe that our common European Democracy is under attack in similar fashion. Not by an angry mob, but in more stealthy ways through erosion. This erosion emanates from the national governments, both individually and collectively in the European Council. It is deliberate, and it has picked up speed in recent years. As I alluded to a few sentences back, this is about power.

DOI: 10.4324/9781003281559-20

The European Council is eating away at the already weak separation of powers that exists at the EU level. I go into this problem in the featured section on the '*trias politica*'. Member States actively undermine the enforcement of EU rules and laws in two major ways. First, by ignoring the European Court of Justice. Second, by co-opting the European Commission and rendering its independence moot. Political ties between parties in national government and Members of the European Parliament do the rest. The Council is not just getting more powerful, it is actively grabbing power. In the process, it is doing real damage to the democratic nature of our Union.

European Democracy is not something people identify as such. When people do not care for a democracy, then there will not be the aforementioned angry mob rising up to smash it at the orders of a vaunted strongman. Conversely, and more importantly: when people do not care for our common European Democracy, they will also not come to its defence. National government leaders are relying on this. For years, decades even, they have told their constituents that the EU is an apolitical technocratic arena. One that people should not care for. In my book, I call this the 'Fiction of the technocratic eunuch'. The chapter on this subject I have included as well.

Probably thanks to the technocratic fiction, we do not have open violence in the halls of the European Parliament. The mob wouldn't know where to go in the first place; Brussels or Strasbourg? A little joke, but with a serious undertone. The European Parliament cannot decide its own seat. If it could, it would have moved out of Strasbourg years ago. It is however the Council who decides, and some members of the Council are all too happy with the controversy that goes with the expensive 'moving circus' from Brussels to Strasbourg every month. This weakens the Parliament, both internally and in the eyes of the public. Furthermore, the principle is important to them; it is a form of absolute power over the Parliament, however symbolic it may be.

A more serious issue of symbolic dominance is the matter of nominating and choosing a Commission President. Only once did the European Parliament succeed in getting its candidate nominated; Jean Claude Juncker in 2014. In doing so, Parliament grabbed the political initiative. It pushed its power beyond what it formally possessed, and it showed to the Commission that it has to answer to Parliament. Five years later already, it gave up that initiative. Parliament lost its momentum, while the national governments once again have a president that primarily listens to them. Thus, the pendulum swung from a supranational EU to an intergovernmental one. That motion is still ongoing. The EU will only swing back when the European Parliament throws its weight on the scale. As stated, I believe the shift of power means erosion of European democracy. The defence of democracy is not optional for a Parliament, it is imperative. Two sections featured here deal with this very point. 'The twig and the trunk' is an analysis of the current democratic framework, while 'European Parliament: watchdog or lapdog' deals with Parliament's obligation to exercise democratic accountability.

The democratic framework we have as a Union has always been a bit rickety, but now it is under pressure. From where I sit, in the European Parliament, I can see how the Council has turned against the EU's legislative process, thus stifling the EU's ability to legislate. Opaque ad hoc deals in camera now trump robust legislation. This method has limitations, as we can see from the truly impressive list of files stuck at the Council for years. Migration and asylum? Stuck in the European Council for more than one Parliamentary mandate now. A banking union, following the financial crisis? Unfinished and stuck in the European Council. European defence? Currently unable to make a stand in Ukraine without the Americans, and indeed stuck in the European Council. The list goes on. I think it is fair to say that almost anything meaningful that gets done through the normal legislative procedure, then goes to the European Council to sink into oblivion.

This complete breakdown of legislative performance is just one aspect of the problem I identify in my book. The other major problem is perhaps even more serious. The EU has arrived at a point where laws and values are not enforced. Let us be clear about European values; the European Union and all its predecessors were founded on the principles of democracy and the rule of law. This is not the opinion of the author; it is fact. The proof is right there in the foundational treaties that underpin our Union. Article 2 of the Treaty on European Union, to be precise. One does not have to search long and wide for evidence that these principles are under threat from within the EU.

Hungary is not a real functioning democracy anymore. Poland has a politicised judiciary that helps the ruling party stay in power. Scratch the surface, and you will find that, besides Poland and Hungary, most other EU Member States are also backsliding in one way or another. What is more, this process is now threatening the whole of European democracy. Let me highlight the most important one: national elections are European elections. When authoritarian forces capture an EU Member State, they get membership of the European Council as a bonus. They get to shape legislations, or block it, that touches the lives of all Europeans. We have at least one member of the European Council who has used his membership to serve his own interests, while also stifling European ambitions of fellow Member States.

The European Council's inclination to first serve the narrow interests of its members, even when it goes against democracy or the common good, and increasingly the rule of law, is becoming more dangerous by the day. Whether it is respecting the mandate of the European Parliament, or the ability of national governments to hold their governments to account, democratic accountability is brushed aside routinely. And so are verdicts from the European Court of Justice. Both the ECJ and the European Commission continue to have 27 members, thus preserving an umbilical cord with the Member States. These institutions are increasingly pressured through that national link to weaken enforcement of European norms and laws. To circle back to the overarching theme of this introduction: European democracy is under threat. Not just in a number of EU Member States, but more importantly *from* EU Member States.

Nowhere is this more clear than the case I am currently working on: the abuse of high-powered spyware by national governments. In Hungary and Poland, spyware is a tool in the toolbox of authoritarian European governments. In Greece, it is used to silence journalists and spy on the democratic opposition. When asked about this matter, the Council refuses to give a meaningful answer. This is an institution that chooses to keep the ranks closed and protect its members, rather than do the right thing and clean its house. It has done so now for nearly 15 years, when Viktor Orbán all but demolished democracy and the rule of law in Hungary.

I believe this behaviour is built into the architecture of the EU. The EU has many impressive qualities that still qualify it as a bulwark of democracy and law. At the heart of this Union, however, sits a democratic anomaly that is threatening the European democratic fabric. This anomaly is the European Council: an 'Unidentified Governing Object' (UGO) that plays an ever-bigger role in EU decision-making. I take stock of the European Council as a 'UGO' in the eponymous chapter, and I quote:

> Its nature, role and mandate are unclear and ambiguous: executive or legislator? Governmental or parliamentary body? It is extremely powerful, and yet not accountable to anyone. The argument that its members, the government leaders, are accountable to their own voters is moot, because the European Council as a body cannot be held to account even though it takes decisions that affect all European citizens.

The fact that a body with this level of unaccountability plays such a big role in EU governance is problematic. Many problems in our EU today are logical outcomes of having the aforementioned democratic 'anomaly' at the heart of European decision-making. The European Council is fundamentally at odds with democratic principles, most prominently with the principle of democratic accountability. I argue that this must change, and that the European Parliament must take upon itself the task to make this change happen.

The twig and the trunk

Democracy is not an institution, but a system. A parliamentary democracy is a complete and coherent democratic system, built on a careful inter-institutional balance. At its core are checks and balances, the separation of powers, accountability, and government rule on the basis of a mandate of the people. It is more than a single institution or elections. North Korea and Russia have elections and a parliament, but this does not make them a democracy. The European Union has a parliament and it has elections, but it is not a mature and complete democracy. It is an intergovernmental system with elements of parliamentary democracy, grafted onto it, like a twig grafted onto the trunk of an intergovernmental tree. As the intergovernmental trunk grows bigger, the system becomes increasingly skewed.

The addition in 1979 of the directly elected European Parliament to the profoundly intergovernmental system has not fundamentally changed the actual nature of the system. The European Union is tilting heavily towards intergovernmentalism and executive powers go largely unchecked, whereas the democratic, parliamentary dimension has become dangerously weak. The traditional alliance between the two supranational 'community' bodies, Commission and Parliament, has all but disappeared. It has been replaced by an intergovernmental alliance between Commission and Council. President Von der Leyen gravitates towards power, and she found a natural ally in the European Council.

None of this would be problematic if European integration were limited to mere technical cooperation. But the EU is a political union, taking deeply political decisions that directly and profoundly affect peoples' lives. It shapes and determines our day to day living environment, our society, just as much as national or local government do. It is irresponsible, dangerous, to govern Europe with an incomplete and imbalanced democratic system. Europe needs a mature, robust and resilient democracy. The old saying remains true: power corrupts, absolute power corrupts absolutely. Any new powers must come with countervailing powers and strengthened scrutiny.

But the European Parliament has not kept up with the rapid political evolution of the EU. The European Parliament is an excellent legislator, processing an impressive body of high-quality legislation. However, it should also be a parliamentary watchdog, willing to bite when necessary. Parliament should be exercising tough democratic scrutiny. Scrutiny and critical questions are not anti-European. On the contrary: they will boost public trust in the European Union and give it more robust legitimacy. As Parliament allows itself to be side-lined and weakened, as I will demonstrate later, European democracy becomes endangered. In any healthy democracy, the parliament has to be the countervailing power to the executive, not an extension of it. But increasingly the European Parliament seems to be just echoing the position of the national governments and the Commission, rather than providing the necessary counterweight to Commission and Council and holding them to account.

An assertive European Parliament is crucial for the future of Europe. It must play its full role as parliamentary watchdog, using all the tools in the toolkit and fully exercising its powers. The European Parliament will have to play a pivotal role in transforming the EU into a full-blown parliamentary democracy. Not just by calling for new powers for itself, but by changing the balance between the institutions. Parliament is pretty good when it comes to policies, but it has to become much better in doing politics. The one is about contents, the other about power. Parliament can achieve substantial change by better using its powers. But ultimately a new balance within the institutional framework requires Treaty change. It is alarming that the majority of Member State governments denies the need for change, even categorically rejects Treaty change. Their haughty dismissal of Treaty change is intended to hide the fact they have a vested interest in the current institutional set up, which serves national governments over the citizens.

European *trias politica*

Article 10(1) of the Treaty on the European Union reads: 'The functioning of the Union shall be founded on representative democracy'. In the best EU tradition of fudge, it is left a bit unclear what that means exactly, but one can assume it refers to the EU institutional set-up itself. As argued earlier, the EU is far from being a mature and complete parliamentary democracy.

A coherent and integrated vision is needed to achieve a new balance between the institutions, based on the separation of powers, accountability, checks and balances and a mandate from citizens for the political leadership and its programme. There are too many ambiguous and hybrid elements in the Treaties. These are the result of compromises, and deliberately vague formulations that have often helped to find agreement. But fudge can only patch over fundamental differences for so long. Sooner or later choices have to be made. The EU governance structures have a high degree of elasticity, but at some point, they get overstretched. The EU may be a 'sui generis', hybrid entity with both intergovernmental and community elements, but a modern democracy requires a clear allocation of powers and the accountability that comes with it. The ambiguity has enabled the creeping erosion of democracy.

However, it is not always visible to the naked eye that the *trias politica* is under threat. The lack of public awareness and the absence of a serious and well-informed public debate on institutional matters leave a vacuum in which European democracy is slowly hollowed out.

European Council: 'Unidentified Governing Object'

In this context, clarification of the role of the European Council and its reform should be high on the agenda. There is a paradox in the inverse correlation between the ongoing strengthening and deepening of intergovernmental Europe and the myth of an ever more powerful supranational Europe dominating the Member States. The claims of the anti-EU forces that the EU is a 'superstate', 'dictatorship' or 'EUSSR', where Member States have supposedly been reduced to mere provinces of an all-powerful imperialist European Union are totally grotesque. The opposite is true: over the decades, Member States have tightened their grip on the EU. This has made Europe neither more effective, nor more democratic.

The European Council has arguably become the most powerful European institution, but it is not anchored in a democratic arrangement. It is a kind of UGO, an 'Unidentified Governing Object'. Its nature, role and mandate are unclear and ambiguous: executive or legislator? Governmental or parliamentary body? It is extremely powerful, and yet not accountable to anyone. The argument that its members, the government leaders, are accountable to their own voters is moot, because the European Council as a body cannot be held to account even though it takes decisions that affect all European citizens. (A small illustration of this is that a written parliamentary question by me to the President of the Council was deemed 'inadmissible' since the inter-institutional agreement between Parliament and European Council did not provide for such questions). Some of the members of the European Council – the government leaders – have a dubious reputation, to say the least. But members of this European governance body cannot be made to resign.

Besides, few Europeans will be conscious of the fact that when they cast their vote in the national elections, they are voting for a member of an EU body as well. Given that national governments and national parliaments are part of the EU governance structures, any national election is decisive for the political composition of the leadership of Europe. In a system of intergovernmental decision-making by consensus, or even by unanimity, each national election can tip the scale. This is true of the larger Member States as well as the smaller ones. Of course, it matters for Europe who is in the *Bundeskanzleramt* and in the *Elysée*. But it matters just as much who is in *het Torentje*, *Grasalkovičov palac*, *Stenbocki maja*, *Auberge de Castille*, *Μέγαρο Μαξίμου* or *Roinn an Taoisigh*. Each of these offices has a say in European politics, each of them can bring a majority or block a decision. It can be compared to the German *Bundesrat* or the United States Senate.

Ironically, whereas many Europeans know the ins and outs of the wafer-thin majority of the Biden administration in the US Senate, they are mostly clueless as to the majorities in the Council in the EU. The fact that the EU is a hybrid 'sui generis' entity is really no excuse for not respecting the basic elements of democracy and applying them equally to the European Council. Undefined and unchecked powers have no place in a democracy. In my view, the European Council is a democratic anomaly. But it exists and, at the very least, the Treaties should clarify the nature of the European Council: executive or legislative? Who is it accountable to, and who gives it a mandate?

The increasingly blurred lines between the European Council (government leaders) and the Council (ministers) as a legislator is highly problematic from a democratic point of view. The Treaties provide that if the Council (ministers) is unable to find agreement, the issue will be escalated to the European Council (government leaders). However, this rule, intended for exceptional situations, risks becoming a more regular practice. In times of crisis the European Council steps in, entering the area of both the executive and legislative powers. The COVID pandemic has intensified this, as the position of the Permanent Representatives, who are naturally closer to the government leaders, has become more prominent in the absence of physical meetings of the ministers. The Council has become a kind of sub-committee of the European Council, at the expense of its own role as independent legislator.

A Chinese wall has urgently to be created between the Council in its legislative capacity, and the European Council. Their powers and duties must be very narrowly defined and delineated. At the very least, when the European Council intervenes in the legislative process, its actions must be subject to exactly the same standards of transparency and accountability as that of the Council or the European Parliament. Even better would be for the Council and the European Parliament to become two chambers of a bicameral parliamentary system on equal footing. These chambers should be subject to the same rules of transparency, so that all meetings of the Council as well as the preparatory debates in the Permanent Representatives Committee (COREPER) should be web-streamed, all documents made public and all votes registered. The Council should be seated in a hemicycle, rather than at a round table, to underline that it is a legislative, not an executive body. It could even be envisaged for each Member State to have more than one delegate, as is the case for example in the German *Bundesrat*.

The European Council is increasingly grabbing the monopoly on political agenda setting, and thus competing with the right to legislative initiative of the Commission. Although the tensions between Mrs. von der Leyen and Mr. Charles Michel are legendary, when it comes to its exclusive right of initiative, the Commission seems to accept the European Council trespassing on its prerogative rather passively. Granting the right of initiative to the European Parliament might go some way towards curbing the growing dominance of the European Council. The formal, enforceable right of legislative initiative should be given to the European Parliament at the next Treaty change. However, until then, Parliament will have to maximise its existing options.

In the summer of 2019 Mrs. von der Leyen, then nominee for the presidency of the European Commission, made an election promise to Parliament: that she would treat legislative proposals from the European Parliament as if it had the full right of initiative. Parliament has made little use of this opportunity. Instead of repetitive and frustrated resolutions calling on the Commission to put forward legislative proposals, Parliament should put forward its own legislative proposals. The European Council has to report to Parliament regularly, but it certainly does not feel answerable to Parliament in any way. Parliament should push back against the expansionism of the European Council. For starters, Parliament should re-instate the monthly strategy debates with government leaders on the shape and direction of the European Union. In addition, Parliament can modify the arrangements for the regular report by the President of the European Council and turn it into a proper 'Question Hour' rather than just a podium for a speech by the European Council President.

European Parliament: watchdog or lapdog?

Building a parliamentary democracy should start from a strong European Parliament, but Parliament has been struggling lately. Admittedly, leading the European Parliament in times of COVID is a daunting task. The leadership has succeeded in keeping Parliament up and running, and that is no small feat. The legislative work has continued, albeit in a much-reduced form. In addition, Parliament had to regroup after *Brexit*.

However, in spite of these circumstances, or maybe especially in these circumstances, Parliament should have a vision for renewing EU parliamentary democracy, not just in terms of tweaking the Treaties, but in bringing about a real transformation of the old intergovernmental, paralysed, technocratic

Europe, into a new, political, vibrant, parliamentary Europe. How do we bring about the shift in the power balance between the institutions? How do we give citizens a real say over the shape, direction and leadership of the European Union? How do we achieve a fully fledged European parliamentary democracy, based on the *trias politica* with the separation of powers? How should the European Parliament operate to achieve that goal and what tools does it have?

Parliament has an extensive arsenal: it has legislative powers, budgetary powers and elective powers. It has to vote the Commission into power, has to hold the Commission to account, and it can even adopt a motion of censure. It does not have formal powers to make an individual commissioner resign, but commissioners have to appear regularly before parliamentary committees, and Parliament can of course request the resignation of a commissioner. There is a range of dedicated scrutiny arrangements that gives Parliament huge influence, for example on Europol, Schengen or the Recovery and Resilience Facility. As one leg of the budget authority it has the power of the purse, and it can decide to withhold budget discharge. Many EU bodies and agencies have to report to Parliament, and Parliament has to agree to, or even decide their work programmes and appointments to the management of the agency. Other scrutiny tools include parliamentary questions, parliamentary inquiries and access to information requests. Some instruments only give limited legislative powers to Parliament, like delegated acts or the consent requirement for international agreements. But any instrument that requires Parliament's consent can become a real big bazooka if used in a strategic and assertive manner.

Parliament should be giving full effect to Article 17(8) TFEU and hold the Commission to account in a meaningful way. It is not optional but an obligation under the Treaties. It should start by re-introducing a proper 'Question Hour' with the Commission President, at least twice a month. This should be materially different from the current practice of the Commission President giving a speech in the plenary session, followed by a long series of MEPs reading out one-minute statements. It needs to be based on actual questions and answers, and tough scrutiny, leaving no wriggle room for the Commission. This will create a political arena . . . and the scent of wild animals. Currently, Parliament is treating the Commission with velvet gloves. The Commission knows it has nothing to fear from Parliament. Once the hurdle of the confirmation vote has been cleared, the Commission can pretty much do as it pleases for five years.

The bar for resignation of commissioners and the College as a whole is much higher than it is for national governments and government ministers. This has to change. Not only the Commission President, but also the commissioners should be subject to regular and rigorous scrutiny. The current scrutiny arrangements for commissioners hardly deserve the name. The seating arrangements during scrutiny sessions in Parliament are illustrative of the power relations. Commissioners get to sit on the podium, next to the committee chair, literally looking down on the MEPs. Some Commissioners turn up regularly at EP committee meetings, as required by the inter-institutional working arrangements, but others don't bother. Parliament occasionally grumbles, but it has not called for any political heads. The European Parliament currently cannot officially make individual Commissioners resign (this power should be one of the priorities for Treaty change). However, if Parliament were to call for the resignation of a commissioner in the case of grave transgressions, errors or failure to act, it would be very hard for the Commission President to ignore that political message.

Parliament does have the option to issue a motion of censure on the whole Commission, but this is the nuclear option and it has been used only once. Or rather: Parliament threatened to use it in March 1999, but the Santer Commission stepped down before the motion was actually voted on. The reasons for the resignation of the Santer Commission (irregularities in the management of EU funds and blatant nepotism of Commissioner Cresson who hired a friend, who was a dentist, as political advisor) seem rather petty compared to failures by subsequent Commissions. It seems that triggering the nuclear option once actually raises the bar for doing so a second time. If breaking the COVID social distancing rules by attending a party is considered grave enough to demand the resignation of a commissioner (as in the case of Commissioner Hogan), then the persistent and deliberate failure of the Commission to act against the deep and protracted rule of law crisis in Europe should be serious enough for the European Parliament to consider withdrawing its support for the Commission. As the EU becomes more powerful, the Commission should be held to higher standards. A motion of censure to vote the Commission out of office is the biggest bazooka of all, and one that should not be triggered frivolously, but be reserved only for the gravest failures of the Commission.

But a bazooka will only work as a deterrent if we are willing to use it. The resignation of an executive body is not the end of the world, and even a normal element of democratic accountability. National governments are regularly sent packing by their parliament, even in times of crisis. Yet, the sun still rises the next day. It will be an important test for the separation of powers and the role of Parliament as watchdog, whether Parliament in 2021 will actually take the European Commission to court for 'failure to act' in response to the non-application of the Regulation on Rule of Law conditionality in the EU Budget.

The Regulation was adopted by the legislators – Parliament and Council – in December 2020. This means that it is law and has to be applied. However, the European Council in its summit conclusions added conditions for the application of the regulation, notably the drafting of 'implementation guidelines', a requirement invented on the spot by the European Council, without any legal basis. The Council also stated that the regulation should only be fully applied after the European Court of Justice had ruled on its legality. This refers to a legal challenge to the regulation brought by Hungary and Poland, the two worst rule-of-law offenders that would be the first to be hit by the new conditionality rule. The European Council considered that such a legal challenge would have an automatic suspensive effect on the application of the regulation.

The Commission followed the interpretation of the European Council. However, there is no rule that such legal challenges have a suspensive effect; it is another fantasy rule invented by the European Council. Although European Council Conclusions are not legally binding, the Commission chose to follow them, in blatant violation of the Treaty rule that the European Commission is not allowed to take instructions from any government or body. President von der Leyen clearly chose to ignore the Treaties, and to serve the European Council and the national governments instead. Von der Leyen probably did not want to cross Orbán and risk his veto against the decision on Own Resources for the EU Budget. An understandable political calculation perhaps. But it is not at the discretion of the European Commission whether or not to apply the law.

If the Commission, the guardian of the Treaties, fails to uphold those Treaties, Parliament has a duty to take the Commission to court. Parliament is angry and frustrated about the refusal of the Commission to apply the regulation, but it is hesitating to act. Sometimes Parliament seems to be afraid of its own shadow. It adopted a resolution at the end of March 2021, giving the Commission another two months to start applying the regulation, or else Parliament would take the Commission to court, but the wording was vague enough to make the resolution little more than a political warning shot, rather than the start of legal proceedings.

Early in June 2021, Parliament voted another resolution, this time announcing legal proceedings against the Commission for 'failure to act'. But again, it was worded in such a way to allow the reluctant EPP group to interpret it as just another warning shot. Nevertheless, at the end of June, President David Sassoli did indeed send formal notice to the Commission, with a two-month deadline to act. It did not come to a court-case, as the European Commission eventually triggered the Rule of Law Conditionality Mechanism. In July 2021 the Commission delayed the approval of the Hungarian share of 7 billion euros from the EU Recovery Fund. Although the Commission did not explicitly refer to the Rule of Law Conditionality Regulation, the move has been interpreted by some as a reaction to Orbán's anti-LGBTI laws. The power of the purse is one of the key powers of a parliament. Although the European Parliament does not have full budget powers, it should use the powers it has more strategically and assertively. Within certain limits the European Parliament can shape and modify the annual budget. But it also has the power to block the adoption of the annual budget, to put money in the reserve, to withhold discharge and to demand access to information.

To begin with, Parliament should exercise the toughest possible scrutiny over the way EU money is spent. The bulk of the EU budget is spent by the Member States, under the aegis of the Commission. That arrangement makes it difficult to verify if money is spent correctly and efficiently. This is all the more worrying as Member States are notoriously sloppy when spending EU money. The level of irregularities – errors as well as fraud – is such, that the European Court of Auditors (ECA) has not once been able to give a positive 'statement of assurance', certifying that EU money has been spent correctly. Against this backdrop it is amazing that Parliament continues to duly sign off the budget each year.

The Budget Control Committee of the European Parliament tends to exercise rigid scrutiny. But other parliamentary committees, too, could exercise tougher scrutiny over expenditure in their own policy area. The Civil Liberties, Justice, and Home Affairs Committee ('LIBE') should use its scrutiny powers to get more leverage over policy areas like migration and security. In my experience, the Commission (and Member States) are extremely reluctant to provide full insight into the way money is spent in these areas. In March of 2020, the European Commission pledged 700 million euros in emergency aid to Greece for the reception of refugees. One-and-a-half year later, the reception conditions of refugees seem to have improved marginally at best. There are more showers and toilets in the refugee camps, but refugees are still living in leaky tents, and reception centres have become detention centres in all but name. But despite repeated requests from the European Parliament 'LIBE' committee, the Commission has hardly provided any meaningful information on how the 700 million euros had been spent and why the situation has not improved.

When it comes to internal security, in the past 20 years a raft of new legislative tools for law enforcement and security has been created, such as for the processing of citizens' travel data, communications data or bank data, for the automatic exchange of information between national authorities, and for automated searches in data bases. The budget for the EU security agenda got a massive boost as well, sometimes indirectly, for example by funding the development of surveillance technologies through the EU research budget. Despite the growing activity of the EU in the area of internal security, it is difficult for Parliament to exercise democratic oversight, as much of the EU security agenda is implemented by national authorities. The Commission denies responsibility, and usually fails to give serious answers to parliamentary questions on the matter. However, national parliaments have no means and no interest in exercising parliamentary scrutiny either. This leads to a gap in parliamentary oversight in areas that affect citizens' rights. The European Parliament should close this gap by investing substantially in expertise and capacity for its parliamentary committees and boost their scrutiny power.

The COVID Recovery and Resilience Fund is not part of the regular EU Budget. In principle, the fund's regulation provides for scrutiny of the national recovery plans by the European Parliament, to make sure EU money is spent in line with the agreed priorities and criteria. However, Parliament's scrutiny powers are not very strong in practice. The very first time this procedure was used, in the spring of 2021, Parliament and the Commission clashed over the latter's reluctance to provide all relevant information. Despite the fact that the obligation to fully inform Parliament had been laid down in great detail in an inter-institutional agreement, the old reflex of secrecy in the Commission was strong as ever. The European Parliament should use the power of the purse to revisit the 'inter-institutional agreements' with the Commission and the Council, governing the practical cooperation arrangements between the institutions. Transparency and access to information must become an absolute precondition for cooperation in the budget procedure.

For the long term, it is crystal clear that far-reaching reforms are necessary. The European Parliament should get full powers in all areas of the budget, including the revenue side. In addition, the multi-annual budget cycle should be replaced by a regular annual budget. The current European Union seven-year multi-annual budget (also known by its pet name MFF or Multiannual Financial Framework) is an anachronism. In today's world, seven years is an eternity. In comparison: the average life span of an iPhone is four years and three months. With a seven-year budget it is impossible to react adequately to unforeseen events like a sudden influx of refugees or a pandemic. Even the communists limited their planning to a modest five years. Formally the EU MFF cycle has to be 'at least' five years, but in practice this has been raised to the maximum of seven years by the Member States. This means it does not coincide with the five-year term of the European Parliament, thus reducing parliamentary influence. During the 2014–2019 Parliament no MFF was adopted.

For the European Parliament, acquiring the full right of inquiry will be as important as the right to initiate legislation. Currently Parliament does not have the power to summon witnesses or hear them under oath. Notwithstanding, Parliament has conducted a number of very successful parliamentary inquiries, for example into CIA extraordinary renditions and abductions, the spying scandals of Echelon and Prism, the LuxLeaks and Panama Papers tax evasion scandals, and the 'Dieselgate' emissions scandal. But Parliament is becoming the victim of its own success. It has acquired a reputation of being a tough interrogator, and witnesses are reluctant to show up at hearings. The British intelligence service GCHQ refused to be present at the 2014 EP inquiry into its hack of Belgian telecom provider Belgacom, which serves the EU institutions and other Brussels-based international bodies. In spring 2021 the Slovenian Prime Minister and Culture Minister walked out of a hearing of the EP Rule of Law Monitoring Group, when the chair (myself) did not agree to the immediate screening of a propaganda video on the Parliament official website. They also refused to answer subsequent written questions about attacks on media freedom and independence of the judiciary in Slovenia. The Polish government refused to turn up to a hearing of Parliament's Civil Liberties, Justice and Home Affairs Committee ('LIBE') to answer questions about the democratic backsliding in their country. Facebook CEO Mark Zuckerberg was extremely reluctant to appear before Parliament to answer questions about the abuse of personal data by Cambridge Analytica of 87 million Facebook users, and only agreed to appear before the Conference of Presidents instead of the mighty LIBE committee, where he expected to get much tougher grilling (he was right: the one-hour live-streamed hearing in the Conference of Presidents was a walk in the park for Zuckerberg). When the Parliamentary committee for public health (ENVI) called in the CEOs of pharmaceutical giants to question them about the delivery issues with the COVID vaccines in early 2021, it took considerable arm-twisting to make them come to Parliament.

Parliament has no formal means to summon witnesses. However, it should check what other tools it has that might add some pressure. For example, it could consider including an obligation in the lobby register for businesses and organisations to cooperate fully with parliamentary inquiries, monitoring and scrutiny exercises as a condition for getting an accreditation. Should they refuse to turn up or answer questions, the accreditation should be withdrawn. It is slightly more complicated with governments and government agencies. Member States are constituent parts of the EU, so they cannot be totally banned, but there should be consequences if they refuse parliamentary scrutiny. Parliament should flex its muscle a bit more and up the pressure on national authorities to cooperate.

And finally, Parliament should not be shy in its conclusions. A parliamentary inquiry is only a useful tool for accountability if the findings come with political consequences. In a mature parliamentary democracy, transparency and accountability go hand in hand. But intergovernmentalism and transparency are mutually exclusive. The Commission and Council have a strong instinct for secrecy. This is a relic from the times when Europe was run by diplomats, and discretion and secrecy were the norm. Of course, national governments are no more keen on transparency nowadays and they do not volunteer information to their citizens any more than the Council and Commission do. However, they are used to being under closer scrutiny by parliaments, media and citizens.

The resistance of the Commission and Council against more transparency and access to information is also about power. They cynically calculate that under the current rules, it suffices for them to simply refuse access to information, even if that refusal is not legally justified. An applicant only has one way to challenge a refusal: in court. Court challenges are lengthy and cumbersome, and by the time there is a court decision, the information may no longer be relevant. 'Private enforcement' by individual citizens and civil society has created important case law relating to transparency obligations of the institutions, notably the 'Turco ruling' (on access to opinions of the legal service), the 'In 't Veld ruling' (on transparency of negotiations on international agreements), the 'Access Info ruling' (on transparency of Council minutes) and the 'De Capitani ruling' (on access to the four-column document for legislative 'Trilogue' negotiations).

But the Commission and the Council try and apply case law in the narrowest possible way. In the Access Info case, the practice of the Council was to redact the minutes of the meetings in such a way that names of individual countries were blacked out, so that it was not visible what position each country had taken. The 'Access Info ruling' banned this practice. But instead of no longer redacting the minutes, the Council then simply left out the names of the Member States altogether, thus complying with the letter of the ruling, but ignoring its spirit. Moreover, applicants run a financial risk. An NGO which challenged in court the refusal of its request to Frontex for access to documents lost the case. Frontex then made the unusual move of making the NGO pay not just the costs of the court case, but also Frontex's own legal costs, amounting to a total of 24,000 euro. In the end Frontex agreed to reduce the amount, but such a move will deter any civil society organisation, journalist or citizen who is looking for information. Even for MEPs it is difficult to get access to information. The Commission can afford to ignore requests or take forever to reply.

The transparency rules must be reviewed as a matter of urgency. A proposal for a new transparency regulation has been stuck in Council and Commission since 2011, as neither body has much appetite for a better transparency law. There should be an explicit and enforceable right to information for all citizens. But in the absence of a new law, Parliament should use its weight as an institution, demand more transparency as an institution, and take Commission or Council to court in the case of refusal.

Written parliamentary questions are a simple but important tool for holding an institution to account. MEPs make ample use of the tool, but the quality of the replies is downright insulting, to Parliament and to the citizens. Most of the replies by the European Commission make a complete mockery of accountability. Of course, the quality of the questions occasionally also leaves something to be desired. The European Parliament has self-imposed restrictions on parliamentary questions, such as a maximum number of questions and limits to the topics. But it has not taken any action to oblige the Commission to change its practice of rubbish replies.

Despite the visible weakening of parliamentary democracy, there seems to be little inspiration for radical change within the European Parliament itself. Internal initiatives like surveys and working groups discussing reforms are mainly about internal procedures, such as the arrangements for speaking time in plenary. Some of the reforms are interesting, but they hardly count as fundamental renewal. It is not just the internal working methods that will make Parliament a vibrant political arena and powerful democratic institution. It is its position among the EU institutions.

The current Parliament leadership seems less combative, have less 'Wille zur Macht', than some of their predecessors with regard to claiming a key role for the European Parliament. In an interview, President Sassoli says on the role of Parliament and intergovernmentalism:

> This leads me to mention the sometimes-difficult relationship between the 'community' and governmental bodies. I know that young people hope that the community bodies prevail (which is also my preference). I am also convinced that we are heading in that direction for the future. But today we must approach this future a bit more pragmatically. At this

> time, it is impossible to envision that one body can dominate another because, above all, we need to re-establish a balance. This is a task which will allow us to affirm Europe's relevance. And so, when we are ready, I think that the community body will prevail. Until then, we must always keep our opportunities in mind, both in regard to the European Union and our democratic systems.

European democracy needs more drive and ambition. Ambition is not about waiting for change to happen by itself, but actively making it happen. All the powers that the European Parliament has today have been hard won; they were not handed on a silver platter. It took the strong leadership of visionary and determined members of the House, who were not afraid of confrontation when it was needed. Their legacy is under threat. Parliament sometimes seems afraid of its own shadow, afraid to use its powers, afraid of confrontation with the other institutions. At the same time, many of the new MEPs do have the fighting spirit; they are brimming with energy, talent and idealism, but in the current vacuum, too much of this evaporates for want of direction and guidance.

The fiction of Europe: the technocratic eunuch

The truth is: the European Union is already deeply political. It is addressing political challenges, making political choices and struggling with political dilemmas. The EU's leaders are politicians and organised in political families, and it has its share of power politics. Technocratic Europe is a myth, but a deeply rooted one and carefully cultivated by those who have an interest in keeping the status quo.

National political leaders repeat ad nauseam the jaded claim, echoed by many others, that Europe is remote for citizens, implying that the EU itself is to blame for that. In his famous 2017 Sorbonne speech, French President Emmanuel Macron makes an accurate analysis:

> Because the sad passions of Europe have reared their heads once more and are drawing people in. . . . They are lying to the people, but we have let them do it, because we wanted to establish the idea that Europe had become a powerless bureaucracy. Throughout Europe, we explained that when there was a constraint, it was Europe's fault! When powerlessness was at the door, it was not us but Brussels!'

Language matters. When asked about reform of the EU, national leaders respond with the mantra that, 'Europe has to deliver' if it wants to win the hearts and souls of Europeans. They seem to imply Europe has not 'delivered' so far. This is nonsense: much of our quality of life is entirely the result of European integration. But more seriously: it is a trap. 'Delivering' is management language, implying that there are objective, straightforward and quantifiable material targets. But the European Union is not a factory or a company that merely needs efficient management. It is a political entity that needs ideas, vision, inspiration, leadership and strategy. By using the term 'delivering' this way, the European Union is dismissed as a mere technocratic organisation that does not merit the attention or interest of its citizens. It reduces citizens to consumers and spectators, instead of enabling them to get involved and take ownership.

This has been intensified during the pandemic. Governments got exceptional powers in order to manage the crisis. They relied heavily on experts. Let there be no misunderstanding: listening to the experts and science is the sensible thing to do in a crisis, and I would not want to recommend otherwise. But the – false – impression was created that decisions were apolitical, that politics had been depoliticised and reduced to mere technocratic management on the basis of facts and figures. No need for public debate or parliamentary control. This may work for immediate and short-term emergencies, but in a prolonged crisis like the COVID pandemic, the apparent disappearance of politics in a prolonged state of emergency is a problem. Calls for national unity, all political forces pulling together behind a single goal, serve a purpose for a short while, but public debate, critical questions and close scrutiny are the oxygen of democracy. And indeed, in many countries unease is growing over the impact of the pandemic on democracy. Not just among misguided virus-deniers, anti-vaxxers and populists.

However, this fiction of apolitical technocratic rule is quite similar to the way the European Union has been run for many decades now. The myth of technocratic Europe allows national governments to have unlimited power, to stifle public debate and to keep citizens out of the game. The European Union is rapidly developing as a mature political entity. Not as a deliberate choice, not as a federalist conspiracy, not because successive Commission presidents solemnly declare their Commission to be 'political' or 'geopolitical', but as an inevitable consequence of a changing world. European integration is merely the reaction to events, in much the same way as the creation of nation states or indeed local authorities has been a response to the challenges of that time. The nature and scale of the challenges we are facing today require different answers from those of 70 years ago; therefore, the nature and scale of European integration will change as well.

But the government leaders are in denial. The Council seems to be frozen in time, refusing to adjust to circumstances. And what Darwin said about organisms applies equally to organisations: 'It is not the strongest of the species that survives, nor the most intelligent that survives. It is the one that is most adaptable to change'. The stubborn refusal of national governments to face reality is impeding the entire European Union from advancing. Whether European integration goes too fast or too slow is not a matter of ideology. It is not something to be measured against the ideals of ardent pro- or anti-Europeans. It can only be judged against the EU's ability to respond to the challenges we are facing, to keep up with the pace of a changing world: to 'deliver', in Council terminology.

We have to conclude that Europe is too slow. In many areas Europe is trailing, held back by people who are clinging to the past, and dreaming of the glory of days gone by instead of facing the present and the future.

The political arena

A people's democracy needs a political arena. 'I love the scent of wild animals in this building', the founding father of my party, Hans van Mierlo, famously said about the Dutch Parliament.

He saw politics as an arena, with the smell of blood, sweat and sawdust, a battleground for the confrontation of ideas and ideals, and for the clash of the political titans. In the arena we smell the fear of our opponent, or we smell victory. We smell mortal fear and bloodthirst. Adrenaline rushes, nostrils flare, all senses are on full alert. The public loves the show, they come and watch the fight of the gladiators and the big beasts. Supporters come to support and cheer their team, their champion. Although actual war has never been any fun for the normal people, throughout history warriors and princes have been gung-ho about fighting, in it for the glory. Knights paraded in shining armour, insignia, colourful banners and impressive weaponry, accompanied by the sound of bugles and drums. Battles, rather than bureaucracy, have made material for epics and blockbusters.

Fortunately, in the 21st century Europe we settle our political differences in a relatively tidy and civilised way, without bloodshed. Most of the time anyway. But under the veneer of civilisation, we are political animals, driven by instinct. And as Von Clausewitz famously said, 'War is the continuation of politics by other means'. The opposite is also true. Politics is battle, just by other means. Of course, ultimately politics must be about substance, about the nitty-gritty of policy making, legislation and regulation. It is about good governance and serving the citizens. But without the drama, nobody would be interested.

The fascination of the public with politics lies firmly in the game and the spectacle of the battle: a gladiator fight behind closed doors is not interesting. The fight must be man to man, in the public arena, where people can smell, hear, see and feel the excitement and choose sides. It is about power and might, and about victory and defeat, not about technical footnotes and legal subparagraphs. No number of online meetings can ever replace the experience of the political arena. The only things you will probably smell during an online policy debate are the sweaty socks you have been wearing off camera for three days. Without the scent of wild animals, the scent of the arena, politics remain sterile and cold. People will not feel any connection or identification.

That may explain why Europeans are so fascinated by US Presidential elections: the confrontation between the candidates is a sublimated gladiator fight. The candidates not only seek to persuade and convince the audience with their excellent policy proposals, but they want to beat their opponent. Like gladiators in the arena, they move around and seek the weak spots in their opponent's defences. Although they do not fight physically, the physical dimension is at least as important as the verbal exchange. Remember how during an election debate in 2016 Donald Trump crept up behind Hillary Clinton like a predator, trying to intimidate and unsettle his opponent? If you ask people if they remember the actual topic of that debate, hardly anyone will. But everyone remembers the scene.

This is why autocratic leaders try to avoid public confrontation with their opponents. Thus, there has not been any serious debate with Viktor Orbán for years, as he is well aware of the risks and avoids political debate like the plague. Authoritarian leaders like to show off their bare-chested virility in front of the camera, in carefully orchestrated press conferences with selected media, but they hide from a real showdown behind their mothers' skirts.

And no, fights and battles are not the exclusive domain of men. Women can be gladiators as well. 'Sofagate' was widely seen as a sexist incident, two alpha males relegating the woman in the room to a lower position. The images of Erdogan and Michel making themselves comfortable in the two top seats, leaving Von der Leyen no choice but to sit down on the sofa, the seat of lesser honour. But Von der Leyen struck back. Fully aware of the presence of dozens of cameras, her irritated 'Ahem . . .' and hand gesture at the two men, left Michel badly wounded. No amount of explaining could undo the image of his pasha-like behaviour. There was definitely the scent of wild animals in the little scene.

In October 2019, French EU Commissioner-designate Sylvie Goulard had to go through an exceptional second confirmation hearing in the European Parliament, as questions had arisen in view of a court case against her in France. The meeting room was jampacked, and the media would not miss a second of this battle. When I entered the room at the start of the hearing, I remember vividly being gripped by the strong sensation that I could actually smell the political bloodthirst of the EPP. (Later on, it turned out that indeed EPP had decided beforehand to eliminate her; the hearing was only meant to extend the agony.) The tension was palpable, as it must have been at the start of a gladiator fight.

In the European Union, such moments are rare, and when they occur, they are not visible to the general public. The myth of a technocratic entity has been carefully maintained for decades. European politics are seen as technocratic and boring. There are battles all right, but they mostly take place behind closed doors, with no sensory experience for the citizens. No smell, no blood, no sounds, no cries or growls, no adrenaline. Sterile like an operating room. For the first half century of European integration, the political work was mainly left to diplomats and bureaucrats. The intergovernmental, diplomatic origins of European integration are still visible today. All political choices are carefully disguised as mere technocratic matters, best left to experts. Political fights take place behind closed doors, and only when a compromise has been reached, will it be presented to the public. Even the choice of political leaders of the EU is carefully kept away from the citizens.

The contrast between the election of the political leader of the United States and the political leadership of the European Union could not be greater. The election of the US President is the most visible, mediatised political event in the world, including in Europe. It is a global event, followed closely by billions of people. The primaries, the year before the actual election, serve as a support act to warm up the global audience for the main event: the battle of the gladiators. Come election day, billions of people around the world know the two candidates for the highest office in the US as well as their running mates, they know what is at stake. There is the smell of wild animals, blood and sawdust. . . .

The election of the political leader of the European Union is the total opposite. With the exception of 2014, the choice of Commission President has always been the outcome of an opaque process of horse-trading behind closed doors. The process recalls of the election of the Pope in the Vatican, more than a proper election campaign, where the candidates publicly compete and seek to win the support of the voters. Much like Cardinal electors, government leaders withdraw behind closed doors and negotiate their choice of candidate, usually as part of a package deal including several European top jobs. When there is white smoke, the doors open, and the new leader is shown to the people. This procedure has very little to do with democracy.

Conclusion

On political responsibility and political control in the European Union

Jean Paul Jacqué

There is a natural and almost unconscious reflex to approach questions of accountability and political control in the European Union through the prism of one's nation's constitution. But in this area, more than in others, comparison is not reason. Indeed, the institutional system of the Union still bears clear marks of its origins. For the founding fathers, the European Coal and Steel Community was a technical agency based on the expertise of an independent High Authority. The essential features of this Community have persisted despite the successive revisions of the treaties. Its political organisation is based on a dialogue between a Commission, whose authority is based on independent expertise, and a Council which expresses the common opinion of the Member States. The Commission's proposals are subject to the decision of the Council, but the Commission is given certain powers to preserve its power of initiative, in particular the obligation to act unanimously to modify its proposals. These prerogatives have been permanently weakened by the Luxembourg compromise, one of the lasting consequences of which is the practice in the Council of consensus when the treaty authorises the use of qualified majority voting. In this system, the Council holds both legislative and executive powers, and there is no room for the separation of powers that is one of the foundations of national systems.

In this context, there is little room for a parliament that has the power to consult without any obligation on the part of the legislator to take its opinions into account. It could, of course, vote to censure the Commission, but the requirement of a two-thirds majority makes this unlikely. Moreover, censure could only be exercised over the management of the Commission, which seems to exclude legislative activity. In fact, as is well known, no motion of censure has ever reached the required majority. The increase in the powers of the Parliament, brought about by the election of its members by direct suffrage, has made it a co-legislator without changing the overall architecture of the system. It has tried to increase its influence on the Commission through its power to elect the President by the '*Spitzenkandidaten*' system, but has encountered strong resistance from the Council. The attempt to graft a parliamentary system onto the existing structure has

DOI: 10.4324/9781003281559-21

met with difficulties, so that currently three systems overlap: the community system desired by the founding fathers, the intergovernmental system that is supported by the Council and the European Council, and a draft parliamentary system. This situation makes it difficult to ensure accountability and control.

We will not go back over the various techniques applicable in this field, since they have been remarkably explained in the previous studies, but we will limit ourselves to a few thoughts of a general nature. First of all, responsibility and control require beforehand that one can identify those responsible for the decisions that one wishes to contest, and this is not easy in the Union. The technique of consensus at all levels has the effect of masking the responsibilities of all parties. As far as the Commission is concerned, its power of initiative for important political decisions is frequently exercised under the impetus of the European Council. It is true that it retains responsibility for the technical drafting of proposals, but it acts on the basis of guidelines laid down in the conclusions of the European Council, so that it is questionable whether it is defending its own text or one imposed by the European Council before the legislator. For its part, the European Council acts by consensus and, like the Council, has the capacity to disengage itself from its status as an institution and transform itself into an intergovernmental body adopting international agreements, as shown by the Treaty on the Stability, Coordination and Governance of the Euro Zone, the creation of the European Stability Mechanism or the EU-Turkey declaration on migrants. ln this case, no control can be exercised at the level of the Union and control is left to the national parliaments when the agreement is submitted for ratification. ln the same way, in legislative matters, the Council is pressured into seeking consensus because, in the event of obstruction on their part, the text will be adopted by qualified majority. This technique dilutes responsibilities and can render the control exercised over the members of the Council by their respective parliaments – insofar as such control exists – ineffective.

The rest of the legislative process leaves little room for real control. The Parliament's position is determined by agreements negotiated between political groups under the guidance of the rapporteur and the 'shadow rapporteurs' of the various groups which remain in relative obscurity, even though the Parliament has modified its rules of procedure to allow the position to be determined by the plenary at the request of one tenth of the members. The final agreement is then negotiated between the Parliament and the Council in closed trialogues, with final approval by the co-legislators being a mere formality.

The entire decision-making process is largely out of the public eye, which leads to a lack of control and therefore difficulty in identifying the responsibility of each actor. Admittedly, the actors are aware of the problem and have tried since Maastricht to combat this tendency through a policy of transparency that should help restore a form of political control. As the Court of

Justice has noted on several occasions when condemning the Council's reluctance in this respect:

> It is precisely openness in that regard which, by allowing divergences between various points of view to be openly debated, contributes to reducing doubts in the minds of citizens, not only as regards the lawfulness of an isolated legislative measure but also as regards the legitimacy of the legislative process as a whole . . . and contributes to strengthening the principles of democracy and respect for fundamental rights.[1]

However, one of the consequences of transparency is that the actual debates are shifted away from the formal forums to which it applies to informal meetings between actors, which by nature escape publicity.

It is therefore difficult to instil the features of a parliamentary-type regime into a system that was originally based on different foundations. Attempts to transform the situation through revisions often fail because of the very nature of the Union. It is not enough to revise the legal rules applicable to the institutions in order to change practices that are deeply rooted in the past. The new rules will certainly be respected, since the Union is based on respect for the rule of law, but they are only the tip of the iceberg, and the real game of power takes place in the submerged part on the basis of almost unchanging practices.

In fact, the European Union falls into the category of consociational federalism, which calls for the organisation of states in which cultural, religious or linguistic differences in the population are such that traditional parliamentary functioning is impossible. As David Sinardet writes:

> Political power cannot rest on a simple majority of political representatives, but must rest on as large a majority as possible, including at least the representatives of the various groups considered important in a particular society. . . . The basis of this system is that decisions are taken by consensus and that representatives of one group cannot take decisions on important matters without those representing the other groups.[2]

This is a phenomenon of government by elites who build consensus in order to avoid conflicts between groups. This does not mean that no evolution is possible, but it can only happen gradually as integration between the different political groups develops. Beyond a modification of the treaties, this integration needs vectors. Thus, the creation of a transnational constituency during European elections is likely to promote this integration by allowing the debate

1 CJEU (Full Court), Case C-156/21, *Hungary v European Parliament and Council of the European Union*, 16 February 2022.

2 D. Sinardet, 'Le fédéralisme consociatif belge: vecteur d'instabilité?', *Pouvoirs* 136, no. 1 (2011): pp. 21–35 (translation by the author).

to be shifted from the national to the European level and by encouraging the development of real European political parties. Rather than an inappropriate transposition of national institutional models, the Union should be the object of a global vision that takes into account its own nature and emphasises the elements that will favour its political integration. This is the positive effect of crises when they show that they can only be resolved by deepening solidarity.

Part III

Diversity of legal approaches

Section 5

Democratic perspectives

12 The European convergence of the strengthening of the executive power

Hanan Qazbir

Some say that the executory power does not need to be limited since its action is by definition temporary and execution is limited by nature.[1] It is moreover the 'moving force of a Government', adding 'action to will'.[2] The question of the definition of the executive power thus entails that of the link between the Executive on the one hand and power and authority on the other.[3] The existence of that power is determined by the power of its action.[4] Limiting it would therefore denature it, while it would be natural and desirable that it be reinforced. However, its strengthening, within a democratic regime, is thought-provoking and worrying. It is thought-provoking because it questions the principle of the balance of powers since it has not been accompanied with an increase of responsibility,[5] far from it. There has been a progressive displacement of the decision-making centre. The main justification for such a state of affairs relies on the common idea that,

> The laws only provide for what is general and predictable; it is always necessary to add a discretionary power, the Executive . . . [that representative government] can only enforce its laws thanks to a vigorous execution, but because it is derived from the people, it cannot admit that the legitimacy of the Government be founded on discretionary wisdom.[6]

1 C.-L. de Secondat Montesquieu, *De l'esprit des lois* (1897; reis. Paris: Hachette BNF, 2017), p. 110.

2 J. Necker, *Du pouvoir exécutif dans les grands États*, Tome 1 (1792; reis., Paris: Hachette BNF, 2019), pp. 15–16.

3 See J.-P. Cléro, 'Hume et Montesquieu, Sur deux chapitres de L'Esprit des lois traduits en anglais', *Revue Française d'Histoire des Idées politiques* 1, no. 35 (2012): pp. 73–91. The first part is dedicated to the distinction between authority, power and potency.

4 H. C. Mansfield, 'Gouvernement représentatif et pouvoir exécutif', *Revue Commentaire*, no. 4 (1986): p. 664.

5 See S. Mouton, 'Conclusion: How Do Local Actors Participate in the Strengthening or in the Weakening of the Holding to Account of the Executive within Modern Democratic States?', in this volume, *Regional Accountability and Executive Power in Europe*, eds. M. Morabito and G. Tusseau (Oxfordshire: Routledge, forthcoming).

6 H. C. Mansfield, 'Gouvernement représentatif et pouvoir exécutif', p. 664.

DOI: 10.4324/9781003281559-24

All the European democratic States, despite their diversity, share that analysis. Compliance with the principle of the institutional autonomy allows European States[7] to put in place the political regime they want and to be organised based on their political-legal culture and their institutional priorities. The only limit is the respect of the rule of law, which is a relative limit given the evolution of some European States (Poland, Hungary).[8] Despite the variants in the political organisation of the States, the parliamentary regime is a basis that is common to all the European systems, be they unitary or federal States. Parliamentary monarchy, prime-minister parliamentarianism, with presidential appropriation, directorial parliamentarianism, etc. All the States considered in this study have chosen democracy, the rule of law and the principle of the separation of powers. Moreover, crises are regularly multiplying at the national, European and international levels today, which provides a common context allowing to compare the evolutions of those political regimes. Terrorist acts which aim at disturbing the stability of institutions, financial crises with institutional consequences and, more recently, a health crisis have upset our certainties. States are encouraged to respect an obligation of adaptation of their actions to avoid foreseeable deaths, especially under Article 2 ECHR. The political practices of the leaders of the European States are evolving, but that is not the only evolution. The legislative and administrative norms hammer home what a strong Executive wants to face that issue, which was first a security issue and has become a health one. However, 'aiming to protect life does not allow measures that would disproportionately violate other fundamental rights'.[9] The trivialisation and the normalisation of those exceptional situations are thought-provoking in relation to possible future choices.

Such a convergence implies clear questioning not only of the features of that practice but of the causes of the convergence. How to explain that institutions and regimes which have so distinct characteristics lead to a converging result? Common result, common stimuli? Do the causes of that converging strengthening of the executive power have a common origin? The analysis of those probable causes leads one to consider not only the evolution of the executive power but more broadly the evolution of the State and its missions,

7 France, The United Kingdom, Belgium, Italy, Spain, Portugal, the Netherlands, Greece, Hungary, Poland, Lithuania, Romania, Germany, Switzerland, Denmark, Nordic Countries (Sweden, Finland, Norway), the European Union.

8 L. Popravka, 'Le volontarisme du Parlement européen en matière d'État de droit', *Revue de l'Union européenne* 4, no. 657 (2022): p. 249; J. Heurtaux, 'Les révolutions conservatrices en Europe centrale. L'illusion d'une nouvelle "fin de l'histoire"?', *Revue de l'Union européenne* 4, no. 657 (2022): p. 215; R. Mehdi, 'Heurs et malheurs de l'État de droit, l'Union européenne au défi d'une crise essentielle', *Revue de l'Union européenne* 4, no. 657 (2022): pp. 240 ff.

9 F. Bouhon, A. Jousten, X. Miny, and E. Slautsky, 'L'État belge face à la pandémie de COVID-19: esquisse d'un régime d'exception', *Courrier hebdomadaire du CRISP* 1, no. 2446 (2020): p. 5.

since it implies 'the analysis of the correlation between the transformations of the State and the corresponding evolution of democracy'.[10] Indeed, questioning the Welfare State entails a 'crisis of governability'[11] which constitutes the framework of the strengthening of the executive power. Beyond the circumstantial causes – the financial, political, security and health crises – which support the natural practice of a reinforced Executive which is very often considered to be excessive (I), the strengthening of the executive power in Europe questions the evolution of the democratic State itself, beyond the Executive (II).

The existence of a converging strengthening of the executive power in Europe which is reinforced by a context of permanent crises

In Europe, the executive power is characterised by those trends. They are, most of the time, the tendencies of political practices, of political powers, but they are also institutional trends. Though the techniques are not necessarily identical since they belong to a particular constitutional and institutional culture, their implementation objectives are convergent.[12] Despite those variations, the strengthening is happening in all these States. Such a practice seems unavoidable and structurally related to today's executive power. It remains to be seen whether the symptoms of the strengthening of the Executive are realised in the same way depending on the States and if there is a convergence there too. Indeed, the issue of the existence of a European convergence may be understood at two levels, i.e., the convergence of the strengthening (A) and the convergence of a common form of strengthening (B).

The natural tendency of the Executive to reinforcement as the first cause of the European convergence

In European democracies, the executive power is not characterised by its form. That is shown by the mapping of the structure of the European executive branches, which reveals that there is no link between the strengthening of the latter and their structure. The European States – in a geographical sense – which are mainly parliamentarian ones, adapt the principles of the collaboration of powers to their constitutional history and culture but very often in

10 J.-F. Thuot, 'Déclin de l'État et formes postmodernes de la démocratie', *Revue québécoise de science politique*, no. 26 (Autumn 1994): p. 75.

11 J.-F. Thuot, 'Déclin de l'État et formes postmodernes de la démocratie', p. 91.

12 In that sense, see all the articles on the States considered in this ambitious general reflection on the executive power in Europe supervised by Prs. M. Morabito and G. Tusseau.

favour of a presidentialist variant.[13] It is possible to identify several patterns – admittedly exaggerated ones – of the executive structure.

- The hierarchical two-headed Executive with the primacy of the Prime Minister is the most common case, despite variations in the way it is implemented;
- The two-headed diarchical Executive with the primacy of the President of the Republic or the King, as was the case in France until the 'presidentialising' of the regime was formalised;
- The collegial Executive characterised by Switzerland, which is quite noteworthy due to its rarity and functioning.

As a matter of principle, 'One always governs too much – or at least, one should always suspect that one governs too much'.[14] The criticism of an excess of government[15] must accompany governmentality.[16] Some consider that that strengthening is justified mainly by 'the idea of good governance'.[17] Government problems are natural since there are 'more respectable alternative solutions in a democracy. . . . Government problems will be at the very heart of democracy'.[18] In addition to this idea there are circumstances that foster the development of what was only a tendency at the beginning. The Executive, which manages the exceptional and the unforeseeable,[19] thus encounters circumstances which favour the reinforcement of its role among the imbalanced balance of powers and in all the considered States. The financial, security and health crises offer an explanation of the reinforcement of the executive power in the European States.

The financial crisis is a regular crisis of today's strengthening of the Executive. However, the last financial crises (2005, 2008, etc. until the current economic crisis that is due to the health crisis) have established a new stage in the formalisation of that reinforcement. The government, being shaken by the

13 Rather than the expression 'semi-presidential regime', we prefer that of 'parliamentarianism with presidential appropriation' of A. le Divellec, 'Vers la fin du 'parlementarisme négatif' à la française?', *Jus Politicum*, no. 6 (December 2011), https://juspoliticum.com/article/Vers-la-fin-du-parlementarisme-negatif-a-la-francaise-439.html.

14 M. Foucault, *Naissance de la biopolitique. Cours a Collège de France (1979–1989)* (1979; reis. Paris: Seuil, 2004), p. 324.

15 M. Foucault, *Naissance de la biopolitique*, p. 324. Foucault defines criticism as 'an attitude, a gesture consisting in siding with the ruled and opposing the forms of government, an art of not being really governed'.

16 M. Foucault, 'Qu'est-ce que la critique? Critique et Aufklärung', *Bulletin de la Société française de philosophie*, 84ème année, no. 2 (April–June 1990): p. 324.

17 P. Kruzslicz, 'Hungary', in *Comparative Executive Power in Europe: Perspectives on Accountability from Law, History and Political Science*, eds. M. Morabito and G. Tusseau (Oxfordshire: Routledge, 2023), p. 6.

18 F. Zakaria, 'De la démocratie illibérale', *Revue Le Débat* 2, no. 99 (1998): p. 26.

19 H. C. Mansfield, 'Gouvernement représentatif et pouvoir exécutif', p. 664.

events and the international scope of the crises, is being called upon despite the progressive disappearance of classic public action.[20] The management of financial crises becomes permanent. . . . The crisis becomes an expected situation, and the government revises its role and place in the economic sphere. Once again, the executive power[21] adapts to the situation and its development is justified[22] as it favours regulation in particular.[23]

The health crisis originating in a climate of insecurity because of the risk of terror attacks is also a cause of this reinforcement. A terror attack triggers a security crisis due to the risk it constitutes and very often an institutional crisis because of the reactions it entails. Indeed, the management of risk and its consequences, through the implementation of emergency state regimes, allow the Executive to concentrate an exceptional capacity for action. The characteristic of contemporary terrorism lies in its global dimension. Its impact on the institutions and more precisely on democracy are all the stronger.[24] A terror attack linked to global terrorism aims to 'force the people to submit in order for it to renounce its freedoms on its own and throw itself into the arms of the power'.[25] It inflicts on democracies a damage that is 'particular because of the link between the power and the people which is at the foundation of those regimes',[26] regardless of the regime. In a social climate that is weighed down by terror attacks, the security imperative prevails over all the others. The balance between the principle of freedom, which is the quintessence of democracies, and the security imperative tips towards the limitation of freedoms.[27] The issue behind the non-counterbalanced concentration of the capacity of action in the hands of the Executive, which is not accountable to the holder of the sovereign power, lies in the excess of government which may change democracy into an authoritarian regime. This is the first concern. The primary balance between security and freedom at the foundation of the role of the State is

20 For a development of that idea, see J.-H. Lorenzi, ed., *Qui capture l'État?* (Paris: PUF, 2012), notably the following chapters: J.-P. Pollin, 'L'État dépossédé', pp. 11–18; D. Thesmar, 'Réinventer l'action publique', pp. 81–85; and B. Jacquillat, 'Faut-il renforcer l'État-providence?', pp. 87–89.

21 E. Kopsidi, 'Le renforcement du pouvoir exécutif sous l'effet des crises financières. Les exemples américain, argentin et grec', *RFDC* 4, no. 104 (2015): pp. 823–838.

22 Présidence de la République Française, *Rapport sur la crise financière – Mission confiée par le Président de la République dans le contexte de la Présidence française de l'Union européenne 2008*, by R. Ricol, September 2008, https://sif.wp.imtbs-tsp.eu/files/2017/06/rapport-Pour-Pdt-FRANCE_2008-Crise-Financiere.pdf

23 S. Hamdouni, 'La crise financière et l'État de droit. Quelles évolutions au regard du dispositif des sommets du groupe des vingt pays industrialisés et émergents, le G20', *Revue Études internationales* 41, no. 2 (2010): pp. 205–231.

24 M. Buhot de Launay, 'Terrorisme et Démocratie', *Revue Commentaire* 1, no. 33 (1986): pp. 170–172.

25 M. Buhot de Launay, 'Terrorisme et Démocratie', p. 155.

26 A. Grapon and M. Rosenfeld, *Démocraties sous stress. Les défis du terrorisme global* (Paris: PUF, 2016), p. 155.

27 A. Grapon and M. Rosenfeld, *Démocraties sous stress*, p. 177.

compromised. The State is again in the spotlight against its will and the Executive becomes the leader of immediate action.[28] Thus the increase of the role of the State in front of the security challenge

> leads to a shift in the balance of powers: it results in the reinforcement of the weight of the Executive – which is the only one that is capable of assessing the importance of the threats and of conceiving a consistent strategy to face them; and in the correlated weakening of Parliament.[29]

The corollary of the reinforcement to the advantage of the Executive is an ambiguous taking on of responsibility[30] based on the obligation of security that is owed to the people.

The specificity of the current global health crisis must be viewed within the ongoing use of reinforced executive powers that is considered as excessive, on the condition that the progressive institutionalisation of such a practice be the best way to make that state of affairs durable. The institutional crisis that results from it leads to violent practice, especially towards the legislative power, for it is legitimised by concerted action both at the national and international levels.

Indeed, the relations between the States and international organisations – the World Health Organisation (WHO), in particular – have benefited the national Executives. The fundamental texts of States provide for the calling upon the fast and efficient action of a leading Executive, which holds more or less limited crisis powers. However, the deep health crisis has made it possible to overcome that foreseeable framework and move on to high-performance governance practices to the disadvantage of the Legislative. Far from being an exception, the health crisis has allowed the States to adapt their legislations to compensate for the shortcomings of the applicable texts. However, as the European Council notes, 'such special measures have been taken even when dedicated legal arrangements and coordination mechanisms existed to deal for instance with public health crisis situations'.[31] The relevance of the political

28 After all, 'security is at the very core of the institution of the State: The primary function of the State is to preserve the existence of the social body by imposing a collective order and to ensure the protection of persons and goods against any threat'. J. Chevallier, 'L'État de droit au défi de l'État sécuritaire', *in Le droit malgré tout: Hommage à François Ost* (Brussels: Presses de l'Université Saint-Louis, 2018), p. 306.

29 J. Chevallier, 'L'État de droit au défi de l'État sécuritaire', p. 306.

30 H. Qazbir, 'Le fondement du régime d'indemnisation par l'État des victimes d'actes terroristes: entre responsabilité administrative et garantie sociale?', *Annuaire du Droit* (2018): pp. 187–210.

31 Conseil de l'Europe, *Rapport sur la gouvernance démocratique et COVID-19*, December 2020, p. 11, https://rm.coe.int/cddg-2020-20f-final-rapport-sur-la-gouvernance-democratique-et-covid-1/1680a0beec

decision could lead to people being held politically responsible once the crisis has ended or is at least mastered. According to the Council of Europe, though the sanitary emergency measures justify the granting of exceptional powers to the Executive, there remains that they are conditional upon 'the respect of the principles of legality, necessity, proportionality and limited duration'.[32] Parliamentary check is one of the necessary conditions for the legitimate and democratic strengthening of the Executive. Thus, the Council recommends that 'parliaments would receive from the executive an account of measures taken as well as information on the evolution of the situation, in order to extend as necessary the applicability of special measures'.[33] Moreover, the increased role of the WHO in particular in the management of that pandemic[34] has put into perspective its relation with the members of the international community. The relations between the international organisation and the executive powers of countries of the whole world once again show that in the case of a crisis the Executive has a special role.[35] In addition, the Venice Commission remains vigilant on the issue of the balance between regulation and the guarantees of the rule of law provided for in its Member States.[36] Thus, the efforts of international and regional organisations to question and warn the States support the idea of a natural tendency of the Executives to strengthen their powers, in particular in times of crisis.[37] Their interventions however also reinforce that natural tendency as they push parliaments into the background. The example of the institutional structure of the EU also copies the national institutional structures with their failings, especially their shortcomings in terms of responsibility.[38]

A convergence of those States towards identical features emerges, i.e., it is necessary to look for alternatives to the mechanisms of the classic political responsibility which the considered Executives mostly escape. Indeed, the strongest symptom of the reinforcement of the Executive is the weakening of the political responsibility of the Executive.

32 Conseil de l'Europe, *Rapport sur la gouvernance démocratique et COVID-19*, p. 11.

33 Conseil de l'Europe, *Rapport sur la gouvernance démocratique et COVID-19*, p. 11.

34 F. Dabis, 'L'organisation mondiale de la santé (OMS) à l'ère de la pandémie de Covid-19', *Hérodote: Revue de géographie et de géopolitique*, 4ème trimestre, no. 183 (2021): p. 19.

35 H. Qazbir, 'L'OMS et les exécutifs nationaux dans la gestion de la crise sanitaire', in *Actes du colloque de l'OPEE* (Bordeaux: Université de Bordeaux, forthcoming).

36 Commission européenne pour la démocratie par le droit (Commission de Venise), *Rapport intérimaire sur les mesures prises dans les États membres de l'UE à la suite de la crise de la COVID-19 et leur impact sur la démocratie, l'État de droit et les droits fondamentaux*, 8 October 2020, www.venice.coe.int/webforms/documents/default.aspx?pdffile=CDL-AD(2020)018-f

37 J. Chevallier, 'L'État à l'épreuve du coronavirus', *Pouvoirs* 2, no. 177 (2021): pp. 109–120, notably p. 112.

38 J. Ziller, 'Political Accountability and Role Splitting of the Executive in EU Member States', in this volume, *Regional Accountability and Executive Power in Europe*, eds. M. Morabito and G. Tusseau (Oxfordshire: Routledge, forthcoming), p. 1.

Different reactions in front of the reinforcement of the Executive: the alternatives to classic political responsibility

There is a special difficulty in the implementation of the classic mechanisms of political responsibility of the parliamentary regime – that of attribution. Indeed, the analysis of the European political systems reveals that the exercise of power is complex. Such complexity exists between the executive and legislative powers, as in Belgium.[39] The federalist feature of Belgium has led to an evolution of the multi-level parliamentarianism: 'next to the federal parliamentary regime, there are regional and community parliamentary regimes'.[40] In addition to that multi-level parliamentarianism there are transfers of competences from one level to another, the inflexible sharing of exclusive competence and 'institutional asymmetries'.[41] That specificity results in 'malfunctions clouded by a dilution of responsibilities'.[42]

The difficulty in attributing political responsibility also exists within some executive branches, between politicians and representatives of the administration or agency responsible for the execution of texts. The evolution mentioned in this analysis leads one to note that the government is no longer defined as 'the supreme body of the public Administration but as he general body of the Executive'.[43] That definition applies in most of the European cases in which the Prime Minister and their government either are the Executive (Switzerland) or dominate the other component (president or monarch). Whether or not there is a hierarchical subordinate conditions the attribution of the responsibility of legal acts. The French case of an administration which is the essential tool of the government is not problematic, since it applies the texts in accordance with the indications of the government and ministries. In Sweden,[44] on the contrary, the government being the Executive in the system does not benefit from a hierarchised administration working under its orders. That has unavoidable consequences on the attribution of traditional political responsibility. In the same way, the Scandinavian cases (Sweden, Norway and Denmark) have a specific feature which has an impact on the attribution of political responsibility. The existence of 'negative parliamentarianism'[45] strongly influences the

39 Y. Lejeune, *Droit constitutionnel belge: fondements et institutions* (Brussels: Larcier, 2021); C. Behrendt, *Principes de droit constitutionnel belge* (Brussels: La Charte, 2021).

40 M. Verdussen, 'Belgium', in *Comparative Executive Power in Europe: Perspectives on Accountability from Law, History and Political Science*, eds. M. Morabito and G. Tusseau (Oxfordshire: Routledge, 2023).

41 M. Verdussen, 'Belgium'.

42 M. Verdussen, 'Belgium'.

43 P. Kruzslicz, 'Hungary', p. 7.

44 For a complete presentation of the Swedish political system, see E. Smith, 'Scandinavia', in *Comparative Executive Power in Europe: Perspectives on Accountability from Law, History and Political Science*, eds. M. Morabito and G. Tusseau (Oxfordshire: Routledge, 2023).

45 That is, 'In such a system, the Government has the possibility to remain in power provided the majority in Parliament does not force them by tabling a motion of no confidence.

issue of attribution. Who must be held politically responsible for the political decision? Those who have the executive power and who compromise with the oppositions of the parliamentary majority which tolerates them, or the majority in parliament which has not opposed the bill in question when it could have done so? The triggering of parliamentary mechanisms is affected – in particular the motion of censure.

That vagueness contributes to the Executive's capacity to reinforce itself since it favours an imbalance between power and traditional responsibility, even though whether other types of applicable responsibility in those countries are enough remains to be seen. Indeed, the evolution of the parliamentary mechanisms for holding the Executive politically accountable is illustrated today by the assertion that 'political responsibility does not necessarily result in a sanction'.[46] Thus, to try and counterbalance the assertion of a prevailing position of the executive power over the political institutions, the States, as their political systems evolve, develop alternatives to political responsibility especially through the strengthening of different counter-powers. In the end, the issue is whether the domination of the Executive is unavoidable when that power is being reinforced.[47] The enlightening European examples on that issue show either that it is (France) or that it is not (Switzerland).

The French constitutional culture in particular as to the role of the Head of State is a European specificity. The practice of what Marcel Morabito calls 'presidential hypertrophy'[48] has increased over time. The President of the Republic is 'the embodiment of the State power, . . . and since no useful model can be found in the republican precedents, the President of the Fifth Republic revives the autocratic legacy'.[49] In France,[50] the almost non-existence of a political responsibility of the Head of the Executive – the President of the Republic – strongly partakes in the reinforcement of the executive power which is shared between the president and the government that is composed of the Prime Minister and the ministers. In front of that Executive, the parliament has only little capacity to act or to hold it responsible. There is also the assertion in the French political culture of a 'negative parliamentarianism' which leads the holders of the executive power to consider that the 'the

The condition is however that the Government itself does not resign due to internal tensions or the death or other unavailability of the Prime Minister, or simply because general elections lead to a change in the Parliament such as to open the possibility for a government supported by another political constellation' (E. Smith, 'Scandinavia').

46 M. Verdussen, 'Belgium'.

47 In that sense see Foucault's developments on the internal and external limits of the government reason.

48 M. Morabito, *Le chef de l'État en France* (Paris: LGDJ, 1996), p. 151.

49 M. Morabito, *Le chef de l'État en France*, pp. 150 ff.

50 See C. Geynet-Dussauze and P. Jensel-Monge, 'France', in *Comparative Executive Power in Europe: Perspectives on Accountability from Law, History and Political Science*, eds. M. Morabito and G. Tusseau (Oxfordshire: Routledge, 2023).

interventions of the majority MPs' are 'illegitimate'.[51] Thus, the evolution of the institutions and the practice of power result, in the case of France, in 'a criminalisation of responsibility',[52] and in 'a shift from political to criminal liability'.[53] Such an evolution of the nature of the Executive's responsibility first concerned the members of the government before it was considered and progressively applied to the President of the Republic, who is the real holder of the executive power under the Fifth Republic. It is a compensation for the non-existence in practice of the political responsibility of the holder of the authority. However, while France has chosen to criminalise responsibility, Germany or even Belgium have chosen the judicialisation of responsibility via claims against acts. In Belgium,[54] federated communities may file for annulment before the Constitutional Court without their interest being required, but not the citizen. Criminalisation or penalisation, on the contrary, most often does not result in anything and never interests the media. In fact, there is no legal basis allowing the complaint.

The Swiss case shows that holding the Executive (the Federal Council) politically responsible is not necessary to the good operation of the democratic institutions. The issue of the responsibility of the Executive within the framework of the use of the referendum is not set in the same terms as in France. De Gaulle left a burden on his successors who would like to use national referendums. In Switzerland, on the contrary, 'using direct democracy is . . . amply played down', for the initiative does not come within the competency of the Executive. This consequently cancels any 'plebiscitary dimension'[55] from that referendum responsibility. The influence of the forms of regimes and constitutional culture of the States on the political responsibility of the Executive therefore seems to be fundamental. Though Switzerland may have been called a 'directorial'[56] regime, it is above all characterised by the existence and use of processes of direct democracy. Their use contradicts

51 E. Lemaire, 'Carence du contrôle parlementaire et contrôle politique par les experts. A propos de la mission d'évaluation de l'exécutif sur la gestion de la crise due au Covid-19', *Jus Politicum Blog*, 9 November 2021, https://blog.juspoliticum.com/2021/11/09/carence-du-controle-parlementaire-et-controle-politique-par-les-experts-a-propos-de-la-mission-devaluation-de-lexecutif-sur-la-gestion-de-la-crise-due-au-covid-19-par-elina-lemai/

52 C. Geynet-Dussauze and P. Jensel-Monge, 'France'.

53 O. Beaud, 'Le glissement d'une responsabilité politique vers une responsabilité pénale des ministres: regard critique sur un certain exceptionnalisme français, révélé par le cas de l'épidémie du coronavirus', *Revue de droit d'Assas*, no. 21 (June 2021): p. 151.

54 M. Verdussen, 'Belgium'.

55 T. Tanquerel, 'Switzerland', in *Comparative Executive Power in Europe: Perspectives on Accountability from Law, History and Political Science*, eds. M. Morabito and G. Tusseau (Oxfordshire: Routledge, 2023), p. 5.

56 'That is quite different from the 'assembly regime' that some foreign observers thought they had read in the Swiss Constitution' (M.-A. Cohendet, *Droit constitutionnel*, 5ème éd. (Paris: LGDJ, 2011), p. 458). 'The Swiss regime, once again, is different from classic parliamentary

the classic systematisation between power and responsibility in a law-abiding State. In other words, the constitutional culture of that State, the regime of which is close to a presidential one,[57] raises questions about the systematic link between power and accountability to parliamentary assemblies in relation to the stability of institutions. The necessity of being able to hold the Executive politically responsible has 'receded into the background while government stability has become an asset'.[58] The direct democracy processes – referendum and popular initiative – are threatening enough for the Federal Council to take into account the possible resistances to those bills beforehand. The famous 'Swiss consensus' in action. . . . Moreover, the health crisis has made it necessary, as in all the States, to implement exceptional measures. Switzerland has not avoided that institutionalised form of the reinforcement of the executive power in a period of crisis, since the state of emergency was put in place in March 2020. However, unlike France, it received the support of a majority of the population – 63 percent in April 2020 – for the implementation of the governmental policy for the management of the health crisis.[59] Such a popular counterbalance seems to exist only in Switzerland due to a constitutional culture where direct democracy is especially strong. In a recent article, Dominique Rousseau has pleaded for and suggested specific institutional changes to put an end to the institutional imbalance due to the reinforcement of the executive power. Among his proposals, 'the right to decide a referendum'[60] features prominently.

The reading of the analysis of the European States taken into consideration in that study raises questions. Though the strengthening of the European executive powers is visible, the different deductions depending on the situations seem to show a diversity of cases. Such diversity exists of course, and it is expressed in the marks of the reinforcement as well as the channellings/limitations/counterweights of that reinforcement. It is nonetheless harmonised through a common result: the domination of the Executive in the studied political systems. Pondering on the existence of a common origin is not a big step to take.

---

regimes: Government and Parliament are clearly separated' (T. Tanquerel, 'Switzerland', p. 13).

57 T. Tanquerel, 'Switzerland', p. 17: 'Swiss constitutional law has created a very original form of government, borrowing many features from the presidential regime, with two main exceptions – the strictly collegial character of the Executive and its election for a fixed term by the Parliament'.

58 T. Tanquerel, 'Switzerland', p. 17.

59 A. Robinet-Borgomano, 'Les États face au coronavirus – La Suisse et le principe de responsabilité', *Institut Montaigne Blog*, 14 May 2020, www.institutmontaigne.org/blog/les-etats-face-au-coronavirus-la-suisse-et-le-principe-responsabilite

60 D. Rousseau, 'Avec la Constitution comme seul témoin', *Le Journal du Dimanche*, 7 Novembre 2021.

A convergence of the reinforcement of the Executive resulting from the deep evolution of the State

Beyond circumstantial causes, the source of that legal-political phenomenon is to be found in the evolution of the framework within which that reinforcement is expressed – the State. The link between the evolution of liberalism,[61] neoliberalism and the 'excess of government'[62] – without forgetting the consequences on the mission of the State[63] itself – is the structural source (A). This evolution has its own fate which also impacts democracy as it is known in Western Europe. It seems to support the more or less partial application of 'epistocracy', that is, the choice made by some States of asserting the choice of illiberalism (B).[64]

A structural cause explaining the convergence of the phenomenon: the transformation of the role of the State

In Western Europe, the 'peoples follow the same path, but they do it at their own pace'.[65] The reinforcement of the power of the Executive is therefore an unavoidable phenomenon in the evolution of European liberal democracies. Convergence is a consequence of this irresistible evolution. Thinking of a European convergence makes one wonder about 'the correlation between the transformations of the State and the corresponding evolution of democracy'.[66] Here, there are apparently two tendencies in the observation of the evolution of the political regimes in Western Europe – the need for efficiency and the tendency to the personification of power. Those two elements are 'the main reasons for the tendency of the Executive in democratic States'[67] and thus the common point among the considered States – except Switzerland – in the excessive reinforcement of the executive power. In the Swiss political system, however, 'the efficiency requirement is a constitutional principle at the federal level as well as in some cantons'.[68] That syndrome of the evolution of liberalism also extends within the mission of the State[69] and transforms it into

61 Liberalism is to be understood here 'in its broadest meaning of doctrine founded on the denunciation of the too active role of the State and the valuation of the regulating virtues of the market' (P. Rosanvallon, *La crise de l'État-providence* (Paris: Seuil, 1984), p. 59).

62 M. Foucault, *Naissance de la biopolitique*, p. 326.

63 B. Nabli, 'Les finalités de l'action de l'État', in *L'État. Droit et Politique* (Paris: Armand Colin, 2017), pp. 124–150.

64 'Democratically elected regimes regularly ignore the limits that the Constitution imposes on their powers and deprive their citizens of fundamental rights' (F. Zakaria, 'De la démocratie illibérale', p. 17).

65 B. Chantebout, *Droit constitutionnel* (Paris: Dalloz (Université Sirey), 2009), p. 285.

66 J.-F. Thuot, 'Déclin de l'État et formes postmodernes de la démocratie', p. 75.

67 B. Chantebout, *Droit constitutionnel*, p. 285.

68 A. Flückiger, 'L'essor des actes étatiques incitateurs' *LeGes* 12 (2001): p. 48.

69 For an analysis of the mission of the 'modern' State, see P. Leroy-Beaulieu, *L'État moderne et ses fonctions* (Paris: Guillaume et Cie, 1900), notably pp. 2 ff.

a disruptive State or even a reflexive one. The change from the Welfare State to the propulsive one[70] then to the reflexive one is realised and observed in the evolution of the executive power. A requirement of efficiency insinuates itself in the functions of the State to the point that it influences all its actions. That concept belongs to an apprehension which is neo-modern and not post-modern since, for the supporters of that theory, we are witnessing a 'decisive phase of mutation, but more than its deconstruction it is its radicalisation or exacerbation'.[71] The State has been confronted with requirements which modify its very essence since the application of institutional liberalism. The propulsive State results from those requirements which are no longer satisfied with the fact that the State 'is the helm, it must also become the propeller'.[72]

The permanent reinforcement of the executive power entails the imbalance in favour of the political responsibility that is necessary to the democratic exercise of power. That has a deep impact on democracy which follows its evolution. Two assumptions seem to prevail and offer perspectives of evolution: the choice between an illiberal democracy and an 'epistocracy'.

'Epistocracy' and illiberalism as perspectives of evolution of the European democracy to face the democratic deficit of the reinforcement of the Executive

Expertise is regularly mentioned to justify a short circuit of decision-making as there is a real 'technical complexity of the public affairs to deal with'.[73] A government – the mission of which is no longer 'realising the general will'[74] but assuming the role of a political leader which is seldom accountable – becomes necessary. That idea of the complexity of public affairs sets the principle of calling upon the expert. They may be a political expert – the politician takes decisions without referring to the nation, or even to its parliamentary representatives because the complexity of the case and its emergency character require it. They may be a private expert – the politician who is overwhelmed by the technical nature of an issue calls upon groups of experts. The interest lies in offering the final political decision the legitimacy of expertise.

At first, the idea of resorting to an expert, especially in times of crisis, seems justified. The shock, the new situation, the absence of knowledge, etc., are factors which can result in taking wrong political decisions. Calling upon an

70 'Il convient maintenant, aux yeux des sages du jour et aux yeux de la foule, que l'État soit "propulsive"' (P. Leroy-Beaulieu, *L'État moderne et ses fonctions*, p. 17). See also, C.-A. Morand, ed., *L'État propulsif. Contribution à l'étude des instruments d'action de l'État* (Paris: Publisud, 1991).

71 J. Caillosse, 'Quand l'analyse des politiques publiques se déplace côté "droit"', *Revue Droit et Société*, no. 42/43 (1999): p. 511.

72 P. Leroy-Beaulieu, *L'État moderne et ses fonctions*, p. 17.

73 P. Kruzslicz, 'Hungary'.

74 P. Kruzslicz, 'Hungary'.

expert seems to be a form of humility of the leader in front of the situation, even though 'there could be no objective political decision in the scientific meaning of the word'.[75] Thus asking for the assistance of an expert shows 'an effort at rationality and a concern for output which are factors of management improvement'.[76] There are several difficulties here, however. First, though calling upon an expert is understandable, the fact that they are a private one is questionable. Public research structures are there to enlighten the State, its executive body, to take the 'good' political decision. However, those structures have been dismantled over the past few years[77] in order to favour resorting to private structures. The argument of the lack of public resources does not hold water anymore. The issues of the good spending of public money and that of the trust in research raise serious questions. More generally, the work of parliamentarians consists, as part of parliament's mission of assessment and legislative function, in producing reports analysing an issue falling under their jurisdiction to enlighten the Members of Parliament, the citizens and maybe the members of the government. The original principle of the flexible separation of powers remains that of collaboration. The behaviour of the executive power here devalues the crucial work of the legislative body.[78] Moreover, the Executive, beyond using private organisations on State-related issues, establishes the practice of calling upon specialised committees and counsel,[79] which are chaired by specialists, thus setting aside any debate with the parliament.

In France, the hyperactivity of the Defence Council[80] compared to an excluded parliament applies the principle of government efficiency to the detriment of that of democracy. That in-camera hyperactivity also benefits from classified defence to keep at bay any immediate parliamentary control – thus, the creation of the Scientific Council in March 2020 and of the Analysis Research and Expertise Committee (AREC) aimed at enlightening and helping the president to take the political decisions necessary to the management of the health crisis. It was a shift in the decision-making process.[81] Parliament,[82] which was excluded from normative creation, saw 'science being

75 J. Freund, *L'essence de la politique* (Paris: Éditions Sirey, 1965), p. 56.

76 J. Meynaud, *Technocratie: Mythe ou réalité?* (Paris: Payot, 1963), p. 10.

77 S. Blin, 'Un projet de loi contre l'avis de la recherche', *Libération*, 4 March 2020, www.liberation.fr/france/2020/03/04/un-projet-de-loi-contre-l-avis-de-la-recherche_1780608/

78 E. Lemaire, 'Carence du contrôle parlementaire et contrôle politique par les experts'.

79 T. Desmoulins, 'La formalisation du présidentialisme sous la Cinquième République: le Conseil de défense et de sécurité nationale', *Jus Politicum*, no. 25, pp. 221–255, http://juspoliticum.com/article/La-formalisation-du-presidentialisme-sous-la-Cinquieme-Republique-le-Conseil-de-defense-et-de-securite-nationale-1375.html

80 Ibid.

81 E. Lemaire, 'Carence du contrôle parlementaire et contrôle politique par les experts'.

82 See E. Cartier, B. Ridard, and G. Toulemonde, eds., *L'impact de la crise sanitaire sur le fonctionnement des parlements en Europe* (Paris: Publication de la Fondation Robert Schuman, 2020).

elevated to the rank of a normative source'.[83] In Italy, the disastrous health situation[84] challenged the exercise of parliamentary oversight. Apart from the health and economic issues, parliament could not discharge its duties, in particular that of supervision of the government's action. In a period of sanitary crisis and reinforcement of the powers of the Executive, that is more than unfortunate. Thus it was the current sanitary crisis which revealed that democratic difficulty since 'it cannot be correctly done since the committees hardly worked on other topics than the pandemic-related' sanitary and economic ones.[85] The *Pagano* Bill No 1834 suggests reintegrating the role of parliament within the framework of the supervision of government action in case of difficult times.[86] The Italian case and the reaction via the Pagano Bill[87] thus belong to an approach which is close to survival 'given the way the most democratic institution of our constitutional system has worked and is still working. This implies answering some questions about the role of parliamentary institutions during the pandemic'.[88]

Then, the opaqueness which surrounds the government's calling upon expert cabinets and private interest groups and above all the moment when the latter intervene introduces a form of suspicion as to the final decision. All the work of the past decades for more transparency,[89] especially to put an end to conflicts of interests, is being challenged. Moreover, and that is quite logical, the action of experts has had a more or less important impact on decision-making, without being submitted to any political accountability.[90]

Those issues lead to mentioning the concepts the increasing importance of which challenges the very evolution of democracy in Western Europe – technocracy[91] and even 'epistocracy'. Technocracy is characterised by 'the lack of democratic legitimacy of the power by highlighting, before the norms are created, the primacy of non-elected bodies over classic institutions which are representative of the political system'.[92] Technocracy is to be found in 'the cult for efficiency which shows the will to get a maximum of results for a minimum

83 A. Viala, 'L'épistocratie: proposition de définition', in *Demain, l'épistocratie?* ed. A. Viala (Paris: Mare & Martin, 2022), p. 23.

84 The same number of casualties as in 1944.

85 I. Ciolli and M. Luciani, 'Le Parlement italien dans la pandémie a eu du mal à maintenir sa centralité vis-à-vis du gouvernement et des régions', in *Le Parlement au temps du coronavirus: Italie* (Paris: Fondation Robert Schuman, 2020), p. 74.

86 I. Ciolli and M. Luciani, 'Le Parlement italien dans la pandémie'.

87 I. Ciolli and M. Luciani, 'Le Parlement italien dans la pandémie', p. 72.

88 I. Ciolli and M. Luciani, 'Le Parlement italien dans la pandémie', p. 72.

89 See all the laws adopted in France in favour of the transparency of political life.

90 On the issue of the role of the expert in decision-making compared to their accountability, see J. Meynaud, 'Les techniciens et le pouvoir', *Revue française de science politique*, 7e année, no. 1 (1957): pp. 5–37, notably pp. 7 ff.

91 See J. Rivero, 'La technocratie: mythe, épouvantail ou panacée?', *Annales de l'Université de Poitiers*, no. 3 (1962): pp. 3 ff.

92 A. Viala, 'L'épistocratie: proposition de définition', p. 17.

of effort'[93] and even in 'the granting of some power over collective affairs to the technician'.[94] That is the problem of the notion of technocracy – the legitimacy of the *technician* in decision-making in *collective affairs*. Then, the time for decision-making and the time for debate are elements that should be corrected. The role of the technician is to accelerate the democratic time. Such acceleration is to be found in the aforementioned emergency and also in the hyperactivity of the Executives. However, the idea of efficiency seems to be more a red herring than a real objective. The questionable aspect of technocracy is really there: efficiency is not its advantage, but 'the absence or insufficient control of operations by elected representatives'[95] is!

'Epistocracy' is different from technocracy in that in addition to what characterises technocracy, it is draped in knowledge and expertise – an 'instrument of the normative process'[96] – in order for 'that post-democratic system to make up for such a deficit in legitimacy'.[97] That Anglo-Saxon neologism refers to 'the idea of a power (cratos) exercised by those who have the scientific power (episteme)'.[98] Scientific knowledge is then presented as the truth resulting from the rationality that the political decision-making process is supposed to have. Epistocracy is linked to the reinforcement of the executive power. Epistocracy as 'post-political governance' is even one of its vehicles for it 'gives the executive power some advantage over the legislative power which embodies, through the parliamentary deliberation and partisan balance of power that are characteristic of it, the old political world'.[99] That is why epistocracy is not only a simple variant of a democratic regime but a distinct political regime. Democracy and epistocracy are even opposed since the former is founded on *opinion* while the latter fights against the opinion via knowledge.[100] In its most absolute form, it may even be called a 'form of anti-democratic elitism'.[101] On the contrary, its application is never complete, either in the texts or in practice since no matter the considered State, there are elections and no foundational text establishes an epistocratic regime.

There are many differences among States, even though they are measured more in the intensity of the reinforcement of the executive power or the existence, or not, of counterbalancing mechanisms. The cases of Hungary and Poland show that beyond a favourable situation and factors of increase of the

93 J. Meynaud, *Technocratie: Mythe ou réalité?* p. 8.
94 J. Meynaud, *Technocratie: Mythe ou réalité?* p. 8.
95 J. Meynaud, *Technocratie: Mythe ou réalité?* p. 10.
96 A. Viala, 'L'épistocratie: proposition de définition', p. 18.
97 A. Viala, 'L'épistocratie: proposition de définition', p. 17.
98 A. Viala, 'L'épistocratie: proposition de définition', p. 20.
99 A. Viala, 'L'épistocratie: proposition de définition', p. 23.
100 'In absolute terms, epistocracy is a form of intellectual aristocracy and it opposes the concept of democracy for its excludes the necessity to resort to the people to pass laws' (A. Viala, 'L'épistocratie: proposition de définition', p. 20).
101 A. Viala, 'L'épistocratie: proposition de définition', p. 20.

Executive's capacity for action, the national context and the constitutional and historical culture more or less intensify that legal-political situation. The radical nature of the evolution of the relations between the executive and legislative powers is convincing. Indeed, the Hungarian evolution results in 'the Government [which] had been entrusted with the realisation of the general will now [has] its political role . . . consecrated in the constitutional text without new guarantees being developed to maintain the balance'.[102] In several European countries where the reinforcement of the executive power has occurred (Poland, Romania, Hungary), debates are referred to illiberalism. The theory of the 'illiberal' democracy justifying in particular the constraints of the constitutional mechanisms that limit the Executive is worrying.[103] It questions the principle of the separation of powers and differentiates constitutional liberalism from democracy. While the former 'is concerned with limiting powers', the latter 'is about its accumulation and use'.[104] The States which support that evolution of democracy thus give added value to a particular conception of democracy. It has the merit of justifying the reinforcement of the executive power, but that amounts to 'taking the necessity of a legitimate government for that of a powerful one'.[105]

Calling upon experts and the legitimacy of their words contributes to the devaluation of the work of parliament. Crises – and the current one especially – allow no longer for the reinforcement of the executive power and body, but for its normalisation and even in some States for its formalisation, its institutionalisation. Today, durable evolutions of Western European democracies are being confirmed. Whether the offered alternatives through the introduction of illiberalism and epistocracy are relevant choices remains to be seen. Time will tell if the choices that the considered States have made will create new democratic political regimes or other regimes.

102 P. Kruzslicz, 'Hungary', p. 7.

103 L. Jaume and F. Hourquebie, '"Démocratie illibérale": une nouvelle notion?', *Constitutions: Revue de droit constitutionnel appliqué*, no. 6 (2019): p. 177; G. Grasso, 'Démocratie (libérale) contre démocratie non libérale: le cas des partis politiques européens et du respect des valeurs sur lesquelles se fonde l'Union européenne', *Constitutions*, no. 4 (2018): p. 479; N. Baverez, 'Les démocratures contre la démocratie', *Pouvoirs* 2, no. 169 (2019): pp. 5–17; T. Chopin, '*Démocratie illibérale*' *ou* '*autoritarisme majoritaire*'? *Contribution à l'analyse des populismes en Europe* (Paris: Institut Jacques Delors, 2019); O. A. Macovei, 'L'Etat illibéral dans l'Union européenne, essai de conceptualisation', *Civitas Europa* 1, no. 40 *(2018): pp. 127–144; F. Zakaria, 'De la démocratie illibérale', pp.* 17–26.

104 F. Zakaria, 'De la démocratie illibérale', p. 21.

105 F. Zakaria, 'De la démocratie illibérale', p. 21.

13 Responsibility, accountability and legitimacy of Executives

What role for the people?

Audrey Bachert-Peretti

Though the term 'democracy' has many definitions, it can simply be understood as a regime in which the people control its destiny.[1] Since pure democracy, in which the citizens convene together to decide all public matters, is not prevalent in our contemporary era – not to mention the question of its possibility – the democratic character of political regimes can be assessed regarding to what extent the people is able to have a say in the public decision-making process. This ability can be achieved through two main categories of mechanisms: those that allow the citizens to choose their leaders regularly and those that enable them to influence their decisions. It is not to deny that the term 'people' can be quite evasive,[2] however it will be understood here as the community of individuals holding political rights, that is to say, the electoral body or the citizenry. Therefore, it will be assumed that the more citizens intervene and the more efficient their intervention is, the more democratic the system will be.

For decades now, it has been commonplace to underline that the Executive has become the dominant governing force in our contemporary polities,[3] despite the difficulty to define precisely, on a theoretical level, the concept of 'Executive'.[4] Without further inquiry and for the sole purposes of this chapter, it may be understood as encompassing three main components beside their contingent labels and respective significance in various national settings: the

1 On democracy as autonomy, see H. Kelsen, *La démocratie. Sa nature. Sa valeur* (Paris: Recueil Sirey, 1932).

2 B. Daugeron, 'Les électeurs sont-ils le peuple? Peuple, citoyens, électeurs en droit constitutionnel: essai de distinction théorique', in *La Constitution, l'Europe et le droit. Mélanges en l'honneur de Jean-Claude Masclet*, ed. C. Boutayer (Paris: Publications de la Sorbonne, 2013), p. 163.

3 See, for example, P. Rosanvallon, *Le bon gouvernement* (Paris, Seuil, 2015); S. Rose-Ackerman, *Democracy and Executive Power* (New Haven: Yale University Press, 2021); N. Rousselier, *La force de gouverner. Le pouvoir exécutif en France, XIV-XXIe siècles* (Paris: Gallimard, 2015); A. Schelesinger, *The Imperial Presidency* (Boston: Mariner Books, 2004).

4 See, for example, H. Mansfield, *Taming the Prince* (New York: The Free Press, 1989); A. Vidal-Naquet and P. Jensel-Monge, *Du pouvoir exécutif au pouvoir gouvernant* (Paris: Marc & Martin, 2021).

DOI: 10.4324/9781003281559-25

Head of State; the government and its head; and the administrative services – which should not be neglected in our times of still-pervasive Welfare State, notwithstanding the criticisms they meet with in different national contexts. Because of their fundamental role in the modern State, the democratic quality of these Executives will have a direct impact on the democratic quality of our political systems.

One way to assess the democratic dimension of these Executives is to wonder how consequential the people can be in controlling their composition and decisions. To conduct this assessment, it is then possible to investigate the different moments in which citizens intervene during the Executive's life. When observing the institutional design and the ordinary functioning of countries involved in the REGALIEN project,[5] it can be noted that the people participate only in a limited fashion in the choice of the members of the Executive (I), while they have some devices to influence the decisions that are made, even if they are mostly partial and indirect (II). In this regard, the democratic dimension of our European representative systems is not non-existent but should not be overstated.

Selecting the Executive

While various devices can be used to select the Executive, direct popular elections are obviously the most significant ones from a democratic perspective. However, they are not flawless (A) and are far from being used to designate every Executive official (B).

The imperfect mechanism of elections

Popular elections ensure a form of democratic legitimacy of the elected officials. However, it should be underlined that they do not create strong constraints because of the prohibition of the imperative mandate.[6] While electoral promises are commonplace, they are not binding obligations for the elected rulers who can choose to set them aside. The link between the people's will[7] and the elected Executive is thus limited to choosing men and not measures,

5 M. Morabito, 'Introduction', in *Comparative Accountability of Executive Power in Europe*, eds. M. Morabito and G. Tusseau (Oxfordshire: Routledge, 2023).

6 On the pervasiveness of this prohibition in Europe, see the European Commission for Democracy through Law (Venice Commission), *Report on the Imperative Mandate and Similar Practices*, 16 June 2009, p. 15, www.venice.coe.int/webforms/documents/default.aspx?pdffile=CDL-AD(2009)027-e

7 The notion of 'people's will' or 'popular will' can be understood here quite plainly as the choices made by the citizenry and expressed through legal procedures, without equating it with the 'Rousseauist' concept of general will, which *stricto sensu* cannot be expressed through election but only through legislation.

to paraphrase Burke.[8] This implies a limited responsibility of the elected Executive towards the people in the sense that citizens, when they select decision-makers, are not firmly controlling the decisions that will be made.

This situation is reinforced by the fact that regularly held elections should be considered as imperfect mechanisms of responsibility.[9] Indeed, even if the dimension of *ex post* judgment of elections is often underlined,[10] this assertion should be qualified for several reasons. For sure, voters can sanction incumbent candidates for their past actions by refusing to re-elect them. However, the electoral process presents various limitations. Firstly, it is fragmented and heteronomous. It happens only occasionally; the electoral body is never the sole triggering force of the elections and incumbents can escape their responsibility by choosing not to run for the elections. Secondly, most of the time, it is not possible to sanction them by putting an end to their term of office in advance and more generally the electoral result cannot be explained solely by the will of the people to retrospectively sanction the incumbent; the motivations of voters are diverse and difficult to untangle from one another. Thus, the election cannot be considered as a mechanism to truly hold the Executive responsible, even if it is the main mechanism to ensure its legitimacy from a democratic point of view.

Regarding the responsibility issue, the difficulty can be alleviated if some mechanism allows to terminate the term of office in an anticipated manner, and to choose an alternative Executive that is more aligned with the people's preferences. Here, it should be underlined that this kind of mechanism, which can be encompassed under the general label of recall procedures, are not necessarily linked with the imperative mandate. They can perfectly be conceived in association with the principle of free mandate that informs our representative systems.[11] This will be the case if the procedures are triggered not because officials are not respecting some previously made promises, but only because the decisions are retrospectively considered as bad ones – so bad as to justify the official's dismissal. The more the citizens are controlling these procedures – depending on their ability to initiate them and to be their decisive voice – the greater the democratic character of the responsibility of the Executive and, as a way of consequence, of the system.

8 E. Burke, *The Works of the Right Honorable Edmund Burke*, vol. 1 (Boston: Little, Brown and Company, 1869), p. 531.

9 P. Segur, *La responsabilité politique* (Paris: PUF, 1998), p. 78.

10 P. Avril, 'Responsibility and Accountability', in *La responsabilité des gouvernants*, eds. O. Beaud and J.-M. Blanquer (Paris: Descartes & Cie, 1999), p. 85.

11 C.-É. Senac, 'La révocation populaire des élus. Anatomie d'une institution démocratique', in *Spicilegium Juris Politici, Mélanges Philippe Lauvaux*, ed. T. Pasquiet-Briand (Paris: Éditions Panthéon-Assas, 2021), p. 929.

The rarity of elections in the choosing of the executive team

On a practical level, it should be underlined that many members of the Executive in countries studied in the REGALIEN Project are not directly elected by the people. This is obviously the case for Heads of State in constitutional monarchies such as the United Kingdom or the Netherlands. There, no choice is given to the people and no popular dismissal is possible without a change of political regime amounting to a revolution. In other systems, where no hereditary principle applies, Heads of State can be elected directly by the people, as in France and Portugal. However, they are often elected indirectly, by Parliament itself or by an electoral college in which the Members of Parliament represent the majority. This latter option confers an indirect democratic legitimacy to Heads of State, whose powers can be more or less extended. Indeed, as the Members of Parliaments, or at least some of them, are elected by the people, their intervention in the selection process can be seen as a mediation of the popular will.

No direct popular dismissal of Heads of State is possible in countries studied in the REGALIEN Project, except in Romania where citizens can decide to terminate the mandate of the President in advance after Parliament has called for this kind of recall elections.[12] In other non-monarchical regimes, a dismissal is still possible, but with no popular intervention. However, even if these destitution processes are often understood as forms of criminal or constitutional responsibility, the political dimension of such procedures should not be underestimated, because of the open-textured provisions related to the nature of the relevant offences and the participation of elected political authorities in the proceedings. Here again, we may thus find some sort of mediated popular decision on this issue of deselecting Heads of State.

Parliaments play a major role in the selection of governments. Though this is a guiding principle of parliamentary regimes in which the government is the 'creature' of parliament exercising an 'elective function',[13] it is not specific to it. For example, the Swiss Federal Assembly is also competent to appoint the Federal Counsellors although Switzerland is a directorial regime.[14] Here again, the parliamentary selection of governments is supposed to create a link, at least an indirect one, between the rulers and the ruled, ensuring the former's democratic legitimacy. This link is even more significant when government members are also Members of the House directly chosen by the electoral body. But this is not a pervasive situation in Europe. The constitutions of Belgium and

12 The Constitution of Romania (1991), Article 95.

13 W. Bagehot, *The English Constitution*, 2nd ed. (1873; reis. Cambridge: Cambridge University Press, 2001).

14 T. Tanquerel, 'Switzerland', in *Comparative Executive Power in Europe: Perspectives on Accountability from Law, History and Political Science*, eds. M. Morabito and G. Tusseau (Oxfordshire: Routledge, 2023), p. 12.

France, for example, provide for the prohibition for members of the Executive to be members of the Parliament at the same time.[15] Nevertheless, the relations between governmental officials and the citizenry can be established thanks to the process of parliamentary selection. While this reinforces the place of the people in the selection of its rulers, it should nevertheless be noted that the original reason for this form of selection has more to do with the representative nature of our polities than with their democratic one. Indeed, it is only the extension of the franchise which happened in the 19th century which serves as the basis for the democratically legitimising force of parliamentary selection which had developed previously.[16]

Regarding the ability to put an anticipated end to the mandate granted to the government, citizens' direct intervention is non-existent in countries of the REGALIEN Project. No popular recall procedure can be used against the government as a whole or its individual members.[17] The closest mechanism seems to be the British procedure provided for in the *Recall of Members of Parliament Act 2015* that could theoretically be used against a member of the government who is also a member of the House of Commons. Nevertheless, the reasons that allow to trigger this revocation process are restrictive and its procedural features make the British recall only a limited democratising device of the British representative form of government.[18]

More traditionally, the possibility of repudiating the government is associated with the principles of parliamentary regime and especially its core principle of responsible government, which is grounded in the confidence the parliament must have in the government for the latter to be able to live on. The centrality of the principle of confidence fosters the democratic legitimacy and responsibility of the government of the day, as it makes it possible to dismiss it when the elected representatives of the people find it unsatisfying. In this regard, a democratised parliamentary regime can be theoretically considered to ensure a stronger form of democratic responsibility than its presidential counterpart, which mainly exists outside Europe. However, it should be noted that in these latter systems, forms of criminal or constitutional responsibility, such as the US impeachment, are not so different from the classic political responsibility associated with parliamentarism. Indeed, the same remarks as those already made in relation to the criminal/constitutional responsibility proceedings for Heads of State in countries of the REGALIEN Project can be made. The political dimension of these procedures should be

15 Constitution of the French Fifth Republic (1958), Article 23; Constitution of Belgium (1831), Article 50.

16 B. Manin, *Principes du gouvernement représentatif* (Paris: Flammarion, 2012).

17 In Europe, only two countries seem to authorise a popular dissolution of parliament, which could have an impact on the composition of the government: See the Constitution of Latvia (1922), Article 14; Constitution of Lichtenstein (1921), Article 48.

18 V. Barbé, 'La révocation populaire des parlementaires au Royaume-Uni', in *La révocation populaire des élus*, ed. C.-É. Senac (Paris: Mare & Martin, 2021), p. 243.

underlined because the misdeeds that can be sanctioned thereby are generally framed in strongly open-textured provisions, giving broad discretion to the authorities that are entitled to determine whether they are constituted or not, and because these authorities are generally political authorities whose partisan views are largely incorporated in the judgment they render.[19] In this regard, neither the specificity of parliamentary regimes nor the enhanced responsibility of parliamentary governments should be overstated. Unless the criminal responsibility of members of the Executive, be they a Head of State or a member of government, is aligned with the ordinary one applicable to any ordinary citizens – which is almost never the case – the political dimension of these proceedings should be recognised. As soon as Members of Parliament, who are mainly elected by the people, are the decisive force in the proceedings, a form of mediated popular influence on the question of the continuance of the mandate of the executive members can be recognised and, consequently, a form of democratic responsibility and legitimacy of the Executive as well.

However, the selection and deselection of members of the Executive by elected representatives, who are supposed to ensure an increasingly democratically legitimate and responsible Executive, because of its ability to mediate the popular will, is in practice limited by the logic of political partisanship. Indeed, the significance of the people's will can be weak when political parties are the true controlling players of the parliamentary game. This is especially true in coalition governments where the choice of ministers and the programme of the government will be determined by negotiations between the winning parties subsequent to the elections.[20] In this case, the relation to the electorate's choices is quite loose. While it is stronger in majoritarian systems, since the electoral results are more directly the cause of the selection of the governmental team, the partisan logic produces a practical weakness of the principle of political responsibility. It is only in situations of strong political crisis, such as the recent 'partygate' in the UK,[21] that the majority party will change its leadership in order to avoid setbacks at the next elections. This means that the people's will is not completely obviated. However, responsibility mechanisms will come into play only as safety valves, to ensure the preservation of the system in politically tricky contexts. Furthermore, their triggering rests upon an assessment of the current public opinion, potentially based on opinion polls, which is only a weak palliative for the lack of a stronger influence of the people.

19 R. Albert, 'The Fusion of Presidentialism and Parliamentarism', *American Journal of. Comparative Law* 57, no. 3 (Summer 2009): p. 531; J. Boudon, 'mauvais usage des spectres', *Revue française de droit constitutionnel* 2, no. 78 (2009): p. 247.

20 S. Ceccanti, S. Curreri, G. Passarelli, and G. Stegher, 'Italie', in *La démocratie exécutive*, ed. J.-P. Derosier (Paris: LexisNexis, 2023).

21 T. Helm, M. Townsend, and J. Tapper, '"Partygate": Johnson's Removal is Now Inevitable, Warns Loyalist', *The Guardian*, 5 February 2022, www.theguardian.com/politics/2022/feb/05/partygate-johnsons-removal-is-now-inevitable-warns-loyalist

Lastly, it should be noted that contemporary regimes have witnessed the development of large administrative bureaucracies. Theoretically, they are often considered to be the Executive's military wings, solely implementing decisions made at the political level. In this regard, a hierarchical principle ensures the democratic dimension of the decisions, since administrative agents respond to their political principal in a well-structured chain of command that conveys a chain of legitimacy and responsibility, the political principal being ultimately accountable for the decisions to the people. However, besides the limits of the democratic responsibility of the governments and Heads of States already mentioned, two further qualifications should be underlined. Firstly, the autonomy of administrative agents in very large administrative structures cannot be neglected, since it limits the reality of the idea of a tight chain of responsibilities. This is all the truer with the growing privatisation of public action. The web of public and private actors who are the actual decision-makers results in the responsibility being quite diffuse, if not completely dissolved because of the difficulty to attribute the decision to a clearly identified authority.[22] Secondly, modern States have also developed independent agencies, officially insulated from elected political actors. While their legitimacy is often considered to rest upon their expertise in the fields of their intervention, the question of their responsibility in a democratic society should not be overlooked.[23]

The ability of the people to check and constrain the composition of the Executive is thus limited by many institutional features and partisan considerations. On the one hand, though their legitimacy can be considered to flow from the consent of the people, which is expressed in the elections preceding their selection, this mechanism is not applicable to every executive function. On the other hand, existing procedures allowing to put an end to their mandate appear to be only a safety valve in our representative regimes. In this regard, while the people are not absent in the choice of the European Executives, their place is firmly circumscribed. This could be a very real democratic concern. While it could be alleviated if the people were able to have a grasp on the Executive's decisions, this is in fact the case only partially and indirectly, which limits the democratic character of our polities.

Controlling the Executive's decisions

The most significant way for the people to control the Executive's decisions is to be associated in their making. However, despite recent developments in deliberative democracy,[24] the ability of the people to take part in public decision-making is quite limited (A) and not without its own risks (B).

22 J. Ziller, 'Political Accountability and Role Splitting of the Executive in EU Member States', in this volume, *Regional Accountability and Executive Power in Europe*, eds. M. Morabito and G. Tusseau (Oxfordshire: Routledge, forthcoming).

23 A. Viala, ed., *Demain, l'épistocratie?* (Paris: Mare & Martin, 2022).

24 A. Bächtiger, J. Dryzek, J. Mansbridge, and M. Warren, eds., *The Oxford Handbook of Deliberative Democracy* (Oxford: Oxford University Press, 2018).

The scarcity of popular interventions

Direct popular intervention is far from being a pervasive phenomenon in our polities. The sole situation in which the whole citizenry can be involved is when some initiative and referendum proceedings exist. When such mechanisms do exist, this has a double consequence: it obviously fosters the ability of the people to choose some public decisions, but it also influences the way the Executive acts, rendering it more sensitive to popular preferences.[25] While this is famously the case in Switzerland, it is not a pervading situation in Europe where quite a strong form of defiance towards direct popular decision-making seems to be persistent. Besides initiatives and referenda, there is a growing interest in other procedures, such as participatory budgets, mini-publics and other forms of popular consultations. However, the degree of actual popular influence will vary depending on these proceedings; most of them are only consultative, if not only informative for the citizens, without giving them an actual say in the final decision. Outside formal procedures providing for direct popular intervention, liberal systems with strong freedom of speech, of the press and assembly allow for some kinds of informal popular interventions such as demonstrations and protests as well as wide public discussion and criticism of public decisions, which can sometimes be influential. The development of new technologies has obviously fostered these channels of popular expression. However, culture and traditions have a strong influence on the use of these tools, French people being for example more famous for their strikes than other nations, even if this could evolve.[26]

Eventually, whatever the degree of institutionalisation of popular participation, only a limited role is given to the whole citizenry in controlling the Executive's decisions. More generally, the people are associated in public decision-making only indirectly, by being represented or able to trigger horizontal, inter-institutional mechanisms of accountability and oversight.[27]

It is obviously through the actions of parliament, where the elected representatives of the people sit, that popular intervention is mostly mediated. It is for sure in the exercise of the legislative function that participation is the strongest. However, the various accountability and oversight mechanisms at the disposal of parliament, besides those enabling to dismiss executive members, should not be neglected. Though they are not about repudiating a dissatisfying Executive, they ensure the latter will publicly explain and justify its actions and even, sometimes, change them. Five types of such accountability mechanisms can be identified within parliamentary institutions:[28] the manifold

25 T. Tanquerel, 'Switzerland'.

26 See, for example, A. Bodry, 'Luxembourg', in *La démocratie exécutive*, ed. J.-P. Derosier (Paris: LexisNexis, 2023).

27 M. Dowdle, ed., *Public Accountability: Designs, Dilemmas and Experiences* (New York: Cambridge University Press, 2006).

28 For more details, see A. Bachert-Peretti, 'Le contrôle de la démocratie exécutive', in *La démocratie exécutive*, ed. J.-P. Derosier (Paris: LexisNexis, 2023).

reports the Executive is supposed to present to parliament, especially the ones regarding the budget; the diverse procedures of questions and interpellations; the inquiry committees and more generally the proceedings within parliamentary committees; the parliamentary guidelines for executive actions; and the procedures where parliament must approve the executive decisions for them to be enforced. Their intensity can thus vary from public information to actual constraint on the Executive's choices. To make its control more effective, parliament can rely on the works of other institutions such as ombudspersons and independent authorities which can provide useful information. These institutions also have autonomous oversight functions, either because they are to be consulted, and can thus influence decision-making procedures, or because they can deal with petitions and complaints by individuals or groups from the civil society. Eventually, judicial review and litigations are forceful accountability mechanisms. Their main purpose is to protect individuals from the injuries they can suffer because of public decisions, but they can sometimes be used efficiently to advance some public causes.

Considered in this light, the powerful Executive of the contemporary era is entangled in quite an impressive web of accountability mechanisms. Its power is not unchecked. It must quite often justify its decisions publicly. However, these devices only allow for a limited popular participation and, when they do so, they are not free from risks.

The risks of privatisation and partisan bias

Every time the citizens, or at least some of them, are able to influence public decisions, the risk that some individuals or groups can take advantage of this ability is not far away. The threat of the capture, and thus of the privatisation of public decision-making processes is a pervasive one. This seems to be a growing concern in Europe, as shown by the recent development of legislation to prevent conflicts of interests and regulate lobbying.[29] This risk of capture is present, whether there is an institutionalisation of popular participation or not. Firstly, some participatory processes are specifically centred on the interventions of some groups, such as trade unions, associations, NGOs and lobbies, this being especially the case in countries with a tradition of consociationalism such as the Netherlands.[30] Secondly, when initiatives and referenda exist, these procedures can be diverted from their original purpose of empowering the whole citizenry, since a sort of marketplace seems to be emerging with companies specialised in political activism[31] and mostly available to the

29 A. Bachert-Peretti, 'Le contrôle de la démocratie executive'.

30 L. Besselink, 'The Netherlands', in *Comparative Executive Power in Europe: Perspectives on Accountability from Law, History and Political Science*, eds. M. Morabito and G. Tusseau (Oxfordshire: Routledge, 2023).

31 J. J. Ruiz-Ruiz, 'Espagne', in *La démocratie exécutive*, ed. J.-P. Derosier (Paris: LexisNexis, 2023).

most powerful, well-organised and well-financed groups. Thirdly, mechanisms of individual or collective complaints and petitions before courts and independent authorities face the same dangers. Finally, in the non-institutionalised channels of popular expression, the risk of hearing mainly from the loudest voices, even if they are not necessarily the majority within the civil society, cannot be neglected.

Regarding the various mechanisms of horizontal accountability, the situation of parliament and other institutions which are supposed to be independent should be considered separately. On the one hand, the ability of parliament to be an effective controlling institution of the Executive's decisions is dependent upon the same considerations already mentioned in respect to its constraining capacity as to the composition of the Executive. Its effectiveness is conditioned by partisan considerations, the degree of consistency within the majority, the significance of prerogatives of individual Members of Parliament and the informal relations between members of the Executive and Members of Parliament. On the other hand, the ability of independent authorities to exercise their function of oversight depends upon their actual independence from the Executive. If they are composed of affiliates of the Executive, their supervisory power will in practice be only nominal and can even sometimes serve to advance the Executive's objectives.[32] As such, the risk of partisan bias, loosely understood to encompass the difficulties associated with political and non-political institutions, cannot be neglected.

At the end of this overview, the democratic deficit of our institutional settings should not be overlooked, despite the promise linked to the extension of the franchise in the 19th century. Here Rousseau's words seem to echo: 'The people of England regard themselves as free; but they are grossly mistaken; they are free only during the election of members of Parliament. As soon as they are elected, slavery overtakes it'.[33] As our current systems claim they are true, if not pure democracies, this deficit in the actual capacity of the people to have a say in public decisions, which is more and more acutely felt by the people, may be a cause of the growing popular defiance towards our institutions.

The popular intervention in public decision-making is quite circumscribed; only on rare occasions can the whole citizenry have a direct impact. It happens much more often that their representatives act in their name or that only some of them, as individuals or organised groups of the civil society, will be able to be influential. Both possibilities carry their own risk of distortion of the popular will. In this regard, the representative and liberal dimension of our institutional settings seems to remain more significant than their democratic one.

32 See, for example, G. Tusseau, 'Les juridictions constitutionnelles en contexte illibéral: la figure du complice', in *La démocratie illibérale en droit constitutionnel*, eds. V. Barbé, B.-L. Combrade, and C.-É. Senac (Brussels: Bruylant, 2023).

33 J.-J. Rousseau, *The Social Contract* (1762; reis. London: Penguin, 1998), Book III, Chapter XV.

Furthermore, the relationship between the Executive and the people appears to be displayed mainly as a duty to explain and justify public decisions, echoing the current significance of the transparency principle. It seems however to be only a consolation prize for those who believe that the people should be the true master of their destiny.

Section 6

Disciplinary perspectives

14 Administrative responsibility and responsibility of the Executive

Hafida Belrhali

Administrative responsibility is at the same time wider and narrower than the idea of the responsibility of the Executive. It is broader first, because it can be considered for almost all the public services and for any public person, be it the State, a local authority or a public institution. The State's administrative responsibility for its part can be due to acts of the Executive, but also to the law or even to the Administrative Court. However, this responsibility is limited by restrictive conditions: a *harm*,[1] which can be attributed to the public person that is being sued, must have a *direct causal link* with the *damage* suffered by the victim. When a public person is held liable, it will have to give – in theory monetary – compensation for the consequences of its acts. The State's responsibility then is narrow since the only aim is to impose on that legal person the financial burden of compensating for the consequences of the action or inaction of its bodies when they cause damage to citizen(s).[2]

To what extent can this administrative responsibility of the State support a reflection on the responsibility of the Executive? How can the sentences decided within that framework encourage to govern well or better?

Three remarks can shed light on the articulation between those two responsibilities. The first is related to the limits of administrative responsibility, compared to the Executive's. Some of the Executive's acts cannot trigger administrative responsibility. As a nod to this collective research, I will mention the articulation between the irresponsibility of the public power and the notion of sovereign services. Indeed, some of those services do not fall within the remit of liability action while others do (I). The second remark consists in highlighting a transformation of the compensation action against the State which is especially related to the Executive's action. Traditionally

1 Fault-based responsibility is ordinary-law responsibility; no-fault responsibility regimes have developed in French administrative law, each within a strictly defined field. On the conditions of administrative responsibility, see my book: H. Belrhali, *Responsabilité administrative*, 2e éd. (Paris: LDGJ, 2020).

2 It is possible to consider a more ambitious and more encompassing vision of the responsibility of public action with other scientific tools: See P. Duran, 'La responsabilité administrative au prisme de l'action publique', *RFAP*, no. 3 (2013): pp. 589 ff.

DOI: 10.4324/9781003281559-27

resorted to following accidents, affairs or isolated crises, liability action is now an instrument for citizens who wish to make a public policy change. It then acts as a goad for the Executive (II). The third remark belongs to a critical and comparative analysis of administrative responsibility. Compared to the criminal liability of public decision-makers and to the political responsibility of the government, there are as many potentialities as limits in administrative responsibility (III).

Administrative responsibility is not relevant for all the acts of the Executive – is the sovereign State irresponsible?

There are some limits to the State's administrative responsibility, especially because the prerogatives of the Executive are not all subject to the control of the Administrative Court. Thus, the government's acts related to France's international relations can only entail limited responsibility. The *Conseil d'État* accepts there may be responsibility for breach of equality with regard to public burdens due to an act of the government, but it refuses, even today, to examine possible faults committed in the relations of France with a foreign State.[3] As to the public power which acts in military operations, it is completely immune, since neither fault-based nor no-fault responsibility is available for acts of war.[4] Fight against terrorism also has its own specificities – that police activity only triggers the State's responsibility provided a serious fault is demonstrated.[5]

Should one conclude that sovereign activities are out of the mechanisms of administrative responsibility's reach? This would be inaccurate insofar as police activities are subject to administrative responsibility and in theory for simple fault, like the prison activity. Moreover, the State is responsible based not only on the law but also on international conventions and because of the Administrative Court (admittedly in very limited cases). Sovereign competences therefore only partly escape administrative responsibility.

From a terminology point of view, one could also note that while the Court does not like to talk of fault when it is considered whether the legislator's responsibility is illicit (unconstitutionality or unconventionality), the Executive's act is considered to be administrative and may entail fault-based and/or no-fault responsibilities, subject to the specificities mentioned earlier.

Administrative responsibility as a goad for rulers – is liability action against the State an instrument for citizens?

Administrative responsibility develops in two very distinct areas: it is most often individually raised for unfortunate events, the impact of which is limited

3 On the Evian Agreements, see Conseil d'État (CE) [Highest Administrative Court: Sits in Sub-Section], 27 June 2016, no. 382319, *Bernabé*.
4 Conseil d'État (CE), 23 July 2010, no. 328758, *Sté Touax et a.*
5 As to the *Merah* case, see Conseil d'État (CE), 18 June 2018, no. 411156.

to one or a few victims. Thus, the court works every day to compensate the victims of medical accidents, public works damage. . . . That ordinary responsibility does not change our perception of the art of governing. However, faced with a collective risk, a health scandal, a natural disaster or large-scale pollution, or massive litigation, public policies themselves and the capacity for crisis management are questioned. This second area of administrative responsibility leads to ponder good and bad decisions, especially those which are taken at ministry level. Regulatory equality is then at the heart of the debate. Was it possible to act more, earlier or better? Would it have been possible to take decisions which would have been more adapted to the circumstances in order to avoid a risk or a situation detrimental to rights? A few decided cases will illustrate this (A), then emerging litigation which underlines the exploitation of the compensation litigation to serve as a goad to public action will be mentioned (B).

Assessment of the public action through the lens of main responsibility cases[6]

The important responsibility cases reveal the scope of the Administrative Court's review of public policy choices. First, in the asbestos case, the 3 March 2004 decisions to hold the State liable[7] were founded on the absence of a specific regulation prior to 1977, then on its inadequacy after that date. The activity of the Ministry of Employment and Work Administration was considered to be defective since the measures to protect workers had been late in being implemented. Another example is the case of Chlordecone: exemptions allowed to use that insecticide in the West Indies until 1993, beyond the legal deadline provided for after the withdrawal of the certificate of the substance. The authorisations granted by the Ministry of Agriculture were at fault, according to the 23 June 2002 judgment of the Administrative Court of Paris.[8] The first two examples show that the administrative responsibility of the State can be triggered by the normative action of the Executive: the passing of regulatory acts or individual decisions, such as inertia or lateness in the enactment of norms may constitute wrongdoings.

On 28 June 2022, the Administrative Court of Paris rendered a decision on the management of the Covid-19 crisis.[9] The choices made in the

6 For a presentation of the administrative, civil and criminal parts of those litigations, see H. Belrhali, *Les grandes affaires de responsabilité de la puissance publique* (Paris: LGDJ, 2021).

7 Conseil d'État, Assemblée (CE Ass.) [Highest Administrative Court: Sits in Assembly], 3 March 2004, no. 241153, *Ministre de l'Emploi et de la Solidarité c/Consorts Xueref*, no. 241152, *Ministre de l'Emploi et de la Solidarité c/Consorts Thomas*, no. 241151, *Ministre de l'Emploi et de la Solidarité c/Consorts Botella*, no. 241150, *Ministre de l'Emploi et de la Solidarité c/Consorts Bourdignon*.

8 Tribunal Administratif (TA) Paris [Regional Administrative Court of First Instance], 24 juin 2022, no. 2006925/6-2.

9 Tribunal Administratif (TA) Paris, 28 juin 2022, no. 2012679-3.

management of the stock of masks before the pandemics were characterised as defective. The concrete measures of the Executive and the *Agence Santé Publique France* were examined. Moreover, the court underlined that several government statements indicated, in February and March 2020, that it was not useful, for the population in general, to wear masks. Those statements were considered as blameworthy for being in contradiction with available scientific data. The government's communication, within the framework of the health crisis, was also scrutinised by the Administrative Court.[10]

In the '*Affaire du siècle*', the action for damages against the State was about the policy of fight against global warming, which was deemed insufficient. The Paris Administrative Court indeed considered that it did not match the commitments made by France and found the State liable to compensate (in nature, as provided for in the Civil Code) for the damage caused to the environment.[11] It decided a particular measure of compensation since it was under the form of an injunction to the government. The Court 'ordered the Prime Minister and the competent ministers to take all the useful sector measures to compensate for the damage' and added, 'The content of those measures was for the Government to decide, since it was not for the Court to take the place of the latter'. That decision highlighted the limits of the power of the Court: it did not wish to replace the government and let it decide on the measures to be taken.

Those few examples show that an administrative trial may lead to a discussion on the very content of a public policy and on its adequacy compared to the commitments of the State. The Administrative Court notes the failures in the decision-making process compared to the missions of the national authorities. By judging the administration, it assesses the action of the Executive which is at the latter's apex. New actions for compensation are brought against the State in order to re-orientate a public policy that citizens, associations and local rulers consider is lacking in efficiency.

The fast-growing goading actions

Along the lines of the '*Affaire du siècle*', several associations have filed an action for compensation to have the insufficient protection of biodiversity and the

10 On the originality of this fault, see A. Jacquemet-Gauché, 'Covid-19: l'État fautif, mais pas responsable', *Le blog du Club des juristes*, 1 July 2022, https://blog.leclubdesjuristes.com/covid-19-letat-fautif-mais-pas-responsable-a-propos-de-la-decision-du-tribunal-administratif-de-paris-du-28-juin-2022-par-anne-jacquemet-gauche-professeure-de-droit-public-a-l/. According to S. Brimo, for the pollution linked to chlordecone, 'A faulty – or even contradictory – communication of the health authorities could create a specific damage, as is the case in medical matters'. S. Brimo, 'Note sous TA Paris, 24 juin 2022, no. 2006925/6-2', *AJDA* (2022): p. 2250.

11 TA Paris, 14 October 2021, nos. 1904967, 1904968, 1904972, and 1904976, *Association Oxfam France et autres.*

failures in the legal framing of pesticides acknowledged.[12] More recently, associations of patients and hospital staff have brought an action for compensation in an administrative court. They are asking for regulatory acts defining the rates of patients per staff and reinforcing the workforce to be enacted. After warning public authorities in vain of the worrying situation of public hospitals, those actors are using compensatory actions to have the failure of the State with regard to that deterioration recognised.[13] Other actions are being brought against public powers for the length of the delays in the judicial system and the few means the latter is granted,[14] or to underline the lack of teachers.[15] The insufficient means given to sea rescue, an obligatory public service of the State, could also lead to a compensation action against the State.[16] Thus, individual actions have developed to modify public action in the medical and social services: the action of parents of autistic children and the important monetary compensations that were awarded may have increased the attention public authorities devote to that issue.[17]

Those compensation actions are not only brought by citizens. Local public authorities too file in court. The town of Strasbourg has filed against the State to highlight its failure in providing emergency shelter for the homeless.[18]

12 P. Mouterde, 'Pesticides: des associations attaquent l'État pour n'avoir pas assez protégé la biodiversité', *Le Monde*, 9 September 2021, www.lemonde.fr/planete/article/2021/09/09/pesticides-des-associations-attaquent-l-etat-pour-n-avoir-pas-suffisamment-protege-la-biodiversite. See TA Paris, 29 June 2023, no. 2200534/4-1.

13 F. Groyer, 'Des associations de patients et collectifs de soignants attaquent l'État pour carence fautive dans la gestion de l'hôpital public', *APM News*, 4 November 2022, www.apmnews.com/depeche/30784/389084/des-associations-de-patients-et-collectifs-de-soignants-attaquent-l-État-pour-carence-fautive-dans-la-gestion-de-l-hopital-public

14 J.-B. Jacquin, 'L'État assigné à Lyon pour "faute lourde" en raison des dysfonctionnements de la justice', *Le Monde*, 18 November 2020, www.lemonde.fr/societe/article/2020/11/18/l-etat-assigne-a-lyon-pour-faute-lourde-en-raison-des-dysfonctionnements-de-la-justice_6060195_3224.html. See also, F. Hourquebie, 'Les dysfonctionnements de la justice et les gages de l'État', *Délibérée* 2, no. 16 (2022): pp. 33 ff.

15 S. Lecherbonnier, 'Non-remplacement des enseignants: des parents lancent une procédure coordonnée de recours contre l'État', *Le Monde*, 30 June 2022, www.lemonde.fr/societe/article/2022/06/30/non-remplacement-des-enseignants-des-parents-lancent-une-procedure-coordonnee-de-recours-contre-l-etat. A. Jacquemet-Gauché, 'Faute d'heures de cours, c'est l'heure des recours!', *Le blog du Club des juristes*, 1 July 2022, 1 June 2023, https://blog.leclubdesjuristes.com/faute-dheures-de-cours-cest-lheure-des-recours-lengagement-de-la-responsabilite-de-letat-pour-le-non-remplacement-des-enseignants/

16 H. Belrhali, 'Secours en mer des migrants: le rappel de l'État à ses responsabilités?', *Le blog du Club des juristes*, 23 December 2022, https://blog.leclubdesjuristes.com/secours-en-mer-des-migrants-le-rappel-de-letat-a-ses-responsabilites-par-hafida-belrhali/

17 For a more critical analysis, see N. Klausser, 'Brèves réflexions sur le contentieux de la non-prise en charge des enfants concernés par des syndromes autistiques', *Revue de droit sanitaire et social*, no. 4 (July/August 2022): p. 734.

18 *Libération* and *AFP*, 'Mise à l'abri des personnes à la rue: Strasbourg porte plainte contre l'État pour "défaillance"', *Libération*, 5 December 2022, www.liberation.fr/societe/mise-a-labri-des-personnes-a-la-rue-strasbourg-porte-plainte-contre-letat-pour-defaillance

The development of compensation litigation between public authorities shows that the attribution of means is at the heart of the debates between local and national actors: for example, mayors of Seine-Saint-Denis tried to have the State be held liable for breach of equality after warning the State authorities of their lack of means and personnel.[19] As to the environment, the administrative courts hear many claims aiming to put pressure on the government.[20] After being considered as the last resort by citizens, such as the claimants claiming under the housing DALO Act, to get the effective exercise of social rights, compensation action also seems to be becoming the last resort for citizens, groups and local public rulers wishing to be heard by the Executive and influence its action too. The underlying stakes are not absent either, of course: as B. Faure underlines, local representatives are trying to bring into the litigation area fights they are losing on the political level.[21]

Virtues and limits of the compensation action – the administrative responsibility of the State at the service of good government?

The way responsibility mechanisms are considered, especially from the point of view of other disciplines, is sometimes quite critical. A probabilistic and sociological study will consider that the courts' method of analysis, which revolves around causality, leads to excessive consequences.[22] The criticism mainly targets criminal liability, which is widely used, especially within the framework of the sanitary crisis, with many actions in the *Cour de Justice de la République*.[23]

19 *Franceinfo* and *AFP*, 'Cinq maires de Seine-Saint-Denis déposent un recours contre l'État pour "rupture d'égalité" ', *Franceinfo*, 14 January 2020, www.francetvinfo.fr/france/cinq-maires-de-seine-saint-denis-deposent-un-recours-contre-l-etat-pour-rupture-d-egalite_3784413.html; L. Couvelaire, 'En Seine-Saint-Denis, la faillite d'un État "inégalitaire et inadapté" ', *Le Monde*, 18 May 2018, www.lemonde.fr/societe/article/2018/05/18/en-seine-saint-denis-la-faillite-d-un-etat-inegalitaire-et-inadapte. See T. Ducharme, 'Note sous TA Montreuil, 3 févr. 2023, no. 2000173', *AJDA* (2023): p. 1352.

20 M. Moliner-Dubost, 'Quand les collectivités se rebellent contre l'État: l'exemple de la politique environnementale', *Actualité juridique Collectivités territoriales*, no. 2 (2022): pp. 84 ff.

21 B. Faure, 'Les relations État-collectivités', presented at *Les litiges contentieux entre l'État et les collectivités territoriales: Approche organique*, Université Clermont Auvergne, 17 November 2017, *DA* (2017): ét. n°4.

22 O. Beaud, 'Un entretien avec François Vatin: Décisions de justice et esprit probabiliste', *Jus Politicum Blog*, 24 October 2022, https://blog.juspoliticum.com/2022/10/24/un-entretien-avec-francois-vatin-decisions-de-justice-et-esprit-probabiliste-par-olivier-beaud/

23 According to O Beaud, 'The criminal solution is in a dead-end for legal technical reasons since it implies meeting conditions that are really difficult to fulfil if one really refers to criminal law: The causal link, in particular, is difficult to prove. . . . In short, criminal liability is inadequate to understand management faults of the State. Political responsibility, together with administrative responsibility, is the right solution to compensate victims. Moreover, criminal solution is a dead-end given the operation of the CJR, a court with a hybrid composition, which is the only one having jurisdiction to decide on crimes committed by members of the Government during office' (Olivier Beaud, 'Si les gouvernants ont failli face à la crise sanitaire, la solution

Administrative responsibility too can be appreciated in a nuanced way. Several of its virtues favouring good administration or government will then appear. First, it is responsibility for the malfunctioning of the public service. It therefore allows to analyse a decision that has been taken, the concrete operations of services, without stigmatising a natural person. It has added value compared to criminal liability which is looking for someone responsible and guilty. Going beyond the issue of the responsible-natural person, it comprehends the operation of services and the lawfulness of decisions structurally. Then, administrative responsibility relies on the claim of victims (in the conditions mentioned earlier). It is therefore within the reach of citizens and associations which are victims: it is not linked to the will of political actors. That is how it offers an advantage over political responsibility which may be paralysed by the forces at play (especially the majority rule). One should note however that the activity of review of the government's action completes administrative case law on the cases mentioned earlier: thus, the health scandals lead to court decisions as much as parliamentary reports. The criminal, administrative and political types of responsibility are really complementary. Between the excesses (and disappointments) of the first, the inefficiency of the third, administrative responsibility offers a few intermediary benefits. Compensation action against the State also has the advantage of relative speed compared to a criminal trial: the outcome of the latter may be quite long (for example, the asbestos or the Mediator cases). Last, administrative responsibility (and/or the echo of a case in the media) may, if it is taken seriously, cause a healthy reaction consisting in reforming the competent institutions. After the contaminated blood products case, the ***Établissement Français du Sang*** (EFS) was established, and after that of the Mediator, the *Agence Française de Sécurité Sanitaire des Produits de Santé* was reformed (and became the *Agence de Sécurité du Médicament*). Thanks to its pedagogical function, administrative (and criminal) responsibility may also encourage to be more prudent afterwards: the hyperactivity of national authorities during the Covid crisis may be explained by the fear of being held liable.[24]

Beyond its potentialities, administrative responsibility causes some disappointments with respect to its scope. First, the institutional reforms launched after crises are rarely the most relevant answers to a deficit in risk culture and prevention. The institutional dimension of crisis management is probably overvalued in France and results in conceiving the reform of structures as an obvious solution.[25] Then, administrative responsibility, by

de la plainte pénale n'est pas la bonne', *Le Monde*, 20 April 2020, www.lemonde.fr/idees/article/2020/04/20/olivier-beaud).

24 Responsibility is often perceived as generating a risk of paralysis of public actors, but in the context of a crisis, it can, on the contrary, push them to be hyperactive.

25 See H. Bergeron, O. Borraz, and P. Castel, 'Covid-19: "Aucune leçon n'a été tirée de la gestion de la crise entre mars et mai"', interview by D. Larousserie and H. Morin, *Le Monde*, 22 October 2020, www.lemonde.fr/idees/article/2020/10/22/covid-19

not stigmatising anyone or only a legal person (and therefore an abstract entity), seems to be a poor threat. In that, the administrative trial, which is less therapeutic than the criminal one, and being less broadcast, is less valued. Moreover, the awarded monetary compensation weighs on public budgets and therefore on taxpayers.[26] Being hardly deterrent, convictions may be the object of a miscalculation. There is a risk of public actors integrating their cost and considering that it is always less onerous to pay them than to modify a public policy. Liability action is then a useless fight, unless the amounts of monetary compensation are significantly increased. Last, some decisions have a Platonic scope. Sometimes a court finds the State at fault without finding it liable. Such hypotheses happen when the court is not convinced of the existence of the damage, or of the causal link between the latter and the wrongdoing. Such was the case for the management mistakes during the sanitary crisis, and for the chlordecone case in the judgments of the Paris Administrative Court.[27] The strictness of administrative responsibility then leads to distinguishing someone who is at fault but not liable, which is not easy for citizens to understand. While the court did not find the State liable, the failures of the public authorities in the Covid crisis and the chlordecone case have been recognised by another source – the President of the Republic. The President's words are a traditional reference for the responsibility of the State for historical damage (one could think of speeches on the deportation of the Jews or the abandonment of the Harkis). However, here the Head of State plays an original role (by defining the limits of responsibility, in sanitary matters, which is still to be established).[28]

Within its limited framework, administrative responsibility usefully contributes for me to make the Executive act more responsibly. Beyond administrative responsibility, other cases brought to the Administrative Court lead it to scrutinise the public action in new ways: the 'control of trajectory' highlighted by the *Conseil d'État* as to the environment thus belongs to another way of dealing with the responsibility (in a broad sense) of public

26 Administrative responsibility is that regime 'that nobody cares about since in reality, it is the taxpayers who pay' according to C. Huglo and C. Lepage, *Nos batailles pour l'environnement* (Arles: Actes Sud, 2021), p. 22. See also, P. Yolka, 'Grand tétras: du coq (de bruyère) à l'âne', *AJDA* (2022): p. 1249.

27 The State has also been found at fault, without being liable, for its insufficient measures against air pollution: Cour administrative d'appel (CAA) Paris [Regional Administrative Court of Appeal], 11 March 2021, no. 19PA02868. See TA Paris, 16 June 2023, nos. 1709333, 1810251, 1814405.

28 Regarding President Macron's declarations in 2018 and 2020, see A. Jacquemet-Gauché, 'La parole présidentielle, source pétrifiante du droit de la responsabilité?', *AJDA* (2020): p. 913.

authorities, from a prospective perspective.[29] In reality, what is at stake is not so much the refining of the modes of judicial review as its consequences: though a responsible Executive is one that learns a lesson from its acts, there remains to hope that all those court decisions, for compensation or other claims, will produce real effects.[30]

29 B. Lasserre, 'Introduction', *Regards croisés du Conseil d'État et de la Cour de cassation – L'environnement: les citoyens, le droit, les juges*, Cour de cassation, 21 May 2021, www.conseil-etat.fr/publications-colloques/discours-et-interventions/l-environnement-les-citoyens-le-droit-les-juges-introduction-de-bruno-lasserre-vice-president-du-conseil-d-etat; 'The objectives of the law may be remote in time, –2030, 2040 or even 2050 –, but the Court cannot wait for 10, 20 or 30 years to check that they have been reached, unless it wants to deny that action is urgently needed today, unless it deprives its control of any useful consequence right away given the very important inertia of climate. Reviewing the trajectory amounts then to reviewing compliance in advance, which leads the Court to ensure, when it issues its decision, not that the objectives have been reached, but that they can be reached, that they are being reached, that they follow a trajectory that is believable and verifiable'. The comparison with the traditionally retrospective dimension of responsibility is interesting.

30 H. Belrhali and A. Jacquemet-Gauché, 'Les citoyens qui saisissent la justice contre l'ineffectivité ou l'illégalité de l'action publique défendent l'intérêt général', *Le Monde*, 18 July 2022, www.lemonde.fr/idees/article/2022/07/18/les-citoyens-qui-saisissent-la-justice; H. Belrhali, S. Brimo, and A. Jacquemet-Gauché, 'La responsabilité administrative: quel sens?', *AJDA* (2022): p. 1473; H. Belrhali, 'Pesticides: qui a (encore) peur du juge administratif?', *AJDA* (2022): p. 713.

15 Understanding responsibility through the issue of the environment – towards a bilateral conception of responsibility?

Malik Bozzo-Rey

Introduction

To understand what is at stake in the concept of responsibility and what difficulties and questions it may raise from a philosophical – and more specifically moral – point of view, it seems relevant to rely, at least at first, on a typology of the different meanings of that word. Then, through the issue of responsibility – and specifically moral responsibility – towards the environment, we will try to understand which conception of responsibility may reasonably be realised to allow individuals to take decisions in favour of the protection of the environment. We will then see that the conception of individual responsibility cannot do without a reflection on the institutional context in which people live.

Typology

In addition to the importance that the word 'responsibility' has in philosophy,[1] it is obvious that it is polysemous. In *La panique morale*, Ruwen Ogien presents an interesting typology which gives a good account of the different meanings it can have (be it the noun 'responsibility' or the adjective 'responsible'). Let us consider the following remarks:

1. X is 'responsible' for entrusting his pit-bull to Y;
2. At first sight, Y is a 'responsible' person;
3. When he accepted to look after X's pit-bull, Y took on some responsibilities;
4. The pit-bull bites Z. The bite is 'responsible' for a dangerous infection;
5. X is 'responsible' for the harm suffered by Z;
6. Y feels responsible.[2]

1 R. McKeon, 'The Development and the Significance of the Concept of Responsibility', *Revue Internationale de Philosophie* 11, no. 39 (1957): pp. 3–32.

2 R. Ogien, *La panique morale* (Paris: Grasset, 2004), pp. 209–210.

DOI: 10.4324/9781003281559-28

The first example insists on the voluntary and intentional dimension of X's action. The latter results from a process of decision-making which is often associated with using rational capacities, but which may also involve other faculties or emotions.[3] Ogien calls it 'responsibility-action' and thus underlines that there is an intrinsic link between responsibility, action and will. This implies being capable of defining what a voluntary act is and what the necessary conditions for an individual to exercise their will are.

The second example refers to what belongs to the character of the agent and denotes prudence or concern for the good of the other. It is then possible to speak of 'responsibility-virtue'. Here, responsibility is associated with a specific quality of the agent. Based on the ethics of virtues, which is a form of moral perfectionism, any virtue may be developed in an individual. Applied to responsibility, it would mean that it can be improved both by the repetition of virtuous behaviours and education.[4]

The third example refers to the idea of duty or obligation. Being responsible then consists in conforming to a certain number of duties or obligations, hence the expression 'responsibility-obligation'. In the present case, Y's responsibilities are linked to the pledge of looking after his pit-bull that he has given to X, and this pledge implies a certain number of obligations.

The fourth example may be the most commonly used, even though it consequently reduces the concept of responsibility. Indeed, 'being responsible' means 'being the cause of' here. It is a central aspect of our intuitive or pre-reflective conception of responsibility. It is then possible to talk of 'responsibility-causality'. There still remains the issue of the extent to which causality allows to assess the degree of responsibility of the agent and to identify whether the absence of a causal link may clear an individual. For example, do I have a moral responsibility as to the consequences of an action that I could not foresee though I was at the origin of it?

The fifth example means that Y may be punished or blamed for a specific state of affairs. That is 'responsibility-sanction'. Here we can see that responsibility is associated with the idea of damage inflicted upon the other. However, if, for example, the minimal principle of ethics is not causing harm to one's neighbour,[5] this implies two things: it is necessary first to identify one's neighbour (the victim) who is involved and, therefore, to admit that the absence of identification of the victim does not allow to ethically classify an action. In other words, would we be ready to accept the idea that if there is no victim a person may not be held liable for what they have done?[6]

3 R. Clark, M. McKenna, and A. M. Smith, eds., *The Nature of Moral Responsibility: New Essays* (Oxford/New York: Oxford University Press, 2015).

4 J. Driver, *Ethics: The Fundamentals* (Malden: Wiley-Blackwell, 2006); A. MacIntyre, *Après la vertu* (Paris: PUF, 2013).

5 J. S. Mill, *De la liberté* (Paris: Folio Essais, 1990); R. Ogien, *La panique morale.*

6 R. Ogien, *L'influence de l'odeur des croissants chauds sur la bonté humaine: et autres questions de philosophie morale expérimentale* (Paris: Grasset, 2011).

The last example, which Ogien calls 'responsibility-emotion', refers to a moral emotion such as guilt or regret. That meaning testifies to a return to inwardness and to the fact that the agent has a oneself-to-oneself relation.

That typology gives a good overview of the different meanings that the word responsibility may have. Some elements could however make it more complete and provide elements of analysis which could allow, for example, to get out of an aporetic vision of responsibility which concludes that our responsibility is at the same time unlimited and non-existent, in other words, that we are simultaneously responsible for everything *and* nothing. It is first possible to distinguish *positive* responsibility (which is about what one does) from *negative* responsibility (which is when one lets things happen) while considering responsibility as to *omissions*.[7]

Obviously, that type of distinction calls for thinking degrees within responsibility. Then, though we have tried to identify different meanings of the word responsibility, it is also interesting to look at the necessary conditions of responsibility. Thus, two conditions are individually necessary and jointly sufficient for an agent to be considered as (morally) responsible for an action.[8] The first is a condition of *control* (or *freedom*) which leads us to answer the question: has agent *X* freely performed action *A*? The second is an *epistemic* (or cognitive, mental) condition which raises the question: was agent *X* aware (of the consequences, the moral meaning etc.) of action *A* he was carrying out? In other words, acting under duress and/or without having specific elements linked to the action at one's disposal or without being able to fully use one's cognitive capacities renders the individual less responsible (or even not responsible) for the performed action. Responsibility therefore is also related to the characteristics of the agent *in themselves.*

Last, one must note that all types of responsibility are not equal and that they are not necessarily logically related. Then, the concept of responsibility is often associated with that of morality, but it is necessary to underline now that moral responsibility cannot be limited or amount to causal responsibility. One can indeed be the cause of an action without having to be liable for it. That typology is especially interesting for it shows not only the polysemy of the word 'responsibility' but also the issues it raises.

It also contains the implicit idea of *accountability*,[9] that is, the idea that responsibility implies having to account for one's actions, being accountable

7 R. Clark, M. McKenna, and A. M. Smith, *The Nature of Moral Responsibility*; J. M. Fischer and M. Ravizza, *Responsibility and Control: A Theory of Moral Responsibility* (Cambridge: Cambridge University Press, 1998); D. K. Nelkin and S. C. Rickless, eds., *The Ethics and Law of Omissions* (Oxford/New York: Oxford University Press, 2017).

8 We are relying here on the elements presented in M. Talbert, 'Moral Responsibility', *The Stanford Encyclopedia of Philosophy*, eds. E. N. Zalta and U. Nodelman (Fall 2022 Edition), https://plato.stanford.edu/archives/fall2022/entries/moral-responsibility/

9 Which should be distinguished from attributability. On that point, see D. Shoemaker, 'Attributability, Answerability, and Accountability: Toward a Wider Theory of Moral Responsibility', *Ethics* 121, no. 3 (2011): pp. 602–632.

for one's actions. One is therefore responsible for something or someone to someone else. That is what is at the foundation of the moral relation between two agents, and it implies a sort of reciprocity or, at least, potential reciprocity.

What is at stake in the notion of responsibility: the issue of the environment[10]

The word 'responsibility' is regularly used in the public debate, especially in relation to future generations and the environment – the two questions being often linked. However, it does not appear that a detailed analysis of the concept of responsibility is made available to the public on those issues. Moreover, if one focuses on the issue of the environment, which is increasingly important and pressing, one can quite easily see that it raises a certain number of questions the answers of which are at the same time fundamental and complex.

Examining responsibility unavoidably sends one back to the question of the definition and identification of the object and subject of responsibility. Who is responsible for the environment crisis – individuals, companies, States or all of them? If all shared some responsibility, would each share be equivalent? Depending on the identified responsibilities, would it not be necessary to create obligations that would correspond to that level of involvement? Attributing responsibility for the damage inflicted on the environment may be less obvious than it seems. Though the idea that individuals – at least those of industrialised societies, as citizens and/or consumers –, because they know the impact their actions have on the environment, bear some responsibility is quite common, the issue of its extent is being debated, and some authors talk of a global responsibility of the individual.[11] The responsibility that is mentioned here is in fact *causal* responsibility, but we have seen that it is only one type of responsibility and that it could not completely cover the idea of moral responsibility, which is however so often referred to in relation to environmental issues. Moreover, can one really consider individuals as a homogeneous whole independently of social, political, economic or historical considerations – in other words, independently of the context in which they live? The answers to those questions are far from trivial as they can allow, or not, to avoid the aporetic alternative: either one is entirely responsible for environmental issues, or one bears no responsibility at all for them. Here, one should introduce a

10 We are referring here to the arguments developed in B. Robyns, C. Lenglet, H. Barry, and M. Bozzo-Rey, *Des usagers intelligents pour la transition énergétique et sociétale* (London: ISTE Editions, 2022).

11 M. Micheletti, *Political Virtue and Shopping* (New York/Basingstoke: Palgrave Macmillan, 2010).

distinction between *retrospective* and *prospective* responsibility.[12] It makes it possible to suggest several ideas:

1. Some individuals may not have to be held liable *retrospectively*, especially when no reasonable alternative was available to them;
2. Conversely, individuals having reasonable alternatives may be held liable *prospectively*;
3. This highlights the *prospective* responsibility of the institutions (governments or companies) the substantial content of which is that they must make available to the individuals the alternatives which will allow them to choose the option with the weakest environmental impact. This third point makes it possible to introduce a fundamental concept: the principle of alternative possibilities (PAP)[13] according to which a person is morally responsible for the action they perform if they had the possibility to carry out another one. This amounts to taking into consideration and questioning the conditions in which the action has been performed. Let us take the following example:[14] Marc steals David's meal at the canteen. Usually, one considers that Marc is responsible for that action and is therefore a thief. Would he still be (also) responsible if specific circumstances had pushed him to act that way? Let us assume, for example, that Eric – the big brute of the school – has forced him to steal David's meal. Or let us suppose that Marc has a serious neurological illness which prevents him from controlling himself. In the last two cases, Marc does not have any other option: he must act as he has done, there is a constraint (which may be external or internal) that compels him to steal David's lunch. In other words, the number of possible actions, other options, is suddenly limited. Some actions become mandatory when others are no longer possible. Should one consider that the context in which the decision was taken has no impact on the way responsibility is attributed to individuals? Isn't the reality of alternatives, as such, a condition – which is not the only one, of course – for one to be able to consider that an individual is (morally) responsible?

12 J. N. Fahlquist, 'Moral Responsibility for Environmental Problems: Individual or Institutional', *Journal of Agricultural and Environmental Ethics* 22, no. 2 (2009): pp. 109–124. The rest of our text relies on the positions defended in that article.

13 H. Frankfurt, 'Alternate Possibilities and Moral Responsibility', in *Moral Responsibility and Alternative Possibilities*, eds. M. McKenna and D. Widerker (London: Routledge, 2003); T. Irwin, ed., *Classical Philosophy* (Oxford/New York: Oxford University Press, 1999); R. Pasnau, 'Human Nature', in *The Cambridge Companion to Medieval Philosophy*, ed. A. S. McGrade (Cambridge: Cambridge University Press, 2003): pp. 208–230; W. L. Rowe, 'Two Concepts of Freedom', *Proceedings and Addresses of the American Philosophical Association* 61, no. 1 (1987): pp. 43–64.

14 Based on the example in D. Robb, 'Moral Responsibility and the Principle of Alternative Possibilities', in *The Stanford Encyclopedia of Philosophy*, ed. Edward N. Zalta (Fall 2020 Edition), https://plato.stanford.edu/archives/fall2020/entries/alternative-possibilities/

Let us now go back to the environment issue. To what extent can and should individuals be held responsible for damage inflicted on the environment and therefore be imposed the obligation to actively participate in any policy fighting against it? Let us take two simple examples[15] to debate that point. Marie lives in a society in which public transportation is very well developed. Agnes lives in a society in which public transports are almost non-existent. It seems that the context of Marie's decision-making allows her to choose public transport and thus reduce her impact on the environment. On the contrary, Agnes' context makes it difficult or more complicated, more expensive (and not only in the economic sense) to take the same decision. The alternatives that are offered to them are consequently radically different. Is it then legitimate and justified to ask them both to use public transportation and does such a request have the same ethical force? For Mary, the request seems *at least* reasonable when it may be (probably) too demanding in Agnes' case. This does not prevent the fact that in both cases one thinks that it is morally good to use public transportation.

Let us now imagine that Anne and Sylvie both wish to build a house. Anne lives in a society where several builders offer to build and each time both the building and the use of the house will be low energy. Sylvie lives in a society in which such builders are rare and 40 percent more expensive. It seems here that the moral request of building a low-energy house has a moral and financial price that is more important for Sylvie than for Anne, independently of their positions. Indeed, whatever Anne's position on that issue, it is not difficult for her to build such a house. Conversely, whatever Sylvie's position – *a fortiori* if she wishes to build an environment-friendly house –, taking such a decision is quite expensive. In both cases, and independently of the individual values of the two persons, it seems difficult to consider that the two contexts imply equivalent moral value, or, at least, that the responsibility that can be attributed to each is equivalent.

What do those examples show? First, it seems necessary to introduce the idea of degree of responsibility, since Marie's and Agnes' in the first example and Anne's and Sylvie's in the second are not equivalent. Then, that degree depends on the context in which they have to take their decisions and therefore act. Last, that context, the social infrastructure in which the decisions are made, is part of political and institutional decisions, and this context provides alternatives – or not. Consequently, it is fundamental to acknowledge the importance of the alternatives that are available to individuals when they could be held responsible for some actions. In other words, the attribution of responsibility to individuals cannot be thought uniformly and unilaterally. Moreover, when one mentions the context of decision-making, one is more specifically interested in the institutional context since it is the latter which

15 The first case quotes and adapts the examples in J. N. Fahlquist, 'Moral Responsibility for Environmental Problems', p. 111.

can offer alternatives to individuals. It is crucial to take into consideration the structural and society obstacles which may prevent individuals from taking decisions – and therefore act – for the environment.

Finally, one must define which reasonable alternatives will allow to define the responsibility of individuals, that is, the fact of holding individuals accountable as to actions which have a negative impact on the environment implies that those same individuals be offered reasonable alternatives to the fact of not acting in favour of the environment, and they may be held responsible for such an action. This means that if such alternatives are not available or offered then individuals may not be held responsible. If one follows Fahlquist, it is possible to define what the reasonable alternatives are, based on four factors.[16] The first factor is price: if the price of the action is high and the involved persons have different incomes, demands cannot be the same. Then, 'good', valid possibilities should be offered: if I want to buy locally to reduce the carbon footprint of my food but shops in my area do not offer any, the fact that price is not an issue is not a sufficient criterion. Moreover, the substantial inconvenience that the action implies must be taken into consideration: I cannot really be held responsible for going to work by car if it is dangerous to go by bike because there is no cycle path. Last, it is necessary that each individual have access to the information that allows him to assess the environmental impact of their actions.

What conclusions may be drawn based on that theoretical framework? Individuals cannot be retrospectively held responsible if they did not have reasonable alternatives, but it is still possible, in some cases, to attribute them some prospective responsibility.

The idea of prospective responsibility is actually quite simple: if and when an individual has the possibility to act in a way that protects the environment, they have a moral obligation to perform such an action. Prospective responsibility is therefore inherently linked to the existence of reasonable alternatives. Conversely, as we have just underlined, an individual who does not have that possibility cannot be held responsible for that impossibility and is therefore not subject to the same obligation. The very existence of those alternatives depends on the institutional, social and economic context in which individuals live. The political institutions and the economic (national or international) actors have resources and means far superior to those of individuals, which is why it is possible for them to act for reasonable alternatives to be made available to individuals. Consequently, the political and economic institutions are responsible since they have the means and the power to offer individuals reasonable alternatives.

16 J. N. Fahlquist, 'Moral Responsibility for Environmental Problems', pp. 116–117.

Conclusion

Though it is neither fair nor legitimate to only hold individuals responsible, it would be illusory to release them from any responsibility by transferring it onto the different institutions. It seems, on the contrary, that individual and institutional responsibilities are inherently linked. The more reasonable the alternative the institutions offer – that is, take on their responsibilities – the more responsible the individuals may be held if they do not perform the actions that are morally mandatory – in favour of the protection of the environment here. However, it is not because the institutions do not have a responsible behaviour that it will be possible to expect individuals to act in a responsible manner. While it is the institutions' responsibility to allow the individuals to be effectively responsible, it is up to the latter to ensure they have the adequate institutions.[17] In other words, duties are bilateral and reciprocal – even though they are on different levels. That leads us to think the links between responsibility and the environment through the lens of the concept of bilateral responsibility.

17 H. Shue, 'Mediating Duties', *Ethics* 98, no. 4 (1988): pp. 696–698.

16 A perspective on civil responsibility

Jean-Baptiste Donnier

The secondary character of responsibility

Though surprising it may seem, given the importance that notion has today, civil law has done without using 'responsibility' for a long time. This word, which 'was missing in Roman law',[1] only became the object of doctrinal elaboration in the 19th century, and only in a limited way.[2] This may be due to the secondary character of responsibility. Responsibility, as etymology shows, is only an answer to something,[3] like an echo (which is also said to 'answer')[4] to a pre-existing reality which, in civil law, is an obligation. Civil liability is a legal answer to a prior obligation. Someone who has to answer for a civil obligation that falls to them is responsible under civil law.

In principio erat factum

The issue here is that of the source of civil liability. What does one have to answer for? One could think first that one has to answer for what has been wanted or at least agreed. Liability then seems to be first and foremost contractual in nature. Such approach has been convincingly challenged.[5] In reality, it relies on a confusion between equivalent enforcement and liability. Contractual commitment is always executed,[6] either in nature when the execution is spontaneous, or, most often, by equivalent enforcement when execution is forced. However, equivalent enforcement is only one particular mode of

1 M. Villey, 'Métamorphoses de l'obligation', in *Archives de philosophie du droit (APD)*, vol. 15 (Paris: Dalloz, 1970), p. 287.

2 For example, Demolombe only devotes half a book of his commentary on the Civil Code to responsibility, while seven books are dedicated to his study of general contract law.

3 A. Ernout et A. Meillet, *Dictionnaire étymologique de la langue latine*, 4e éd. *(Paris: Klincksieck, 2001)*, p. 643.

4 L.-N. Bescherelle, *Dictionnaire national*, t. 2, 9ème éd. (Paris: Garnier, 1861), p. 1159.

5 P. Rémy, 'La "responsabilité contractuelle", histoire d'un faux concept', *RTD Civile* (1997): p. 323.

6 The only case of real non-execution of a contractual obligation is that of the insolvency of a debtor which de facto excludes any equivalent enforcement in the form of damages.

DOI: 10.4324/9781003281559-29

executing contractual obligations. There is no need to use the notion of liability.

If one excludes liability from the field of contract, the only thing one has to answer for is not a voluntary commitment but a fact. That is what is expressed – in a periodical style, the form of which shows the meaning of civil liability – in Article 1382 of the French Civil Code, which became Article 1240 after the 2016 reform of the law of obligations:

> Any human action whatsoever which causes harm to another creates an obligation in the person by whose fault it occurred to make reparation for it.[7]

At the beginning there is a fact ('Any human action whatsoever'); at the end there is a right (reparation), and in between, an obligation.[8] The obligation, which is created by a fact, precedes and measures the right,[9] which consists in re-establishing the initial balance which has been upset by the fact causing the harm.

Vinculum juris

Civil liability thus refers to a legal link (***vinculum juris***, which is the core of the notion of ***obligatio***), and a particular legal link, the three characters of which define its specificity.

The first is its general character, which is two-fold. It is first the general character of the generating fact. 'Any human action whatsoever' may give rise to civil liability and not only given causes, which is essential since it reveals that the source of the legal link is in the fact itself and not in positive law.[10] It is also the general character of the repairable harm which characterises the general principle of civil liability stated in Article 1240 Civil Code. The use of the indefinite article in French (***un dommage***, 'a harm') clearly expresses that any damage, of whatever nature, may in itself be repaired through civil liability.

The second character of the legal relation which gives rise to civil liability is the causal link between the generating fact and the harm. That requirement

7 Translations of the French Civil Code can be found at: www.trans-lex.org/601101/_/french-civil-code-2016/

8 One will note that in the French text of Article 1382/1240 Civil Code, the verb 'create an obligation', 'oblige' is exactly at the centre of the text: there are 11 words before and 11 after it, which makes it the 12th word of the ascending period and the first of the descending period. In other words, it is the pivot which re-establishes the balance that has been upset by the harm-causing fact.

9 On the primary character of obligation compared to the right, see *S. Weil, L'enracinement* (Paris: Gallimard, 1949), p. 9.

10 On that point see the controversy between Toullier and Demolombe, in *C. Demolombe, Cours de Code Napoléon: Traité des engagements qui se forment sans convention*, vol. 7 (Paris: Lahure, 1879), pp. 17 ff.

of causal link, which is inherent in civil liability, defines its domain. The occurring of a harm is not enough to trigger civil liability. The harm must also be the consequence of an identifiable fact and must be attributable to its author. This implies a fault on the latter's part being at the direct origin of the harm suffered by the victim. There results that any damage may not necessarily be repaired by civil liability. There is irreparable damage (the 'acts of God' in the common law systems) or damage which can only be repaired by using other means than civil liability, such as a statutory duty, for example. Then it is no longer the fact which gives rise to a relation of obligation, but the law, which excludes reparation from the domain of civil liability.

Last, the third element which characterises the legal relation is the personality of civil liability. It is 'the person' by whose fault it has occurred who must repair the damage that has been caused. Civil liability relies on a personal fault which can be attributed to its author. It is a condition of the existence of a relation of obligation which gives rise to the right of the victim to get compensation.

A contrasting picture

From those three characteristics result at the same time a function and a foundation which are specific to civil liability. The specific function of civil liability is expressed in the last word of Article 1240 French Civil Code, which indicates the aim of the obligation: the reparation of the harm. The objective is to correct – thanks to an act of justice which is precisely called corrective (or commutative) – the inequality that has been created by the damaging fact resulting from the fault that has been committed. This aim contains its foundation in and of itself: the fault committed by the author of the damage. Such are the function and the foundation of civil liability, which are reduced to their initial simplicity in the wording of Article 1240 French Civil Code.

Comparing this archetype to case law practice and legislative evolution, as well as to the attempts at theoretical elaborations to which they have given rise or which have sometimes caused them, reveals a contrasting picture. On the one hand, the renewal of the foundations of civil liability (II) may be considered as a homogeneous development of potentialities contained in the principle, but, on the other hand, the ends attributed to civil liability seem to be quite blurred (I).

Blurred purposes

The confusion of purposes

Traditionally, the object of civil liability is what differentiates it from criminal liability. While the latter aims to 'punish the author of the harm', civil liability aims at 'repairing the harm'.[11] Today, that distinction has been weakened as

11 J. Carbonnier, *Droit civil: Les biens, les obligations*, vol. 2 (Paris: PUF, 2004), p. 2253.

a result of a two-fold movement. First, civil liability no longer only aims to repair the damage, but may also be punitive.[12] Second, criminal liability does not any longer aim to only punish the offender, but it increasingly also aims to recognise the victim,[13] such recognition being meant to help the latter to 'make a fresh start'. The restorative aim of civil liability thus pervades criminal liability, while the punitive objective of the latter is not quite foreign to the former.

Liability without reparation

That weakening of the recognised specificity of civil liability is furthered by an endless multiplication of the objectives which are attributed to such liability. To the reparation of the damage other purposes are aggregated in addition to the punishment of the author of the injury, such as the prevention or the termination of the unlawful act.[14] Those new purposes which are attributed to civil liability modify its nature insofar as they open the road to the implementation of civil liability for other purposes than the reparation of a harm. Thus, there is liability without reparation, which upsets not only the end, but also the temporality of civil liability. Whereas civil liability's restorative objective necessarily happens after the damage has been caused in order to re-establish the initial balance, its preventative purpose aims to intervene before the damage in order to prevent it. There is a deep evolution of the legal relation between the victim and the author of the harm, the latter having to answer not only for what they have done, but also for what they are *capable of avoiding*.

Reparation without liability

Moreover, while there may be liability without reparation, cases of reparation without liability tend to increase, which blurs the purposes of civil liability even more. Not only is the latter attributed other ends than reparation, but, at the same time, reparation may be ensured by other means than civil liability.

Thus, in order to avoid the limits that are inherent in civil liability, the law organises the transfer of the reparation of some harms to insurance or to guarantee funds. That is the case of the 5th of July 1985 Act on road accidents, which ensures that the victim gets immediate compensation through an insurance mechanism and relegates the issue of civil liability into the background, on the level of a possible claim against the person responsible for the accident. That is the case, which is even more important, of situations in which the

12 See the preface by G. Viney in S. Carval, *La responsabilité dans sa fonction de peine privée* (Paris: LGDJ, 1995).

13 D. Schnapper, 'Les victimes et le procès pénal', *Commentaire* 3, no. 179 (Autumn 2022): p. 589.

14 See the preface by R. Bout and the foreward by Ph. Le Tourneau in C. Bloch, *La cessation de l'illicite* (Paris: Dalloz, 2008).

compensation of victims is transferred to guarantee funds.[15] The issue of liability is then completely hidden in aid of a collectivisation of risks which blurs the frontier between victim and liable person, since the victim indirectly contributes, as a member of the community, to their own compensation.

Aiming to also compensate the victims of damage that may not be repaired via civil liability, the law occasionally imposes on the author of the harm the reparation of the detrimental consequences of a fact that cannot be attributed to them. The most characteristic example of it, which is already an old one,[16] is that of the compensation of harm caused under the influence of a mental disorder. Pursuant to Article 414–3 of the French Civil Code, the author of the damage is 'nevertheless obligated to provide reparation', even though their mental disorder prevents them from being attributed a fault which, alone, would allow to hold them liable. The law here directly takes over from civil liability to create an obligation of compensation which is completely autonomous and separated from any idea of liability.

A transformation of the relation of obligation

Such a blurring of the purposes of civil liability is not without consequences for its foundations, which themselves become blurred. Indeed, not only does civil liability not have the exclusiveness of the reparation of the harm and may fulfil other functions, but it also does not necessarily rely on a legal relation between the victim and the author of the damage. This is a more recent evolution, emerging with the issue of compensation for the environmental damage and harm caused by robots. The absence of personality of the victim (nature in the first case) or of author of the damage (the robots in the second) makes the existence of a relation of obligation[17] – and consequently the foundation of such a liability – problematic. By questioning its purposes, it is therefore the

15 Fonds de garantie des victimes des actes de terrorisme et d'autres infraction (Loi n° 90-589 du 6 juillet 1990, mod. Loi n° 2008-644 du 1er juillet 2008) [Guarantee Fund for Victims of Terrorist Attacks and Other Offences (Law no. 90-589 of 6 July 1990, Model Law no. 2008-644 of 1 July 2008)]; Fonds de garantie des assurances obligatoires de dommages (Loi n° 2003-706 du 1er août 2003, mod. Loi n° 2007-1174 du 17 décembre 2007) [Compulsory Damage Insurance Guarantee Fund (Law no. 2003-706 of 1 August 2003, Model Law no. 2007-1174 of 17 December 2007)].

16 That compensation regime was established by Loi n° 68-5 du 3 janvier 1968 portant réforme du droit des incapables majeurs [Law no. 68-5 of 3 January 1968 on the reform of the law on incapacity].

17 That difficulty tends to be overcome by attempts of personification either of natural elements or robots. Thus, laws granting rivers legal personhood were enacted in New Zealand in 2014 and in 2017, while the European Parliament adopted on 16 February 2017 a resolution offering to establish the legal personhood of autonomous robots (see *G. Loiseau, 'La personnalité juridique des robots, une monstruosité juridique', La Semaine juridique – Édition général (JCP G)*, no. 22 (2018): p. 597). That headlong rush towards an increasing artificialisation of the legal relation badly hides the unsettled issue of the legal foundation of the liability that is to be established.

very notion of liability that is being blurred, hence the necessity to renew its foundations.

Renewed foundations

A contradictory inspiration

While the need for the renewal of the foundations of civil liability is the consequence of the blurring of its purposes, it cannot be said that what inspires that needed renewal is perfectly consistent. The causal role of the fault in the implementation of civil liability is probably the most significant manifestation of that inconsistency. The classical conception of liability as it is expressed in Article 1240 of the French Civil Code expressly links fault and reparation. It is the fault which, by causing the damage, obliges who has committed it to repair the detrimental consequences that result. However, that link between fault and reparation today is being undermined by the purely utilitarian aim of facilitating the compensation of the victim while reparation is no longer the sole function of civil liability.

Reparation without fault

The rupture of the necessity relation between fault and reparation of its resulting damage is seen in liability for damage caused by things as well as in vicarious liability.

As to liability for damage caused by 'things under one's custody',[18] a decision of 7 April 2022[19] is quite revealing. The *Cour de Cassation*, considering that 'only the victim at the exclusive origin of the damage they suffer is an obstacle to the examination of the liability of the custodian of the thing', has held the lessor of a lodging liable as the custodian of a window from which the tenant had fallen at night after consuming alcohol and drugs. The fall of the tenant having caused his death, the lessor was held to be solely liable – as the custodian of the window – for the death of the victim, the imprudence of the latter not being the *exclusive* cause of the damage, for it would not have happened if the lodging had not had a window from which one could fall. . . . The absurd reasoning clearly shows the evolution from the liability of the custodian to a guarantee mechanism which imposes on the lessor (and its insurer) the consequences of the victim's inappropriate use of the window given the state he had put himself in.

The same disassociation between the fault and the reparation appears in vicarious liability. This is shown in the evolution of the responsibility of the

18 Code civile (C. civ.) [Civil Code], article 1242, (Ancien Article [Formerly Article] 1384).

19 Cour de cassation, deuxième chambre civile (Cass. 2ème civ.) [Supreme Court for Judicial Matters, Second Civil Chamber], 7 April 2022, no. 20-19.746, D. 2022, 1454, note S. François.

father and mother for the acts of their minor children towards full responsibility. This has been consecrated by the *Cour de Cassation* in its *Bertrand*[20] decision and which obliges the father and mother to repair any damage cause by their minor children even though they are not at fault. There again, the solution could lead to absurd results. As has been underlined by a distinguished commentator,

> one could imagine that the first student to have failed a competitive exam asks for reparation to the parents of the last one to have passed it – supposing the latter is a minor – because of the damage that the success of their child causes them![21]

Those converging evolutions of the liability of the custodian as well as that of the father and mother show that the repairing purpose of civil liability prevails over the link with the fault, which is not devoid of paradox, insofar as reparation has ceased to be the sole function – or even the dominant one – of civil liability. There is some inconsistency here which may cause the specificity of civil liability to disappear to transform it into a mechanism of compensation among others, which is far from being the most efficient one. That is all the more regrettable as case law has, alongside, shown it was inventive enough to design, based on the nature of civil liability, an authentic renewal of its foundations.

The invention of authority

That authentic renewal was conducted through the invention of a general principle of vicarious liability founded on authority. Unlike liability 'for the things one has custody of', which case law discovered as early as the end of the 19th century based on Section 1 of Article 1384 of the Civil Code,[22] it was only in the 1991 *Blieck*[23] decision that a general principle of liability 'for people one has to answer for' was asserted. The foundation of that general principle of liability is the authority exercised over the other. The judicial invention of that new case of civil liability relies on the idea that the exercise of authority, by drawing the support of who is subjected to it, may be at the origin of a detrimental behaviour. The relation established between the one who exercises authority and the behaviour of the one subjected to that authority justifies the

20 Cour de cassation, deuxième chambre civile (Cass. 2ème civ.), 19 February 1997, no. 94-21.111; H. Capitant, F. Terré, Y. Lequette, and F. Chénedé, *Grands arrêts de la jurisprudence civile*, t. 2, 13ème éd. (Paris: Dalloz, 2015), pp. 217–219.

21 H. Capitant, et al., *Grands arrêts de la jurisprudence civile.*

22 Cour de cassation, section civile (Cass. civ.), 16 June 1896, *Teffaine*, D. *1897, 1, 433, note* R. *Saleilles; S.* 1897, 1, 17, note A. Esmein.

23 Cour de cassation, assemblée plénière (Cass. ass. plén.), 29 March 1991, *Grands arrêts de la jurisprudence civile*, no. 218, p. 343.

obligation. For the one who, based on their authority, is at the origin of the detrimental behaviour is to repair its consequences.

Looking for the unity of the functions and foundations of civil liability

That creative interpretation, which discovered a new possible foundation for liability, shows that it is possible to renew those foundations while keeping them consistent with the functions attributed to civil liability. The recognition of a liability founded on the exercise of authority indeed allows the development of both the repairing and preventative functions of liability. It does this by encouraging the one who exerts an authority to integrate the prevention of any resulting damage into the use they make of it. To do so, it is still necessary, however, to keep the link between fault and reparation in order not to transform civil liability into a simple guarantee nor to make the one who exercises an authority the easy scapegoat of irreparable misfortunes that they are not liable for, properly speaking.

17 The responsibility of the Executive

Cross-read approaches

Amaia Errecart

Anyone who is interested in the concept of responsibility will note that it seems to operate like a *credo* in our society. A legal notion at the beginning, responsibility has become a principle of action which has progressively been extended to all domains, from individual to collective action, be it economic, political, public or other.

This chapter offers an approach of the notion of responsibility which is anchored in information and communication sciences (ICS), an area which is inherently interdisciplinary, originating in different fields of humanities and social sciences. This text also presents a sort of 'step aside' compared to the topic of the symposium, insofar as it relies on works focused more on 'corporate social responsibility' (CSR) than on the responsibility of the Executive as such, and makes the assumption that a certain number of features shared by the economic and political spheres as to responsibility – which is the sign of an increasingly visible porosity between the different social worlds – may be revealed.

First a (short) genealogy of the notion of responsibility will be presented, then this chapter will focus on the case of the economic actors that companies are through the issue of the scope of the field of responsibility that characterises them today. Last, the elements which seem structuring as to the specific input of an approach of the concept of responsibility through the information and communication sciences will be examined.

A short genealogy of the notion of responsibility

As Nicole D'Almeida underlines in a book on unlimited liability companies (*L'entreprise à responsabilité illimitée*), in which she explores the different aspects of responsibility in today's economic sphere by relying on a double philosophical and communicational anchorage, the notion of responsibility, which is historically recent, emerged in the 18th century in a society which was becoming secularised, and which granted individuals what used to be the prerogative of divine power: 'The irruption of responsibility corresponds, in society as in the (economic, social or political) organisations, to the refusal of transcendence, the supreme and remote cause of human future which has

DOI: 10.4324/9781003281559-30

the features of God or fate'.[1] Then, 'being responsible means being capable of accounting for (*respondere*) freely chosen acts. The idea of responsibility supposes that events do not happen either by chance or out of necessity, but are produced by a freedom which is a capacity of initiatives'.[2]

In his article published in *Esprit* in 1994 which presents a semantic analysis of the concept of responsibility, Paul Ricoeur specifies that, in the classic legal use, that concept is defined, in civil law, by the obligation to remedy the damage one has inflicted and, in criminal law, by the obligation to suffer a punishment.[3]

Paul Ricoeur also notes that

> it is outside the semantic field of the verb 'answer', regardless of whether it means 'answer to' or 'account for' that the foundational concept must be looked for, that is, in the semantic field of the verb impute, . . . Imputing an action to someone means attributing it as to its true author, as if to ascribe it to them and making them accountable for it.[4]

It is a question of making someone accountable for a reprehensible act, for a fault. Responsibility becomes an 'obligation to do which goes beyond the frame of compensation and punishment'.[5] The extent of the field of responsibility thus goes with a transformation of meaning that Paul Ricoeur highlights: responsibility now refers less to the damage or to the consequences of the act than to the relation between who acts and who suffers. Being responsible is not only being capable of accounting for one's acts, it is increasingly expressing a concern for the other. Responsibility is less individual than relational, its contrary being negligence (its Latin etymology, *neg-ligere*, means 'cut the link').

Thus, there is a shift from a paradigm of compensation to one of imputation: 'Everything happens as if the narrowing of the legal field were compensated by an extension of the moral field of responsibility'.[6]

It is to be noted that the legal-philosophical notion of imputation is used by researchers in information and communication sciences like Nicole D'Almeida, who links it to two close terms – deputation and reputation. Imputation and deputation refer to two distinct positions:

> Imputation consists in attributing an act to a presumed author, who is the object of a positive (praise) or negative (blame) judgement while

1 N. D'Almeida, *L'entreprise à responsabilité illimitée. La citoyenneté d'entreprise en questions* (Paris: Éditions Liaisons, 1996), p. 155.

2 N. D'Almeida, *L'entreprise à responsabilité illimitée*, p. 155.

3 P. Ricœur, 'Le concept de responsabilité. Essai d'analyse sémantique', *Esprit*, no. 206 (November 1994): p. 28.

4 P. Ricœur, 'Le concept de responsabilité', p. 30.

5 P. Ricœur, 'Le concept de responsabilité', p. 29.

6 P. Ricœur, 'Le concept de responsabilité', p. 42.

> deputation consists in taking charge of a public interest mission. Imputation happens *a posteriori*, it implies an obligation to do (repair, bear the consequences of one's act) while deputation is a will to do which is stated *a priori*. Imputation is decided by another and implies an answer, while deputation is self-stated and includes some sovereignty. Imputation is a notion that refers to the law (to the mechanism of attribution of responsibility and answer, *respondere*) whereas deputation refers to the self-determined sphere of morals and political commitment.[7]

Imputation therefore represents a debtor pole that submits to the assessment of a third party. Its place is the court. Declaring one's deputation symmetrically represents a voluntarist pole, an ethical or political declaration of intent and the modes of its implementation. It belongs to the platform. Reputation has become 'an economic variable in its own right and that old word is regaining its strength, defeating close notions like renown, fame or image'.[8]

In its contemporary meaning, the notion of responsibility thus oscillates between those three poles or positions of imputation, deputation and reputation. An individual principle of action at the beginning, it has become a political principle which applies both in the political and economic domains. The obligation to account for one's acts, as to render accounts, is imposed like an injunction on individuals and organisations alike by a society which is looking for meaning and transparency, and is permeated by logics of generalised media coverage, in which the role of opinion – or audience – is increasingly significant.

The case of economic actors: the extension of the field of responsibility

Companies, which today are (re)defining their missions and (re)building a weakened legitimacy, like most institutions, do not escape that trend: today they have to account for their activities, and are accountable – in line with the Anglo-Saxon perspective of accountability – to an increasingly greater number of people (shareholders, personnel, journalists, customers, public authorities, elected representatives, associations, etc.). Indeed, though in the neo-classic economic theory the company is essentially destined to look for profit and the maximisation of it, the attribution of the responsibility to the company implies taking into account criteria that are beyond the strict framework of economic activity. The economic system is not perceived as independent from the social sphere: the company is given a role as a social actor insofar as it is integrated into society. Its function is no longer to only maximise its profitability and

7 D'Almeida, *La société du jugement. Essai sur les nouveaux pouvoirs de l'opinion* (Paris: Armand Colin, 2007), p. 117.

8 D'Almeida, *La société du jugement*, p. 110.

increase its profits, but to consider and even to take charge of the general interest.

Thus, the notion of 'corporate social responsibility' is inspired from theories which have been developed for some 50 years by management sciences and organisational studies aiming to elaborate a vision of the relations that companies should have with their external environment. It has progressively become prevalent in the management concerns of companies, by offering a systemic vision of the relations between the company and society, the company being caught, 'embedded' in a network of relations with its different stakeholders.[9]

From a communicational perspective, 'corporate social responsibility' is translated into 'ethical declarations',[10] voluntarist justification discourses, those 'written texts of the CSR' based on the structuring principle of the 'promise'.[11] Companies are compelled to question anew the role they have in society, to adopt new positions which in particular translate into a re-characterising of their activities in the register of general interest, which may create a difference 'in a competition domain where trade battles are won in the field of image'.[12] As the company has become a 'society matter',[13] the economic organisations have to justify their activities and their contribution, not only based on the profit they make but also in relation to social, societal and environment dimensions as to which they are being questioned.

It is therefore the place of the company within society which is being challenged. While Max Weber had underlined that the dynamic of capitalism could not be reduced to objective factors, but that entrepreneurship could be motivated by religion, ethics and psychology,[14] Luc Boltanski and Ève Chiapello have shown that, in line with his work, and in front of increasing scepticism and criticisms from society, capitalism has been led to justify itself, to demonstrate that it contributes to the general interest and the common good.[15] That looking for justification, which is accompanied with a search for legitimacy, leads it to draw from the beliefs and values which have a persuasive power in society.[16]

Thus, 'ethics (which is characteristics of CSR discourses) constitutes in itself a communicational phenomenon of dislocation of the norms that are

9 K. Polanyi, *La grande transformation. Aux origines politiques et économiques de notre temps* (Paris: Gallimard, 1983).

10 C. Renouard, 'L'éthique et les déclarations déontologiques des entreprises', *Études* 410, no. 4 (2009): pp. 473–484.

11 R. Huët and C. Loneux, 'Une analyse communicationnelle des "écrits de la RSE": le cas des chartes et codes de conduite', *Revue de l'organisation responsable* 4, no. 1 (2009): p. 59.

12 G. Lipovetsky, *Le crépuscule du devoir. L'éthique indolore des nouveaux temps démocratiques* (Paris: Gallimard, 2000), p. 337.

13 R. Sainsaulieu, ed., *L'entreprise, une affaire de société* (Paris: Presses de Sciences Po, 1992).

14 M. Weber, *L'éthique protestante ou l'esprit du capitalisme* (Paris: Plon, 1985).

15 L. Boltanski and E. Chiapello, *Le nouvel esprit du capitalisme* (Paris: Gallimard, 1999).

16 L. Boltanski and E. Chiapello, *Le nouvel esprit du capitalisme*, p. 70 in particular.

traditionally admitted and acknowledged in companies. Systems are implemented to produce real things, to act on the world order in order to produce consistent relations between different elements'.[17] Accordingly, companies seem to be constantly looking for 'acceptability' and legitimacy. They have understood that, to establish that legitimacy, they have to adopt symbolic or effective strategies of image and conformity to the dominating values of society. Legitimacy may then be defined as 'the shared impression that the actions of the organisation are desirable, suitable or appropriate as to a socially built system of social norms, values and beliefs'.[18]

However, the legitimacy of the company cannot be self-declared, it can only be recognised. Thus, companies may lose at any time their so-called licence to operate, in the sense of 'intervening', for neglecting the negative perceptions that their activities may generate in public opinion. Here the aforementioned notions of imputation, deputation and reputation are implicitly associated with CSR.

Let it also be specified that responsibility becomes a principle of action which emphasises coercion less than incentive, on the individual level as well as on the level of organisations. The very principle of CSR entails a precise conception of a type of privileged regulation. It is incentivising and voluntary, and it is an alternative to regulatory regulation – since this non-constraining character may be understood as a limit to the exercise of that responsibility because it depends on the willingness of the actors and their own commitment.

The specific input of an approach from information and communication sciences

Moving away from the management approach, which is often quoted on those topics, the communicational approach of the CSR shifts the usual representation of companies. The latter are no longer perceived as a place of production of goods and services, which have a more or less extended responsibility, but also as spaces where discourses are made, which will participate in the shaping of the specific representations of the social world. The company is then understood as a real speaker subject. It is composed of individuals and groups which make discourses and try to give some consistency to the world where it acts. Economic organisations are social actors that are places of production and circulation of signs and meaning, which evolve and are transformed depending on society's changes, of which they make themselves the mirror and the indicator.

17 C. Loneux, 'Analyse critique de la "Responsabilité Sociale des Entreprises" (RSE): changement/permanence, la normalisation comme processus', in *Communication & Organisation: Perspectives Critiques*, eds. T. Heller, R. Huët, and B. Vidaillet (Villeneuve d'Ascq: Presses Universitaires du Septentrion, 2013), p. 133.

18 M. Capron and F. Quairel-Lanoizelée, *Mythes et réalités de l'entreprise responsable. Acteurs, enjeux, stratégies* (Paris: La Découverte, 2004), p. 105.

As to the production of CSR discourse, communication is sometimes perceived and presented as only belonging to greenwashing, i.e., as façade discourses in which the ethical and responsible commitment is only a statement without effective content. Thus,

> the proliferation and high heterogeneousness of those communicational objects have led some actors to consider CSR as a simple play on words. Companies are then accused of creating the illusion of a change and the CSR policies are only marketing and communication strategies without direct associated effects. That criticism is problematic in that it prevents thinking of communication as an effectively meaningful activity producing social effects beyond the intentions of their authors.[19]

Communicational work on CSR indeed works as engineering of the symbolic, in which social representations, beliefs, imaginaries, forms of narrative, but also discourse and rhetorical strategies – which are precisely the object of the analysis of the researcher in ICS – are used.

One question can be raised from that perspective of research: would 'corporate social responsibility' be testifying to a will of re-enchantment, as a mode of responding (*respondere*) to the expectations and requirements of the different publics in these times of 'endless crisis'?[20]

It is to be noted that that rhetoric is also present in the discourses of other social players, especially public and political ones, which may allow enlarging the focus of that questioning.

Conclusion

Starting from the definition of responsibility by the law – which makes the distinction between civil responsibility, which aims first and foremost to repair the damage that has been inflicted, and criminal responsibility, which is characterised by its objective of punishment – we have referred to Paul Ricœur's philosophical approach which shows that,

> All the contemporary story of what is called the *law of responsibility* in the technical sense, tends to make room for the idea of *no-fault responsibility*, under the pressure of concepts such as solidarity, security and risk which tend to take the place of the idea of fault.[21]

19 R. Huët and C. Loneux, 'Une analyse communicationnelle des "écrits de la RSE"', p. 55.
20 M. Revault d'Allonnes, *La crise sans fin. Essai sur l'expérience moderne du temps* (Paris: Seuil, 2012).
21 P. Ricœur, 'Le concept de responsabilité', p. 40.

There is a development of both the moral and political dimension of the concept of responsibility, as it can be seen at work in the economic sphere through the implementation of so-called corporate social responsibility policies.

Works about the legitimacy of the activities of the companies compared to the dominating values of society, after Luc Boltanski and Ève Chiapello, are particularly enlightening to understand the (re)positioning of companies and its evolution. However, as shown by the approach of the information and communication sciences, while discourses on CSR are not devoid of ambiguity, they 'oblige' those who make them: in front of the necessity of anticipating risks – be they environmental, social or of opinion – the companies are forced to reassess their place in society, and to adopt new positions which in particular are translated into a re-characterisation – in the discourse at least – of their activities in the register of the general interest.

One can consequently assess here the evolution of the concept of responsibility through its different semantic migrations from its original legal meaning.

18 The unique nature of political responsibility

Cécile Guérin-Bargues

Conceiving a multidisciplinary approach of the concept of responsibility and applying it to the very specific object of the Executive is an ambitious objective. From the angle of political responsibility, the project even seems to be quite a tall order. As early as 1835, Pellegrino Rossi, the first holder of a constitutional law position, already distinguished 'moral and political responsibility' from 'judicial responsibility'.[1] Since it is only an obligation in a weak sense, political responsibility is clearly different from administrative responsibility and even more from civil or criminal liability.

In order to demonstrate the uniqueness of political responsibility, let us first try to briefly define the notion of 'Executive'. Pursuant to the provisions of the French Constitution[2] and in particular the combined reading of Articles 10 and 13 on the President of the Republic, Article 20 on the government and Article 21 on the Prime Minister, the Executive first refers to the group made up of the President of the Republic and the government headed by the Prime Minister. Article 20 of the Constitution pursuant to which '[t]he Government shall determine and conduct the policy of the Nation. It shall have at its disposal the civil service and the armed forces' is quite valuable to grasp that notion. Admittedly, it only imperfectly describes the reality of the operation of institutions, since in case of concordance between the presidential and parliamentary majority, the authority of the Head of State prevails over that of the Prime Minister and the government. Because of what some people have referred to as the presidential appropriation of the regime,[3] in practice it falls to the President of the Republic to determine the nation's policy. This is not essential for our reflection, though. What is crucial is what is said about the Executive in Article 20, even when it is dominated by the Head of State. By

1 Excerpt from his *Cours de droit constitutionnel*, quoted by Marcel Morabito in *Histoire constitutionnelle de la France de 1789 à nos jours*, 17è éd. (Paris: LGDJ, 2022), p. 251.

2 All of the references from the Constitution of 1958 in this text are taken from: www.conseil-constitutionnel.fr/en/constitution-of-4-october-1958

3 A. Le Divellec, 'Parlementarisme négatif et captation présidentielle. La démocratie française dans la "cage d'acier" du présidentialisme', in *Les soixante ans de la Constitution. 1958–2018*, eds. Le Cercle des Constitutionnalistes and É. Balladur (Paris: Dalloz, 2018), pp. 73–87.

DOI: 10.4324/9781003281559-31

letting the dimensions of anticipation, initiative, conception and execution show through, the article makes one think that G. Burdeau's expression – of 'government function'[4] – would be more adequate to account for modern political and administrative practices than the idea of subordination inherent in that of executive power.[5] However, one can only partially agree with G. Burdeau's idea here. He recommended to include the legislative function in the government one in order to differentiate two constitutional powers only: the 'autonomous and unconditioned'[6] government function and the 'subordinate and limited'[7] administrative one. The classic distribution of powers within the State however profits from the 'brilliant consecration of positive law'[8] which does not subject administrative and legislative acts to the same legal regime. Here, the notion of Executive will therefore refer to the government function, in a broad sense, but from which legislative activity is definitely excluded. This does not amount to negating the extension of the notion especially since the Executive could not be reduced only to the constitutive elements which are at the highest level of the State. The existence of local executive authorities, the prerogatives and budgets of which increased as decentralisation developed, indeed leads us to include their responsibility in our analysis.

The political system of the Fifth Republic shows a strong concentration of powers to the benefit of the Executive, be it at the national or decentralised level. At the national level, the preponderance of the executive power is provided for and organised in the Constitution which, via Article 5, makes the President of the Republic the 'keystone' of the regime (Michel Debré), while the government has many attributions.[9] At the local level, the same tendency appears. The distinction between the deliberating and executive bodies is underlined in the General Code of Local Authorities, which entrusts the former with 'conducting the business' of the community and the latter with preparing and executing the decisions of the Assembly.[10] The decision-making power of the assemblies badly resists the concentration of powers in the hands of the Executives, at all the local levels. That concentration has been facilitated by the presence of the Executive in the local assembly and reinforced by the strengthening of decentralisation which has resulted in a real marginalising of the assemblies.[11]

4 G. Burdeau, 'Remarques sur la classification des fonctions étatiques', *Revue du droit publique* 51, no. 61 (1945): p. 214.

5 A. Le Divellec and M. de Villiers, 'Pouvoir exécutif', in *Dictionnaire du droit constitutionnel* (Paris: Sirey, 2022), p. 289.

6 G. Burdeau, 'Remarques sur la classification des fonctions étatiques', p. 218.

7 G. Burdeau, 'Remarques sur la classification des fonctions étatiques', p. 220.

8 G. Burdeau, 'Remarques sur la classification des fonctions étatiques', p. 204.

9 See, in particular, Articles 20, 39, 44, 45 and 49 of the Constitution.

10 See for example Article L2511-2 CGCT (General Code for Local Authorities) for Paris, Lyon, and Marseille.

11 S. Cadiou, 'Les exécutifs locaux', *Revus française d'administration publique* 2, no. 154 (2015): p. 338.

That power of the Executives, at the national and decentralised levels, would not be really problematic if the essential principles of liberal democracy were fully respected. The latter implies that with power come responsibilities, but also and above all, responsibility. In other words, to quote the suggestive distinction made by Paul Ricoeur, 'responsibility-burden' (to have responsibilities) implies 'responsibility-attributability' (to account for).[12] The concentration of powers to the benefit of the Executives should therefore be compensated by a full effectiveness of the principle of responsibility.

However, that responsibility of the Executive – one should say the Executives – is particular. It expresses the idea that the rulers, entrusted with the conduct of public business, must account for how they exercise their power. The adjective that is added to it – political – naturally allows to differentiate it from other types of responsibility – administrative, civil or criminal – to only mention the law. It first refers to the specificity of some persons who are destined to fulfil it (the political personnel) or to hold to account (the political personnel, the people, the *polis*, the city). It then echoes the originality of its modes of implementation (motion of confidence, of censure, vote) and its sanction (destitution or *a minima* loss of authority). Last, it allows to isolate that type of responsibility in all its uniqueness since, unlike administrative responsibility, for example,[13] political responsibility is fundamentally different from private law responsibility.

The very definition of political responsibility still remains uncertain. Should its conception be 'technical and legal' and should it be assimilated to the loss of power only, for example the resignation of the government (Const. Article 50) or the destitution of the President of the Republic (Const. Article 68)? Should it on the contrary be understood in a more flexible way, taking into consideration the 'reputational' mechanisms of responsibility? Political responsibility then becomes diffuse and goes beyond the framework of the constitutional rule, at the risk of diluting the notion outside the border areas of the law.[14] In such an assumption, emphasis is laid on the fact that responsibility is exerted before different instances of various sorts, be they the parliamentarians of a committee of inquiry, or, even more broadly, public opinion. There results a broader conception of political responsibility which is no longer reduced to a mechanism of sanction but seems to be a process of assessment of the action of rulers. Responsibility will then be defined here as a mechanism of attribution of value to the acts of the Executive. It aims to encourage – rather than oblige – the rulers to render account, following a determined procedure and

12 P. Ricœur, 'Le temps de la responsabilité', in *Entretien sur l'éthique*, ed. F. Lenoir (Paris: Fayard, 1991).

13 B. Seiller, *Droit administratif*, vol. 2 (Paris: Flammarion, 2021), p. 282.

14 P. Ségur, 'Qu'est-ce que la responsabilité politique?', *Revue du droit publique* 6, no. 2 (1999): p. 1601.

before an authority invested with conducting that supervision, for acts done during office.[15]

For some 30 years now, France has been the place of a strange historical reversal, which shows in the criminalising of public life.[16] This can be explained in particular by the rise in importance of the figure of the victim, which has been favoured by the multiplication of incriminations, the progressive objectification of responsibility over the 20th century and the assertion of an increasing number of individual rights. To the emergence of a society which is inherently risk-adverse is added the attraction of the principle of equality, which contains the claim of a strict subjection of political authorities to ordinary law.

Those evolutions of society are combined with the weakness of the mechanisms of political or administrative responsibility. On a constitutional level, the rationalising of the notion of censure has been added to the optional character of the inauguration of the government and the absence of individual political responsibility of the ministers in the name of ministerial solidarity. Thus, the idea that the minister is more accountable for his actions to the President of the Republic or the Prime Minister than to Parliament has taken root. From the point of view of civil or administrative responsibility, the landscape is not better, since, because of a solidarity credo, administrative case law has led to an increasingly narrower conception of personal fault, the few leftovers of which are diluted in the notion of fault not deprived of any link with the service. The increase in the resorting to criminal law aiming to give back some meaning to personal responsibility thus will not come as a surprise. It is nonetheless quite worrying given the evolution of political institutions. It is indeed a form of regression, since the very principle of the political and collective responsibility of the government, which is at the heart of the parliamentarian regime, has gained ground thanks to the progressive weakening of the criminal liability of the ministers.[17] It should also draw the attention of the jurist who is attached to categories, so immeasurable political responsibility and criminal liability seem to be. From the point of view of its nature, political responsibility has a collective and functional dimension which criminal liability lacks (I). It is also particular because of the superfluous character of the fault and incrimination alike (II) and the specificity of the sanction (III) which are not relevant in matters of criminal, civil or administrative responsibility.

15 We are modifying and extending the meaning of the definition of P. Ségur in 'Qu'est-ce que la responsabilité politique?', p. 1609.

16 On recent evolutions on that matter, see my article: C. Guérin-Bargues, 'L'emprise du droit pénal sur la responsabilité des gouvernants dans un contexte de crise sanitaire', *Actualité juridique Pénal* 12 (December 2021): pp. 569–572.

17 The history of the progressive falling into disuse of the impeachment procedure in 18th-century England is an example of it. See D. Baranger, *Parlementarisme des origines* (Paris: PUF, 1999), pp. 255 ff.

The collective and functional dimension of political responsibility

While criminal liability is an individual and personal responsibility, political responsibility fundamentally seems to be a collective responsibility which may be exercised for the other.

Criminal liability, unlike civil liability, can only be imposed on whoever (author or accomplice) has actually committed a criminal offence. It is therefore personal, as specified in Article 121–1 of the Penal Code pursuant to which 'No one is criminally liable except for his own conduct'[18] which is a principle with a constitutional value.[19] There result from that fundamental characteristic of criminal liability several consequences each of which moves it away from political responsibility.

First, criminal liability could not be strict since it is founded on a quality. Conversely, political responsibility is precisely responsibility because of an office.[20] The minister, who holds authority in the political and administrative domains, is the only one to have received power democratically, even if indirectly. They therefore have normally to be held liable for the acts of those who work under their direction.[21]

Then, criminal liability could not be vicarious, despite seeming exceptions to the principle of personal responsibility.[22] There results that in criminal matters transfers of liability are impossible in theory. On the contrary, political responsibility, pursuant to the principle of ministerial solidarity, is precisely 'vicarious liability'.[23] It is the government as a whole which is accountable for the acts of each of its members, as for those of the civil servants working under the authority of the ministers.[24] Unlike criminal liability, political responsibility thus allows to attribute, through a fictitious link, 'to whoever is liable all the acts of the Executive, no matter their real origin'.[25]

Last, criminal liability, unlike political responsibility, could not be collective: in case a crime has been committed by several persons, an individual can only be found criminally liable if it is possible to determine their precise participation in the commission of the fact constituting the crime. Conversely, the principle of ministerial solidarity, which is shown in the resignation of the

18 All citations of the French criminal code (Code pénal) can be found at: www.equalrightstrust.org/ertdocumentbank/french_penal_code_33.pdf
19 Conseil constitutionnel (CC) [Constitutional Court], 16 juin 1999, no. 199-411 DC.
20 O. Beaud, *Le sang contaminé* (Paris: PUF, 1999), p. 116.
21 O. Beaud, *Le sang contaminé*, p. 125.
22 On those exceptions, which are partly a consequence of the criminal liability of legal persons, see in particular, J. Larguier, P. Conte, and V. Peltier, *Droit pénal général*, 24è éd. (Paris: Dalloz, 2022), p. 92.
23 P. Avril, 'Pouvoir et responsabilité', in *Mélanges G. Burdeau, Le pouvoir* (Paris: LGDJ, 1977), p. 9.
24 P. Ségur, 'Qu'est-ce que la responsabilité politique?', p. 1606.
25 D. Baranger, *Parlementarisme des origines*, pp. 151–152.

whole government as provided for in Article 50 of the Constitution, shows the collective dimension of political responsibility. However, one should note that, in practice, under the Fifth Republic, the ministers tend to be accountable to the President of the Republic, because, in particular, of the latter's power of appointment provided for in Article 8 of the Constitution.[26] Political responsibility then has an individual dimension which is excluded before the National Assembly, since the latter can only censure the government as a whole.

The superfluous character of incrimination and fault alike

Criminal liability is founded on the attribution of an illegal fact to a person who is considered to have committed a criminal offence. However, the committing of a crime implies the meeting of at least three constitutive elements: the material element, of course, but also the moral and the legal ones. The last two seem to be fundamentally exogenous to political responsibility.

The moral component of criminal liability implies that the author of the act has committed a fault. Guilt is indeed necessary to the existence of the moral element, without which there could be no crime.[27] In political matters, on the contrary, responsibility is disassociated from guilt.[28] The establishment of political responsibility is not subordinated to the existence of a fault or a mistake that the Executive could be held accountable for.[29] The shared feeling of the incompetence of the government in office could in theory be enough. A persisting divergence of points of view between the government and the National Assembly could perfectly lead to the adoption of a motion of censure by the latter against the former.[30]

Moreover, as to criminal liability, the principle is that of the lawfulness of incriminations and sentences, which is set in Article 8 of the Declaration of the Rights of Man and the Citizen and repeated in Article 111–3 of the Penal Code. What is at stake is the exclusion of arbitrariness and the protection of individual freedoms.[31] The increasing role of the case law interpretation admittedly results in 'a fuzzier determination of the limit between what is allowed and what is prohibited, which does not exclude doubt'.[32] However, in criminal liability matters, the principle *nulla poena sine lege* still prevails.

26 'The President of the Republic shall appoint the Prime Minister. He shall terminate the appointment of the Prime Minister when the latter tenders the resignation of the Government. On the recommendation of the Prime Minister, he shall appoint the other members of the Government and terminate their appointments'.

27 J. Larguier, P. Conte, and V. Peltier, *Droit pénal général*, p. 39.

28 That is what Georgina Dufoix had tried to express in vain during the trial of the contaminated blood, when she said, 'responsible but not guilty', a formula the legal accuracy of which was inversely proportional to political opportunity. . .

29 P. Ségur, 'Qu'est-ce que la responsabilité politique?', p. 1606.

30 P. Ségur, 'Qu'est-ce que la responsabilité politique?', p. 1606.

31 J. Larguier, P. Conte, and V. Peltier, *Droit pénal général*, p. 14.

32 J. Larguier, P. Conte, and V. Peltier, *Droit pénal général*, p. 16.

On the contrary, political responsibility is characterised by the fundamental indeterminacy of the faults and mistakes that may be politically sanctioned. The legal framework is much looser than in criminal liability matters.[33] This is shown for example in Article 68 of the Constitution which provides for a procedure of destitution of the Head of State in case of a 'breach of his duties patently incompatible with his continuing in office'. It would be perfectly possible to launch such a procedure outside any criminal offence committed by the Head of State, for example because of a violation of the Constitution or a behaviour which would be patently incompatible with the continuing holding of office. The field of facts that could lead to political responsibility being imposed is therefore much broader and indeterminate than that of the sole crimes provided for in the Penal Code. Holding someone responsible does not depend on a text, on a legal classification of facts made by a judge, but a more subjective assessment of a given behaviour. It therefore does not respond to a principle of lawfulness but opportunity.[34] It incidentally puts up with alleged facts quite well, while 'legal' (criminal, civil or administrative) responsibility implies that proof of the incriminated behaviour has been brought.[35]

The specificity of sanctions

For criminal liability, there is a scale of sanctions which is all the more precise as the principle of lawfulness applies to sentences as well as to incriminations. While today judges apply increasingly personalised sentences, they could not create new ones. Only the law on crimes or the regulation on infractions could do that. There results a hierarchy of sentences which are differentiated, depending on their nature in French law, into serious, hybrid or minor ones.

Here again, political responsibility could not be that precise. The attraction exerted by the parliamentary regime in that field has for a long time led the constitutional doctrine[36] to limit the mechanisms of sanction of political responsibility to the sole possibility for the Parliament to force the government to resign. If one accepts that reduction of political responsibility to the legal mechanisms of revocation though, one must note that it is rather the principle of irresponsibility which prevails under the Fifth Republic. The president is politically irresponsible while in office, except if the exceptional procedure provided for in Article 68 of the Constitution is launched. As to the

33 O. Beaud, *Le sang contaminé*, p. 117.

34 O. Beaud, *Le sang contaminé*, p. 117.

35 O. Beaud, *Le sang contaminé*, p. 118.

36 See, for example, A. Esmein, *Éléments de droit constitutionnel français et comparé* (1914; reis. Paris: Panthéon Assas, 2001), p. 811: 'La responsabilité politique, caractéristique du gouvernement parlementaire, consiste simplement dans la perte du pouvoir, dans l'obligation morale de démissionner, qui s'impose aux ministres, lorsqu'ils ont perdu la majorité dans le parlement. . . . La responsabilité politique est la seule qui aboutisse nécessairement devant le parlement et ne puisse aboutir ailleurs'.

government, the recurring use of Article 49, except for once in 1962, has never led to its overthrow. Local Executives cannot be dismissed based on an initiative of citizens, or a motion of no confidence or censure.[37]

There is however no reason why political responsibility should be reduced to a few procedures that are known for being incapable of yielding any result because of the government's prudence or the majority fact, i.e., calling to account based on a general policy statement provided for in Article 49, Section 1[38] and possibility for the Assembly to adopt a spontaneous (Article 49, Section 2) or prompted (Article 49, Section 3) motion of censure. Political responsibility is indeed 'quicksilver',[39] the modes of which cover the whole range of means compelling the Executive to 'render account', that is, to justify its action. One should include, at least, all the instruments and tools provided for in the Constitution, the Organic Law or the Standing Orders of the Assemblies which allow the Parliament to supervise the government as provided for in Article 24 of the Constitution: committees of inquiry (Article 51–2), oral questions (Article 48, Section 1), written questions to the Prime Minister and on the government's general policy. . . . Political responsibility, unlike criminal liability, could therefore not be content with a narrow conception which determines its existence based on the possibility of a sanction. It must be grasped more broadly, beyond Articles 49 and 50, as a more flexible mode of assessment of the way the Executive performs its functions.

Be it from the point of view of its nature, its modes of exercise or its effects, political responsibility is little related to criminal liability. If one had to continue the judicial metaphor, one could also say that it often looks like a sort of trial without verdict, or debate without sanction . . . or maybe public disapproval or *satisfecit*, for which one may hope electoral consequences. One can therefore only be sorry that 'the social resurgence of the accusation'[40] has established a confusion of classes in minds. Examples of this could be the current claim in the *Cour de Justice de la République* to decide the liability of ministers as to how they have dealt with the pandemics.[41]

37 For a defence speech in that sense, see O. Beaud, 'L'affaire Perdiau, Le maire et la démocratie locale', *Jus Politicum Blog*, 1 October 2022, https://blog.juspoliticum.com/2022/10/01/laffaire-perdriau-le-maire-et-la-democratie-locale-par-olivier-beaud/

38 It only requires the absolute majority of the votes cast (and not of the Members of the Assembly) to force the government to resign. The Prime Minister, who decides, only risks it when they have some guarantees.

39 D. Baranger, 'L'affaire Benalla et la Constitution: le Sénat, organe de contrôle politique de l'exécutif', *Jus Politicum Blog*, 23 September 2018, https://blog.juspoliticum.com/2018/09/23/laffaire-benalla-et-la-constitution-le-senat-organe-de-controle-politique-de-lexecutif/

40 We borrow that expression from P. Ricoeur, 'Le concept de responsabilité. Essai d'analyse sémantique', *Esprit* 1, no. 18 (November 1994): p. 41.

41 On the confusion of responsibilities from which the existence and operation of the CJR proceed, see my book, C. Guérin-Bargues, *Juger les politiques: la Cour de justice de la République* (Paris: Dalloz, 2017).

19 Responsibility and sports

Some remarks on a particular couple

Clémentine Legendre

The subject of this chapter may be surprising at first sight. And indeed, the contribution of sports to the study of the founding concepts of responsibility is nothing but obvious. Sport may however, despite appearances, constitute a fertile laboratory of analysis of those concepts, for different reasons.

First, sport is a challenge for the fundamental notions of responsibility. The models of responsibility are, for example, thought in general with reference to a normal behaviour, that of the reasonable person. Conversely, what is expected from a sportsman is rarely a normal or reasonable behaviour. Practising sport very often implies taking risks, adopting more dangerous behaviours than usual or even using violence. Responsibility also often implies the identification of one responsible person. It may be difficult to identify that person in collective sports, of course, but also in phenomena such as violence in stadiums. The main principles of responsibility may consequently be ill-treated in sports matters.

Second, sport may allow a special highlighting of the founding notions of responsibility because of the diversity of the perspectives it calls upon. The damage that is caused during the practice of sport may lead to the author of the damage being held liable, of course, but other responsibilities may also be found: criminal liability in violent sports, administrative responsibility when a federation which is the holder of a public service concession is involved, or even disciplinary responsibility. Sports organisations overview the organisation of each sport and sanction, under the supervision of the Administrative Court, any breach of their rules. Responsibility in sports matters thus may draw upon multiple rules – State as well as sport ones – and courts – civil, criminal and administrative as well as private ones, such as the arbitrators of the Court of Arbitration for Sport. Such diversity makes sport a very valuable observation post of the central concepts of responsibility.

What could be noted from that lookout post? How do the classic notions of responsibility flourish in sports matters? The issue could justify a large-scale study.[1] The ambition of this contribution is more modest, since only some

1 See G. Durry, 'L'adéquation des notions classiques du droit de la responsabilité au fait sportif', in *Les problèmes juridiques du sport: responsabilité et assurance* (Paris: Economica, 1984),

DOI: 10.4324/9781003281559-32

trends, which disturb civil and administrative liabilities in sport, will be studied. Within those two types of responsibility two tendencies can be noted. First, in civil liability, the conditions of involvement of the responsibility of the sportsman are being increasingly hardened (I). Then, in disciplinary liability matters, the evolution on the contrary is towards a simplification of the possibility to hold a person liable (II). The will to reinforce the efficiency of sports rules leads to the fairly frequent sanctioning of sports players. Each of those trends calls for a few clarifications.

The restrictive admission of civil liability

Civil liability and sports will of course meet frequently. Sports practice necessarily leads to accidents and damage which are directly linked to the law of civil liability. The meeting could be explosive since the logics at work in those two disciplines are likely to be opposite. Civil liability has been for many years permeated by a logic of compensation, an 'ideology of reparation'.[2] Thus, the founding concepts of responsibility are thought to allow for the awarding of damages to the victim. In order to reach that objective, case law, for example, flexibly interprets the different facts creating liability. The strict application of such a logic in sports could seriously disturb the organisation of sports. Boxing is a good example of it. If each blow could allow to characterise a civil fault to guarantee the victim's compensation, the future of the discipline would obviously be compromised. To avoid those unfortunate consequences, the liability of the sportsman, be it based on fault (A) or actions of things (B), is admitted in a restricted way in case law.

Liability of the sportsman based on fault

First, the *Cour de Cassation* has hardened the conditions of the classification of fault in sport.[3] In its classic meaning, fault refers to 'the breach of a pre-existing duty'[4] or of the standard of the reasonable person. Practising a sport often means taking risks and therefore adopting little reasonable behaviours. Case law, which is aware of that state of affairs, has consequently raised the

pp. 19–38; J. Mouly, 'Les paradoxes du droit de la responsabilité civile dans le domaine des activités sportives', *La Semaine Juridique – Édition Générale (JCP G)* 1 (2005): p. 134; J. Mouly, 'La spécificité de la responsabilité civile dans le domaine du sport, légitime résistance ou inéluctable déclin?', *Revue Lamy Droit Civil (RLDC)*, no. 29 (2006); C. Albiges, S. Darmaisin and O. Sautel, *Responsabilité et sport* (New York: LexisNexis, 2007).

2 On which see, L. Cadiet, 'Sur les faits et les méfaits de l'idéologie de la réparation', in *Le Juge entre deux millénaires: Mélanges P. Drai* (Paris: Dalloz, 2000), p. 495.

3 On the specificity of the assessment of fault in sports, see D. Voinot, 'La faute en matière sportive', *RLDC* 15, no. 609 *(2005); P. Jourdain, 'A propos de la faute en matière sportive', in Le monde du droit, Écrits en l'honneur de J. Foyer* (Paris: Economica, 2008), pp. 559–567.

4 M. Planiol, *Traité élémentaire de droit civil*, 2e éd. (Paris: Pichon et Durand Auzias, 1901).

standard in that matter. It has made the characterisation of the fault conditional on the existence of quite a serious breach of the rules of the game.[5] It could be, for example, a disloyal behaviour or one that is against the spirit of the game.[6] The standard of the fault has thus been raised to take into account the specificities of sport.

The *Cour de Cassation*, which usually easily finds fault to make compensation easy, on the contrary, accepts some distance from that imperative in sports matters to adapt to their specificity. That restrictive admission of the liability of the sportsman also exists in liability caused by the action of things.

Liability of the sportsman based on the action of things

As to liability caused by the action of things, case law also tends to restrict the admission of the liability of the sportsman especially through its interpretation of the notion of custody. For liability caused by the action of things to be admitted, it must be possible to identify a custodian and, in principle, one only, but, in sports, the identification of the sole custodian is far from obvious each time. To be convinced, one only needs to think of the existence of a rugby or soccer match in which players pass the ball rapidly. If the ball causes a damage to one of the players during the game, it may be difficult to identify a custodian, since none of them seems to really control that ball. To deal with that difficulty, the *Cour de Cassation* has admitted that custody may be exercised in common when several persons have the same powers on the thing.[7] Then the different players are co-custodians. That common custody may however produce severe consequences on the victim player. Indeed, case law considers that being a custodian and a victim at the same time is not possible. The victim sportsman will not be able to have the other players held liable based on the action of the thing because they are a co-custodian.[8] Only the liability for fault could be admitted, but, as we have seen, on restrictive conditions.

The theory of the acceptance of risks also illustrates that restrictive admission of the liability of the sportsman because of the action of things. According to that theory, when an athlete participates in a sporting activity, they accept the normal risks linked to that activity. But accepting would amount

5 Among several decisions see, Cour de cassation (Cass.) [Supreme Court for Judicial Matters] 2e civ., 23 September 2004, no. 03-11.274, D. *2005, p. 551, note B. Brignon; Cass. 2e civ., 13 January 2005, no. 03-12.884, D.* 2005, p. 2435, note E. Cornut; *La Revue trimestrielle de droit civil (RTD Civ.)* 2005, p. 410, obs. P. Jourdain.

6 See Cass. 2e civ., 15 May 1972, *Bull. Civ.* II, no. 149; Cass. 2e civ., 21 June 1979, *Bull. Civ.* II, no. 196, D. 1979, IR 545, obs. F. Alaphilippe et J.-P. Karaquillo.

7 On the application of that theory in sports see, Cass. 2e civ., 20 November 1968, *Bull. Civ.* II, no. 277; *RTD Civ.*, 1969, 335, obs. G. Durry, and, more recently, Cass. 2e civ., 13 January 2005, no. 03-12.884, D. *2005, p. 2435, note E. Cornut; RTD Civ.*, 2005, p. 410, obs. P. Jourdain.

8 See Cass. 2e civ., 20 November 1968, *Bull. Civ.* II, no. 277; *RTD Civ.* 1969, 335, obs. G. Durry.

to renouncing to resort to liability caused by the action of things against the other competitors. When a damage happens during a sporting activity among sportsmen, the liability caused by the action of things of the sportsman causing the damage will not be admitted if that damage is the realisation of a normal risk related to that activity. The application of the theory of common custody and of the acceptance of risks therefore may result in harsh consequences for the victim since they both may neutralise liability due to the action of things.

That harshness against sports victims, which has been admitted for a long time, seems to be decreasing. Indeed, common custody is now used sparingly by judicial courts.[9] The theory of the acceptance of risks was completely abandoned by the *Cour de Cassation*, in its 4 November 2010 decision,[10] before it was reintroduced by the legislator in the Act of 12 March 2012[11] but only for material damage. A sportsman therefore cannot be held liable, based on the action of things, for the material damage inflicted on another sportsman if the damage is the realisation of a normal risk linked to that activity.

The observation of a strict framing of the conditions of the finding of the liability of the sportsman to protect sports interest has thus lost some of its force without completely disappearing. It still exists for fault-based liability and partly for liability caused by the action of things. As to disciplinary liability, the tendency is quite different.

The extensive admission of disciplinary liability

The conditions for imposing disciplinary liability on the contrary seem to be made more flexible. Sports organisations are trying to guarantee that any violation of their rules will be sanctioned, even in cases in which the classic conditions of liability are not strictly met. Two examples, which are far from isolated cases, clearly illustrate that phenomenon. The first is about the disciplinary liability of clubs for the violence caused by their supporters (A), the second is about disciplinary liability in doping matters (B).

The disciplinary liability of clubs for the violence caused by their supporters

Football, like other disciplines, faces an important issue of violence in stadiums. That violence is generally committed by the supporters of the teams they

9 For an example, see Cass. 2e civ., 14 April 2016, no. 15-17.732, D. 2017, p. 667, obs. Centre de droit et d'économie du sport de Limoges; *Jurisport* 2016, no. 164, p. 9; D. 2017, p. 24, obs. O. Gout; *Dalloz actualité*, 4 May 2016, obs. T. Coustet; *JCP G.* 2016, no. 22, act. 610.

10 Cass. 2e civ., 4 November 2010, no. 09-65.947, D. *2010, p. 2772, obs. I. Gallmeister; D.* 2011, p. 632, chron. J.-M. Sommer, L. Leroy-Gissinger, H. Adida-Canac et S. Grignon Dumoulin; D. 2011, p. 690, chron. J. Mouly; D. *2011, p. 703, obs. Centre de droit et d'économie du sport, Université de Limoges; RTD Civ., 2011, p. 137, obs. P. Jourdain; JCP* 2011.12, note D. Bakouche.

11 Loi n°2012-348 du 12 mars 2012 tendant à faciliter l'organisation des manifestations sportives et culturelles [Law no. 2012-348 of 12 March 2012 to facilitate the organisation of sporting and cultural events].

have come to support. Sports organisations, whether national or international ones, are *a priori* helpless against those supporters. First, they face a difficulty, which is common to any mass phenomenon, and which is that of the identification of the responsible person. The second difficulty is no less embarrassing since it is linked to the limits of the sports federations' disciplinary power. It can only be exerted against their own members. Supporters are not members of those organisations. They are therefore in theory out of reach of the sports federations. Those obstacles have not dissuaded sports associations from acting. For example, the disciplinary regulation of the French Football Federation imposes liability for those misbehaviours onto its members, the clubs.[12] In case of violence of the spectators of a match, the club may be found liable at a disciplinary level.

The nature of that liability is ambiguous. First, it seems to be vicarious. The idea behind that system is to sanction the clubs in order to harm spectators *in fine*. This is not sanctioning the club for its own good but for that of the supporters. The arbitrators of the Court of Arbitration for Sport seem to agree with that analysis and admit the liability of the clubs even without fault.[13] The Paris Administrative Court has analysed that system as vicarious liability too, and therefore ruled it was illegal because it was against the principle of personal liability, which has a constitutional value.[14] Vicarious liability is not recognised in disciplinary matters, in which a certain number of principles of criminal law, such as the principle of personal liability, apply.[15]

Another analysis prevailed before the *Conseil d'État*, which had to decide upon the lawfulness of the system. For it, that liability is a liability for one's own acts which is based on an obligation of safety of result. The club is not liable because of its supporters but because of its own failure in the organisation of the safety of the event.[16] That obligation being a duty of result, any failure will be a fault. The club will therefore automatically be sanctioned in case of misbehaviour of its supporters. Quite fortunately, the means used by the club to avoid those misbehaviours may justify the modulation of the sanction.

12 See Article 2.1 of Règlement disciplinaire et barème disciplinaire de la fédération française de football 2021/2022 [Disciplinary Regulations and Disciplinary Scale of the French Football Federation 2021/2022] (annexe 2).

13 See, for example, Court of Arbitration for Sport (CAS) 2002/A/423, *PSV Eindhoven c. UEFA*, award of 3 June 2003; JDI *2004, p. 295 note E. Loquin; CAS 2013/A/3094, Hungarian Football Federation c. FIFA*, award of 14 January 2014.

14 Tribunaux Administratifs (TA) Paris [Regional Administrative Courts of First Instance], 16 March 2007, no. 0505016/6-3, *Société Paris Saint Germain*, AJDA *(2007), p. 1890, note M. Maisonneuve, D.* 2007, p. 2292, note S. Marciali.

15 For an assertion of the application of the constitutional principle of personal responsibility in criminal matters to disciplinary and administrative sanctions, see Conseil d'État (CE) [Highest Administrative Court], 29 Octobre 2007, no. 307736, *SASP LOSC Lille Métropole*, AJDA *(2008), p. 919, note J.-M. Duval; D.* 2008, p. 1381 note M. Maisonneuve; Gaz. Pal. 3 January 2008, no. 3, p. 11, concl. E. Prada Bordenave; Gaz. Pal. 21 October 2008, no. 295, p. 33, comm. G. Simon; *Cah. dr. Sport* 2008, no. 10, p. 133 note V. Forti.

16 CE, 29 October 2007, no. 307736, *SASP LOSC Lille Métropole, AJDA* (2008), p. 919 note J.-M. Duval.

The solution is still quite severe for the clubs which will be sanctioned in case of misbehaviours of supporters even though the means available to them to avoid that violence are limited. Indeed, it is public authorities and not the clubs which may, for example, forbid access to the stadium to supporters who have already been violent or dissolve some associations of supporters.[17] Clubs only have limited means to avoid misbehaviour. They will however be held systematically liable.

To reinforce the efficiency of the fight against violence in stadiums, sports organisations and courts therefore do not hesitate to admit the liability of the clubs, even if it means distorting some principles of liability, in particular that of personal liability. The same phenomenon exists in doping matters.

Disciplinary liability in doping matters

The World Anti-Doping Code is also an illustration of the relaxing of the conditions to impose disciplinary liability. The Code provides that a sportsman commits a disciplinary crime as soon as prohibited products or substances are found in their body.[18] That crime will be automatically characterised, no matter whether the sportsman is at fault or not, whether they have voluntarily ingested the substance or not.[19] The sportsman may however avoid the sanction if they prove they have committed no fault. It is therefore a real presumption of fault that weighs on the sportsman and that is contrary to the classic models of liability. The severity, again, is necessary to guarantee the efficiency of the fight against doping. In the name of the efficiency of the fight against violence in the stadiums or doping, the liability of the sports players is thus admitted more easily. It is not sure that justice really prevails here.

At the end of that short confrontation of sports and the fundamental notions of responsibility, one cannot but observe that in sports matters, both disciplinary and civil liability evolves in reverse of the general trend of civil liability which is focused on the imperative of the compensation of the victim. Sport therefore does not seem, in those circumstances, to be at the service of a unity of the founding concepts of responsibility. It is however not forbidden to consider that sport could also be a pioneering figure to think some concepts of responsibility anew. One only needs to think of the current debate

17 In that sense see, M. Maisonneuve, 'Violence des supporteurs et responsabilité disciplinaire des clubs', note sous CE (avis), 29 Octobre 2007, *Société sportive professionnelle LOSC Lille métropole*, D. 2008, p. 1381; J.-M. Duval, 'Responsabilité des clubs de football du fait de leurs supporters', *AJDA* (2008), p. 919.

18 Article 2.1.1 of the World Anti-Doping Code 2021 specifies that 'It is the Athletes' personal duty to ensure that no Prohibited Substance enters their bodies. Athletes are responsible for any Prohibited Substance . . . found to be present in their Samples. Accordingly, it is not necessary that intent, Fault, Negligence or knowing Use on the Athlete's part be demonstrated in order to establish an anti-doping rule violation under Article 2.1'.

19 Article 2.1.1 of the World Anti-Doping Code 2021.

on the liability of international sports organisations in the human and environment damage caused by the World Cup in Qatar. The alleged breach of human rights, by Qatar, especially for the building of the stadiums, are edifying. Thousands of workers are supposed to have died during that building.[20] The International Football Federation is of course not the direct author of those violations, but could it be found liable because it abstained from using its influence to have those massive violations of human rights stop?[21] That type of responsibility would undeniably be innovating. It would be a case of finding a private person liable because they have failed to use their power of influence on a State to prevent it from committing violations of human rights. Future will tell if sport will, in that respect, be a trailblazer.

20 See the press release of Human Rights Watch, available at: www.hrw.org/fr/news/2022/05/18/qatar-la-fifa-devrait-payer-pour-le-mal-cause-aux-travailleurs-migrants

21 On that hypothesis, see F. Latty, 'FIFA and Human Rights in Qatar', in *Global Private International Law: Adjudication without Frontiers*, eds. H. Muir Watt, L. Bizikova, A. Brandao de Oliveira, and D. Fernandez Arroyo (Cheltenham: Edward Elgar Publishing, 2019), pp. 152–160; C. Legendre, *La coordination du Mouvement sportif international et des ordres juridiques étatiques et supra-étatiques* (Paris: LGDJ, 2020), p. 105.

20 The difficulty of thinking about executive responsibility in a republic

A historical perspective

François Quastana

The history of the responsibility of the executive power in France, as it is usually told, seems to owe much to an approach the main lines of which were set by the constitutional doctrine of the Third Republic, which relied on the theoretical legacy elaborated under the July Monarchy by liberal authors like Guillaume Hello or Prosper Duvergier de Hauranne. Considering, quite classically, that based on the English example of constitutional monarchy, responsibility in the parliamentarian sense derives from criminal responsibility, that approach focuses on the political responsibility of ministers. The history of the responsibility of the Executive therefore becomes confused with that of the ministers, which was characteristic of the emergence of the parliamentary regime in France from the Bourbon Restoration onwards.

Within that framework, responsibility is above all considered as the right of a political assembly to remove members of the Executive. Though it is admitted that such a right may exist in practice without being consecrated in texts, the historical approach of responsibility then most often consists in looking for that right to remove under the different regimes, and the different means that allow the chambers to obtain the removal of members of the government. Apart from the fact that it tends to leave aside the other forms of responsibility, one of the drawbacks of that presentation is that it has a tendency to underestimate the historical importance of the Revolution as an inaugural moment of the emergence of the principle of the responsibility of the Executive. Another disadvantage of that classical approach is that it leads to hide another fundamental issue that was also raised as early as the Revolution – that of the link between the responsibility of the Executive and the form of the government.

Can the responsibility of the Executive in a republic be considered in the same way as under a monarchical government? That issue, which does not hold much attention, was actually central until 1875, and Benjamin Constant even considered it as 'the most important, but also, in a republican government, the

DOI: 10.4324/9781003281559-33

most difficult of all the constitutional issues'.[1] This issue will be the common thread of this presentation.

It is interesting to note that the word 'responsibility' placed right next to 'Government' appeared in a symptomatic way in the French language a few years before the Revolution, which seems to have placed it immediately within the field of public law.[2] The notion of responsibility, linked to that of 'rendering of accounts', is to be found often in the List of Grievances[3] and emerged with the Revolution in a climate of distrust towards the executive power which is often likened to 'ministerial despotism'. The responsibility of the Executive, which only had a role of execution of the laws at the beginning, is exercised within the framework of its natural submission to the legislative power. That responsibility is first penal or civil in nature, in that it aims to repair a fault committed by a member of the Executive or the sanction of a crime. But the stakes that are attached to it are at once eminently political for its implementation entails the loss of power.

At the beginning of spring 1791, the first Republicans rejected the idea that the monarch was not accountable due to his 'inviolability', which was a corollary of the throne being inheritable,[4] but it was in July 1791, following the arrest of Louis XVI at Varennes, that the debate on the responsibility of the King gained in conceptual and ideological substance and that for the first time in France the idea of a link between republic and the responsibility of the Head of the Executive imposed itself both among its supporters and its opponents.[5]

The *Dictionnaire de la Constitution et du Gouvernement français* by Pierre Nicolas Gautier, which was published in the fall of 1791, was the first to devote a specific article to responsibility. The author indicated that it was a 'word recently formed' which meant 'obligation to be accountable, to be responsible for something'. The interest of that book is that it offers a critical vision of the 1791 Constitution and of the responsibility of the public powers by an author with a republican mind. Though he specifies that it is above all upon

1 B. Constant, *Œuvres complètes, IV, Discours au Tribunat. De la possibilité d'une constitution républicaine dans un grand pays (1799–1803)*, eds. M. L. Sanchéz Mejía and K. Kloocke (2005; reis. Berlin: De Gruyter, 2017), p. 590.

2 J. F. Féraud attributes the first use of the word to Necker who mentions 'the responsibility of the Government', '*la responsabilité du gouvernement*' (*Dictionnaire critique de langue française* (Marseille: Mossy, 1788), p. 456).

3 *Déclaration des droits de l'homme et du citoyen* [Declaration of the Rights of Man and of the Citizen], 26 August 1789, Article 15: 'La société a le droit de demander compte à tout agent public de son administration' [Society Has the Right to Require of Every Public Agent an Account of His Administration].

4 See, for example, 'De l'inviolabilité du roi et de responsabilité des ministres', *Les Révolutions de Paris*, no. 92 (9–16 April 1791): pp. 1–14, https://gallica.bnf.fr/ark:/12148/bpt6k1051200j/f12.item.

5 M. Morabito, 'La responsabilité du chef de l'État', *Giornale di storia costituzionale* 2, no. 28 (2014): pp. 43–49.

the ministers that the 'new law of responsibility' weighs, and that due to the countersignature they are answerable for the execution of the laws and orders given by the King, he nonetheless thinks that, pursuant to Article 15 of the Declaration of the Rights of Man, it is not normal either that the monarch be, among all public servants, 'the only one not to be accountable'.[6] Such irresponsibility that heredity implies is, according to him, prejudicial and should not exist within a republican government where the Head of the Executive is elected and where the right to choose and dismiss ministers is reserved to the people, to whom they are accountable.[7]

The Report by Hérault de Séchelles, which was presented on 22 February 1792 and which aimed to explain how responsibility should be understood in the 1791 Constitution and why a specific law on the responsibility of ministers did not seem to be necessary, is also worthy of attention. In that text, the author proposes to consider responsibility as the 'Penal Code of authority', '[t]he long chain of all the duties of a minister and the punishment or the reparation which corresponds to each of the links'.[8] Making the distinction between several types of responsibility of the executive power – 'general', 'particular', 'penal' and 'civil' – he claims that in order to be a real guarantee of public liberty, ministerial responsibility should not simply be about the 'direct and obvious wrongdoings'. It must extend to the 'negligence', and even 'inertia' of the agents of the Executive, whose fault is sometimes not easy, or even impossible to establish, but which could ruin the common weal if they remained unpunished.[9] To 'positive' responsibility, of which crimes are set in the Penal Code, is therefore added 'negative' responsibility, which must be sanctioned. That punishment is imposed within the framework of a trial before a National High Court, a court that is charged with all the so-called political crimes.[10]

From the Revolution onwards, a specific procedure and a specific court thus appeared to rule on the responsibility of ministers, impeached by the National Assembly outside ordinary courts. According to the author, the minimal punishment that should be imposed in case of negative responsibility should be destitution, the loss of power, which he likens to a case of treason.[11] However, Hérault de Séchelles also admits that there are cases in which the legislative power will be able to encourage the King to dismiss one of his ministers, even without evidence, by simply declaring that he has lost the trust of the nation.[12]

6 P. N. Gautier, *'Responsabilité', in Dictionnaire de la Constitution et du gouvernement français* (Paris: Guillaume Jeune, 1792), pp. 521–524.

7 P. N. Gautier, 'Responsabilité'.

8 *Archives parlementaires de 1787 à 1860, première série (1787 à 1799), tome XXXIX du 22 février au 14 mars 1892*, Archives parlementaires règne de Louis XVI, Assemblée Nationale Législative, 1792, p. 9.

9 *Archives parlementaires*, p. 9.

10 *Archives parlementaires*, p. 10.

11 *Archives parlementaires*, p. 11.

12 *Archives parlementaires*, p. 11.

The fall of the monarchy did not allow for such a system to really operate, but it directly raised the issue of holding the Executive accountable within a republican framework for the first time.

In revolutionary republican constitutions, the principle is always that of the subordination of the Executive to the Legislative. Even though the degree of subordination varies, the executive authority, which is periodically and partially renewed, is deprived of any participation in the legislative function, but intervenes in the decision to wage a war and in the conclusion of treaties.

The choice of an Executive elected by the people and accountable is a necessary feature of the Girondist constitutional project. The accountability of ministers is exercised through their impeachment by the legislative body for crimes related to their office, but they can also be prosecuted for misconduct or simply removed. Condorcet did not aim to make the ministers the 'creatures' of the legislative power and entrusted a national jury elected by the people with deciding whether dismissal was needed.[13]

After the Girondist project failed, the Constitution of 1793 introduced some dualism within the executive branch which implied a double system of responsibility. A separate Executive Council nominated and dismissed ministers while being itself accountable to the legislative body. In addition to its power to appoint members of the Council, the legislative body could impeach them for malpractice, non-execution of the laws and decrees and non-denunciation of the abuses they were aware of.[14]

The Constitution of the Year III set the principle of a double accountability within the framework of a complex Executive composed of a collegial body – the Directory, which exercised the government office and specialised ministers, who were general agents of the executive power charged with executing the laws. The idea of the inviolability of the Directory, which was mentioned for some time, was quickly rejected as incompatible with the nature of the republican government. The debates of the Committee of the Eleven also show that the idea of only one agent being elected and ministers nominated with him by the implementation of a double mechanism of accountability to the legislative body, entrusted with declaring loss of trust, was also considered.[15]

Let us note that the expression 'political responsibility' seems to have been first penned at that time by Roederer who defined it as 'that by which one accounts for one's office for the bad use one makes of it' and differentiated it from capital, pecuniary and moral responsibilities. According to him, 'All those responsibilities must be imposed on the rulers, they are auxiliaries the one for

13 Constitutional draft presented to the National Convention on the 15th and 16th of February 1793, Title V, Section I, Article XXVI.

14 Constitution of 24 June 1793, Articles 71 and 72.

15 P. Colombo, 'La question du pouvoir exécutif dans l'évolution institutionnelle et le débat politique révolutionnaire', *Annales historiques de la Révolution française*, no. 319 (January–March 2000): p. 15.

the other, and it is easier and more necessary to establish them in a republic than in any other form of government'.[16]

While the importance of the responsibility of the Executive in republican constitutionalism is unanimously admitted, not everyone shares the same optimism as to its implementation. Thinking about *the possibility of introducing a republican constitution in a big country*, Benjamin Constant echoed it directly: at the origin it seemed impossible to conceive one or several Heads of the Executive who would not be accountable while ministers would be. In a republic, responsibility, which is a guarantee against the abuses of the Executive, must weigh on all the degrees of the constitutional hierarchy. However, whereas in a monarchy the irresponsibility of the hereditary king easily allows to combine the responsibility of the ministers, it is only with difficulty that an elected complex republican Executive can admit the responsibility of the ministers, because it could backfire and make it useless.[17] It is in order to fix this problem posed by responsibility that Constant proposed for the first time in this text the establishment of a 'preserving power', the example of which was partly drawn from the Spartan *ephors* and the *balia* of the Florentine Republic. In his project, that original institution, which was composed of members elected for life, had at the same time the right to dissolve the legislative body as well as the discretionary power of dismissal, without charges or judgement, of members of the Executive when they breached their duties. Responsibility before the courts only remained for the individual crimes of the ministers, the political ones resulting in the destitution of the whole Executive.[18]

Already quite deeply analysed in Constant's works under the Directory, the issue of the responsibility of the Executive in a republic was only raised again in 1848 with the introduction, for the first time, of a president elected by universal suffrage. Within the Constitution Committee, everybody thought, as Tocqueville recalled, that '[i]t was in the essence of the Republic that the Head of State be responsible'.[19] Thus the 1848 Constitution led to the unprecedented consecration of presidential responsibility combined with ministerial responsibility. However, though providing for criminal liability, it remained vague on the question of political responsibility. The debates of the Committee testify to the fact that a certain number of members would have liked to give the President real power by making him the soul and spirit of the Executive. The latter, entrusted with acts of high policy, must be politically responsible, but the ministers had to share that responsibility, since the implementation of the presidential policy necessitated their involvement. By depriving him of the direct legislative initiative and of the right of dissolution, the Constitution nonetheless significantly weakened the President by preventing him from having the active power – which the acknowledgement of his responsibility

16 P. L. Roederer, *Du gouvernement (1795) in Œuvres*, t. VII (Paris: Firmin Didot, 1858), p. 28.
17 B. Constant, *De la possibilité d'une constitution républicaine dans un grand pays*, pp. 590–594.
18 B. Constant, *De la possibilité d'une constitution républicaine dans un grand pays*, pp. 619–621.
19 A. de Tocqueville, *Souvenirs* (Paris: Gallimard, 1964), p. 190.

seemed to induce – at his disposal. The existence of a responsibility of the ministers before the chambers in the presence of a president elected by the people and responsible himself seemed to be an aporia for some people. Odilon Barrot thus thought that ministerial political responsibility is a characteristic and condition that cannot be transferred from the constitutional monarchy to the republican regime.[20]

While the 1848 constitutional text, in its silence, seems to concede the political responsibility of the ministers to the Assembly, it provides, in line with the revolutionary republican tradition, for a High Court of Justice to which the National Assembly may bring the ministers and the President of the Republic, 'republican liberty' requiring as Marrast, the reporter for the Committee, said, 'a real responsibility, not troublesome but not disappointing either'.[21]

Despite the issues it raised, that republican dogma of the responsibility of the President as Head of the Executive remained untouched until 1875. It was, as is well known, the 1875 constitutional laws which broke down that conceptual barrier by operating a fundamental break through the transposition of the royal inviolability to a republican Head of State, while officially introducing for the first time, next to the criminal liability of ministers, their political and collective responsibility to the chambers.[22] Despite the government instability that it caused, ministerial political responsibility was presented as significant progress by the constitutional doctrine from that time on, which was to send criminal liability, an archaic and primitive form of the rulers' responsibility, to the dustbin of history. As we all know, contemporary political history has belied that prediction.

In line with the Third and the Fourth Republic, the Fifth kept the irresponsibility of the President, while introducing in 2007 a very limited possibility of destitution in case of violation of the duties of his office by the Parliament acting as a High Court. It constitutionally consecrated the mechanisms of involving the political responsibility of the government within the framework of the so-called rationalised parliamentarism.

That consecration has not been realised much in practice where there has been an evanescence of political responsibility due to the majority rule and the 'presidentialisation' of the regime. The government has won stability but the combination of those two factors has made accountability of the ministers to Parliament illusory, resulting in an increased recourse to the criminal path. Such recourse does not seem contrary to the original republican tradition even though some have considered it to be a regress of constitutional law.[23]

20 O. Barrot, *Mémoires posthumes*, t. 2 (Paris: Charpentier, 1875), pp. 366–367.

21 A. Marrast, *Rapport fait au nom de la Commission de constitution*, 30 août 1848, Assemblée nationale constituante, 1848–1849, Tome IV. no. 393 (Paris: Impr. de l'Assemblée nationale, 1849).

22 Loi constitutionnelle du 25 février 1875 [Constitutional Law of 25 February 1875], Article 6.

23 O. Beaud, 'La responsabilité politique face à la concurrence d'autres formes de responsabilité des gouvernants', *Pouvoirs*, no. 92 (2000): pp. 17–30.

The central problem seems to be elsewhere. Responsibility has become an empty noun. The fact that the reality of power is in the hands of a Head of State who is no longer a referee, but the real leader of a majority with an increasingly narrow democratic foundation, has raised the question, which was thought to have been forgotten, of the political responsibility of the President to the people, which grants him an authority which, in a republic, implies rendering accounts. That question leads to another – that of the nature and the forms that ministerial responsibility should have. Those are perilous issues to which an urgent answer is needed, if we do not want, the *res publica*, like responsibility, to become a *nomen vacuum*, to paraphrase Cicero. Responsibility, which was born in a context of domination of the Legislative over the Executive, must now be thought anew in the light of the great shift that is characteristic of contemporary times, in which the Executive has become the prevailing power.

21 Of sheep and straw men

The accountability of the Executive from the perspective of political science

Olivier Rozenberg

The idea that who takes decisions must account for them may be a universal dimension of the political – not that it is implemented everywhere, but the full legitimacy of the decision-maker implies some dialogue, some oversight, a possible sanction, in short, something that goes beyond the law of the strongest or the most efficient.[1] The responsibility of power, that 'restoring force'[2] of political systems consists both in *answering* questions and criticism and *accounting for them*, i.e., in pledging something important in the answer – one's reputation or position. In modern times, the principle of responsibility has been legally formalised, with the obligation for members of government to justify their acts before parliaments, and the possibility for the latter to overthrow them if they are not convinced. That mechanism, which is at the heart of the parliamentary regime, is operating almost everywhere in Europe.[3]

A perspective from political science reminds us that despite the generalisation of the principle of the political accountability of the Executive, the latter results from a long-term power struggle among institutions and social groups. More precisely, it refers to subtle institutional balances which contribute to adapt its scope and sometimes to moderate it. Above all, focalising on the political, social and economic balance of powers which is at the basis of the institutional responsibility of the Executive helps to understand its contemporary evolutions. This chapter claims that the principle of the accountability of the Executive tends to be diluted today. That word is understood first through the multiplication of the bodies and groups to which the government is accountable, beyond parliament. It also refers to the multiple and partly victorious strategies of the European executives to escape their responsibilities and exempt themselves from the threat of sanctions, at a time of democratic

1 P. Clastres, *La société contre l'État: recherches d'anthropologie politique* (Paris: Éditions de Minuit, 1974).

2 P. Rosanvallon, *Good Government* (Harvard: Harvard University Press, 2018 [2015]).

3 There are three types of exceptions: a presidential regime at Cyprus, a few presidents of republics who are not accountable to the parliament but who have some exceptional prerogatives and the French regime, in which the responsible part of the Executive is usually less powerful than the irresponsible part.

DOI: 10.4324/9781003281559-34

distrust. The process of the assertion of the accountability of the Executive and its modes will be dealt with in a first part, and the different aspects of its dilution in a second part.

The historical assertion of the government's accountability to parliament

The formalisation of the accountability of the power through specific constitutional mechanisms belongs to a long history where political, social and economic considerations are intertwined. The generalisation of parliamentary regimes in Europe covers a diversity of situations related to both the principle of accountability and its scope.

In the absence of bailiffs

Historically speaking, the formalisation of the responsibility of the power comes from the establishment of *impeachment* in the 14th-century English Parliament.[4] The procedure was an individual one and was triggered for serious offences and betrayals, rather than political choices. It contributed both to limit the powers of the King, since his ministers could be condemned, while preserving his function insofar as the Crown could not be impeached. From the 17th century onwards, *impeachment* became political as it included broader claims in relation to bad administration and a collective dimension with the possible resignation of the whole Cabinet. That evolution contributed among other things to make the sanction civilised, since resignation replaced beheading, and regulated conflicts between the Crown and the assemblies.

Political economy provides an enlightening interpretation of that process.[5] Many works indeed associate parliamentarianism and the financial needs of monarchies, whether those needs came from domestic and foreign security or from the financing of medieval and modern proto-bureaucracies. The central idea was that the Kings renounced some prerogatives, accepted to account for public spending and progressively consented to their ministers being sanctioned by representative assemblies because of their need for money.

The approaches of political economy borrowing from the game theory show that the Crown suffered from a structural lack of credibility in the eyes of its creditors because it possessed coercive weaponry.[6] More simply, the

4 D. Baranger, *Parlementarisme des origines* (Paris: PUF, 2002). See also, P. Rosanvallon, *Good Government.*

5 For the whole section: W. R. Clark, M. Golder, and S. N. Golder, *Principles of Comparative Politics*, 3rd ed. (New York: Sage, 2018), Chapter 6.

6 And, to a lesser extent, the power to pass bills. What the economists call a problem of credible commitment. D. North and B. Weingast, 'Constitutions and Commitment: The Evolution of Institutions Governing Public Choice in Seventeen Century England', *Journal of Economic History* 49, no. 4 (1989): pp. 803–832.

main national and European creditors hesitated to lend money to the King for they knew that they would not be reimbursed in case of default on the latter's payments. Similarly, the land aristocracy or urban bourgeoisie were reluctant to contribute via taxes, which were considered as a form of spoliation fuelling the way of life of the power. 'Parliamentarisation' then is understood as a strategy of the Crown to establish its financial credibility. In the absence of bailiffs and accountants, there were parliamentarians. As his spending became supervised and the budget was progressively submitted to the assemblies, the King sent the sign that he was a responsible economic actor and that it was rational to lend him money or to pay taxes. Note that that reasoning is as true of the main European banks, which can refuse to lend money, as of the wealthy national taxpayers who can escape paying taxes by masking or relocating their economic activities. As to the latter, the nature of the current economic assets is a key issue of the parliamentarisation of regimes for their liquidity and their volatility make the threat of an *exit*[7] credible. That is why English sheep in the 17th century contributed more to democracy than French cereals at the same period or Middle East hydrocarbon in the 20th century.

The complete victory of the principle of responsibility

While the assertion of political accountability cannot be reduced to a story of finances, the political economy approaches have the merit of enlightening the economic and social struggles operating behind the legal formalisation of the parliamentary regime and the marginalising of Heads of State. That model became predominant in Europe in the course of the 19th and 20th centuries. It not only resulted in the marginalising of monarchies and the disassociation, within the Executive, of the Head of State and Head of Government. What is crucial is not that some people may have the title of Head of State outside heredity, but that the prerogatives of that head be limited.

For the 19th-century French and English thinkers, the King or president must indeed intervene as little as possible, except in case of institutional and political crises.[8] The Head of State is a sort of third party who suggests solutions or redefines rules if tension rises among actors. Their duties – choosing the prime minister, vetoing the choice of ministers and dissolution – are important but exceptional. By contrast, power is in the hands of a government team which is under tight supervision of parliament, *a minima*, because a majority of members may force that team to resign as they wish, and *a maxima* because ministers come from parliament or even sit there.

7 *Exit* may be a relocation of the economic activity or its minimalisation via fraud, which is made possible by the liquidity of assets. Moreover, the degree of dependence of the Crown to wealth produced by private actors is a second incentive to parliamentarianisation.

8 W. Selinger, *Parliamentarism. From Burke to Weber* (Cambridge: Cambridge University Press, 2019).

Unlike the crisis powers of the Head of State, which are by nature exceptional, the rulers' accountability to parliament is constant and ordinary. It may be found in an array of instruments some of which, after being forgotten for decades on the shelves of assemblies, are brought back into fashion thanks to the evolution of communication technologies, for example televised hearings of investigation inquiries or e-petitions. Above all, parliament's supervision of the government is theoretically complete: nothing justifies nor allows to escape it, it covers any topic and may operate at any moment. The accountability principle, like that of sovereignty or the general will, may not be divided and operates in its entirety. Moreover, parliamentarians do not have to legally justify a motion of censure. They must formulate it, often orally and in writing, then vote upon it, but without common criteria of the political validity of the government's action being defined beforehand.

The victory of the government's accountability to parliament in Europe can be seen through the marginalising of the part of the Executive which is not accountable – the State chiefdom. Quite noticeably, and France excepted, Heads of State keep limited duties and powers even when they are directly elected and could therefore claim some popular legitimacy. This is far from insignificant in Western Europe and even more so in the former popular democracies or Soviet republics. In most of those countries, parliament keeps a monopoly on the government's accountability and the president may not, *de jure*, demand that the prime minister resign.[9]

Specific modes of implementation

Whereas the principle of accountability exists in almost all the European countries, works of comparative politics show differences in the modes and scope of the latter. It is possible to make four distinctions.[10]

First, the idea of the accountability of the Executive to parliament is all the more relevant as the latter has delegated many prerogatives to the former. The democratic necessity of supervision is more important when the government plays a key role in the preparation and implementation of laws or even has some delegated legislative means. In the United Kingdom, the progressive establishment of the accountability of the government to parliament went historically along the increase in power of the cabinet vis-à-vis the Crown.[11]

The comparison of public policies fields and especially budget policies[12] suggests that European democracies followed different institutional paths in

9 Exceptions are Austria (where the president has renounced that prerogative), Iceland and Russia (where it contributed to an authoritarian stiffening in the years 2010s).

10 See also, O. Rozenberg, 'Comparer les parlements', in *Politique comparée*, eds. J.-M. de Waele and Y. Déloye (Brussels: Bruylant, 2018), pp. 303–364.

11 D. Baranger, *Parlementarisme des origines*.

12 J. Wehner, 'Assessing the Power of the Purse. An Index of Legislative Budget Institutions', *Political Studies* 54, no. 4 (2006): pp. 767–785.

that matter. In some countries, a peaceful or on the contrary watchful constitutional history, the constant necessity of a partisan coalition or frequent minority governments contributed to placing parliaments at the heart of the making of public policies. Laws are more amended by parliamentary majorities in the legislative phase or before it. The necessity of a tight supervision of the Executive's acts is less obvious given the limited scope of parliamentary delegation. The reasoning is at the same time historic and practical: parliamentary groups have not felt it necessary to amend the rule towards more control, the agenda is focalised on the legislative procedure rather than on oversight and parliamentarians who are busy legislating have only limited energy to do anything else.

Comparative works provide a partial confirmation of such balances: Swedish, Norwegian and German Parliaments play an active role in the day-to-day conception of public policies but are not good supervisors.[13] The Irish, Greek or Spanish are in the opposite situation. However, many cases depart from a balance between the supervision of the delegation and the direct action of parliaments. The Danish, Austrian and German Parliaments are strong on the two dimensions, while the British and French Assemblies at the same time take little part in the supervision and direct action. Those exceptions, which are many, are due to singular constitutional histories (like the strong rationalisation of French parliamentarianism in 1958) but also to a second factor that explains the scope of parliamentary supervision, that is, the coalition character of the Executive. The multiplication of the number of parties in the government and the frailty of the main component from which the prime minister comes is a powerful vehicle of the parliamentary monitoring of the government, whether about getting more prerogatives or using them.[14] The supervision work by parliament committees especially may be understood as a partisan police operation of the coalition agreements: the Minister of party A forming a coalition with party B must convince during hearings led or encouraged by party B that she is not betraying the coalition agreements made between A and B at the beginning of the legislature. In other words, the Executive is, in fact, all the more accountable as it is divided.

The third dimension of the implementation of the accountability principle is linked to the timing of the parliamentary supervision of government. Delegation theoreticians have showed that the delegating power had two non-exclusive strategies to ensure the quality of the delegate.[15] Before delegation, it must ensure to choose the best profile, which it thinks is the most capable

13 U. Sieberer, 'The Institutional Power of Western European Parliaments: A Multidimensional Analysis', *West European Politics*, 34, no. 4 (2011): pp. 731–754.

14 L. W. Martin and G. Vanberg, *Parliaments and Coalitions* (Oxford: Oxford University Press, 2011).

15 D. Epstein and S. O'Halloran, *Delegating Powers. A Transaction Cost Politics Approach to Policy Making under Separate Powers* (Cambridge: Cambridge University Press, 1999).

and loyal one. Afterwards, it may assess the action of the delegate by summoning and questioning him or delegating that to third parties. Though the two operations belong to the supervision of the delegate by the delegating power, the notion of accountability of the delegate is not understood in the same way. *A priori*, the delegate is assessed as to their reputation and commitments; *a posteriori* as to their acts and explanations. In one case they try to seem responsible (in the sense of a *responsible* attitude); in the other they are (in the sense of being the author of an act).

The constitutional provisions as to the formation and fall of governments account for that duality of the notion of responsibility. Once again, some balance may be found when European democracies are compared.[16] In some cases belonging to so-called positive parliamentarianism, the crucial influence of parliament is on the formation of the government. A parliament gives itself more means to choose a prime minister who corresponds to what it wants if the nomination is mandatory and procedurally favourable.[17] In other cases of so-called negative parliamentarianism, the leeway of parliament to overthrow the government may be made easier by technical provisions such as the required type of majority.[18] The comparison shows that there is a form of exchangeability of accountability with on the side of demanding nomination and difficult censorship Germany, Slovenia or Poland, and on the side of easier censorship without nomination vote Denmark, the Netherlands, Norway and Austria. As for the degree of delegation, but to a lesser extent, some countries still escape the exchangeability between the *a priori* and *a fortiori* supervision of the Executive by the Legislative – for example the United Kingdom, which is dominated by the Cabinet, or Finland, which is in the opposite situation.

The fourth mode of parliamentary responsibility of the Executive is due to statutory and sociological proximity among parliamentarians and ministers. The selection of ministers along parliamentarians is a powerful vehicle of *a priori* supervision of the Legislative over the Executive. Though there are rare cases in which belonging to parliament is a requirement to be in the government (only in the United Kingdom and Ireland), the majority of ministers in Europe are usually former parliamentarians. That is another dimension of the European parliamentarian model which ranks institutional positions and

16 U. Sieberer, 'Hire or Fire? The Link between Cabinet Investiture and Removal in Parliamentary Democracies', in *Parliaments and Government Formation: Unpacking Investiture Rules*, eds. B. E. Rasch, S. Martin, and J. A. Cheibub (Oxford: Oxford University Press, 2015), pp. 309–330.

17 Among the procedural elements favourable to parliament, there is: the motion of introduction of candidate representatives, the requirement of an absolute majority of members or secret ballot.

18 And also the absence of requirement of an agreement on the substitutive prime minister as in the so-called constructive motion of censure provided for in Germany, Armenia, Belgium, Spain and Hungary.

makes parliament an airlock, which is not mandatory but frequent, towards the ministerial top of power.

That model of career is doubly important for holding the Executive to account. First, the ministers are not only controlled by people who have delegated them some power, as is stated in the theory of delegation, but by competitors. The will of the parliamentarian to be a minister is a powerful vehicle to mobilise them to practice efficient control, including within the majority. Second, the comparison of political careers and institutional provisions shows an opposition between long-term control via socialisation and daily procedural control.[19] British ministers spend a good decade on the benches of Westminster before they become a Cabinet member. They are judged and assessed by their peers and learn applicable norms. Once ministers are in place, parliament needs all the less to check each of their actions as it has selected and, in a way, trained them. Dutch ministers come less than in other countries from parliament but must more frequently account for their action to it. On the one hand making the Executive aware of its responsibilities, and on the other holding it to account – the choice of an institutional model rather than another obviously depends on the level of cohesion within the political elite and more generally on the degree of social trust. However, the current evolution of those two elements (elite cohesion and social trust) contributes, in different forms, to the ongoing dilution of the accountability of the Executive.

The multiform dilution of the accountability of the Executive

Dilution refers to different evolutions. The accountability of the Executive to parliament faces significant challenges. However, based on recent political crises, it can be said that parliamentary oversight is not totally gutted. Obviously, parliament has competitors as to the supervision and sanction of the Executive, especially the courts and public opinion. Against those evolutions, European executives have implemented different, sometimes successful strategies, consisting in discarding part of their responsibilities, in the facts or in the way the latter are represented. The following second part successively examines those three dynamics.

The uncertainties of parliamentary responsibility

In the course of the 20th century, the implementation of the Executive's responsibility to parliament had to face many challenges which could wrongly make one think that it had become purely formal. Admittedly, for example,

19 T. Saalfeld, 'Members of Parliament and Governments in Western Europe: Agency Relations and Problems of Oversight', *European Journal of Political Research* 37, no. 3 (May 2000): pp. 353–376.

the presence of British[20] or Canadian[21] prime ministers in parliament decreased over the century. From the point of view of parliaments, the 2000 governments were less easily controllable than those of 1900 in three respects.

The first is due to the increase of bureaucracy and the fact that public action has become more complex. According to the delegation theory, the delegating authority's information deficit has increased and, in fact, offers more important leeway to the delegate not only to conduct the policy they want but also to let the delegator know what they are doing. The increasing complexity of action justifies the deepening of controls, the increase of means and instrumentation, which are all elements that seem to be operating in European parliaments today, as is shown by the evolution of the number of questions,[22] inquiry committees,[23] or the assessment of public action.[24] It remains doubtful though that those efforts may really bridge the gap between the expertise capacities of the State Administration and those of Parliament, including in countries where assemblies are rather well endowed with power, such as the United States or Germany.

The second challenge is a political one. The progressive nationalisation of legislative elections and the 'partification' of political life have led to control of parliamentary troops. Governments in Europe can generally rely on a strong parliamentary basis that is reinforced both by the electoral calculation of majority backbenchers as well as their career ambition and their ideological proximity with ministers. Admittedly, the situation is not identical from one parliament to the next. There still remains that the political control of party leaders on their troops makes parliament's institutional supervision of the Executive more uncertain. It lays a good part of calling the government to account on the shoulders of the opposition in parliament. However, and that is the third challenge parliaments face, procedural provisions may greatly reduce the capacity of parliament to control the Executive in general, and of the opposition to act in particular. The rules about the *negative agenda control*,[25] that is, the centralisation of parliamentary procedure in order to

20 P. Dunleavy, G. W. Jones, J. Burnham, R. Elgie, and P. Fysh, 'Leaders, Politics and Institutional Change: The Decline of Prime Ministerial Accountability to the House of Commons, 1868–1990', *British Journal of Political Science* 23, no. 3 (1993): pp. 267–298.

21 J. Crimmins and P. Nesbitt-Larking, 'Canadian Prime Ministers in the House of Commons: Patterns of Intervention', *Journal of Legislative Studies* 2, no. 2 (1996): pp. 145–171.

22 O. Rozenberg and S. Martin, 'Questioning Parliamentary Questions', *Journal of Legislative Studies* 17, no. 3 (2011): pp. 394–404.

23 O. Rozenberg, 'Inquiries by Parliaments: The Political Use of a Democratic Right' (Study Requested by the Committee on Constitutional Affairs), Policy Department for Citizens', *Rights and Constitutional Affairs of the European Parliament*, March 2020, www.europarl.europa.eu/RegData/etudes/STUD/2020/648709/IPOL_STU(2020)648709_EN.pdf

24 P. Norton, 'Post-Legislative Scrutiny in the UK Parliament: Adding Value', *The Journal of Legislative Studies* 25, no. 3 (2019): pp. 340–357.

25 B. E. Rasch, 'Parliamentary Floor Voting Procedures', in *Legislatures: Comparative Perspectives on Representative Assemblies*, eds. G. Loewenberg, P. Squire, and D. R. Kiewiet (Ann Arbor: University of Michigan Press, 2002), pp. 269–287.

limit obstruction, have multiplied in favour of a modernising feature centred around procedural efficiency. Today's obsession for digital immediacy took over from the 20th-century technocratic myth of a depoliticised governance. There results not only some increased delegation of responsibilities to the Executive, but also a frequent difficulty of the opposition to hold the Executive to account.

The ascendency of the Executive and the different difficulties of parliament to operate authentic supervision of the latter's acts may have led some to think that the accountability of the Executive has become purely formal. One can note that the motions of censure resulting in the fall of the government are rather rare: the last one dates back to 1962 in France, 1979 in the UK and 1982 in Germany.[26] However, deeper attention paid to national political lives shows that the principle, even reduced, of parliament holding the Executive to account remains operating especially in periods of social and political tensions. When a coalition or a majority are divided and/or a power is clearly contested by public opinion with, for example, the increase of street movements, parliament remains a place where a part of the crisis develops and unravels. The government undergoes rough question time sessions, finicky inquiry committees and motions of censure. It may be pushed to resign by the reversal of alliances the balance of which depends on the numerical strength of parliamentary groups. Finally, it is (rarely) censored like the Prodi Cabinets in Italy in 2008, the Rajoy Cabinet in Spain in 2018, Citu in Romania in 2021 or Löfven in Sweden in 2021. Most often, the fall of the government is followed by the victory of the opposition in legislative elections, which shows a form of continuity between parliamentary and popular control.

Outside exceptional crises caused by economic difficulties or a political affair, the principle of accountability of the government may also contribute to a sort of cyclical regulation of relations among branches of power. British political life provides good examples.[27] The trust of majority MPs tends to wane with time and the unpopularity of the Executive or the disappointment of simple elected members who would like to have a role in the government. The comparison in that respect between M. Thatcher and T. Blair is striking, as they were pushed out in the middle of a parliamentary session after ten years in power. Eventually, the accountable feature of the British Government has contributed to limit the expansion of personal power by putting an end to the functions of those leaders who at the same time have left their mark on their era and aroused strong domestic oppositions. The structural contribution of

26 Except, in Germany the motions of censure caused by the government to get a dissolution of the *Bundestag*. Y. Mény and Y. Surel, *Politique comparée*, 8è éd. (Paris: Montchrestien, 2009), pp. 272 ff.

27 O. Rozenberg, 'Order and Disorder. Le Brexit ou la victoire amère des études parlementaires', *Revue française de science politique* 71, no. 4 (2021): pp. 599–621.

parliament to the moderation of power and civil peace, which is at the heart of the concerns of parliament theoreticians,[28] is therefore not anachronistic.

The end of the parliament monopoly regarding governmental accountability

Like legislative activities,[29] the tendency of parliament to be the only one to politically hold the Executive to account has been countered by the assertion of other political actors and even institutions, starting with voters themselves. In modern democracies, the Executive in indeed doubly accountable to public opinion.

It is first accountable during elections since, most of the time, the candidates in legislative elections are elected on the basis of their party membership rather than their own virtues. That is a sort of retrospective judgement on past policies which allows to sanction or approve the incumbent team. Political science works have multiplied to try and evidence that phenomenon.[30] They focalise on economic issues and underline that the incumbent government tends to be assessed on the macroeconomic evolution of the country rather than on the personal situation of everybody.[31] More precisely, different analyses show that though a government may not necessarily get credit for good results, by virtue of Tocqueville's paradox that an objective improvement of the situation may be a source of frustration, on the contrary, the incumbent team may be sanctioned for bad results or because it was unlucky enough to be governing the country in a time of crisis.

The work of H.P. Kriesi on the electoral consequences of the Great Depression of the years 2000 and 2010 gives precise result in that respect.[32] It shows that the increase in budget deficits resulted in an electoral defeat of the governments in office everywhere in Europe during the 2008–2011 period. The regression methods that were used allow to say that the result is robust including when other explanations are introduced in the analysis. All other things

28 W. Selinger, *Parliamentarism. From Burke to Weber.*

29 A. Le Divellec, 'Parliament in Constitutional Law', in *Handbook of Parliamentary Studies: Interdisciplinary Approaches to Legislatures*, eds. C. Benoît and O. Rozenberg (Cheltenham, RU: Edward Elgar, 2020), pp. 102–120.

30 See A. Healy and N. Malhotra, 'Retrospective Voting Reconsidered', *Annual Review of Political Science* 16, no. 1 *(2013): pp. 285–306. For a presentation of theoretical stakes: J. Mansbridge, 'Rethinking Representation',* *The American Political Science Review* 97, no. 4 (2003): pp. 515–528; and A. Przeworski, S. C. Stokes, and B. Manin, eds., *Democracy, Accountability and Representation* (Cambridge: Cambridge University Press, 1999).

31 R. M. Duch and R. T. Stevenson, *The Economic Vote. How Political and Economic Institutions Condition Election Results* (Cambridge: Cambridge University Press, 2008).

32 K. Hanspeter, 'The Political Consequences of the Economic Crisis in Europe. Electoral Punishment and Popular Protest', in *Mass Politics in Tough Times: Opinions, Votes and Protest in the Great Recession*, eds. L. Bartels and N. Bermeo (Oxford: Oxford University Press, 2014).

being equal, an additional point of public deficit resulted in a point less of support in the votes in Eastern Europe and 0.5 point in Western Europe.[33]

In that respect, the democracies that were based on a majority system – i.e., those close to the British one – rather than on consensus, appear much more prone to the retrospective vote of voters. The increased tendency of the citizens and observers to attribute the responsibility of the policies to the governments in office and to identify those governments translates into greater electoral reactivity.[34] It results, as measured by comparative studies,[35] that the rate of realisation of electoral pledges is much higher in the majority system. The government is at the same time led to respect its programme and be more capable of doing it, as there is no coalition compromise. Besides, it is logical that mono-partisan governments are more accountable to the citizens, insofar as, as we have seen in the first part of this chapter, whether there are coalition partners is a determining factor in parliament's effective holding of the Executive to account.[36]

Second, it is to be noted that the opinion's judgement of the government is not limited to electoral periods. It is actually continuous and manifest, or even manipulated, via numerous processes, from opinion polls to social movements. Bernard Manin's work underlines both that the fact that opinion which is free to express itself *up to the door of parliament* has been one of the central principles of representative government since it was first described and that our times which he calls 'the public's democracy' highlights it even more.[37] According to his analysis, the progressive reduction of the representative collective – from parliamentarians to party leaders to a leader – is the counterpart of constant and almost obsessive attention of those in power to the public opinion. In other words, the weight of opinion polls is all the more important

33 For difficult-to-understand reasons, the same study shows that the unemployment rate has electorally penalised governments in Western but not Eastern Europe, the situation being the reverse as to the fall of the GDP.

34 G. Bingham Powell Jr. and G. D. Whitten, 'A Cross-National Analysis of Economic Voting: Taking Account of the Political Context', *American Journal of Political Science* 37, no. 2 (May 1993): pp. 391–414.

35 R. Thomson et al., 'The Fulfillment of Parties' Election Pledges: A Comparative Study on the Impact of Power Sharing', *American Journal of Political Science* 61, no. 3 (2017): pp. 527–542. See also I. Guinaudeau and S. Persico, 'Tenir promesse. Les conditions de réalisation des programmes électoraux', *Revue française de science politique* 68, no. 2 (2018): pp. 215–237.

36 From that point of view, France is in an intermediate position. As a majority democracy, its governments are encouraged to hold their promises and to that end have a powerful concentration of powers in the hand of the President. However, the fact – which is unique – that a two-round first-past-the-post election can be the determining moment of the granting of power, with the presidential elections, contributes to multiply and radicalise promises, which makes them less realisable and even not doable. On that topic: E. Grossman and N. Sauger, *Pourquoi détestons-nous tant les politiques?* (Paris: Presses de Sciences Po, 2017).

37 B. Manin, *The Principles of Representative Government* (Cambridge, UK: Cambridge University, 1997 [1995]).

as the traditional vectors of public, parliamentarian or activist expression are discredited. The perpetual and chaotic dialogue between a leader who is both powerful and powerless, and a public which is both vindictive and apathetic is therefore an essential dimension of today's governance. The immaterial public space is the place of an informal but powerful mechanism of questioning of the accountability of rulers which may lead to the renouncing of some projects, to the resignation of ministers or even, in the two-headed French system, to that of the prime minister, who has sometimes had to resign in place of the president, even when parliament did not demand it.

Outside public opinion, challenge of the Executive also tends to be carried out by judges. Many elements indeed show that the classic theoretical distinction between the sanction for political choices, which is in the hands of parliament, or for violation of the law, which is in those of the judges, is no longer relevant. The encroachment is in fact double. The examination of real or alleged breaches of ministers sometimes leads judges to consider only the political opportunity of past decisions. Let us note that the spectrum of a government of the judges should not be perceived through the lens of an alleged will of power of judges who have long been subordinated to their political masters. It is also to be explained, as in the case of COVID-19 in France,[38] by the fact that people who think they are victims of the government's action file in court. The judicialisation of political accountability is supported by a part of society and . . . politicians.

That movement is accompanied by the symmetrical evolution, which is less obvious, of the importance of judicial considerations in the questioning of the government by parliament. Purely political questions being in a certain way neutralised by the coalition agreements, the nationalisation of the vote or partisan loyalty, only exceptional facts can break the trust that the Executive normally enjoys for the duration of the term. Among them, violations of the common rules, whether they are proven or not, figure prominently. It is often less a violation of the law than of principles of prudence, common sense, probity or sincerity. Examples include the suspicion of failure as to risks of spying (Willy Brandt in Germany in 1974), of opinion manipulation (Tony Blair in the UK in 2007), of party corruption (Mariano Rajoy in Spain in 2018) or of violation of health measures (Boris Johnson in the UK in 2022). To sum up, it has been contended that the accountability of the Executive tends to be less to parliament and more to the public opinion or to the judicial power, but also that judges and members of parliament sometimes exchange, if not their duties, at least the records of the checks they carry out.

38 M. Callon and P. Lascoumes, 'Covid-19 et néfaste oubli du principe de précaution', *AOC Media*, 27 March 2020, https://aoc.media/analyse/2020/03/26/covid-19-et-nefaste-oubli-du-principe-de-precaution/

The Executives' strategies of liability limitation

The dilution of the accountability of power is not only due to the multiplication of direct or indirect sources of oversight, but also to the partly winning strategies of the executives to escape it.[39] Most of the time, governments aim to avoid the oversight and sanction of parliamentarians and public opinion, the emphasis laying more on one of them depending on the countries and times.[40] Two main strategies of accountability reduction, which have been implemented throughout Europe, may be distinguished: delegating and networking – France[41] and the UK[42] standing out in that respect.

Widely used in political science,[43] the concept of delegation offers an analytical lens shared by *a priori* very different phenomena, like 'agencification', devolution or the constitutional courts' rise in power, which are all evolutions that have been happening in Europe since the 1970s. From the point of view of the government, delegating to a third party the realisation of one political function or another offers different advantages most of which are not related to the issue of accountability.[44] However, delegating is a means

39 Here we refer to institutional strategies, which result in the creation of bodies, and set aside more traditional discursive strategies which, for example, consist in blaming the previous government for current difficulties.

40 To that has been recently added a will to avoid possible criminal proceedings as shown by the management of the COVID-19 crisis (2020–2022) during which the governments systematically relied on the advice and recommendations of health authorities.

41 The French Fifth Republic is a specific case of liability reduction relying on another strategy, i.e., the increase, within the Executive, of a part of it which is not accountable to Parliament. It is to be noted that though the political system is actually led by a president who is powerful and above control, important dependency on public opinion is the price for that limitation of accountability, which is reinforced by the weakness of the system of circulation of information, warning and even catharsis that the parliamentary arena provides. See G. Tusseau, 'Le présidentialisme de la Cinquième République: la part de l'autosuggestion dans la culture constitutionnelle', in *La Ve République démystifiée*, eds. O. Duhamel, M. Foucault, M. Fulla, and M. Lazar (Paris: Presses de Sciences Po, 2019), pp. 27–36.

42 In the UK, the increase in the number of paid government positions – almost a hundred – which have been granted to parliamentarians, doubly contributes to limiting the accountability of the government. On the one hand it dissolves the frontier between the branches of power, which gives the Executive an onion-like structure. On the other hand, it limits any wish on the part of majority members, who are attracted by those positions, to exercise any control. See S. Berlinski, T. Dewan, K. Dowding, and G. Subrahmanyam, 'Choosing, Moving and Resigning at Westminster', in *The Selection of Ministers in Europe*, eds. K. Dowding and P. Dumont (London: Routledge, 2009), pp. 58–78.

43 For a conceptualisation of regimes from that perspective: K. Strøm, W. C. Müller, and T. Bergman, eds., *Delegation and Accountability in Parliamentary Democracies* (Oxford: Oxford University Press, 2003). For an integration of heterogenous institutional phenomena from that angle: E. Grossman and N. Sauger, *Introduction aux systèmes politiques nationales de l'UE* (Bruxelles: De Boeck, 2007), Chapter 7.

44 The other aims are reducing the financial or administrative costs of public action (or sending such a signal to third parties), limiting the capacities for action of later governments and making the policy credible by erasing partiality and patronage.

to escape sanctions by public opinion (or at least to hope avoiding them) if results are bad.[45] In many ways, devolution measures are an illustration of the will of the central government to leave it to local authorities to decide public policies which are at the heart of citizens' everyday life – social policies, or school matters, for example. Though such a strategy may be efficient, the price to pay is important as it entails the loss of some prerogatives and the building of information asymmetries and moral hazards.

Recently, the strategies of blame avoidance through delegation have taken on another dimension in Europe as straw men or women were chosen as heads of government. Thus, in Poland, the two prime ministers who have ruled since 2015 are commonly considered to be less influential than the leader of the main majority party, Jarosław Kaczyński, who, after enjoying the role in 2006–2007, has preferred to be less exposed on the political and media level. This practice, though rare,[46] is a challenge for contemporary democracies, which are founded on a strong correspondence between the identity of the formal and real holder of power.

The second strategy of liability limitation consists for the governments of a regional zone to act in a network. Thus, they can both hide their own share of responsibility in a given policy and shift the blame onto others and hope they will profit from the power or aura of their peers. That tactic is close to, but different from delegating however: by participating in regional cooperation policies, the governments delegate power to a network to which they belong and to which they give visibility. The political notion of Member State of the European Union as a replacement for the Nation-State, as was developed by Chris Bickerton,[47] places at its heart that networking of European executives which try to compensate for their domestic loss of legitimacy by relying on the leaders of other States. In a more mundane way, the density of the policies developed in a regional organisation like the EU and the partially diplomatic character of negotiations entail a major information gap which makes the national governments less accountable. Though Members of national Parliament have reacted by granting themselves specialised procedures,[48] it is often difficult for them to know what their ministers have done at a Council meeting. Beyond the informal character of negotiations, national parliamentarians indeed struggle with the uncoupling of the political agreement[49] – i.e., the

45 K. Weaver, 'The Politics of Blame Avoidance', *Journal of Public Policy* 6, no. 4 (1986): pp. 371–398.

46 There are also more classical practices of straw men when the majority leader is judicially prevented from governing, as for example in Romania in 2018.

47 C. Bickerton, *European Integration. From Nation-States to Member States* (Oxford: Oxford University Press, 2012).

48 C. Hefftler, C. Neuhold, O. Rozenberg, and J. Smith, eds., *The Palgrave Handbook of National Parliaments and the European Union* (London: Palgrave Macmillan, 2015).

49 The original expression of 'political agreement' is partially misleading as it often results from a compromise between high civil servants rather than ministers, which emphasises how difficult it is to exercise parliamentary oversight.

confidential agreement of the Council members – and the later display of the votes of the ministers.[50]

Without reducing European integration to a strategy of avoidance of parliamentary oversight, one may see that it takes part in it. However, as for delegation, networking entails a price to pay for the governments. Some public policies can be imposed on them or refused to them. Moreover, when they rely on their peers to escape domestic constraints, the heads of government run the risk of being abandoned by their peers and of having to pay the price for it at the national level. In November 2011, the fall of Silvio Berlusconi, who had been Head of Council in Italy for three years, may admittedly be explained by relations within his coalition, the people's discontent and mobilisation, and, quite simply, by bad results. His resignation was doubly precipitated yet by the international dimension: the European institutions had obtained from Italy a cost cutting plan a few months before, then implied that they did not trust the Prime Minister to implement it. A few days before he resigned, the G20 summit at Cannes had concretely shown the isolation of S. Berlusconi to whom bilateral meetings had been refused.[51]

Conclusion

The analysis of today's state of the accountability of governments thus reaches mixed conclusions: the parliament seems to be domesticated when the government is being held to account, but it keeps a unique role in periods of crisis; the bodies assessing and judging the government's policies have multiplied, but they sometimes trigger victorious strategies on the part of governments to avoid them. From the point of view of political economy approaches, which were mentioned in the first part of this chapter, those evolutions are disturbing. As has been said, parliamentary accountability has developed by accompanying the development of the trade economy, especially because assets were mobile. Parliament lent credibility to the kings' capacity to borrow money. In today's globalised economy, the mobility of assets has reached an extraordinary level, as shown in the relocation of manufactures and the digital financialisation of the economy. However, in such a context, the credit of borrowing States does not go through the level of constraint exercised by parliament on the Executive, either because that constraint no longer seems credible in the eyes of financiers (parliament will vote a deficit budget if the government asks it to do so), or because it is perceived as a part of the problem (parliament will push the government into deficit). Thus, there appears a form of uncoupling between the principles of political liberalism and financialised global economy,

50 Once the agreement has been reached by qualified majority on a given version of the text, the ministers adopt an official position, which was not necessarily theirs. See S. Novak, *La prise de décision au Conseil de l'Union européenne. Pratiques du vote et du consensus* (Paris: Dalloz, 2011).

51 P. Ridet, 'C'est terminé, Silvio, inutile de t'accrocher', *Le Monde*, 7 November 2011, www.lemonde.fr/europe/article/2011/11/07/c-est-termine-silvio-inutile-de-t-accrocher

which is reminiscent of the so-called authoritarian capitalism of some States, in a manner that is in many ways much less tragic as to fundamental rights.

Moreover, democracy does not only suffer from violations 'from the top' but from the often-fantasised nostalgia that arouses 'from the bottom'. In reaction to the rulers' strategies of financial credibility and to their attempts to avoid accountability to parliament and public opinion, there developed in the 2010s different populist movements. Their vindictive character and their frequent call for direct democracy may have made observers forget that populisms most often agree to claim a capacity to act from the political power.[52] The Brexiters' motto 'take back control' is quite revealing in that respect and may be partly understood as a reaction to the aforementioned strategies of accountability avoidance taking the form of delegation and networking. Many understand the constraint discourse of the rulers as a form of negation of the capacity of the political power to collectively act upon society. The reaction of part of the public opinion thus points to the limits of accountability avoidance strategies implemented by the executive powers. Such government may admittedly emphasise that it could not be held accountable for the unemployment rate, but some voters end up challenging the legitimacy of a system in which their rulers seem so powerless.

By taking a little distance from the analyst's position, I would like to underline that those evolutions call for the implementation of a subtle constitutional engineering which distinguishes between parliamentary loss of accountability monopoly and the Executives' strategies of accountability avoidance. The first dynamic must surely be accepted by strengthening the articulations among the different – parliamentary, popular and judicial – types of supervision of the Executive. The people's democratic vigilance between two elections may be institutionalised by being linked to the prerogatives of the parliamentary arena.[53] In that respect, vigilance against the attempts at manipulating public opinion is crucial, whether they originate in economic or diplomatic games. On the contrary, what has been assimilated in this chapter to logics of accountability avoidance on the Executives' part should be fiercely fought against. That does not mean that delegating or networking is necessarily noxious, but that authentic democracy cannot survive in the shadow of a power that would not take responsibility for what it has done. Despite their rationalisation, parliaments, via the pulpit offered to the opposition, keep a central role to denounce, beyond the government's policy, its attempts at hiding itself.

52 That is especially the case as to economic issues. P. Rosanvallon, *The Populist Century: History, Theory, Critique* (Cambridge, UK: Polity Press, 2021 [2020]).

53 P. Rosanvallon, *Good Government*.

Conclusion

For a common concept of 'responsibility' from a multidisciplinary perspective

Xavier Magnon

The synthesis of this symposium will be organised around a double dimension: that of the *meta-discourse*, and, therefore of the framework of the discourse, which refers to an issue of method and a reflection on the very possibility of establishing a common concept in multidisciplinary research, and another dimension under that of the *discourse on the law* itself, on the concepts, with a proposal of general and common concept of 'responsibility'.

The meta-discourse: the possibility of a common concept within the framework of a multidisciplinary reflection

A multidisciplinary approach of responsibility was chosen for this symposium, and each contributor, who came from a different disciplinary field within social or political science, reported the meaning that that object has in their field. This symposium presupposes that *concepts can be communicated among social sciences* and shows that there is a scientific interest in knowing the different definitions of a common concept, or which is at least known under the same name, in disciplinary fields which do not share the same object, or which understand it differently and which, *a fortiori*, do not use the same methods to describe it.

Social sciences have identical objects, for example the State, and each of them has an interest in knowing the intensions of that concept in other sciences to question its own definitions, no matter the result of that approach; whether definitions show that they are radically closed to one another, or highlight similar directions, in other words, whether they affect his own vision of the concept or not. Questioning one's object and one's vision of it anew are scientific interests in themselves within a multidisciplinary approach. Indeed, questioning anew amounts to doubting, and, whatever the results of the latter, it allows to test one's vision of things.

Beyond the communicability of concepts, which shows the interest of mobilising different definitions of a same object that are suggested by the discourses of different social sciences, it is possible in some situations like that of responsibility to consider some conceptual unity and therefore set a common interdisciplinary concept.

DOI: 10.4324/9781003281559-35

It is still very difficult to identify, in a general way, the situations in which such conceptual unity is possible. Without starting some research that would go well beyond the frame of this analysis, one could consider that all the realities that are to be described which immediately imply a normative dimension, which may be described by the use of the deontic logic of permission, prohibition or obligation of behaviours, may be given a common definition. This does not mean concepts which *may be* made legal by being enunciated under the form of an obligation, permission or prohibition, but which, in themselves, necessarily imply that they must be formulated that way. A distinction could be made here between the *immediate normative concepts* and the *mediate normative ones*, i.e. the *concepts that can be made normative*. The State could be considered as a set of norms and may therefore be made legal, while other social sciences would see very different features in it. It should therefore be seen as a mediate normative concept. On the contrary, responsibility, and reading works in different areas seems to confirm this, appears to be a purely normative mechanism which may therefore be immediately formulated that way.

Thus, it is possible to make the distinction in science of law among *immediate normative concepts*, which make it necessary to account for the described reality from a normative angle, and *concepts that can be made normative*, which have objects which, without having a normative dimension, can be made normative. It is possible to understand the reality that is described by an immediate normative concept directly, through permissions, obligations or prohibitions; that which is apprehended by a concept that can be made normative may be translated by permissions, obligations and prohibitions of behaviours without being reduced to that one dimension and may therefore be understood differently. Some interdisciplinary conceptual *uniqueness* is therefore possible for the first ones, whereas only some *communicability* is possible for the second. 'Responsibility' is an immediately normative reality, which may be described based on duties to act, whereas the 'State' is a reality that may be made normative.

That reading will therefore be made concrete based on the concept of responsibility which is considered as an immediate normative concept and which may be defined in a unique way, independently of the involved social sciences.

A common concept to analyse responsibility

Before tackling issues of meaning, a preliminary one on *the very axiological possibility of a responsibility* should be dealt with, as A. Errecart noted, or, to use another term, on the very conditions of responsibility, which refers to the moral presupposition on which the mechanism of responsibility is based. The Judaeo-Christian and liberal presuppositions on which responsibility is founded must be underlined: free will, individualism and the autonomy of the will. That dimension is present in Aristotle: 'If then, as is commonly said, the virtues are voluntary (because we at least cooperate in producing our moral states, and we assume the end to be of a certain kind according as we are ourselves of certain characters), the vices must be voluntary also, because the cases are exactly similar'.[1] It is also present in Saint Augustine:

> The mind commands the mind to will, and yet though it be itself it does not obey itself. . . . the will does not will entirely; therefore it does not command entirely. For as far as it wills, it commands. And as far as it does not will, the thing commanded is not done. For the will commands that there be an act of will – not another, but itself.[2]

Marcel Gauchet considers that 'Responsibility is one of the most immediate correlates of the individualistic foundation of our legal systems'.[3] He highlights a double internal and external dimension of responsibility: 'Crediting the individual with a responsibility is granting them full inside self-government . . . depending on which it is possible, for the outside, to impute to that individual who has been granted self-government the whole of what they do and are'. The free and therefore responsible individual is consequently supposed to own the 'subjective responsibility of their objective behaviour and condition. That is what the fact that they are responsible for, what happens to them means'.[4]

That precondition being set, the polysemy of the word was highlighted several times during debates. Malik Bozzo-Rey and Ruwen Ogien identified six meanings of the word responsibility. Keeping only classifications and referring to their contributions for explanations, there is: responsibility-action, responsibility-virtue, responsibility-obligation, responsibility-causality, responsibility-sanction and responsibility-emotion.

Among those different meanings, many belong to everyday language and though it is possible to build a common concept, it could not be a scientific one.

The suggested general definition, because it concerns all the disciplines that use the concept, will be the following: ***responsibility is a normative mechanism pursuant to which a behaviour, which causes a damage, be it a personal or a social one, implies duties to act (obligation of retribution) on the part of the author of the behaviour for who has suffered the damage***. And, undoubtedly, that is close to the original formula of the French Civil Code, according to which, 'Any

1 Aristotle, *Ethique à Nicomaque [Nicomachean Ethics]* (Paris: Flammarion, Le monde de la philosophie, 2008), p. 99.

2 Saint Augustin, *Les confessions* (Paris: Flammarion, Le monde de la philosophie, 2008), p. 196.

3 M. Gauchet, 'À la charnière de l'individuel et du collectif', in *De la responsabilité solidaire. Mutations dans les politiques sociales d'aujourd'hui*, eds. C. Bec and G. Procacci (Paris: Éditions Syllepse, 2003), p. 24.

4 M. Gauchet, 'À la charnière de l'individuel et du collectif', p. 24.

human action whatsoever which causes harm to another creates an obligation in the person by whose fault it occurred to make reparation for it'.[5]

The different elements of the proposed definition have been referred to by the different contributors, even if the formulation remains quite original. The fact that responsibility implies obligations has been underlined by Jean-Baptiste Donnier, in his elegant way: 'At the beginning, there is a fact . . ., at the end there is a right (reparation), and in between, an obligation'. Cécile Guérin-Bargues sees responsibility as

> a mechanism of attributing value to the acts of the Executive. It aims to encourage – more than oblige – rulers to be accountable, following a determined procedure, and to an authority that has been invested with exercising that oversight, for acts committed during office.

She thus refers to the concrete modes of the obligation of reparation which follows the implication of political responsibility. H. Belrhali notes that the responsibility of the State consists in 'imposing on that legal person the financial burden of compensating for the consequences of the action or inaction of its bodies when they cause damage to citizen(s)'.

The mechanism of responsibility, as it was defined, spreads out into several different fields, each of which gives it different characteristics. It is possible to differentiate criminal, civil and administrative liability, political and social responsibility. The first three types are dealt with by the law, i.e., there are legal norms which frame the mechanisms of responsibility, while *social responsibility* is not covered by the law. It refers to a spontaneous mechanism of responsibility, which leads to some damaging behaviours being condemned socially by those who consider themselves as their victims.

Criminal liability is that for which the obligation of retribution is the strongest since it can consist in depriving the author of the damaging act of their freedom. The intensity of the retribution is strong because the damage is considered to be a collective one, and even as affecting the essential elements of the operation of society. The obligation of retribution has a strong dimension of exemplariness. Given the intensity of the retribution, the behaviours which may be condemned must be defined precisely by the law – this is the principle of the lawfulness of crimes to avoid any arbitrariness. Any behaviour may not lead to the implication of some criminal liability; since only those which have been precisely defined beforehand may. The intensity of the retribution then imposes reinforced procedural modes of incurring and assessing responsibility in terms of procedural and substantive guarantees in favour of those who have displayed the condemned behaviour and legitimacy of the

5 Access to the new provisions of the French Civil Code created by Ordonnance n° 2016-131 of 10 February 2016 translated into English at: www.justice.gouv.fr/sites/default/files/migrations/textes/art_pix/THE-LAW-OF-CONTRACT-2-5-16.pdf

competent authorities to validly judge it. 'Judicialising' the procedure is obviously necessary, following a liberal logic.

Civil and administrative liability are founded on the same logic and may therefore be assimilated. They aim, in theory, to repair a personal damage, even though the latter may affect a group of people. In that case, the damage remains specific to a category of people who have their own characteristics and not, as for criminal liability, society as a whole. Within that framework, retribution can extend to the implementation of a physical constraint on goods, for example the seizure of goods, and not on people. The behaviours that may trigger the mechanism of responsibility are *a priori* indeterminate. In theory, any damaging behaviour may give right to compensation. It is the existence of a damage which makes it possible to understand which behaviour has caused it. That is complete adaptability of those responsibilities to the *de facto* concrete situations, the implementation of which is only conditioned by the existence of a damage. A judicialisation of the procedure is also necessary following a liberal logic.

Political responsibility is the most flexible and least constraining. It may concern any behaviour which challenges the normal behaviour that voters or representatives are entitled to expect from a political representative. The damage lies here in the existence of a behaviour which goes outside the expected frame and the obligation of compensation may have different forms which may range from a simple obligation of public explanation of one's behaviour to the loss of one's office. However, Audrey Bachert-Peretti has perfectly evidenced the limits of political responsibility which are consubstantial with the limits of the democratic character of the European Executives: the participation of the people in power is limited, in practice, to designating their representatives. Whatever the mechanisms provided for by the system, the sole involvement of the term of office for the election makes the participation of the people to power concrete. No specific requirement of judicialisation is *a priori* necessary given the considered field.

The suggested definition should however be explained even more. It seems first important to distinguish *who is responsible* from *responsibility* itself. Who is responsible is who is at the origin of a detrimental behaviour; responsibility, once who is responsible has been identified, consists in compensating for the consequences of that behaviour. In other words, *responsibility* implies that *who is responsible* be first determined. There are two periods in the mechanism of responsibility, based on a distinction that is found in Paul Ricoeur[6] and which has been referred to by J.-B. Donnier and A. Errecart: the first which belongs to a *logic of attribution*, which makes it necessary to establish who is liable, and the second within which a *logic of retribution*, which implies that the damage deriving from the behaviour that has caused it should be compensated

6 P. Ricoeur, 'Le concept de responsabilité. Essai d'analyse sémantique', *Esprit*, no. 206 (Novembre 1994): pp. 30 ff., in particular.

for, develops.[7] Hans Jonas also distinguishes two movements in responsibility: 'responsibility as causal attribution of acts that have been committed' and 'responsibility for what is to be done: the obligation of power'.[8]

Those two logics make it possible to answer two different questions: who is at the origin of the behaviour (***attribution***)? How to compensate for the damage due to the behaviour (***retribution***)? Within the logic of retribution, three elements need to be distinguished: the detrimental behaviour, the obligation of retribution and the proportionate character and scope of the obligation of retribution which refer to a logic of justice. From that presentation there appears attribution, the behaviours at the origin of the use of the mechanism, the obligation of retribution and the relation between the behaviour, the damage and the obligation of retribution. That division allows to highlight different characteristics of responsibility, which have been revealed by the different presentations made by the contributors to this symposium.

Attribution: the linking of a behaviour to one person or to a group of them

Linking a detrimental behaviour to a person or to several of them, who are therefore responsible for it, may refer to reality, but also to fictions. In the first case, there is an issue of evidence to causally link the behaviour and a person; in the second, in the name of a certain value, another person than who is at the origin of the behaviour may be held responsible. Administrative responsibility, for example, is linked to the responsibility of the agent, and therefore to who is at the origin, in reality, of the behaviour, but also to the State, in a fictitious way, while the agent is an agent of the State and their personal action obliges more broadly the community in the name of which they act. Because the State gives its agents the means to act, any action of the agent can be linked to the action of the State, even though, from the point of view of reality, the State cannot be at the origin of the detrimental behaviour at all. The link between the behaviour and the liable person is here supposed or fictitious; in most cases, the action of the agent will imply that of the State, no matter the behaviour of the agent; the share of personal responsibility which may be attributed to the agent compared to collective responsibility, the breach of the administrative duty, which is linked to the State, being most often weaker. There may be presumptions of attribution of detrimental behaviour. There are such presumptions in sports law, as C. Legendre underlined. Football clubs are thus considered to be liable for the acts of their supporters.

7 On that double dimension of responsibility see: X. Bioy, 'Avant-propos', in *Constitution et responsabilité: Actes du Colloque de Toulouse, 5 et 6 octobre 2007*, ed. X. Bioy (Paris: Montchrestien-Lextenso éditions, 2009), particularly pp. 10–12. See the contribution of A. Errecart for a presentation of responsibility based on the principles of imputation, deputation and reputation.

8 H. Jonas, *Le Principe responsabilité* (Paris: Flammarion, 1990), pp. 179, 182.

Among the justifications relied upon to attribute a behaviour to another person than who has adopted the detrimental behaviour, there may be a concern about the compensation of the harm. That dimension is a strong one in the field of administrative responsibility, as the State is always more creditworthy than its agents. From that perspective, the concept of 'breach of an administrative duty' allows to capture a great number of behaviours of the agents which may be linked to the State and to find the latter responsible. One could see in the responsibility of the State due to its agents the responsibility due to people one is liable for, in French civil responsibility, which has been consecrated by the *Cour de Cassation* as a general principle, although it is expressly provided for in Article 1384, Section 1 of the French Civil Code.[9]

The very fact that a behaviour can be linked to a person may also depend on the capacity of the latter to be liable for their acts and, more precisely, on the consideration that the person may be fully liable for their acts, which is the issue of the autonomy of the will. The liability of parents for their children's acts belongs to that dimension. That responsibility for another's acts is interpreted today in a radical way by the *Cour de Cassation*. The latter obliges the parents to compensate for any damage committed by their minor children, even though they are not at fault.[10] There is here a double presumption. The first one implies a certain age and/or a certain mental capacity to be validly linked to a behaviour, while the second, if the first one does not apply, imposes a transfer of responsibility onto other people.

Conversely, as J.-B. Donnier has said, the law may impose 'on the author of the harm the reparation of the detrimental consequences of a fact that cannot be attributed to them'. While the damaging behaviour is not to be assigned to a person, in terms of capacity, the law still imposes on that person an obligation to compensate. Such is Article 414–3 of the Civil Code, about the compensation for damage caused when subject to a mental disorder: 'He who has caused harm to another while under the control of a mental disturbance is nevertheless obligated to provide reparation'. This is again a fiction which aims to defend a value, that of the compensation of victims. One can see how different the solutions of positive law may be, in the name of that same value. Faced with the same problem of mental capacity, in some cases who was at the origin of the detrimental behaviours, the behaviour of children, will not be found liable, but there will be a transfer of attribution to other people, i.e., their parents; in other cases, despite the mental incapacity of the author of the detrimental behaviour, in case of mental disorder, they will be found liable.

That fictitious dimension of attribution allows to link behaviours which are not caused by people but by things or animals, to people. J.-B. Donnier has quoted the radical formula of the *Cour de Cassation* as to civil responsibility about things that one has authority over, provided for in Article 1242

9 Cass. Ass. Plén., 29 March 1991, no. 89-15.231, quoted in that sense by J.-B. Donnier.
10 Cass. 2è civ., 19 February 1997, no. 94-21.111, quoted in that sense by J.-B. Donnier.

section 1 of the French Civil Code, according to which 'only the victim at the exclusive origin of the damage they suffer is an obstacle to the examination of the liability of the custodian of the thing'. That solution leads to an absolute attribution on principle of the custodian of the thing, unless, and that is an exceptional circumstance, the damage is only caused by the victim.

Last, O. Rozenberg has shown that the 'strategies of accountability avoidance of the Executives' that the latter have put in place have been developed to escape their responsibility and, more precisely, the attribution of their policies. Two strategies have thus been revealed: the *concept of delegation*, in the political science meaning, the Executives delegating their political action to other bodies through 'agentification', decentralisation and constitutional courts, and *the network action* within a given regional area, the European Union then possibly being a scapegoat to avoid assuming political choices. That double strategy allows the Executives to avoid being held liable for their policies.

Resorting to fictions is therefore frequent, whatever the justifications which prescribe that use, to extend or move the people at the origin of the detrimental behaviour.

Retribution

Retribution itself is divided into three parts: the detrimental behaviour; the obligation of retribution; and the relation between the obligation, the damage and the behaviour.

The detrimental behaviour

Potentially, any behaviour may be at the origin of a mechanism of responsibility provided it causes a damage, any damage. The 'blameworthy' character of a behaviour or the fact that it may be different from an expected average behaviour seems to be less decisive than the damage it may cause, be the latter suffered by a person or a group of persons. Finally, it is the damage that triggers the liability for a determined behaviour, rather than the behaviour itself. That disassociation of the behaviour and the fault is obvious, provided responsibility is considered to be due to unlawful norms, which in turn may be considered as a behaviour linked to the production of norms. Unlawfulness is not the fault, and it is indeed the damage resulting from the illegality which triggers the imposition of liability. That remark may *a fortiori* be transposed to the cases of no-fault liability. Depending on the types of liability, the damage that is likely to be covered by the mechanism of responsibility is more or less encompassing: physical, material or moral, the latter may be understood in a very broad way too when it comes to political responsibility.

While any behaviour, as soon as it is detrimental, may lead to the implementation of the mechanism of liability, the behaviour itself may be taken into account depending on the liability mechanisms in question. While criminal liability requires a criminal behaviour, civil or administrative liability in principle excludes the taking into account of what is at fault in the behaviour, while taking into consideration the degree of the fault to authorise the implementation of the responsibility mechanism. Political responsibility seems to take into account even more broadly any behaviour whatsoever. Behind the fact that the blameworthy character of the behaviour is taken into consideration, there is the gradation of the damage. The damage is collective in criminal matters, individual in civil or administrative ones, quite indeterminate in political responsibility, while, as O. Rozenberg said, there is a 'the multiplication of the bodies and groups to which the Government is accountable' and representatives are accountable to the public opinion.

It is still possible to extend the reflection around the image of a scale of behaviours which refers to different responsibilities, from criminal to civil or administrative liability, to political and social responsibility, the latter only resulting in spontaneous social disapproval of some behaviours. On that scale, some behaviours may escape, for example, administrative liability, a situation which was described by H. Belrhali, within military operations, for example. However, in such a situation, political responsibility is still possible, as well as social responsibility, for the Executive that commands war operations. Here one can see what H. Belrhali has also mentioned that 'types of responsibility are really complementary'. Insofar as the object of each of those responsibilities is not the same, they can either be added up, as criminal liability sometimes goes with civil liability, or compensate each other, since the absence of administrative responsibility may be counterbalanced by political responsibility, while social responsibility is always required, for, being spontaneous, it develops outside legal norms.

Obligations of retribution

In the mechanism of responsibility, the damage caused by a behaviour imposes obligations on who is at the origin of the harm. Those obligations may take the form of a sanction which may extend, in a legal system, to the implementation of a physical constraint on goods or persons, or to compensation for the harm. It is from that angle of the obligations resulting from the existence of a damage that the sanction/compensation opposition should be situated. While the logic of sanction belongs to a logic of collective retribution, compensation refers to individual retribution. Compensation may consist in rescission and, when necessary, may be the obligation to do something, i.e., paying monetary compensation. Sanction does not necessarily have radical forms like deprivation of freedom. In the political domain, a representative may sometimes only have to publicly explain a behaviour, that sanction being either informal and resulting from a political-media balance of power, or formalised, e.g., an obligation to answer the questions of parliamentarians during question time or inquiry committees. This is close to a logic of accountability, that is, an obligation to render accounts, to explain one's acts.

The obligations of those who have caused a damage may also be considered as the consequence of the acknowledged rights of the victim of the damage. Here 'right' means the conferring of power on a determined person which allows them to demand a certain behaviour from another person. The victim of the damage may also require obligations on the part of the author of the detrimental behaviour and claim for them to be respected in court. F. Quastana has thus showed, 'The history of the responsibility of the Executive therefore becomes confused with that of the ministers. . . . Within that framework, responsibility is above all considered as the right of a political assembly to remove members of the Executive'. The obligation of retribution of the latter thus reflects a guaranteed right to the advantage of a political assembly.

The relation between the obligations, the behaviour and the damage

This relation implies a proportion between several elements which will contribute to establishing a fair retribution. Within that retribution, it is possible to distinguish an *instrumental dimension*, in the relation between the behaviour and the damage with the establishment of a causality link, and a *substantial dimension* of proportionality between the behaviour, the damage and the obligations.

The mechanical *instrumental dimension* of the proportion refers to the causal link between the behaviour and the damage allowing for a fair retribution in the compensation of the harm depending on the share that the behaviour has in the realisation of the damage.

From the angle of causality, the identification of the detrimental behaviour and, in turn, of the liable person is not always easy, as C. Legendre showed, in sports law. In combat sports, in particular, in which there are precisely risks of injury, it is quite difficult to identify who is responsible for an injury and which behaviour(s) are at the origin of the damage. Though one immediately thinks of the opponent, it is also quite possible to think of the responsibility of the referee, of the injured person themselves, given their lack of training, of that of their coach or even of their doctor, or more broadly, of a member of their medical staff. The causal diagram here is delicate to establish.

The *substantial dimension* may be understood from the perspective of distributive justice and proportional equality as developed by Aristotle,[11] even though some consider that responsibility belongs more to corrective justice.[12]

11 Aristotle, *Ethique à Nicomaque*, Book 7, pp. 174 ff.: 'Ce qui est juste, c'est quelque chose de proportionnel (le proportionnel, en effet, constitue une propriété non seulement du nombre, formés d'unité, mais globalement de la quantité dénombrée) dès lors que la proportion est une égalité de rapports et qu'elle implique quatre termes au moins', p. 176.

12 J.-B. Donnier considers that the reparation of the harm within the framework of civil responsibility makes it necessary 'to correct, by an act of justice precisely classified as corrective (or commutative) the inequality caused by the detrimental fact resulting from the committed fault'. Aristotle rejects the proportional in corrective justice: 'But the Just which arises in transactions between men is an equal in a certain sense, and the Unjust an unequal, only not in the way of that proportion but of arithmetical. Because it makes no difference whether a robbery, for instance, is committed by a good man on a bad or by a bad man on a good, nor whether a good or a bad man has committed adultery: The law looks only to the difference

That dimension includes not two but four elements. One must therefore take into account, on the one hand, the behaviour, the damage and the obligation of compensation, and, on the other, the situation of the person who is at the origin of the detrimental harm and that of who has suffered the latter. The substantial proportion between the behaviour, the damage and the obligation of compensation thus takes into consideration several elements: in case of a theft, what must be taken into account is what has been stolen, the circumstances of the theft, the damage suffered, but also the situation of who steals and who has been the victim of a theft. One must balance those different elements to establish a fair retribution. There are elements which allow to offset the retribution: theft when in a situation of need, the fair place of the harm depending on what is owned by who has been the victim of a theft. In that substantial dimension, there must be a balance between the behaviour, the damage and the obligations of retribution. The more or less blameworthy character of the behaviour, the scope and the characteristics of the damage must be balanced with the obligation of retribution in order to obtain a fair result in the application of the mechanism of responsibility.

At the end of this synthesis, it is for the different contributors to judge that unitary and interdisciplinary approach of responsibility in order to test it and nurture it. We wish this reading could have benefited from those perspectives.

created by the injury and treats the men as previously equal, where the one does and the other suffers injury, or the one has done and the other suffered harm. And so this Unjust, being unequal, the judge endeavours to reduce to equality again' (*Nicomachean Ethics*, Book 5, Chapter 7). 'Dans les rapports contractés entre personnes . . ., ce qui est juste, c'est une sorte d'égalité (et non pas de proportionnalité), certes, et ce qui est injuste, une sorte d'inégalité, mais l'égalité ne traduit pas la proportionnalité exigée dans le premier cas: elle traduit au contraire la proportion arithmétique' (*Éthique à Nicomaque*, V, 7, p. 179). 'Peu importe en effet qu'une spoliation soit commise par un honnête homme aux dépens d'un vilain ou l'inverse, ou que l'auteur d'un adultère soit honnête homme ou vilain. Ce qui importe, au contraire, c'est le dommage occasionné, et la seule chose que considère la loi, traitant les personnes sur un pied d'égalité, c'est de savoir si l'une a commis une injustice dont l'autre a été victime, autrement dit, si l'un a causé un dommage dont l'autre a été victime' (*Éthique à Nicomaque*, V, 7, p. 179). 'Si bien que, devant ce traitement injuste, qui introduit de l'inégalité, le juge s'efforce de rétablir l'égalité' (*Éthique à Nicomaque*, V, 7, p. 179) 'ce qui est juste à titre de correctif, c'est le milieu entre perte et profit ' (*Éthique à Nicomaque*, V, 7, p. 180).

Concluding remarks

A kaleidoscopic approach to make (necessary) interdisciplinary communication possible

Guillaume Tusseau

1. Addressing regional accountability and executive power in Europe, the REGALIEN Project has focused on notions that are familiar to every legal scholar, as well as to every actor of public life, be it at the local, national, supranational or international levels. Responsibility truly appears as a building block of contemporary constitutional theory. In this respect, it undoubtedly deserves to be identified as part of what Corrado Caruso and Chiara Valentini call the 'grammar of constitutionalism', on a par with notions like constitution, sovereignty, democracy, rule of law, separation of powers, political representation, secularism, pluralism, security, economic constitution, constitutional adjudication, fundamental rights, equality, citizenship, property, work and duties.[1] It could equally easily be added to the list of fundamental notions Francois Venter identifies and discusses in his book *The Language of Constitutional Comparison*.[2] Like the concepts of nation, sovereignty, State, citizenship and nationality, democracy, rule of law, constitutionalism and judicial review, the concept – or, as is now evident after reading the foregoing chapters, the concept*s* – of responsibility compellingly deserves to be added to the list of the most salient and structuring concepts that form the architectonic lexicon of contemporary constitutionalism.

However, like all these 'constitutional keywords', the contributions gathered in this volume bear witness to the diffraction of the theme of the responsibility of the executive power. After being the subject of a study including national monographs which provided a rich comparative synthesis,[3] this topic had to be considered at multiple levels and through multiple prisms. Without claiming, in Kelsenian terms, to offer a 'nomostatics' as well as a 'nomodynamics' of executive accountability,[4] this book provides a mapping

1 C. Corrado and V. Chiara, eds., *Grammatica del costituzionalismo* (Bologna: Il Mulino, 2021).
2 F. Venter, *The Language of Constitutional Comparison* (Cheltenham: Edward Elgar, 2022).
3 M. Morabito and G. Tusseau, eds., *Regional Accountability and Executive Power in Europe* (Oxfordshire: Routledge, 2023).
4 H. Kelsen, *General Theory of Law and State*, trans. A. Wedberg (Cambridge: Harvard University Press, 1945).

DOI: 10.4324/9781003281559-36

of existing situations, identifies evolving patterns, highlights practical transfers and interactions, and describes part of the doctrinal puzzlements that ensue. It especially sheds light on the multiplicity of stakeholders that are in fact involved in a widely interactive institutional intellectual process.

2. The responsibility of the Executive is ordinarily analysed from a purely horizontal perspective, i.e., by focusing on the relationship between the national executive and legislative powers. Taking into account the teachings of the first book published within the framework of the REGALIEN Project,[5] the authors whose contributions are gathered in this volume decided to proceed otherwise. They helped adopt a multidimensional approach to the topic.

   From 'below', the responsibility of national executive powers towards local actors has been examined. Depending on the case, the situation or the circumstances, subnational actors influence, reinforce, mitigate or imperil the responsibility of the national Executive in contemporary States. The expertise of practitioners from various countries with differing local organisations, and from various local levels has been invaluable to supplement that of the academics. The existence of more or less unsuspected forms of responsibility of the national Executive towards these local actors has thus been documented. Its modalities and effects have been debated by the stakeholders who are primarily concerned. A rather complex landscape appears. Multiple strata of actors – *communes*, *départements*, *régions*, *métropoles*, *regioni*, *Länder*, *Städte*, *Gemeinde*, associations of collectivities, etc. – interact with one another as well as with the national Executive.[6] Various legal instruments, which appear to distort traditional understandings of the term,[7] are involved and serve as vehicles for complex interactions. Thus, many organic and functional configurations appear, which testify to a multifaceted and interactive dimension of the phenomena of executive responsibility.

   From 'above', several contributions address the fascinating case of the European Union,[8] and the way it progressively appropriated the grammar of the State's political organisation, while at the same time modifying

5 M. Morabito and G. Tusseau, eds., *Regional Accountability and Executive Power in Europe*.

6 See the chapters contributed under Part I of this volume, 'The responsibility of the national executive power from the point of view of local territories'.

7 See the chapters contributed under Part II of this volume, 'Diversity of legal approaches'.

8 See J. F. López Aguilar, 'Parliamentarianism and Accountability of the Executive Power on a European Scale: The Experience of the European Parliament (Chapter 11)'; S. in 't Veld, 'The Scent of Wild Animals (Chapter 12)'; P. Ponzano, 'The Accountability of the EU Commission as the EU's Executive (Chapter 7)'; J. P. Jacqué, 'On Political Responsibility and Political Control in the European Union (Conclusion, Part II)'; F. Péraldi-Leneuf, 'Political Accountability within the European System (Chapter 9)'; J. Ziller, 'Political Accountability and Role Splitting of the Executive in EU Member States (Chapter 8)', in this volume, *Regional Accountability and Executive Power in Europe*.

it. In this specific sphere, the competing rationalities that lie beyond the legal technicalities of responsibility become apparent. Responsibility has been a vehicle for the politicisation of this European supranational institutional environment. It has helped reinforce democracy within it against its propensity to appear as a form of 'epistocracy',[9] bureaucracy or technocracy. The internal mechanism of political responsibility that emerges within this framework, which has been established by international treaties and secondary law instead of domestic constitutions, testifies to a complex logic. Once again, it makes it necessary to pay attention to several forms of interactions with many other institutional actors. Competing rationalities are thus highlighted depending on the multiplicity of audiences these actors are accountable to, both horizontally in the supranational sphere, and vertically with respect to national and subnational actors, not to mention the way all these actors are or should be answerable to the people themselves. The complex picture that emerges bears witness to the dimension of 'Unidentified Governing Object'[10] to which Sophie in 't Veld refers in her analysis of the European Council.

3. Such distorted intertwined landscapes and such unstable multipolar dynamics tend to blur familiar notions and distinctions and to destabilise the traditional understanding of responsibility. As Olivier Rozenberg puts it, one is currently witnessing a 'multiform dilution of the accountability of the Executive'.[11] This is why the contributions to this volume also propose to take a step backward and ponder over the very notion of responsibility. While the responsibility of the Executive is intuitively perceived as a constitutional lawyer's issue, other perspectives are worth exploring in this context. An interdisciplinary approach is necessary. This is why, along with constitutional law,[12] hints coming from civil law,[13] sports law[14] and administrative law[15] have first proved valuable to offer a more precise mapping of the legal conceptual apparatus. Secondly, other disciplines have been worth exploring to delineate the roots of the puzzlements. Insights coming from

9 See H. Qazbir, 'The European Convergence of the Strengthening of the Executive Power (Chapter 13)', in this volume, *Regional Accountability and Executive Power in Europe.*

10 S. in 't Veld, 'The Scent of Wild Animals (Chapter 12)', in this volume, *Regional Accountability and Executive Power in Europe.*

11 O. Rozenberg, 'Of Sheep and Straw Men: The Accountability of the Executive from the Perspective of Political Science (Chapter 22)', in this volume, *Regional Accountability and Executive Power in Europe.*

12 C. Guérin-Bargues, 'The Unique Nature of Political Responsibility (Chapter 19)', in this volume, *Regional Accountability and Executive Power in Europe.*

13 J.-B. Donnier, 'A Perspective on Civil Responsibility (Chapter 17)', in this volume, *Regional Accountability and Executive Power in Europe.*

14 C. Legendre, 'Responsibility and Sports: Some Remarks on a Particular Couple (Chapter 20)', in this volume, *Regional Accountability and Executive Power in Europe.*

15 H. Belrhali, 'Administrative Responsibility and Responsibility of the Executive (Chapter 15)', in this volume, *Regional Accountability and Executive Power in Europe.*

philosophy,[16] political science,[17] history,[18] and information and communication sciences[19] have helped identify the roots of our current predicament, as well as make clear the boundaries of a serious and well-informed discussion about the responsibility of the Executive. The conceptual apparatus of which the notion of responsibility is part is indeed much more than a mere toolkit. Like the other major notions that form the grammar of constitutionalism, it has to do with the *forma mentis juris*, i.e., the very mindset of jurists.

Both from a synchronic and a diachronic viewpoint, these reflections contribute to what Paul Veyne conceives as a kaleidoscopic exploration of the topic.[20] They associate the perspective of the *Begriffsgeschichte*[21] to the dynamic mapping of the concrete uses of the vernacular of responsibility. These involve complex conceptual circulations, starting with the founding experiences and then spreading across the whole legal landscape. Far from being a fixed notion, the more the Executive's responsibility is studied, the more it appears as the focal point of controversies and battles. The apparent fluidity of the term and the rather messy portrait of the legal field that appears when one concentrates on the regional and European dimensions of the topic, illustrate a plurality of attempts to make use of this idea, both to call into question a form of whatever type of governance or to justify its action. This is the reason why an approach that makes room for the actors' own understanding and manipulation of the term is worthwhile to go beyond black letter law or law in books and rather understand law in action.[22] The fact that a multiplicity of configurations in which responsibility is involved exists is not pathological.[23] As it is exposed here, it testifies

16 M. Bozzo-Rey, 'Understanding Responsibility through the Issues of the Environment: Towards a Bilateral Conception of Responsibility? (Chapter 16)', in this volume, *Regional Accountability and Executive Power in Europe.*

17 O. Rozenberg, 'Of Sheep and Straw Men: The Accountability of the Executive form the Perspective of Political Science (Chapter 22)'.

18 L. Lacchè, 'Are there Common National Traditions Regarding the Responsibility of the Executive Power? (Chapter 6)', in this volume, *Regional Accountability and Executive Power in Europe*; F. Quastana, 'On How Difficult It is to Think about the Responsibility of the Executive in a Republic – from a Historical Perspective (Chapter 21)', in this volume, *Regional Accountability and Executive Power in Europe.*

19 A. Errecart, 'Responsibility of the Executive: Cross-Read Approaches (Chapter 18)', in this volume, *Regional Accountability and Executive Power in Europe.*

20 P. Veyne, *Comment on écrit l'histoire* (Paris: Editions du Seuil, 1971).

21 See especially, L. Lacchè, 'Are there common national traditions regarding the responsibility of the executive power?' (Chapter 6).

22 On this classical opposition, see R. Pound, 'Law in Books and Law in Action', *American Law Review* 44 (1910): pp. 12–36.

23 See also, G. Tusseau, 'Conclusion: A Culture of Constitutional Cultures', in *Comparative Executive Power in Europe: Perspectives on Accountability from Law, History and Political Science*, eds. M. Morabito and G. Tusseau (Oxfordshire: Routledge, 2023).

to the vitality and creativity of legal discourse and argumentation. It consequently calls for innovative scientific protocols from the academia.

This situation does not rule out any attempts at designing, on a metalinguistic level, a concept of responsibility. Xavier Magnon, for example, suggests the following definition in order to address the contemporary situation: 'responsibility is a normative mechanism pursuant to which a behaviour, which causes a damage, be it a personal or a social one, implies duties to act (obligation of retribution) on the part of the author of the behaviour for who has suffered the damage'.[24] On the contrary, this theoretical effort is even more necessary. As all the foregoing contributions prove, this effort is not only for the sake of theorisation or academic obsession. From the field, from the viewpoint of the legal actors that are directly in touch with the people, such research conditions the existence, availability and understandability of a vocabulary that allows citizens to express their demands in front of those who are supposed to exercise their power 'in the name of the people'.[25]

4. Precisely because the stakes eventually appear to be so high, it has been evident for all the participants in the REGALIEN Project that such a diffracted picture of the practice of executive responsibility imposes a combination of approaches. The success of the enterprise is a matter for debate, and a matter for the reader to decide.

An optimistic viewpoint would conclude that '*ab esse ad posse valet consequentiam*'. Because multiple perspectives have been confronted, communication has taken place. Cross-fertilisation has been possible and has helped refine each viewpoint in light of other perspectives and methodologies. A shared understanding has been possible to contribute to a more self-conscious analysis of responsibility. A pessimistic perspective would on the contrary insist on the gaps between approaches. It would suggest that different disciplines and different actors, although they use the same words, truly speak different, hermetic, languages. Responsibility in public law is not the same as responsibility in private law. Responsibility in constitutional law is not the same as responsibility in administrative law. Responsibility for a law professor is not responsibility for a French mayor, senator or *préfet*.[26] An epistemological distance necessarily surfaces and makes discussion impossible.

24 X. Magnon, 'For a Common Concept of "Responsibility" from a Multidisciplinary Perspective (Conclusion, Part III)', in this volume, *Regional Accountability and Executive Power in Europe*.

25 See A. Bachert-Peretti, 'Responsibility, Accountability and Legitimacy of Executives: What Role for the People? (Chapter 14)', in this volume, *Regional Accountability and Executive Power in Europe*.

26 See the chapters contributed under Part I of this volume, 'The responsibility of the national executive power from the point of view of local territories'.

Borrowing from the methodology of *sentipensar*,[27] my *feeling* – no more, no less – is that it may not be necessary to take sides in this controversy. Like indigenous peoples, the participants in the REGALIEN Project have accepted to adopt 'spiral thinking'. Rejecting the idea of a linear determinism between particular fixed substances, it highlights the interconnected processes that operate in the movement of thought. The spiral thus elegantly integrates all the parts and stages of reasoning, both practical and theoretical, as if they contributed equally to its own dynamics. This interdependent movement has no logical or temporal end, but functions through the constantly renewed inclusion of new elements, placed in a relationship of complementarity and reciprocity.[28] From this perspective, one accepts to deprive oneself of absolute certainties, and to move forward with others. We may have been going round and round in circles, but we have never gone back to exactly the same place. Ultimately, because of the results it delivers, but most of all because of the path that was collectively followed, there is no doubt that the approach of the REGALIEN Project has been fruitful.

27 A. Escobar, *Sentipensar con la tierra: Nuevas lecturas sobre desarrollo, territorio y diferencia* (Medellín: UNAULA, 2014); L. Zóttola, *Indisciplinados aproximaciones a sentipensar la investigación* (Santiago del Estero: EDUNSE Editorial Universitaria, 2018); R. Santamaría, *La utopía del oprimido. Los derechos de la pachamama (naturaleza) y el sumak kawsay (buen vivir) en el pensamiento crítico, el derecho y la literatura* (Bogotá: AKAL/Universidad Andina Simón Bolívar, 2019), pp. 398, 253–261.

28 See especially V. M. Gavilan Pinto, *El pensamiento en espiral. El paradigma de los pueblos indígenas* (Santiago: Nuke Mapuforlaget, 2012).

Index

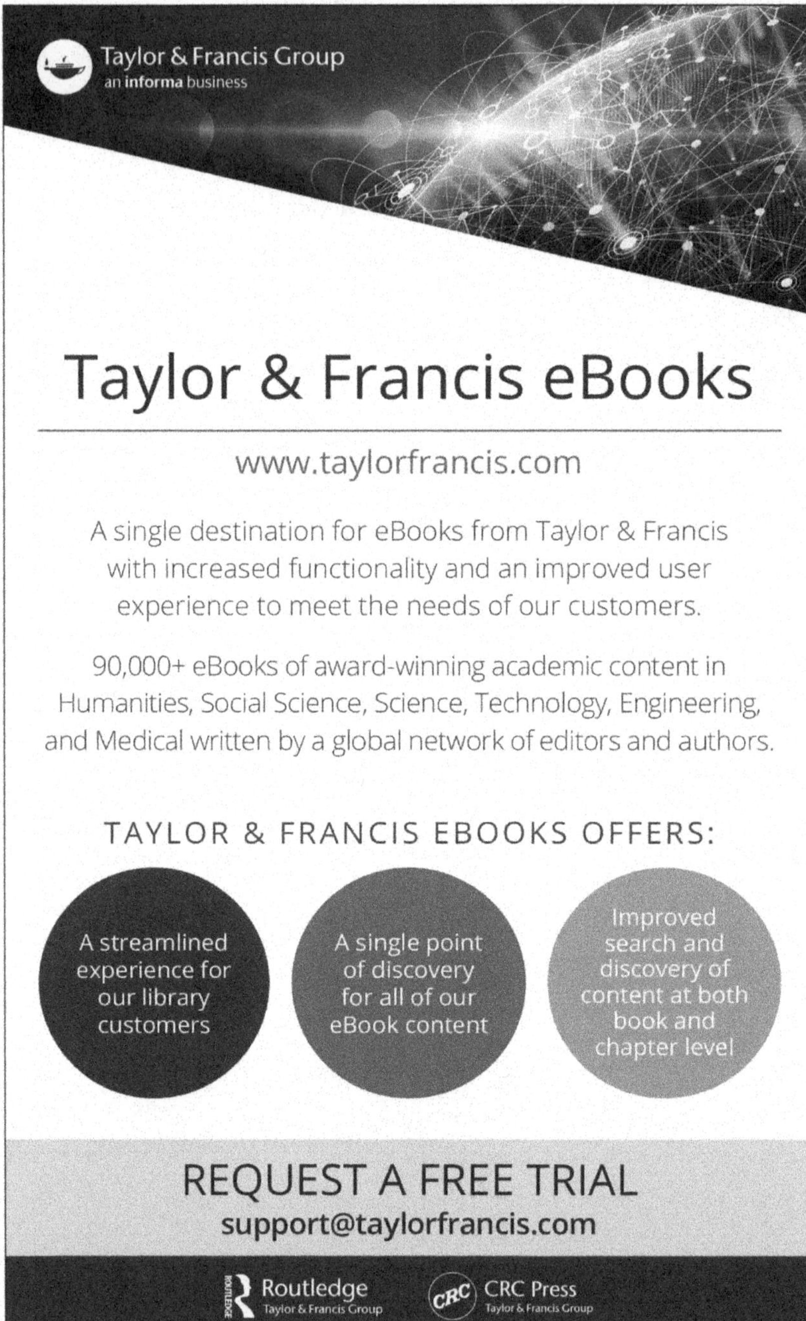
Taylor & Francis Group
an informa business
Taylor & Francis eBooks
www.taylorfrancis.com
A single destination for eBooks from Taylor & Francis with increased functionality and an improved user experience to meet the needs of our customers.
90,000+ eBooks of award-winning academic content in Humanities, Social Science, Science, Technology, Engineering, and Medical written by a global network of editors and authors.
TAYLOR & FRANCIS EBOOKS OFFERS:
A streamlined experience for our library customers
A single point of discovery for all of our eBook content
Improved search and discovery of content at both book and chapter level
REQUEST A FREE TRIAL
support@taylorfrancis.com
Routledge
Taylor & Francis Group
CRC Press
Taylor & Francis Group